Surveys in International Trade

Surveys in International Trade

Edited by

DAVID GREENAWAY
AND
L. ALAN WINTERS

BLACKWELL
Oxford UK & Cambridge USA

Copyright © Basil Blackwell Ltd 1994

First published 1994
Reprinted 1994, 1995

Blackwell Publishers, the publishing imprint of
Basil Blackwell Ltd
108 Cowley Road
Oxford OX4 1JF, UK

Basil Blackwell Inc.
238 Main Street
Cambridge, Massachusetts 02142
USA

British Library Cataloguing in Publication Data
A CIP catalogue record for this book is available from the British Library.

Library of Congress Cataloging-in-Publication Data
Surveys in international trade / edited by David Greenaway and L. Alan Winters.
    p.   cm.
  Includes bibliographical references and index.
  ISBN 0–631–17892–9. — ISBN 0–631–18589–5 (pbk.)
  1. International trade.   2. International economic relations.
3. Commercial policy.   I. Greenaway, David,   II. Winters, L. Alan.
HF1379.S87   1994
382—dc20   93–5453
                                                               CIP

Typeset in 10.5 on 12.5 pt Times by Pure Tech Corporation, Pondicherry, India

This book is printed on acid-free paper

CONTENTS

LIST OF FIGURES

LIST OF TABLES

LIST OF CONTRIBUTORS

James E. Anderson, Boston College
John Cantwell, University of Reading
Paul Collier, University of Oxford
Rodney E. Falvey, Australian National University
David Greenaway, University of Nottingham
Jan Willem Gunning, Free University, Amsterdam
Robert C. Hine, University of Nottingham
Didier Laussel, Université d'Aix-Marseille II
Edward E. Leamer, University of California, Los Angeles
Stephen P. Magee, University of Texas at Austin
Christian Montet, University of Montpellier
André Sapir, Université Libre de Bruxelles
Alasdair Smith, University of Sussex
Chantal Winter, Université Libre de Bruxelles
L. Alan Winters, University of Birmingham

1

INTRODUCTION AND OVERVIEW

David Greenaway and L. Alan Winters

1.1 CONTEXT

This volume of specially commissioned essays is designed to offer an up-to-date overview of the theory of international trade and its application. The essays are written to be accessible to graduate students and advanced undergraduates, but also to allow professional economists a ready insight into the main developments in the subject over the last decade. They introduce recent theory and evidence, place them in their intellectual context, and offer thorough, if not exhaustive, guides to the recent literature on international trade.

In designing the volume we have included contributions only from leading scholars in the various fields and have encouraged each to explore the topics he/she considers most important in his/her area and to use the techniques he/she feels most appropriate. We have not sought to impose a uniform approach or notation, so that, while the coverage of topics is fairly comprehensive, the reader is introduced to a wider menu of analytical tools than most textbooks would permit. The readings thus provide both a thorough supplement to existing textbooks and a suitable introduction to international trade for more advanced courses where students have some experience and an ability to follow up references for themselves.

International trade theory is an important part of the economist's tool kit. Practically, most countries trade at least 10 per cent of their GDP and several trade more than 50 per cent; all have large bureaucracies making and administering trade policy. Intellectually, the theory of the composition of trade is probably the major application of general equilibrium theory, while trade policy analysis exploits both general and partial equilibrium modes of thought. Both aspects now make use of and develop theories of imperfect competition and industrial organization, and utilize a wide range of empirical and econometric techniques. Thus as well as covering some of the most important of practical issues, this branch of economics offers the challenge and interest of employing a variety of analytical approaches to address them. This book is intended not only to point out the issues and techniques involved, but also to communicate to the student some of the intellectual excitement that they can generate.

The 1980s were an exciting time for international trade research. Academic progress stems from the conjunction of two forces: the existence of pressing practical problems or puzzles, to which answers must be sought, and the emergence of new techniques which allow them to be examined from new perspectives. Of course, the two are not wholly independent, but their separate effects can be identified in the case of recent international trade research. The problems or challenges of the 1980s included trying to explain: why so much international trade was of an intra-industry nature; why different countries had such different growth and development histories, and the ways in which the laggards might be helped resurrect their fortunes; why the internal deregulation of many industrial economies was not accompanied by a corresponding external liberalization; why pervasive use was made of economically inefficient instruments of trade policy such as voluntary export restraints (VERs); whether increasing economic integration would stimulate economic activity and welfare; what is different between goods and services trade, and what explains the patterns of the latter; and the commercial interest in services, intellectual property and investment policy in the Uruguay Round.

Among the analytical developments that have helped to unlock these issues are: the ability to model internal economies of scale and imperfect competition formally but simply – which arose out of parallel work in industrial organization; the development and refinement of methods of duality in international trade; the insights of directly unproductive profit-seeking activities (DUPs) and the theories of endogenous policy; the simple matrix representation of general equilibrium trade models, which has both made the nature of trade models more transparent and facilitated their empirical implementation; and the development of computable general and partial equilibrium models.

The ways in which the conjunction of these forces has advanced the study of international trade and trade policy over the last decade can be seen in a number of examples. For instance, the advent of models of imperfect competition has enlivened pure trade theory, allowing a more fruitful discussion of the location of production, the volume of international trade, and, at the level of differentiated versus homogeneous goods, the composition of trade. (The new models have not yet contributed much on the composition of trade within the class of differentiated goods.) It has also formalized a long-discussed but previously unmodelled benefit of international trade – its pro-competitive effect. This, in turn, has extended our analysis of trade liberalization and even more so of international economic integration. The traditional analysis of customs unions (CUs) suggested that European integration might have increased economic welfare by up to 1 per cent of GDP, but the recent theoretical advances coupled with their implementation in numerical models allowed an altogether more optimistic – and probably realistic – assessment of policies such as the EC's single market programme and the North American Free Trade Agreement.

Imperfect competition also spawned a new look at international trade policy. The pressure to protect an industry typically comes from all factors of production in that industry. Traditional theory, however, suggests rather that it would come only from the owners of particular factors, but from all such owners no matter in which industry they were employed. This is because traditional theory has no supernormal profits, so that the returns to protection can be felt only via its effects on the overall demand for factors. Imperfect competition, on the other hand, introduces supernormal rents which can accrue to any or all of the factors in a particular industry. These rents mean that any policy which increases sales increases profits. Moreover, if the effect is to increase net sales abroad, so that domestic consumers do not suffer the cost of paying prices in excess of marginal costs, such policies potentially increase national welfare. This insight lies at the heart of strategic trade policy, by which governments may be able to help their own firms to push rivals out of markets and increase national welfare. The nature of the policies required for this vary dramatically from case to case, however. Thus strategic trade policy is essentially non-operable in the real world, as well as usually being antisocial; nevertheless it generated significant academic interest during the 1980s.

Interest in trade policy during the 1980s also extended to contingent protection – anti-dumping duties and non-tariff barriers – as such policies became more prominent and attracted more attention in liberalization debates. The analysis of the political economy of such instruments has made clear why they are preferred to simple tariffs – e.g. their lack of transparency, their bureaucratic rather than legislative nature and the private rents they generate. Recent approaches to measuring their intensity are being developed to help measure their effects and plan reform packages.

At a more practical level, the need for substantial structural adjustment in many economies over the 1980s and the recognition in the 1970s that import substitution was a failed development strategy combined to produce a large measure of trade liberalization in developing countries. Planning for and studying these episodes have led to a more thorough – albeit still incomplete – understanding of the consequences of liberalization and the ways in which it should be tackled and sequenced. Issues such as the need for policy credibility, the second-best implications of partial reform, and the interaction of current and capital accounts have all figured in these developments, and many of them have proved critical to the formulation of plans for the transition of the Eastern European and ex-Soviet economies.

The surveys in this book are self-contained and present the reader with a coherent and relatively complete view of their fields. Their objective is not merely to illustrate recent developments but also to place them in their contexts. Nevertheless the theme that a combination of advances in technique and the pressure of practical problems and puzzles has made the 1980s a fruitful decade in international trade research will keep recurring. We hope that this book will help to persuade a new generation of researchers to roll that progress into the 1990s.

1.2 OVERVIEW OF THE SURVEYS

As noted earlier, there have been a number of classic surveys of international trade, but fewer surveys of specific topics in international trade – hence this volume. Each of the chapters which follows is self-contained and free-standing. In chapter 2 Rod Falvey provides a comprehensive review of the pure theory of international trade. After a brief résumé of the Ricardian model he derives the core theorems of the H–O model relating to trade and factor returns, the pattern of trade, factor returns and product prices, and outputs and factor endowments. Of course most of this is well known and Falvey spends much more time evaluating the consequences of relaxing the standard assumptions of the model to allow for *inter alia*, taste differences, technology differences and non-traded goods. Two extensions in particular are emphasized, specific factors and higher dimensions. The former, sometimes known as the Ricardo–Viner model, has proved to be a useful framework for thinking about trade problems when some factors are sector specific – as they often are in the short run. Falvey traces out the consequences of the specific factors model for the standard trade theorems, then does the same in the final section when describing a setting of many goods and many factors. Higher dimensionality makes life rather more complicated for the theorist. Falvey traces out in a straightforward way the consequences of higher dimensions for the standard theorems, most of which carry over, albeit in somewhat weaker form.

The one area which Falvey steers away from is imperfect competition and international trade. Since the key contributions of Dixit and Stiglitz (1977) and Lancaster (1979), this has been a vibrant research field. So much has been done on this issue that we commissioned a separate survey on it by Alasdair Smith. This is the subject of chapter 3. Smith begins by asking why we should study trade with imperfect competition – his answer is that since so much trade is between countries with similar factor endowments, we have a gap to fill which is left by the 'HOS model'. The literature on imperfect competition being a large one, Smith organizes his survey around a number of the central themes. He sets out a general framework, and uses this to evaluate: the impact of trade on domestic competition and product variety; the role of external economies; the effects of trade restrictions and economic integration; imperfect competition in a general equilibrium setting; the multinational corporation (MNC); and trade and growth. The comprehensiveness of Smith's treatment accurately conveys the flavour of the richness and diversity of work in this area.

Ever since the publication of Leontief's famous paradox, testing trade theory has been a major preoccupation of applied economists. In chapter 4 Ed Leamer surveys the huge literature which has accumulated. Leamer begins with a discussion of the key methodological difficulties of testing, lamenting the lack of real interaction between economists who are interested in the properties of models, and econometricians, who are primarily interested in the properties of data. The core of his chapter is then taken up with an evaluation of the results of empirical studies of the Ricardian, Ricardo–Viner and Heckscher–Ohlin models, as well as an overview of the growing literature on intra-industry trade and imperfect competition. The survey concludes with a discussion of empirical studies of the effects of demand, and growth and openness. Leamer's survey is both descriptive and prescriptive. He provides an organized and comprehensive overview of a vast literature; in addition, however, he also gives a clear prescriptive steer on the way in which trade analysts should do things in order to produce empirical work which is better focused and methodologically more secure.

Although not as extensively surveyed as the theory of international trade, the theory of protection has been the subject of a number of major treatises. James Anderson's survey in chapter 5 differs from previous surveys in two important respects. First, the emphasis is on providing a general framework which can be used to illustrate the power of simple tools. Second, the entire analysis is conducted via the dual approach. The result is an evaluation which is both elegant and clear. Following an outline of the dual method, Anderson develops a trade policy accounting framework for evaluating the welfare consequences of trade policy changes. Both standard allocative effects and rent-seeking losses are discussed. From early contributions by Bhagwati and others, it is well established that there are important non-equivalences between instruments. Anderson uses his framework to investigate optimal intervention in the presence of both domestic and international distortions. Another important area for development has been the structure of protection, and this too is investigated, with particular reference to the theory of effective protection. Policy conditionality has been an important ingredient in the lending programmes of the World Bank over the last ten years or so, in which trade policy reforms have figured prominently. In the final part of his survey Anderson investigates timing and sequencing issues from a theoretical standpoint, showing that the issues are not quite as simple as they appear to be at first blush.

At times Anderson touches upon endogenous trade policy. He does no more than that however, as chapter 6 by Stephen Magee is a survey of the political economy of trade policy. As with a number of the other topics addressed in this volume, we have seen an enormous amount of work on this issue, both theoretical and empirical. Magee has been at the forefront of this work. In the first part of his chapter he surveys the early literature which concentrated on explaining the pattern of tariffs across activities and across countries, as well as refining the concept of rent-seeking. Following this, endogenous policy theory is explained. This begins from the presumption that wealth is accumulated by production and predation – the former increases total wealth, the latter simply redistributes it. In general production is co-operative and predation non-co-operative. Magee, Brock and Young (1979) formally develop a model on the basis of these presumptions. As well as raising some interesting welfare problems, the framework explains a number of important features of protection in the 'real world'. The chapter concludes with a review of recent empirical work, focusing in particular on the structure of protection and the revealed preference on the part of policy-makers for relatively inefficient instruments like voluntary export restraints.

Another key area for innovative work in recent years has been strategic trade policy. This was stimulated by insights from the imperfect competition and international trade literature, and employs the tools of modern game theory to model strategic interaction. This literature is surveyed in chapter 7 by Didier Laussel and Christian Montet. The seminal work on strategic trade policy is Brander and Spencer (1984a, b). There, the notion that rents could be systematically shifted by government intervention in oligopolistic industries was first explored. Laussel and Montet formally outline the Brander–Spencer model and show how, even in a relatively simple setting, the results are sensitive to assumptions regarding conjectural variation. The analysis is then extended to a two-stage game-theoretic setting where firms choose location or R&D expenditure prior to competing on price or quantity. Conclusions regarding optimal policy are much harder to pin down in this more complex setting. On the other hand, however, it does permit investigation of industrial policy and trade policy.

Laussel and Montet take a broader view of strategic trade policy than that associated with Brander and Spencer and go on to investigate strategic interactions between governments. Again, making use of the tools of modern game theory, they show how we can gain insights into co-operative and non-co-operative behaviour on the part of governments, and the factors which are likely to result in one rather than the other. The burgeoning theoretical literature on strategic trade policy has stimulated a literature directed at quantification. This is the subject of the final part of the chapter. Not surprisingly perhaps, the results reported are mixed. However, if any conclusion can be reached thus far, it is that the conditions for successful intervention in oligopolistic industries are likely to be rare, and the pro-competitive and scale benefits available reaffirm the superiority of free trade.

The appropriate role of international trade in economic development has long been a controversial issue. Recent work, both theoretical and empirical, suggests that protectionist policies are likely to be damaging to development prospects, and this has been influential in stimulating extensive liberalization. In chapter 8 Paul Collier and Jan Gunning briefly review the literature on the structure of protection in developing countries and the factors which explain relatively high levels of protection. The bulk of their survey is, however, directed at two more recent developments – trade shocks, and liberalization attempts and consequences.

Developing countries are especially susceptible to trade shocks, given their relatively concentrated export structure. Two features of shocks appear to be important: first, asymmetries in the gains/losses associated with positive/negative shocks; second, the tendency for temporary shocks to stimulate permanent increases in protection. Collier and Gunning outline a framework within which one can analyse the consequences of trade shocks, and explain the subtle interactions between a given shock and the structure of protection. The other important issue which Collier and Gunning address is the process, and progress, of liberalization. Recent work emanating from the World Bank seems to suggest that it is a relatively straightforward process. If so, why do so many liberalizations get aborted? The authors assess recent work and point up the role of appropriate sequencing, policy compatability, timing, and support measures. The key point which they emphasize is the role which the exchange rate can, and should, play in a liberalization episode.

Regionalism in the world economy is currently a major theme in policy discussions, stimulated by the deepening of integration arrangements in Europe, North America and East Asia. In chapter 9 Robert Hine surveys the literature on international economic integration. Following a brief taxonomy of integration arrangements, he reviews the classic Vinerian framework and its many extensions and refinements. As well as bringing out the key concepts, he assesses the contribution which this paradigm has made to our understanding of the customs union issue. He concludes that, until relatively recently, the legacy of this literature had been a relatively small number of insights. Extensions into higher dimensions, non-marginal tariff changes and imperfect competition, have enhanced its usefulness. As in other areas, the theoretical literature has spawned a large empirical literature which Hine also surveys. As well as reviewing early work using elasticities and trade share approaches, he evaluates the output of recent computable general equilibrium modelling exercises. Although most of the discussion concentrates on the EC it also extends to recent work on the North Amerian Free Trade Area (NAFTA). In general, the results point to net gains from integration. Of course, even when we identify net gains, there may nevertheless be important policy issues arising from the distribution of those gains. In the final section of the chapter Hine discusses allocational issues and other policy problems associated with harmonization and external trade policy.

The focus of international trade theory and policy has tended to be merchandise trade – trade in goods. Trade in services, however, now amounts to about one-third of the value of merchandise trade. As trade in services has become increasingly important, so analysts have become increasingly more interested in explaining the phenomenon. Chapter 10 by André Sapir and Chantal Winter is devoted to services trade. They begin by trying to pin down the exact nature of a service – something which is actually quite difficult. In fact, different types of service transaction can be identified, depending upon where production and consumption occur, and the interaction between consumers and producers. Having defined the characteristics of services, Sapir and Winter then go on to explain the determinants of international trade in services. They show how, if perfect competition prevails, we can explain services trade using the same technology as we do to explain trade in goods. Since, however, much of the provision of services occurs under conditions of imperfect competition, much work remains to be done. This also applies to empirical analysis of trade in services. Work here is hampered partly by the relatively narrow theoretical base on which it is built, and partly by the deficiencies of official data. What limited evidence we do have suggests that relative factor endowments are an important explanatory factor. Finally, Sapir and Winter evaluate welfare implications and the role of commercial policy, both in theory and in practice. Work thus far suggests that there are mutual gains from trade in services, and that liberal trade policies are therefore appropriate. As they show in their discussions, this has not prevented trade in services from being contentious in the Uruguay Round.

When suppliers from one nation set up a branch in another nation to provide goods or services, we have foreign direct investment (FDI), and a link is generally established between international trade and international production. This is the subject of chapter 11 by John Cantwell. It has been a major research programme over the post-war period, and has recently enjoyed a revival, partly because of the emergence of the new industrial economics. Cantwell begins by assessing the various ways in which the emergence of MNCs can be explained. Since his theme is international trade and international production, he then goes on to show just how important intra-firm trade is to MNCs, and to explain how it arises. A prominent feature of this intra-firm trade is that it also tends to be intra-industry trade. This can be due to both horizontal and vertical specialization, and Cantwell shows how recent work on imperfect competition and international trade can help explain this. Cantwell shows how the relationship between international trade and international production is an essentially complementary one and investigates how the changing structure of international production impacts on the trade of MNCs.

As noted at the outset, the volume does not claim to be completely comprehensive. It does, however, endeavour to cover most of the fields where important work in international trade – theory and policy – is under way. We hope that this collection of surveys is sufficiently comprehensive to meet the needs of most specialists in international trade.

REFERENCES

Brander, J. and Spencer, B. 1984a: Trade warfare: tariffs and cartels. *Journal of International Economics*, 16, 227–42.

Brander, J. and Spencer, B. 1984b: Tariff protection and imperfect competition. In H. Kierzkowski (ed.), *Monopolistic Competition and International Trade*, New York: Oxford University Press, 194–206.

Dixit, Avinash K. and Stiglitz, Joseph E. 1977: Monopolistic competition and optimum product diversity. *American Economic Review*, 67, 297–308.

Lancaster, Kelvin 1979: *Variety, Equity and Efficiency*. New York: Columbia University Press.

Magee, S. P., Brock, W. A. and Young, L. 1989: *Black Hole Tariffs and Endogenous Policy Theory*. Cambridge: Cambridge University Press.

2

THE THEORY OF INTERNATIONAL TRADE

Rodney E. Falvey

2.1 INTRODUCTION

The theory of international trade is concerned with the effects of trade on resource allocation and income distribution both among and within each of the participating countries. Three related issues have been the focus of attention. First, what determines the pattern of trade (i.e. who trades what with whom and at which prices)? Second, what are the sources of any gains from trade, and how are these distributed among the trading partners? Third, what are the implications of trade for the structure of production and returns to factors within each trading country? Answering these questions requires the development of general equilibrium models involving at least two countries, two products (an importable and an exportable), and two factors (in order to generate a factoral distribution of income that can be affected by trade).

Early developments concentrated on the construction of simple (or 'low dimensional') models. These were designed to highlight those specific aspects or interrelationships thought to be most relevant and to illustrate basic principles that were expected, at least implicitly, to carry over to more complex situations. The advantage of considering a variety of simple economic models is that it allows the examination of a range of relationships, each of which is likely to be important in some, but not necessarily all, contexts. The focus can then be placed on important aspects, which would tend to be obscured in more general models. The disadvantage is that the generality of the results may be unclear.

Subsequent developments have aimed at capturing important aspects excluded from these simple models. This has involved both examining the extent to which the propositions derived in simple models can be generalized, and searching for new propositions which might only emerge in a more general context. From this approach a general body of theory has been developed which has informed discussions of trade theory and policy over the last several decades.

In presenting this theory it is useful to follow the same process of generalization. Not all topics in trade theory can be considered here, however. Many of the other surveys in this volume cover important aspects of trade theory, particularly its most recent developments. In consequence this chapter will concentrate on what has been labelled the 'traditional' theory and examine only some of its potential extensions. I hope the outcome is both a useful survey and helpful background to the other chapters.

2.2 THE STANDARD ASSUMPTIONS

The models that trade theorists have traditionally chosen to work with have had a number of common features. This has provided familiarity and has allowed the implications of individual assumptions to be examined in isolation. It is therefore helpful to specify at the outset a set of 'standard' assumptions which will carry through most of the chapter, with variations noted as they occur.

1 *Dimensionality*. There are two countries, *n* products and *m* factors of production. Each country is endowed with a fixed stock of each of the factors.
2 *Mobility*. Factors can move costlessly among industries within a country, but are completely immobile internationally. There are zero transport costs and no other impediments to the international flow of products. There are no non-traded products, and all products are final products.
3 *Competition*. All agents are price-takers in product and factor markets. Producers maximize profits and factor returns adjust to ensure full employment of all factors.
4 *Technology*. Production functions for all products exhibit constant returns to scale and diminishing marginal products of factors. Each country has the same productive technology for each good. There are no factor intensity reversals (see section 2.4.2 below).
5 *Tastes*. Consumers everywhere have identical homothetic utility functions.

Under these assumptions producers of each product choose that input mix which minimizes the cost of producing their chosen level of output. Given constant returns to scale, this cost-minimizing input mix depends only on relative factor returns and is independent of the level of output, so that one can write

$$a_{ij} = a_{ij}(\mathbf{W}) \quad i = 1, \ldots, m; j = 1, \ldots, n$$

where a_{ij} denotes the number of units of factor *i* used to produce each unit of output *j* and $\mathbf{W} = (w_1, \ldots, w)$ is the vector of factor returns. The unit cost of production for each product

$$C_j(\mathbf{W}) = \sum_{i=1}^{m} a_{ij}(\mathbf{W}) \cdot w_i \quad j = 1, \ldots, n$$

is then independent of the level of outputs.

In aggregate, production is subject to resource constraints (full employment conditions) that

$$\sum_{j=1}^{n} a_{ij}(\mathbf{W}) \cdot X_j = V_i \quad i = 1, \ldots, m \tag{2.1}$$

where X_j is the output of product j $(j = 1, \ldots, n)$ and V_i is the economy's endowment of factor i $(i = 1, \ldots, m)$. Competition ensures that in equilibrium the unit price for product j (p_j) is no greater than its average cost, i.e.

$$C_j(\mathbf{W}) \geqslant p_j \quad j = 1, \ldots, n \tag{2.2}$$

with equality holding for those products actually produced.

On the demand side aggregate consumption is constrained by aggregate income. The budget constraint can be represented in two equivalent ways as

$$\sum_{j=1}^{n} p_j D_j = \sum_{j=1}^{n} p_j X_j \tag{2.3a}$$

or

$$\sum_{j=1}^{n} p_j M_j = 0 \tag{2.3b}$$

where D_j is the aggregate demand for product j, and M_j $(= D_j - X_j)$ represents net imports of product j (so that $M_j > 0$ if product j is imported, and $M_j < 0$ if product j is exported). With this general structure in the background, we can begin to investigate specific trade models.

2.3 COMPARATIVE ADVANTAGE: THE RICARDIAN MODEL

The most fundamental, and famous, result in trade theory – that the trade pattern will be based on relative and not absolute efficiency in production – can be demonstrated quite simply. Suppose we adopt the standard assumptions, except that technologies are not identical across countries. Suppose further that there are only two products $(n = 2)$ and one scarce factor – labour $(m = 1)$. Production in any country is then constrained by the single full employment condition that

$$a_{L_1} X_1 + a_{L_2} X_2 = L \tag{2.4}$$

Given constant returns to scale, the frontier of this production set is linear with a slope which depends only on relative labour productivities in the two products.[1]

If both products are to be produced in autarky, the zero profit conditions

$$a_{L_j} w = p_j \quad j = 1, 2$$

12   RODNEY E. FALVEY

where w is the wage rate, imply autarky relative product prices are

$$p_2/p_1 = a_{L_2}/a_{L_1}$$

At any other relative price producers would find it profitable to specialize in the production of only one of the goods.

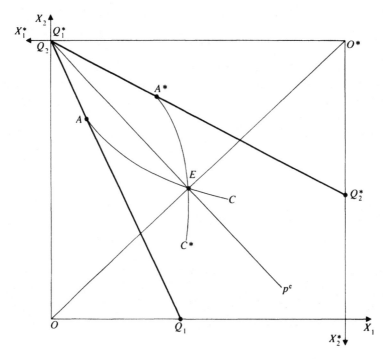

Figure 2.1 Trading equilibrium for two countries

A trading equilibrium for two such countries (home and foreign) is illustrated in figure 2.1. There the home and foreign production sets are represented by OQ_1Q_2 and $O^*Q_1^*Q_2^*$ respectively, under the assumption that

$$\text{(home)} \quad \frac{a_{L_2}}{a_{L_1}} < \frac{a_{L_2}^*}{a_{L_1}^*} \quad \text{(foreign)}$$

so that the home country has the lower autarky relative price of product 2. In the trading equilibrium the world relative price ratio must lie in the (closed) range $[a_{L_2}/a_{L_1}, a_{L_2}^*/a_{L_1}^*]$, for at any other relative price ratio producers in both countries would attempt to specialize in the production of the same product. For any price ratio in the interior of this range, countries will specialize, each producing only that product in whose production it is relatively most efficient[2] (or alternatively stated, that product in the production of which this country has a *comparative advantage*). In our example, the home country would produce and export product 2 and import product 1. It is important to note that this trade would occur even if one country had a superior technology (*an absolute advantage*) in the production of both goods (that is, a_{L_j} exceeds or falls below $a_{L_j}^*$ for $j = 1$ and 2).

While the trade pattern is determined by differences in technology, the actual trading equilibrium also depends on preferences. In this equilibrium consumers in both countries have identical homothetic tastes and face identical relative prices. They will be consuming the two products in equal proportions therefore. For equilibria in which both countries are specialized, the consumption allocation will lie somewhere on the diagonal OO^* in figure 2.1. The exact location on this diagonal will depend on tastes, and can be found by tracing out the desired consumption allocations for each of the countries for each of the price ratios in the closed range. Allocation A represents the home country's autarky consumption allocation and locus AC traces out its desired consumption path as the relative price of product 2 is increased beyond its autarky level. Similarly locus A^*C^* traces out the desired consumption path of the foreign country. Allocation E, where these loci intersect, is the free trade equilibrium, with the corresponding world price ratio (or *terms of trade*) indicated by the slope of p^e.[3] The gains from trade are demonstrated by the fact that both countries are consuming outside their production sets.[4] Again the potential for such gains results from comparative advantage, and is independent of whether or not one country has an absolute advantage in the production of both products. Obviously absolute technical efficiency is important in determining income and welfare levels, but the basic point that emerges in this Ricardian framework is that it is comparative and not absolute advantage that is the source of trade and the gains from trade.

2.4 FACTOR PROPORTIONS:
THE HECKSCHER–OHLIN MODEL

While the Ricardian framework usefully illustrates basic determinants of the pattern and gains from trade, it has limitations when it comes to analysing other questions of interest to trade theorists. A one-factor model can say nothing about the effects of trade on a country's factoral distribution of income. Further its prediction of widespread production specialization is generally inconsistent with empirical observation.[5] Nor is it comforting to have trade patterns predicted on the basis of exogenously given differences in technology, when technology itself is tradable. Recognition of these limitations underlay the development of alternative models which return to the assumption of identical technologies but which allow for more than one factor. In such models the trade pattern is determined by differences in national factor endowments and the way the (common) technologies allow factors to be combined in the production of different products. Hence the label 'factor proportions' models of trade.

The pre-eminent model of this type is known as the Heckscher–Ohlin (or HO) model. It makes the standard assumptions listed in section 2.2 while

restricting the dimensionality of both products and factors to two
($n = m = 2$). As we shall see, both the low dimensionality (2) and the equality
($n = m$) are crucial to the results obtained. The low dimensionality does have
the advantage that the results can be illustrated diagrammatically, however.
For convenience of exposition the factors will be labelled labour and capital.

2.4.1 The Gains from Trade

Figure 2.2 depicts the production set (OQ_1Q_2) of the home country, given its
factor endowments and technology and assuming that the cost-minimizing
input combinations used in the two products are not identical.[6] In autarky
this country's consumption possibilities are constrained by this set. Suppose
A indicates the autarky equilibrium production and consumption allocation.

Now consider the possibility of trade. Suppose this country is small on
world markets and faces given world prices as indicated by p^e in figure 2.2. If
production occurs at X^t consumption can then occur at any point on C_1C_2
(where trade will be balanced). This locus lies outside the autarky consumption possibility set everywhere but at X^t. Only if world prices equal autarkic
prices (whence $X^t = A$) will there be no trade and therefore no gains from
trade.

If the home country is large, world prices will depend on the desired volume
of trade. The more the country wishes to import (and export) the worse its

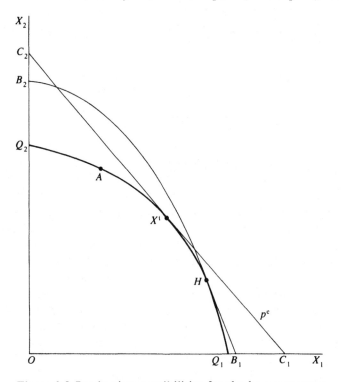

Figure 2.2 Production possibilities for the home country

terms of trade, other things equal. A consumption possibility set can also be constructed in this case, and its frontier is represented by the 'Baldwin frontier' $(B_1 B_2)$ in figure 2.2.[7] Since trade itself does not 'shrink' the production set there are potential gains from trade through the ability to consume outside it. The internal distribution of these gains is a separate issue, of course.

2.4.2 Trade And Factor Returns: The Factor Price Equalization Theorem

With more than one factor, factor returns depend on relative product prices and (possibly) factor endowments. One area of interest to trade theorists has been the effect of trade on factor returns. Since product trade indirectly allows competition between the same factor in different countries, should we expect a tendency to equalization in their rates of return? In the HO model we actually get more than this.

If w is the wage rate, and r the rental on capital, the competitive profit conditions become

$$a_{L_j}(Z)w + a_{K_j}(Z)r \geq p_j \quad j = 1, 2 \qquad (2.5)$$

where $Z = w/r$. If both goods are produced, this becomes a system of two (non-linear) equations in two unknowns (w, r) for given product prices. As long as both countries are non-specialized in production, trade equates relative product prices internationally, technologies are identical across countries (so that cost-minimizing factor inputs are identical functions of relative factor returns) and factor proportions are not identical across industries,[8] equation (2.5) will have a unique solution, i.e. trade will equalize factor returns internationally. This is the *factor price equalization* (FPE) theorem.

This is a very strong result. But the technology and factor endowments do limit the possibilities of a non-specialized trading equilibrium with FPE. In figure 2.3 loci $x_j x_j, j = 1, 2$ represent the unit value isoquants for the two products, at the given equilibrium relative product prices (i.e. the isoquants corresponding to output levels equal in value to one unit of the numeraire). Cost minimization by producers implies that the input combinations actually employed will be such that the marginal rate of technical substitution between inputs (the slope of the isoquant) will be equal to (minus) their relative factor returns (the slope of the relevant isocost line). In equilibrium then, if both the zero profit conditions are satisfied, so that both goods are being produced, factor returns must be such that both unit value isoquants are tangent to the same (unit value) isocost line (that shown by $F_1 F_2$ in figure 2.3).[9]

The uniqueness of this tangent is essential to FPE. If the unit value isoquants coincided over some range, or if isoquants of different products could intersect more than once,[10] there would be more than one potential tangent, and hence more than one set of factor returns consistent with these product prices.

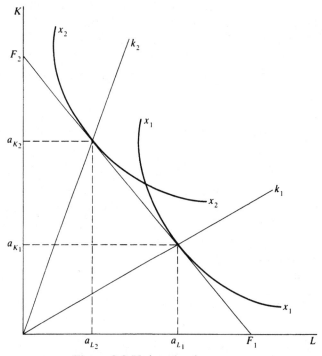

Figure 2.3 Unit value isoquants

Along with equilibrium factor returns, figure 2.3 indicates the equilibrium capital/labour ratios ($k_j = a_{K_j}/a_{L_j}$, $j = 1, 2$) used in the two industries. Given the full employment conditions

$$L_1 + L_2 = L \tag{2.6a}$$

$$K_1 + K_2 = K \tag{2.6b}$$

the allocation of factors can be determined. Dividing both (2.6a) and (2.6b) by L, and rewriting in terms of capital/labour ratios, one obtains

$$\lambda_{L_1} + \lambda_{L_2} = 1 \tag{2.7a}$$

$$\lambda_{L_1} k_1 + \lambda_{L_2} k_2 = \bar{k} \tag{2.7b}$$

where λ_{i_j} is the share of the endowment of factor i employed in sector $j (\lambda_{i_j} \geq 0, \lambda_{i_1} + \lambda_{i_2} = 1, i = K, L, j = 1, 2)$ and $\bar{k}$ is the economy's endowment ratio ($\bar{k} = K/L$). From these two equations the equilibrium allocation of labour can be directly determined, and then the corresponding allocations of capital solved from the k_j.

These equations also indicate the limitation that factor endowments place on factor prices for a non-specialized equilibrium, since from (2.7b), $\bar{k}$ must be a positively weighted average of k_1 and k_2. Consider figure 2.4, where

$k_j(Z)$ depicts the relationship between the cost-minimizing input mix for product j and the wage/rental ratio. This diagram is constructed under the assumption that product 2 is everywhere 'relatively capital intensive' – that is $k_2(Z) > k_1(Z)$ at any common factor price ratio.[11] If the economy's factor endowment ratio is $\bar{k}$, then full employment requires a wage/rental ratio somewhere in the range $[Z_1, Z_u]$. At Z_1, the economy would be specialized in the production of the relatively capital-intensive product (corresponding to production at Q_2 in figure 2.2). As Z increases, labour becomes relatively more expensive, cost-minimizing capital/labour ratios increase in both sectors and, for full employment to be maintained, resources must move towards the relatively labour-intensive product (production moves down the production frontier in figure 2.2). Such increases in Z could continue until Z_u is reached, at which point production would be specialized in the relatively labour-intensive product (at Q_1 in figure 2.2).[12]

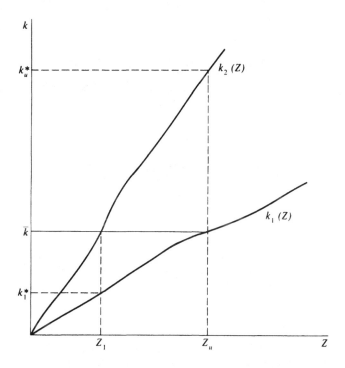

Figure 2.4 Cost-minimizing input combinations and factor prices

Given factor endowment ratios and identical technologies internationally, FPE is only possible if the ranges of factor return ratios consistent with non-specialized equilibria in the two countries overlap. In figure 2.4, this would require that the foreign factor endowment ratio be somewhere in the range $[k_1^*, k_u^*]$. A requirement for FPE is therefore that factor endowment ratios be 'sufficiently similar'. If they are not, then one or both countries must be specialized in production in the trading equilibrium.[13]

2.4.3 The Pattern of Trade: The Heckscher–Ohlin Theorem

If one or both countries are specialized in production in the trading equilibrium, then the trade pattern will be obvious. But what if the trading equilibrium meets the conditions for FPE? What determines 'comparative advantage' then?

With identical relative prices and identical homothetic tastes the products are consumed in the same proportions in the two countries. Home consumption of product j can then be written as

$$D_j = \alpha \cdot (D_j + D_j^*) = \alpha \cdot (X_j + X_j^*) \quad j = 1, 2$$

where α is equal to the home share of world income, i.e.

$$\alpha = \frac{(w + r\bar{k})L}{(w + r\bar{k})L + (w + r\bar{k}^*)L^*} \tag{2.8}$$

If the full employment conditions (2.6a) and (2.6b) are rewritten as

$$a_{L_1}X_1 + a_{L_2}X_2 = L \tag{2.9a}$$

$$a_{K_1}X_1 + a_{K_2}X_2 = K \tag{2.9b}$$

one can solve for outputs in terms of factor proportions and endowments. Defining β_j as the share of home output in total world output of good j, i.e.

$$X_j = \beta_j \cdot (X_j + X_j^*)$$

in the free trade equilibrium one has that

$$\beta_j = \frac{(k_h - \bar{k}) \cdot L}{(k_h - \bar{k})L + (k_h - \bar{k}^*)L^*} \quad j, h = 1, 2 \quad j \neq h \tag{2.10}$$

Then $M_j = D_j - X_j = (\alpha - \beta_j)(X_j + X^*)$.

The home country therefore imports (exports) product j as $\alpha > (<)\beta_j$ or, from (2.8) and (2.10), as

$$\frac{\bar{k} - \bar{k}^*}{(k_h - \bar{k})L + (k_h - \bar{k}^*)L^*} > (<) \, 0$$

If the home country is relatively capital abundant ($\bar{k} > \bar{k}^*$) then $\beta_2 > \alpha > \beta_1$ and it will export (import) the relatively capital (labour)-intensive product. This is the 'quantity version' of the *Heckscher–Ohlin (HO) theorem*: if the conditions for factor price equalization are met and both countries have identical homothetic tastes, then in free trade each country will export the product making relatively intensive use of its relatively abundant factor. Here relative factor abundance is defined in terms of the relative quantities of the factors in the two countries' endowments.

The intuition underlying this result is straightforward. Identical technologies and factor prices imply identical factor proportions are used in each industry across countries. For full employment then, the relatively capital-abundant country will have to employ relatively more of its resources in the capital-intensive sector. With products consumed in the same proportions in each country, this implies that the capital-intensive product will be exported.

2.4.4 Factor Returns and Product Prices: the Stolper–Samuelson Theorem

The relative product price changes that accompany the opening of the economy to trade will affect the real incomes of factor owners. One question of interest is whether the gains from trade are automatically passed on to all factors in terms of higher real incomes? Or are some factors winners and others losers in terms of the effects of trade on their real incomes?

The implications of trade for the internal factoral distribution of income can be obtained via the competitive profit conditions. For concreteness consider the effects of a small product price change from an initial non-specialized equilibrium. From (2.5) one can solve for

$$\Theta_{Lj}\hat{w} + \Theta_{Kj}\hat{r} = \hat{p}_j \quad j = 1, 2 \tag{2.11}$$

where Θ_{ij} is the share of factor i in the unit cost of product j, and a circumflex denotes a proportional change.[14] Equation (2.11) can be solved for the individual factor return changes, i.e.

$$\hat{w} = \frac{\Theta_{K_2}\hat{p}_1 - \Theta_{K_1}\hat{p}_2}{|\Theta|} \qquad \hat{r} = \frac{\Theta_{L_1}\hat{p}_2 - \Theta_{L_2}\hat{p}_1}{|\Theta|} \tag{2.12}$$

where $|\Theta| = \Theta_{L_1} - \Theta_{L_2} = \Theta_{K_2} - \Theta_{K_1}$ and $|\Theta| > 0$ if product 2 is relatively capital intensive. If the relative price of product 2 rises (i.e. $\hat{p}_2 > \hat{p}_1$), one obtains the 'magnification effect' (Jones, 1965) that

$$\hat{r} > \hat{p}_2 > \hat{p}_1 > \hat{w} \tag{2.13}$$

Equations (2.12) and (2.13) demonstrate the *Stolper–Samuelson (SS) theorem*: a small increase in the relative price of the relatively capital-intensive product will increase (reduce) the return to capital (labour) in terms of both products.

The same result applies to large price increases, for given factor endowments, provided there are no factor-intensity reversals. In figure 2.2, as the relative price of (capital-intensive) product 2 declines, and production moves from Q_2 towards Q_1 along the production frontier, the real return to labour is rising and the real return to capital is falling.

The SS theorem implies that the gains from trade are not passed on automatically in terms of higher real returns to both factors. But trade offers opportunities for potential Pareto improvements, in that the winners could fully compensate the losers and remain better off than in autarky, provided appropriate non-distortionary redistribution mechanisms were available (e.g. lump-sum taxes and subsidies).[15]

This relationship between product and factor prices also provides a 'price version' of the HO theorem. The country with the higher autarky relative price of the capital-intensive good will have the higher autarky real return to capital. Interpreting factor abundance in terms of factor returns (i.e. the relatively labour-abundant country is that with the lower real return to labour in autarky), then each country will have the lower autarky relative price of the product making intensive use of its relatively abundant factor, and will export that good in the trading equilibrium.

2.4.5 Outputs and Factor Endowments: The Rybczynski Theorem

One further area of interest to trade theorists has been the link between changes in factor endowments and changes in the composition of output at given product prices. What are the effects of population growth or capital accumulation on a country's industrial structure? For 'small' endowment changes (i.e. those that do not move the country outside its original 'cone of diversification') the country remains non-specialized in production, and constant product prices imply constant factor rentals and hence unchanged input/output coefficients. Differentiating the full employment conditions (equations (2.9a) and (2.9b)):

$$\lambda_{L_1}\hat{X}_1 + \lambda_{L_2}\hat{X}_2 = \hat{L} \qquad (2.14a)$$

$$\lambda_{K_1}\hat{X}_1 + \lambda_{K_2}\hat{X}_2 = \hat{K} \qquad (2.14b)$$

Solving for output changes,

$$\hat{X}_1 = \frac{\lambda_{K_2}\hat{L} - \lambda_{L_2}\hat{K}}{|\lambda|} \qquad \hat{X}_2 = \frac{\lambda_{L_1}\hat{K} - \lambda_{K_1}\hat{L}}{|\lambda|} \qquad (2.15)$$

where $|\lambda| = \lambda_{L_1} - \lambda_{K_1} = \lambda_{K_2} - \lambda_{L_2}$ and $|\lambda| > 0$ under our factor intensity assumption. If the economy's capital/labour endowment ratio rises (i.e. $\hat{K} > \hat{L}$) then we again have a magnification effect

$$\hat{X}_2 > \hat{K} > \hat{L} > \hat{X}_1 \qquad (2.16)$$

Equations (2.15) and (2.16) demonstrate the *Rybczynski (R) theorem*: at constant relative prices, a small increase in the economy's capital/labour endowment ratio will increase (reduce) the output of the relatively capital (labour)-intensive good, relative to both factors.

The intuition underlying this theorem is also straightforward. Suppose the economy's capital stock increases. Then, if both industries are to continue using unchanged input mixes, the only way this additional capital can be employed is by expanding the output of the relatively capital-intensive industry and contracting the output of the labour-intensive industry. Since the latter releases more labour per unit of capital than is used by the former this adjustment generates some labour to be employed with the additional capital.

A large change in endowments may require that the economy specialize in production to maintain full employment at the given product prices. In this case factor returns would also alter. In particular the real return of the now relatively more abundant factor would fall.

These then are the major results of the HO model. Because of its simple structure, this framework generates quite precise answers to the three questions posed in the Introduction. The intuition obtained from studying this framework has guided economists' views of trade and trade policy for several decades. From this perspective the importance of extending this framework of analysis is apparent. One needs to know how sensitive these results are to the quite restrictive assumptions underlying the model, particularly since early attempts at empirical verification suggested a 2×2 framework was quite inadequate for explaining the trade pattern.[16]

2.5 RELAXING THE STANDARD ASSUMPTIONS

In order to isolate the significance of specific assumptions, the usual procedure has been to relax them one at a time where possible. This approach will also be followed here.[17]

2.5.1 Factor Intensity Reversals (FIRs)

The major theorems of the HO model rely on an ability to characterize goods as relatively capital or labour intensive. But what if there are FIRs, i.e. factor return ratios at which the $k_j(Z)$ schedules intersect in figure 2.4? Each product is then relatively capital intensive at some factor return ratios, and relatively labour intensive at others. We have also lost the monotonic relationship between relative product prices and relative factor returns.

Suppose the two countries' factor endowment ratios lie on different sides of an FIR in figure 2.4. Then any common product price ratio will be consistent with two quite different factor return ratios in the two trading partners[18] (the relatively capital-abundant country will have the higher w/r ratio). FPE will not then obtain. The relatively capital-intensive product in one country will be the same product as the relatively labour-intensive product in the other. Since both countries cannot export (or import) the same product in equilibrium, both must be exporting either their labour-intensive or their capital-intensive products and hence one country must violate the HO theorem. Neither the price nor quantity versions of this theorem can hold. Note, however, that the relatively capital-abundant country will use relatively more capital-intensive techniques to produce both products, so that this country's exports, whichever product they turn out to be, will be more capital intensive than the labour-abundant country's exports. In this sense the spirit of the HO theorem is maintained.

The SS and R results will continue to hold for small changes. For large changes that move the equilibrium across an FIR, there are obvious difficulties since relative factor intensities are no longer well defined.

2.5.2 Taste Differences

The implications of taste differences can be dealt with very briefly. If the relatively capital-abundant country has a sufficiently large taste bias towards the relatively capital-intensive good, for example, the trade pattern would be the reverse of that predicted by the HO theorem. The other results, which relate solely to the production structure, should be unaffected.

2.5.3 'Dissimilar' Factor Endowments

Although trade is generated by factor endowment differences in the HO theory, if these differences are too great then some of the standard theorems will not apply. The HO theorem will still hold, but FPE will not and nor will the SS or R theorems in the specialized economy. As long as it remains specialized, an increase in the relative price of the produced product will generate equiproportionate rises in both factor returns, and an increase in any one factor endowment will see a less than proportionate increase in the output of the produced product.

2.5.4 Technology Differences

The assumption that technologies are identical across countries is basic to the HO framework and is a major point of departure from the Ricardian model. None the less it is clear that this assumption is restrictive, particularly in the short run. A large literature dealing with technology differences exists, much of it developed during the 1960s. In addition, considerable attention has been devoted to the dynamic aspects of the generation and transfer of technology internationally, and the implications this has for the product pattern of trade over time.[19] Rather than attempting to summarize this large literature, we will simply note the implications of existing technology differences for the standard trade theorems.

Technology differences can be divided into two major categories, although in practice most are likely to be a combination of both.

1 *Product augmenting*: where one country can produce a larger output from the same factor inputs in a particular sector (or sectors). Product-augmenting technical changes act very much like product price changes.

2 *Factor augmenting*: where a factor (or factors) in one country is uniformly more productive than the same factor in the other, independent of the sector in which the factor is employed. Factor-augmenting technical changes act very much like factor endowment changes.

Equalization of product prices will not give equalization of factor returns if there are technology differences, whether product or factor augmenting, even if both countries are non-specialized. The left-hand sides of (2.5) will be different functions of factor returns in the two countries.

When considering the trade pattern one has the problem that technology differences themselves can provide a basis for trade – as illustrated by the Ricardian model. Even with identical factor endowments, countries would have a different mix of outputs at the same product prices. If technology differences are purely factor augmenting the trade pattern might be explained in terms of 'effective' factor endowments, i.e. adjusting units of measurement to take account of the effects of technology differences on factor productivity. But to the extent technology differences are product augmenting there are now two potential determinants of the pattern of trade, and, indeed, it may be difficult to classify goods in terms of factor intensities.

The SS and R theorems will be unaffected by international technology differences, since they deal with small changes in only one country. Obviously these effects need no longer be the same in the two countries.

2.5.5 Transport Costs and Non-traded Products

Included in the mobility assumptions of traditional trade models is the assumption that products face zero international transport costs. This assumption has been relaxed to allow for 'wastage' as products are transported, and to include an additional industry producing transport services (Casas, 1983). One simple means of highlighting the potential significance of transport costs, however, is to draw a distinction between traded products for which transport costs are zero, and non-traded products for which they are prohibitive.

In general there are three features non-traded products might add to the standard framework. First, since each country must produce its own requirements of these products it cannot specialize away from them. Second, the factors available for producing traded products, and hence the 'endowment' relevant for determining the pattern of trade, are the total resource endowment minus the factors employed in producing non-traded products. Third, since the markets for non-traded products are country specific, one would expect their domestic prices (and quantities) to adjust to ensure domestic market clearing, so that trade would not necessarily result in the equalization of all product prices internationally.

With these features in mind, one can see that the results generated by adding a third non-traded product to the standard two-traded-product two-factor trade model will be interesting but rather special (Ethier, 1972). If product trade equalizes factor returns internationally (equation (2.5) still holds for the traded products), then non-traded product costs and hence prices will also be equalized internationally, provided the assumption of identical technologies is extended to cover the non-traded product. It is then only the output of non-traded products that adjusts to clear their domestic markets, and product price and factor return equalization are preserved.

It is important to emphasize, however, that this result (and the analogues for the other standard theorems) reflects the rather special properties of the HO framework when it is extended to allow for more products than factors ($n > m$), rather than the effects of 'non-tradedness' *per se*. If the number of factors exceeds the number of products, equalization of non-traded product prices (or factor returns) would not be expected in general. Questions relating to the relative numbers of products and factors are discussed in more detail in section 2.7.

Models including non-traded products have proved particularly useful in the analysis of trade issues facing small open economies. The 'Dutch disease' or 'booming sector' literature is an example (Corden and Neary, 1982). There the main issue is the effects of an expansion in one traded sector, on other traded sectors. An important element in the analysis is the adjustment in the 'real terms of trade' (the relative price of non-traded products in terms of traded products).

2.5.6 Intermediate Products

The standard assumption is that all products are final products, that is, they enter directly into household consumption and are not intermediate inputs or components that enter into the production of other products. Yet a significant proportion of trade is in fact composed of raw material and intermediate input flows.

The existence of intermediate products also has significant implications for the standard trade models (Chacholiades, 1979; Ethier, 1979). First, they introduce the possibility of international trade in (produced) inputs. Are final product and intermediate input trade flows substitutes or complements? Second, a distinction can now be made between produced (intermediate) and primary (factor) inputs, with the cost of the latter being referred to as *value added*. If b_{h_j} represents the number of units of intermediate input h used per unit of output j, the competitive profit conditions can be rewritten as

$$\sum_{h=1}^{n} b_{h_j} p_h + \sum_{i=1}^{m} a_{ij} w_i \geqslant p_j \quad j = 1, \ldots, n$$

and value added in industry $j(\pi_j)$ is

$$\pi_j \equiv p_j - \sum_{h=1}^{n} b_{h_j} p_h = \sum_{i=1}^{m} a_{ij} w_i$$

It should be clear from this relationship that it is now the value added prices that will be relevant to the SS theorem.

Third, a similar distinction must be made between the *gross* and *net* outputs of a product. The net output takes account of the product's use as an intermediate input and measures the output actually available for final use. If X_h denotes the gross output of product h and x_h its net output then

$$x_h \equiv X_h - \sum_{j=1}^{n} b_{hj} X_j \quad h = 1, \dots, n.$$

Net output can be negative in a trading equilibrium (provided the product is imported).

Fourth, since factors are now used in production both directly (in value added) and indirectly (through the intermediate inputs) there are now two alternative measures of 'factor intensity' – direct (value added only) and total (direct plus indirect). Which measures will be relevant for the analogues to the standard trade theorems? (Hamilton and Svensson, 1983).

Simply adding inter-industry flows (i.e. the use by one industry of the other's output as an intermediate input) to the standard two-sector trade model does not change its basic results. Total factor intensities are an average of direct factor intensities, and the ranking of products by direct and total factor intensities is the same. Adding a pure intermediate product brings with it problems associated with unequal numbers of products and factors, which are left to section 2.7.

2.5.7 Variable Factor Supplies

An obvious move towards realism in the HO framework is to allow the supply of (at least) one factor to respond to changes in its real return. While most results continue to hold, the trade pattern can no longer be explained by differences in factor endowments. Instead one must refer to differences in factor *usage*. The effects of product price changes on real factor returns can be predicted, as before, from the SS theorem. The effects of the induced changes in factor supplies on outputs can then be determined from the R theorem.[20] With identical technologies, FPE will occur as long as both countries are non-specialized.

The implications of variable factor supplies for the HO theorem depend crucially on the sign of the relevant factor supply elasticities. If these elasticities are positive, then the HO theorem can simply be restated in terms of 'relatively abundant utilization'. Allowing variable factor supplies then makes no qualitative difference to the HO model. But negative elasticities (i.e. backward-bending factor supply functions) of sufficient magnitude can generate circumstances where an increase in a product's relative price leads to a fall in its output. Such perverse responses pose problems in predicting the trade pattern, but appear unlikely to occur in practice (Martin and Neary, 1980).

2.6 LIMITED FACTOR MOBILITY:
THE SPECIFIC FACTORS MODEL

Perhaps the most obviously restrictive features of the HO model are its small
dimensions – only two goods and two factors – and the equal number of
goods and factors. Considerable research effort has been devoted to extending the analysis to an $n \times m$ model, both with $m = n$ and $m \neq n$. The results
are considered in section 2.7. But before moving to this general literature it
is helpful to examine a simple $n < m$ model to complement our Ricardian
($n > m$) and HO ($n = m$) results. One then has some intuition for all three
cases.

The specific factors (or 'Ricardo–Viner') model has the same structure as
the HO except that capital is assumed to be product specific (i.e. capital does
not move between sectors). This can be viewed both as an interesting
framework in its own right, and as a 'short-run' version of the HO model,
aimed at highlighting the possibility that one factor (say labour) may be more
mobile than the other over some time frame.[21]

The competitive profit conditions are now

$$a_{L_j}w + a_{K_j}r_j \geqslant p_j \quad j = 1, 2 \tag{2.17}$$

where r_j denotes the return to capital in industry j. Even when both products
are produced, (2.17) is now a system of two equations in three unknowns, so
that factor returns cannot be determined on the basis of product prices alone.
Adding the full employment conditions

$$a_{L_1}X_1 + a_{L_2}X_2 = L \tag{2.18a}$$

$$a_{K_j}X_j = K_j \quad j = 1, 2 \tag{2.18b}$$

where K_j is the endowment of capital j, provides a system of five equations
in five unknowns (outputs and factor returns). Factor returns depend on both
product prices and factor endowments so that product price equalization
through trade will not ensure FPE in general.

Our interest here is in examining the effects of product price and factor
endowment changes on outputs and factor returns in order to derive the
analogous results to the standard theorems of the HO model. Consider figure
2.5 where the horizontal axis measures the labour endowment, and the
vertical axes measure the wage rate. Each T_jT_j locus represents the value of
the marginal product of labour in industry $j(VMPL_j)$ as a function of the
labour employed in that industry (L_j), given its stock of (sector-specific)
capital and product prices. In equilibrium, profit maximization ensures that
the wage rate is equal to the $VMPL$ in each sector, and the wage rate adjusts
to ensure labour is fully employed. The initial equilibrium in figure 2.5 is
denoted by E^0, with a wage of w^0 and an allocation of labour of OL^0 to
product 1, and L^0L to product 2. The value of outputs are given by the areas

under the respective *VMPL* curves up to the equilibrium employment.[22] Subtracting the wage bill (e.g. Ow^0 times OL^0 in industry 1) from the value of output in each industry leaves the corresponding value of payments to capital.

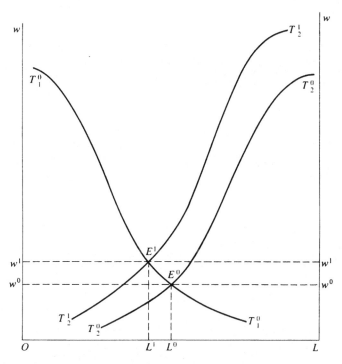

Figure 2.5 The specific factors model

Now suppose the relative price of product 2 rises. For any given employment in sector 2 this will raise the $VMPL_2$ in equal proportion to the product price increase. That is, T_2T_2 shifts upward (to $T_2^1 T_2^1$) equiproportionately to the rise in product price. The new equilibrium is at E^1 with:

1 An increase in the wage rate (from w^0 to w^1) that is less than proportional to the increase in p_2 (to be equiproportional E^1 would have to be vertically above E^0).
2 Changes in capital returns which can be derived by differentiating equation (2.17) to get

$$\Theta_{Lj}\hat{w} + \Theta_{Kj}\hat{r}_j = \hat{p}_j \quad j = 1, 2 \tag{2.19}$$

Since $\hat{p}_2 > \hat{w} > \hat{p}_1 (= 0)$, the magnification effect from (2.19) is

$$\hat{r}_2 > \hat{p}_2 > \hat{w} > \hat{p}_1 > \hat{r}_1 \tag{2.20}$$

Equation (2.20) provides the analogue to the SS theorem. An increase in the relative price of product j increases the real return to the factor specific to that sector, reduces the real return to the factor specific to the other sector, and has an ambiguous effect on the real return to the mobile factor.[23] Like the HO model, every relative price change results in a real winner and a real loser among the factors. But unlike that model, it is not clear here that for every factor we can find some relative price change that makes it a winner (or loser).

3 A shift in employment (of $L^1 L^0$) from product 1 to product 2, and, given unchanged stocks of specific factors, a corresponding increase in output of product 2 and decline in output of product 1.

The effects of endowment changes can also be inferred from figure 2.5. Suppose the capital endowment in sector 2 increases. This will raise the marginal product of labour for any given employment in that sector, so that $T_2 T_2$ will again shift up (but not necessarily equiproportionately) to say $T_2^1 T_2^1$. The new equilibrium is again represented by a point such as E^1, where:

1 The wage has risen in terms of both products. With no change in product prices, equation (2.19) implies a corresponding decline in the real returns to both specific factors.

2 Labour has moved from industry 1 to industry 2. However, since the marginal products of labour in both sectors have risen, the capital/labour ratios have increased in both sectors, so that the output increase in sector 2 is less than proportional to the capital increase in that sector.

It should also be clear, from figure 2.5, that an increase in the labour endowment, *ceteris paribus*, results, in general, in a decline in the real wage, an increase in the real return to both specific factors and an increase in the labour employment and outputs in both sectors.

In seeking an analogue to the R theorem (noting that constant product prices do not imply constant factor returns in this case), we have seen that an increase in either specific factor endowment leads to an increase in its own output (but less than proportionate to the endowment increase), and a decline in the other output. An increase in the mobile factor endowment leads to a decline in neither output, and while the proportionate increase in one output may exceed that of the labour force, it need not (Jones, 1971). Thus only some predictions of the R theorem carry over to a framework with more factors than products.

As this section has demonstrated, changing the (relative) dimensions of the model can have significant implications for its results. If these results are to guide our thinking on trade issues it is important, therefore, to consider the extent to which they can be generalized to the full $n \times m$ context (while maintaining the other standard assumptions) and what reinterpretations, if any, are required in this process. That is the task of section 2.7. Fortunately most of the insights of the simple models carry over if only in a somewhat weaker form.

2.7 MANY GOODS AND FACTORS[24]

At this point it is useful to switch to vector and matrix notation, and to represent the implications of profit maximization in terms of a national product function $G(\mathbf{P}, \mathbf{V})$ (Ethier, 1984, pp. 133–4). This function is defined by

$$G(\mathbf{P}, \mathbf{V}) = \max_{\mathbf{X}}\{\mathbf{P} \cdot \mathbf{X} : \mathbf{X} \in Y(\mathbf{V})\}$$

where $\mathbf{P}$ is, as before, the vector of output prices, and $Y(\mathbf{V})$ represents the technologically feasible set of (net) outputs, given the economy's vector of factor endowments $\mathbf{V}$ (i.e. $Y(\mathbf{V})$ is the production set). Function $G(\mathbf{P}, \mathbf{V})$ therefore represents the maximum value of output for this economy, given $\mathbf{P}$, $\mathbf{V}$ and its technology. Since the value of output $(\mathbf{P} \cdot \mathbf{X})$ is equal to the value of factor income $(\mathbf{W} \cdot \mathbf{V})$, the national product function also has a dual interpretation as the minimum payment made to factors, subject to price being no less than average cost for any product, i.e.

$$G(\mathbf{P}, \mathbf{V}) = \min_{\mathbf{W}}\{\mathbf{W}\mathbf{V} : \mathbf{W}\mathbf{A}(\mathbf{W}) \geqslant \mathbf{P}\}$$

2.7.1 The Gains from Trade

Consider two feasible equilibria for this economy, and let $\mathbf{P}^i$, $\mathbf{X}^i$, $\mathbf{D}^i$ and $\mathbf{M}^i$ denote the price, output, demand and net import vectors in equilibrium i $(i = 0, 1)$. Profit maximization and the budget constraint in equilibrium 1 imply that

$$\mathbf{P}^1 \cdot \mathbf{D}^1 = \mathbf{P}^1 \cdot \mathbf{X}^1 = G(\mathbf{P}^1, \mathbf{V}) \geqslant \mathbf{P}^1 \cdot \mathbf{X}^0$$

Using the market clearing $(\mathbf{X}^0 = \mathbf{D}^0 - \mathbf{M}^0)$, and trade balance $(\mathbf{P}^0 \cdot \mathbf{M}^0 = 0)$ conditions in equilibrium 0, one can substitute for $\mathbf{X}^0$ and rewrite this inequality as

$$\mathbf{P}^1 \cdot \mathbf{D}^1 - \mathbf{P}^1 \cdot \mathbf{D}^0 \geqslant [\mathbf{P}^0 - \mathbf{P}^1] \cdot \mathbf{M}^0 \tag{2.21}$$

This equation yields two important results. First, suppose equilibrium 1 is free trade and 0 is autarky. Then $\mathbf{M}^0 = 0$ and equation (2.21) illustrates the gains from trade. At free trade prices $(\mathbf{P}^1)$, the value of the consumption bundle actually chosen $(\mathbf{P}^1 \cdot \mathbf{D}^1)$ is no less than the value of the autarky consumption bundle at these prices $(\mathbf{P}^1 \cdot \mathbf{D}^0)$. Therefore the autarky bundle $(\mathbf{D}^0)$ could have been consumed, and the free trade bundle $(\mathbf{D}^1)$ is revealed to be preferred.

Second, suppose both equilibria represent trading equilibria, but with different world price vectors. Then a sufficient condition for trading equilibrium 1 to be preferred to trading equilibrium 0 is that

$$[\mathbf{P}^0 - \mathbf{P}^1] \cdot \mathbf{M}^0 \geqslant 0$$

That is, a shift in the terms of trade (from $\mathbf{P}^0$ to $\mathbf{P}^1$) such that the original net import vector ($\mathbf{M}^0$) would cost less at the new prices ($\mathbf{P}^1$) than it did at the original prices ($\mathbf{P}^0$), will raise home welfare. This shift is then referred to as an *improvement* in the terms of trade.

2.7.2 Comparative Advantage

Under the standard assumptions product prices will equal marginal costs in equilibrium, and autarky prices therefore reflect autarky marginal costs or 'comparative advantage'. In two product models, one can predict the trade pattern on the basis of differences in countries' autarky relative prices (i.e. the country with the higher autarky relative price of product 2 will import it and export product 1). Does this property generalize when there are more than two products?

Again suppose equilibrium 0 is autarky and 1 free trade. The gains from trade result just derived (viz. that $\mathbf{D}^1$ was preferred to $\mathbf{D}^0$) implies that bundle $\mathbf{D}^1$ could not have been purchased at autarky prices ($\mathbf{P}^0$), i.e. that

$$\mathbf{P}^0 \cdot \mathbf{D}^1 \geqslant \mathbf{P}^0 \cdot \mathbf{D}^0 = \mathbf{P}^0 \cdot \mathbf{X}^0 \qquad (2.22)$$

Profit maximization at autarky prices implies that

$$\mathbf{P}^0 \cdot \mathbf{X}^0 = G(\mathbf{P}^0, \mathbf{V}) \geqslant \mathbf{P}^0 \cdot \mathbf{X}^1$$

Combining this with equation (2.22) yields

$$\mathbf{P}^0 \cdot [\mathbf{D}^1 - \mathbf{X}^1] = \mathbf{P}^0 \cdot \mathbf{M}^1 \geqslant 0$$

Taking account of trade balance at free trade prices ($\mathbf{P}^1 \cdot \mathbf{M}^1 = 0$) then gives

$$[\mathbf{P}^0 - \mathbf{P}^1] \cdot \mathbf{M}^1 \geqslant 0 \quad \text{or} \quad \sum_j (p_j^0 - p_j^1) \cdot \mathbf{M}_j^1 \geqslant 0 \qquad (2.23)$$

Equation (2.23) implies that, on average, $p_j^0 - p_j^1$ and $\mathbf{M}_j^1$ have the same sign, i.e. if the free trade price for product j is less (greater) than its autarky price, then product j tends to be imported (exported). Alternatively one can say that vectors $\mathbf{P}^0 - \mathbf{P}^1$ and $\mathbf{M}^1$ are *positively correlated*.

The same relationships hold for the trading partner, i.e.

$$[\mathbf{P}^{*0} - \mathbf{P}^1] \cdot \mathbf{M}^{*1} \geqslant 0$$

and since $\mathbf{M}^{*1} = - \mathbf{M}^1$, this equation combined with (2.23) yields

$$[\mathbf{P}^0 - \mathbf{P}^{*0}] \cdot \mathbf{M}^1 \geqslant 0 \qquad (2.24)$$

There is therefore a positive correlation between autarky price differences and trade flows. The trade pattern can be predicted on the basis of autarky price differences on average. However, because of the complex substitution and complementarity relationships that can arise among products when there are many products and factors, it will not necessarily be true that the direction of trade flow in each individual product can be predicted on the basis of its autarky price difference.

2.7.3 Factor Price Equalization

In matrix form the full employment conditions and competitive profit conditions (equations (2.1) and (2.2) respectively) are

$$\mathbf{A(W)} \cdot \mathbf{X} = \mathbf{V} \qquad (2.25a)$$

$$\mathbf{W} \cdot \mathbf{A(W)} \geqslant \mathbf{P} \qquad (2.25b)$$

with

$$[\mathbf{P} - \mathbf{W} \cdot \mathbf{A(W)}] \cdot \mathbf{X} = 0 \qquad (2.25c)$$

Here $\mathbf{A(W)}$ denotes the $m \times n$ matrix of input/output coefficients (which depend on relative factor returns) and equations (2.25b) and (2.25c) together state that price equals average cost for products with positive outputs, and average cost exceeds price for outputs that are not produced.

FPE requires that two conditions be met. First, that equation (2.25b) yields a unique factor return vector for any product price vector. This requires that the number of products be no less than the number of factors ($n \geqslant m$),[25] and if $n > m$ that price still equals average cost in all commodities. Second, that there is some non-negative output vector such that the full employment conditions (2.25a) are satisfied at these factor returns. As before, this limits international differences in factor endowments, requiring that endowments be in the 'cone of diversification' spanned by the columns of $\mathbf{A(W)}$. For any price vector $\mathbf{P}$, all countries with endowments in the associated cone of diversification will have equal factor returns in free trade. Thus FPE can be extended as long as there are at least as many products as factors.[26]

2.7.4 The Standard Theorems as Correlations

The Stolper–Samuelson theorem

What, if anything, can be said concerning the relationship between changes in relative product prices and relative factor returns in these general models? Take two trading equilibria $i = 0, 1$, where $\mathbf{P}^i = \mathbf{W}^i \cdot \mathbf{A(W}^i)$, and consider only those products produced in both equilibria. One can then construct a function

$$J(\mathbf{W}) = \mathbf{W} \cdot \mathbf{A(W)} \cdot [\mathbf{P}^1 - \mathbf{P}^0]$$

and by applying the mean value theorem (Ethier, 1984) to this function show that there exists some factor rental vector $\bar{\mathbf{W}}$ such that

$$[\mathbf{W}^1 - \mathbf{W}^0] \cdot \mathbf{A}(\bar{\mathbf{W}}) \cdot [\mathbf{P}^1 - \mathbf{P}^0] > 0 \qquad (2.26)$$

Equation (2.26) demonstrates a positive correlation between vectors $\mathbf{W}^1 - \mathbf{W}^0$ and $\mathbf{A}(\bar{\mathbf{W}}) \cdot [\mathbf{P}^1 - \mathbf{P}^0]$ (or between vectors $[\mathbf{W}^1 - \mathbf{W}^0] \cdot \mathbf{A}(\bar{\mathbf{W}})$ and $\mathbf{P}^1 - \mathbf{P}^0$). On average positive values of $w_i^1 - w_i^0$ are associated with positive values of $\Sigma_j\, a_{i_j}(\bar{\mathbf{W}}) \cdot [p_j^1 - p_j^0]$, that is large values of $a_{i_j}(\bar{\mathbf{W}})$ when $p_j^1 - p_j^0 > 0$ and small values of $a_{i_j}(\bar{\mathbf{W}})$ when $p_j^1 - p_j^0 < 0$. In this sense there is a tendency for an increase in the returns to factors employed most intensively in those products whose prices have risen and a decline for the others. But again this is an average result, and not necessarily one that need hold for each instance.

The Rybczynski theorem

In general the relationship between endowment and output changes is sensitive to whether the endowment change requires a change in factor returns to maintain full employment at the given product prices. Consider two endowment vectors $(\mathbf{V}^0, \mathbf{V}^1)$ in the same cone of diversification. Then

$$\mathbf{V}^i = \mathbf{A}(\mathbf{W}) \cdot \mathbf{X}^i \quad i = 0, 1$$

and

$$[\mathbf{V}^1 - \mathbf{V}^0] \cdot \mathbf{A}(\mathbf{W}) \cdot [\mathbf{X}^1 - \mathbf{X}^0] = [\mathbf{V}^1 - \mathbf{V}^0] \cdot [\mathbf{V}^1 - \mathbf{V}^0] > 0 \qquad (2.27)$$

Equation (2.27) can be interpreted in an analogous fashion to equation (2.26). There is a tendency for an increase in those outputs using intensively those factors whose endowments have risen and a decline for the others.

The Heckscher–Ohlin theorem

Recall that section 2.4 provided two versions – a 'price' and a 'quantity' version – of the relationship between factor abundance and trade flows. Both versions can be generalized to some degree.

Price version. If one reinterprets the equilibria in equation (2.26) as corresponding to the home (1) and foreign (0) autarkic equilibria respectively, then this equation illustrates a positive correlation between autarky price differences, factor intensities and relative factor abundance (in the return sense), i.e.

$$[\mathbf{W}^0 - \mathbf{W}^{*^0}] \cdot \mathbf{A}(\bar{\mathbf{W}}) \cdot [\mathbf{P}^0 - \mathbf{P}^{*^0}] > 0$$

From equation (2.24)

$$[\mathbf{P}^0 - \mathbf{P}^{*^0}] \cdot \mathbf{M}^1 \geqslant 0$$

Combining, one has

$$[\mathbf{W}^0 - \mathbf{W}^{*^0}] \cdot \mathbf{A}(\bar{\mathbf{W}}) \cdot \mathbf{M}^1 \geqslant 0 \qquad (2.28)$$

Equation (2.28) implies that, on average, the home country is importing ($\mathbf{M}_j^1 > 0$) products 'intensive' (large $a_{i_j}(\bar{\mathbf{W}})$) in the use of its relatively scarce ($w_i^0 - w*_i^0 > 0$) factors, where factor intensity is measured at some intermediate factor price ratio.

An alternative version of this relationship can be derived (Deardorff, 1982; Ethier, 1984) by defining the factor content of trade as $\mathbf{V}^m \equiv \bar{\mathbf{A}} \cdot \mathbf{M}^1$ where $\bar{\mathbf{A}}$ is the matrix formed by taking the input/output coefficients actually used in the country exporting these products. These coefficients will be the same internationally if the conditions for FPE are met, but otherwise they will differ. Given identical technologies, the home country could produce its free trade consumption vector ($\mathbf{D}^1$) from a factor endowment of $\mathbf{V} + \mathbf{V}^m$. However, this would not necessarily be the profit-maximizing output combination for this endowment at these prices, so that

$$G(\mathbf{P}^0, \mathbf{V} + \mathbf{V}^m) \geq \mathbf{P}^0 \cdot \mathbf{D}^1$$

Further, since $G(\mathbf{P}^0, \mathbf{V} + \mathbf{V}^m)$ also represents the minimum factor cost, we have that

$$\mathbf{W}^0 \cdot [\mathbf{V} + \mathbf{V}^m] \geq G(\mathbf{P}^0, \mathbf{V} + \mathbf{V}^m)$$

Combining these with the gains from trade result $\mathbf{P}^0\mathbf{D}^1 \geq \mathbf{P}^0\mathbf{D}^0$ gives

$$\mathbf{W}^0 \cdot \mathbf{V}^m \geq \mathbf{P}^0 \cdot \mathbf{D}^0 - \mathbf{W}^0 \cdot \mathbf{V} = 0$$

Similarly in the foreign country $\mathbf{W}^{*^0} \cdot \mathbf{V}^{*m} \geq 0$, and since $\mathbf{V}^m = -\mathbf{V}^{*m}$ we have

$$[\mathbf{W}^0 - \mathbf{W}^{*^0}] \cdot \mathbf{V}^m \geq 0 \qquad (2.29)$$

Countries tend to import ($V_i^m > 0$) their relatively scarce ($w_i^0 - w*_i^0 > 0$) factors.

If FPE does not hold, one can use a similar approach to show that (Helpman, 1984)

$$[\mathbf{W}^1 - \mathbf{W}^{*^1}] \cdot \mathbf{V}^m \geq 0$$

Again countries tend to import their relatively scarce factors, where scarcity can now be measured using free trade factor return differences.

Substituting for $\mathbf{V}^m$ in (2.29) gives an expression analogous to equation (2.28)

$$[\mathbf{W}^0 - \mathbf{W}^{*^0}] \cdot \bar{\mathbf{A}} \cdot \mathbf{M}^1 \geq 0 \qquad (2.30)$$

While (2.28) used some intermediate technology, equation (2.30) measures factor content according to the country of origin of the traded products.[27] Again if FPE does not hold one has (Helpman, 1984)

$$[\mathbf{W}^1 - \mathbf{W}^{*^1}] \cdot \bar{\mathbf{A}} \cdot \mathbf{M}^1 \geq 0$$

with a similar interpretation.

Quantity version. The assumptions and arguments used in section 2.4.3 can also be extended. Suppose FPE holds, and let $\alpha(\alpha^*)$ denote the home (foreign) share of world income as before. If $V^w(= V + V^*)$ is the world factor endowment vector, then in equilibrium the vector of factors required to produce the vector of home consumption is αV^w. The factor content of home trade (V^m) can then be specified directly as

$$V^m = \alpha V^w - V = \alpha V^* - \alpha^* V \qquad (2.31)$$

Turning to the product composition of trade, since

$$V = A(W) \cdot X^1 \qquad (2.32a)$$

$$V^* = A(W) \cdot X^{*1} \qquad (2.32b)$$

where X^1, X^{*1} denote home and foreign free trade productions respectively, then multiplying (2.32a) by α^*, and (2.32b) by α and subtracting, one obtains

$$[\alpha V^* - \alpha^* V] \cdot A(W) \cdot [\alpha X^{*1} - \alpha^* X^1] = [\alpha V^* - \alpha^* V] \cdot [\alpha V^* - \alpha^* V] > 0$$

Substituting in V^m from (2.31) and using the home net import vector

$$M^1 = \alpha(X^1 + X^{*1}) - X^1 = \alpha X^{*1} - \alpha^* X^1$$

gives

$$[\alpha V^w - V] \cdot A(W) \cdot M^1 \geq 0 \qquad (2.33)$$

On average, a country tends to import ($M_j^1 > 0$), those products that use intensively (large $a_{ij}(W)$) its relatively scarce factors ($\alpha V_i^w - V_i > 0$), where scarcity (abundance) is defined as a world factor endowment share (V_i/V_i^w) less (greater) than the corresponding world income share (α), at the common factor returns.

2.7.5 Factor Returns and Product Prices

Along with the general relationships between endowments and outputs, product prices and factor returns, etc. that have been considered thus far in this section, the standard propositions of trade theory make quite specific predictions about the effects of endowment and product price changes on outputs and factor returns. The SS theorem states that any change in relative product prices will raise one factor's real return (a winner) and reduce the other's (a loser). One can show that this result generalizes to the $n \times m$ case.

Consider the effects of an increase in the relative price of some good j produced both before and after the price change.[28] From equation (2.2) we have

$$\hat{C}_j = \Theta_{1j}\hat{w}_1 + \ldots + \Theta_{mj}\hat{w}_m = \hat{p}_j \qquad (2.34)$$

with

$$\sum_{i=1}^{m} \Theta_{ij} = 1 \qquad \Theta_{ij} \geq 0 \quad i = 1, \ldots m$$

The proportional change in unit cost is thus a positively weighted average of the proportional change in factor returns, and equals the proportional change in the product price. Then, for at least one factor – say factor 1 – we have

$$\hat{w}_1 \geq \hat{p}_j > 0 = \hat{p}_h \quad h \neq j, h = 1, \ldots, n$$

So at least one factor's real return must increase.

Suppose in the new equilibrium factor 1 is also used to produce some other good (k) before and after the price change. Then for this good

$$\hat{C}_k = \Theta_{1k}\hat{w}_1 + \ldots + \Theta_{mk}\hat{w}_m = \hat{p}_k = 0 \qquad (2.35)$$

Since $\hat{w}_1 > 0$, equation (2.35) implies that there is at least one other factor – say factor 2 – for which

$$\hat{p}_j > \hat{p}_k = 0 > \hat{w}_2$$

So at least one factor's real return must fall. Relative product price changes therefore produce both winners and losers as before. The difference is that their identities can no longer be predicted directly from factor intensities.

2.7.6 Outputs and Factor Endowments

The predictions of the R theorem can be generalized using similar arguments, although now the assumption that factor returns remain constant as factor endowments are varied limits our analysis to cases where the conditions for FPE are met.

Consider an increase in the endowment of some factor i. From the full employment conditions

$$\lambda_{i_1}\hat{X}_1 + \ldots + \lambda_{i_n}\hat{X}_n = \hat{V}_i \qquad (2.36)$$

and hence for at least one product – say product 1 – we must have

$$\hat{X}_1 \geq \hat{V}_i > \hat{V}_h = 0 \quad h \neq i, h = 1, -, m$$

If product 1 also uses some other factor (k) then, from its full employment condition, we have

$$\lambda_{k_1}\hat{X}_1 + \ldots + \lambda_{k_n}\hat{X}_n = \hat{V}_k = 0 \qquad (2.37)$$

Since $\hat{X}_1 > 0$, equation (2.37) implies there is at least one other product – say product 2 – for which

$$\hat{V}_i > \hat{V}_k = 0 > \hat{X}_2$$

In combination $\hat{X}_1 \geqslant \hat{V}_i > \hat{V}_k = 0 > \hat{X}_2$, a result analogous to the R theorem.

2.7.7 The Reciprocity Relations

One further aspect of the SS (R) theorem is its implication that each factor (industry) has a 'natural friend' in the sense of at least one product (factor) whose price (endowment) increase will increase the return to that factor (output of the industry) more than proportionately. Similarly each factor (industry) has a 'natural enemy' whose price (endowment) increase generates a fall in the relevant return (output). These results can also be generalized to some extent.

To show this we need to draw on some properties of the national product function – namely that its partial derivative with respect to a product price yields the corresponding net output (i.e. $\partial G(\mathbf{P}, \mathbf{V})/\partial p_j = \mathbf{X}_j$), and that its partial derivative with respect to a factor endowment yields that factor's return (i.e. $\partial G(\mathbf{P}, \mathbf{V})/\partial \mathbf{V}_i = w_i$). Taking advantage of the equality of cross-derivatives one then obtains the *reciprocity relations*[29]

$$\frac{\partial \mathbf{X}_j}{\partial \mathbf{V}_i} = \frac{\partial G(\mathbf{P}, \mathbf{V})}{\partial \mathbf{V}_i \partial p_j} = \frac{\partial G(\mathbf{P}, \mathbf{V})}{\partial p_j \partial \mathbf{V}_i} = \frac{\partial w_i}{\partial p_j} \qquad (2.38)$$

That is, the effect of an increase in the endowment of factor i on output j, for given product prices, is equal to the effect of an increase in the price of product j on the return to factor i, for given factor endowments.

These reciprocity relations can be combined with the results of sections 2.7.5 and 2.7.6 to further generalize the SS and R theorems. Two cases will be considered as illustrations.[30]

1 Suppose $m \geqslant n$. Then the reciprocity relations and results of section 2.7.5 imply that each industry has a 'natural enemy' and a 'natural friend' among the factors. That is, an increase in one factor endowment (the 'enemy') leads to a fall in this industry's output while an increase in another (the 'friend') leads to an increase in this industry's output sufficiently large to reduce the total value of all other outputs.[31]
2 Suppose $m = n$ and the other conditions of section 2.7.6 are satisfied. Then each factor has a 'natural enemy' and a 'natural friend' among the products. That is, an increase in one product's price (the 'enemy') leads to a decline in this factor's real return, while an increase another's price (the 'friend') leads to an increase in this factor's return of such magnitude that the aggregate income of the other factors falls.[32]

Before concluding this section, some comment should be made concerning the sensitivity of some of these results to the relative number of products and factors. If $n > m$, we find that countries tend to specialize in production, and a small change in relative prices could induce a large change in the composition of output. If $n = m$, production responses may be less extreme, but the possibility of FPE means that factor returns may be (locally) insensitive to changes in factor endowments. If $n < m$, factor returns will be sensitive to both endowments and product prices. Whether n is greater or less than m therefore has important implications for the responses of outputs and factor returns to changes in relative prices and endowments, etc. Should one be concerned that our results depend on what is presumably an arbitrary feature of tastes and technology?

In considering this issue one should recall that there is inevitably imprecision in determining distinct factors and products. Products may differ in terms of both their technologies and their consumption characteristics, and both of these will generally be changing over time. Similarly the degree to which factors are mobile between sectors will be sensitive to the time allowed for adjustment and the incentives to adjust. Given sufficient time, and sufficient stability in the exogenous variables, it may even be appropriate to regard 'capital' as a single factor. In view of this ambiguity, and given the difficulties of explicitly modelling the adjustment process, the best procedure would appear to be to examine a variety of cases. If nothing else this highlights the way in which the implications of changes in the terms of trade or growth can be sensitive to the degree of adjustment that has taken place. No single model exists which is likely to capture 'reality' at all stages in this adjustment process.

2.8 CONCLUSIONS

This chapter began by putting forward a set of 'standard' assumptions from which a series of general equilibrium models of international trade could be developed and analysed. Following the literature, our procedure involved working from simple 2×2 models towards a more general $n \times m$ framework. In each case the three questions concerning the pattern, gains and income distributional implications of trade, posed in the Introduction, were examined.

As was their purpose, the simple models analysed in sections 2.3, 2.4 and 2.6 gave quite precise (though not always identical) answers to these questions. While this has clearly helped with our understanding of the issues and relationships involved, it is also important to determine the degree to which these results could be generalized. This was the task of sections 2.5 and 2.7. What then are the general predictions of the 'traditional' theory of international trade?

First, that there are potential gains from trade as long as the terms of trade differ from autarky relative prices. The internal distribution of these gains, however, will depend, *inter alia*, on the pattern of factor use as well as factor ownership. The gains will not automatically accrue to everyone.

Second, trade volumes will be positively correlated with differences in factor endowments (measured either in price or quantity terms). In this sense the pattern of trade reflects differences in endowments on average, although one cannot expect to be able to predict the direction of trade in each individual commodity on this basis.

Third, changes in relative product prices will have magnified effects on real factor returns, in general. Policies that change relative prices should therefore have both opponents and supporters among the factors. Detailed knowledge of the production structure may be required to identify the winners and losers, however. The concepts of factor intensity and specificity employed in the simple models may suggest where to look.

Fourth, changes in an economy's factor endowments may similarly have magnified effects on its industrial structure, depending on the technology. One would therefore expect an economy's path of development to be characterized by the rapid expansion of some sectors and the contraction of others, rather than a uniform expansion across the board (Deardorff, 1984). Such movements will be reflected in shifts in the composition of trade.

Finally, predicting the effects of trade on factor returns appears a risky enterprise indeed. The possibility of FPE is extremely sensitive to the production structure of the model. Where it does not occur there is no reason to expect that factor returns will necessarily be drawn closer by trade.

The empirical success of these predictions, and the implications of relaxing other assumptions, must be left to the chapters that follow.

NOTES

Earlier versions of this chapter were written while visiting the Institute for International Economic Studies at the University of Stockholm and the Centre for Research in Economic Development and International Trade at the University of Nottingham. I am grateful to the editors and Norman Gemmell for helpful comments.

Several surveys of the theory of international trade already appear in the literature. The state of the theory in the early 1960s is captured in the surveys of Mundell (1960), Bhagwati (1964) and Chipman (1965–6). This material, plus the important developments over the next two decades, are extensively examined in *The Handbook of International Economics*, vol. I (Jones and Kenen, 1984). Readers should consult the Handbook, particularly Jones and Neary (1984) and Ethier (1984), for more advanced treatments of some of the material presented below.

1 Equation (2.4) implies $dX_2/dX_1 = -a_{L_1}/a_{L_2}$ for a given L.
2 Since $a_{L_2}/a_{L_2}^* < a_{L_1}/a_{L_1}^*$ the home country is relatively more efficient at producing product 2 when compared with the foreign country.
3 Note that this is not the only possible outcome. Depending on tastes and country sizes it may be that the only free trade equilibrium price ratio corresponds to one country's autarky price ratio in which case that country does not specialize in production. The other does, however, and the trade pattern continues to reflect

comparative advantage. Such an equilibrium would occur, for example, if AC were to cut $Q_1^* Q_2^*$ in the range $Q_1^* A^*$. In this case the home country would specialize in the production of product 2, and the foreign country would produce both products.

4   More generally, at least one country will be consuming an allocation unattainable without trade.

5   Although specialization in particular varieties of products is quite common.

6   Otherwise the production frontier would not be 'bowed out' but linear as in the Ricardian framework.

7   This frontier is the envelope curve found by sliding the origin of the foreign offer curve around the home production possibility frontier. The slope of H, where $B_1 B_2$ is tangential to $Q_1 Q_2$, corresponds to the foreign autarky price ratio. See Baldwin (1952). In fact $C_1 C_2$ is a degenerate Baldwin frontier for the case where world prices are constant.

8   If they are, then (2.5) would yield two inconsistent equations unless $p_1 = p_2$.

9   In figure 2.3, output units have been chosen equal to value units at these product prices. Consequently the input–output coefficients are as depicted.

10   See the discussion of factor intensity reversals (FIRs) below.

11   Thus there are no FIRs, i.e. no factor return ratios such that one product is relatively capital intensive for higher factor return ratios and relatively labour intensive for lower factor return ratios. If there is an FIR at Z' say, then $k_1(Z') = k_2(Z')$.

12   Clearly product prices must adjust to maintain the competitive profit conditions. The movement from Q_2 to Q_1 requires a declining relative price of product 2.

13   Alternatively, for any given factor return ratio one can define a 'cone of diversification' of k such that if both endowments lie in this cone then FPE will occur. For example, the cone for Z_1 would be k_1^* to $\bar{k}$.

14   That is $\Theta_{Lj} = a_{Lj} w / p_j$, etc, and $\hat{a} = da/a$. Note that the cost minimization condition $w\, da_{Lj} + r\, da_{Kj} = 0$ has been used in the derivation of (2.11).

15   Redistribution without lump-sum instruments may also be possible. See Dixit and Norman (1986) and Kemp and Wan (1986).

16   Thus many extensions of the HO model were put forward in response to the Leontief paradox. See ch. 4 in this volume.

17   Most of the topics examined here are treated only briefly. References are provided to more detailed discussions. Topics covered in detail in other chapters will not be dealt with. For example, chs 9 and 10 allow for international factor mobility and ch. 3 allows for economies of scale and imperfect competition.

18   For a fuller discussion of FIRs see Sodersten (1980, pp. 63–7). Deardorff (1986) shows how preferences can have similar implications to FIRs in an $n > m = 2$ context, and that FIRs can be arbitrarily created and removed by appropriately redefining the commodities. He argues that FIRs themselves are therefore unimportant.

19   Cheng (1984) surveys the work on 'technology-based trade' and the 'product cycle'. For a recent treatment, and references, see Markusen and Svensson (1985).

20   A production set which allows for variable factor supplies can then be derived. An alternative approach would be to add 'leisure' as a third, non-traded product, produced only by labour (forgone), thus generating a special case of the models described in section 2.5.5. For this and other results, see Martin (1976).

21   This second view imposes further restrictions on the 'short-run' equilibrium since it must be consistent with the 'long-run' (HO) equilibrium (Neary, 1978). The specific factors model also has the advantages that it can readily be extended to

many sectors, and that its results are broadly consistent with those one would obtain from a simple partial equilibrium analysis (Jones, 1975).

22 Since total output is the sum of the marginal products of the labour employed to produce it.

23 Ruffin and Jones (1977) argue that, once consumption patterns are taken into account, there is a presumption that an increase in the relative price of the importable will reduce the real return to the mobile factor.

24 This section draws heavily on the material in Ethier (1984) which the reader should consult for a more rigorous and detailed treatment. A useful extension of the Ricardian model to a continuum of products is given in Dornbusch, Fischer and Samuelson (1977). More than two countries can also be considered, although this extension is of somewhat less interest since the two-country results can be interpreted in terms of a home country and the 'rest of the world'. For some purposes, however, multi-country models are important – for example, the testing of trade theories using bilateral trade patterns. See Helpman (1984) for an analysis of comparative advantage and the HO theorem in the multi-country case.

25 The specific factors model illustrated the case when $n < m$, and FPE did not occur.

26 Even when FPE fails one might wonder if factor prices are at least drawn closer by trade. Counter-examples exist showing that this need not occur, however (Deardorff, 1986).

27 As Ethier (1984) notes, this is to avoid 'higher dimensional analogues of factor intensity reversals' (p. 175).

28 Other cases are also considered by Ethier (1984).

29 These relations require that the relevant derivatives be well defined. In general this requires $n \leq m$, for if $n > m$, then the full employment output mix is undefined and so are $\partial X_j / \partial V_i$, etc.

30 The results are sensitive to the relative numbers of goods and factors. The interested reader should consult Ethier (1984) for further details.

31 From section 2.7.5 for any product j, there exists:

(a) Some factor 1 such that

$$\frac{p_j}{w_1} \frac{\partial w_1}{\partial p_j} > 1$$

From (2.38) this implies

$$\frac{p_j}{w_1} \frac{\partial X_j}{\partial V_1} > 1$$

From the properties of $G(\mathbf{P}, \mathbf{V})$ we have

$$w_1 = \frac{\partial G}{\partial V_1}(\mathbf{P}, \mathbf{V}) = \sum_h p_h \frac{\partial X_h}{\partial V_1}$$

Hence

$$\frac{1}{w_1} \sum_h p_h \frac{\partial X_h}{\partial V_1} = 1$$

and so

$$\sum_{h \neq j} p_h \frac{\partial X_h}{\partial V_1} < 0$$

– the 'natural friend' result.

(b) Some factor 2 such that $\partial w_2 / \partial p_j < 0$. From (2.38) this implies $\partial X_j / \partial V_2 < 0$ – the 'natural enemy' result.

32 From section 2.7.6 for each factor i, there exists:

(a) Some product 1 such that

$$\frac{V_i}{X_1} \frac{\partial X_1}{\partial V_i} > 1$$

From (2.38) this implies

$$\frac{V_i}{X_1} \frac{\partial w_i}{\partial p_1} > 1$$

From the properties of $G(P, V)$, we have

$$X_1 = \frac{\partial G}{\partial p_1} (P, V) = \sum_k \frac{\partial w_k}{\partial p_1} V_k$$

Hence

$$\frac{1}{X_1} \sum_k \frac{\partial w_k}{\partial p_1} V_k = 1$$

and so

$$\sum_{k \neq i} V_k \frac{\partial w_k}{\partial p_1} < 0$$

– the 'natural friend' result.

(b) Some product 2, such that $\partial X_2 / \partial V_i < 0$. From (2.38) this implies $\partial w_i / \partial p_2 < 0$ – the 'natural enemy' result.

REFERENCES

Baldwin, Robert E. 1952: The new welfare economics and gains in international trade. *Quarterly Journal of Economics*, 66, 91–102.

Bhagwati, Jagdish N. 1964: The pure theory of international trade: a survey. *Economic Journal*, 74, 1–84.

Casas, F. R. 1983: International trade with produced transport services. *Oxford Economic Papers*, 35, 89–109.

Chacholiades, Miltiades 1979: Intermediate products in the theory of international trade. In Maurice B. Ballabon (ed.), *Economic Perspectives: an annual survey of economics*, Vol. 1, New York: Harwood Academic Publishers, 151–72.

Cheng, Leonard 1984: International trade and technology: a brief survey of the recent literature. *Weltwirtschaftliches Archiv*, 120, 165–89.

Chipman, John S. 1965–6: A survey of the theory of international trade. *Econometrica*, 33, 477–519, 685–760; 34, 18–76.

Corden, W. Max and Neary, J. Peter 1982: Booming sector and de-industrialisation in a small open economy. *Economic Journal*, 92, 825–48.

Deardorff, Alan V. 1982: The general validity of the Heckscher–Ohlin theorem. *American Economic Review*, 72, 683–94.

Deardorff, Alan V. 1984: An exposition and exploration of Krueger's trade model. *Canadian Journal of Economics*, 17, 731–46.

Deardorff, Alan V. 1986: FIRless FIRwoes: how preferences can interfere with the theorems of international trade. *Journal of International Economics*, 20, 131–42.

Dixit, Avinash and Norman, Victor 1986: Gains from trade without lump-sum compensation. *Journal of International Economics*, 21, 111–22.

Dornbusch, R., Fischer, S. and Samuelson, P. 1977: Comparative advantage, trade and payments in a Ricardian model with a continuum of goods. *American Economic Review*, 67, 823–39.

Ethier, Wilfred J. 1972: Nontraded goods and the Heckscher–Ohlin model. *International Economic Review*, 13, 132–47.

Ethier, Wilfred J. 1979: The theorems of international trade in time-phased economies. *Journal of International Economics*, 13, 225–38.

Ethier, Wilfred J. 1984: Higher dimensional issues in trade theory. In Ronald W. Jones and Peter B. Kenen (eds), *Handbook of International Economics*, Vol. I, Amsterdam: North-Holland, 131–84.

Hamilton, Carl and Svensson, Lars E. O. 1983: Should direct or total factor intensities be used in tests of the factor proportions theory? *Weltwirtschaftliches Archiv*, 119, 453–63.

Helpman, Elhanan 1984: The factor content of foreign trade. *Economic Journal*, 94, 84–94.

Jones, Ronald W. 1965: The structure of simple general equilibrium models. *Journal of Political Economy*, 73, 557–72.

Jones, Ronald W. 1971: A three factor model in theory, trade and history. In Jagdish N. Bhagwati et al. (eds), *Trade Balance of Payments and Growth*, Amsterdam: North-Holland, 3–21.

Jones, Ronald W. 1975: Income distribution and effective protection in a multicommodity trade model. *Journal of Economic Theory*, 11, 1–15.

Jones, Ronald W. and Kenen, Peter B. 1984: *Handbook of International Economics*, vol. I, Amsterdam: North-Holland.

Jones, Ronald W. and Neary, J. Peter 1984: The positive theory of international trade. In Ronald W. Jones and Peter B. Kenen (eds), *Handbook of International Economics*, vol. I, Amsterdam: North-Holland, 1–62.

Kemp, Murray C. and Wan, Henry Y. 1986: Gains from trade with and without lump-sum compensation. *Journal of International Economics*, 21, 99–110.

Markusen, James R. and Svensson, Lars E. O. 1985: Trade in goods and factors with international differences in technology. *International Economic Review*, 26, 175–92.

Martin, John P. 1976: Variable factor supplies and the Heckscher–Ohlin–Samuelson model. *Economic Journal*, 86, 820–31.

Martin, John P. and Neary, J. Peter 1980: Variable labour supply and the pure theory of international trade. *Journal of International Economics*, 10, 549–59.

Mundell, Robert A. 1960: The pure theory of international trade. *American Economic Review*, 50, 67–110.

Neary, J. Peter 1978: Short-run capital specificity and the pure theory of international trade. *Economic Journal*, 88, 488–510.

Ruffin, Roy and Jones, Ronald W. 1977: Protection and real wages: the neoclassical ambiguity. *Journal of Economic Theory*, 14, 337–48.

Sodersten, Bo, 1980: *International Economics*, 2nd edn, London: Macmillan.

3

IMPERFECT COMPETITION AND INTERNATIONAL TRADE

Alasdair Smith

3.1 WHY STUDY INTERNATIONAL TRADE WITH IMPERFECT COMPETITION?

The previous chapter of this book has given an account of the preoccupations of the 'conventional' theory of international trade. Trade is explained by comparative advantage: international differences in relative prices. In turn, comparative advantage is explained by technological differences between countries (as in the Ricardian model) or by differences in countries' factor endowments (as in the Heckscher–Ohlin (HO) model). Trade arising from comparative advantage gives rise to gains from trade: increases in national income. However, when trade arises from factor endowment differences, it is also associated with large effects on factor prices, so that gains in 'national' income can be associated with reductions in the real income of some groups within the country. Moreover, the generalization of the Stolper–Samuelson (SS) theorem tells us that such swings are not confined to the textbook two-good two-factor Heckscher–Ohlin–Samuelson (HOS) model.

These are interesting stories which, correctly interpreted, seem to tell us a great deal about the real world. If we are interested in the forces underlying trade between the developed economies and the newly industrializing countries of South-East Asia and the impact on income distribution of that trade, or if we are interested in predicting how the reforming economies of Eastern Europe will fit into the pattern of world trade at the beginning of the twenty-first century, then the theories presented in chapter 2 offer us a surprisingly powerful toolbox. There are, however, very important aspects of world trade that are either left unexplained by or, even worse, seem to contradict the predictions of that theory.

The explanation of trade by comparative advantage implies a strong tendency for trade between countries to be greater the greater the differences (in technology or in factor endowments) between countries. In reality, trade flows are greatest where countries are most similar to each other: the greatest part of world trade consists of trade flows between the countries of Western Europe, North America and Japan. A high proportion of world economic activity is located in these countries, so it is natural for there to be much international trade between them – what is surprising in the light of the conventional theory is that they account for a higher proportion of world trade than their proportion of world income. The same phenomenon is seen when we make comparisons over time rather than across countries: as national income grows, international trade takes an increasing share of national economic activity.

A measure of the problem for the conventional theory is provided by the success of the gravity model of trade, which seeks to explain trade flows between countries by their incomes, populations and other measures of their economic proximity. One recent example is Hamilton and Winters (1992), who explain 70 per cent of the variation in trade flows between 76 countries in 1984–6 by such variables. Gravity models explain aggregate trade flows between countries rather than the commodity composition of trade on which the technological and HO theories focus, but nevertheless it seems that we can predict a great deal about trade flows without resorting in any way to the textbook theories.

When we examine trade flows between developed countries, we find that a high proportion consists of intra-industry trade, where, for example, Germany exports motor vehicles to France and France exports motor vehicles to Germany. Some intra-industry trade is purely a statistical phenomenon, as the collectors of statistics allocate to the same statistical categories goods that are in reality quite different. The finer the goods classification used to report trade flows the lower is the proportion of intra-industry trade, but even at the finest classifications, there is still much intra-industry trade. The very concept of comparative advantage does not admit the possibility of a country having both a comparative advantage in a particular good (and therefore exporting it) and having a comparative disadvantage (and importing it). Faced with intra-industry trade in 1.5 litre petrol-engined four-seater four-door saloon cars with manual transmission and power steering, one can resort to the tautological formula that France has a comparative advantage in Renault cars and Germany in Volkswagens, but it is better to admit that we have a phenomenon that is not explained by comparative advantage.

Next, consider what the conventional theory suggests about political reactions to trade flows. Trade will be associated with substantial income redistributions and should therefore be politically controversial, as the losers object to the effects of trade on their incomes. This prediction is borne out in respect to some kinds of trade: European farmers lobby hard against competition from American and Australian farmers; textile workers in the USA object to competition from Hong Kong; newly unemployed workers in Poland or eastern Germany object to the effect on their livelihoods of the opening of these economies to trade. On the other hand, the growth of trade in Western Europe over the past 30 years (much of it intra-industry trade) has been accompanied by little of the political squealing that should have happened if it had been associated with sharp redistributions of income. The predictions of the conventional theory seem not to hold.

Greenaway and Milner (1986) provide a comprehensive discussion of intra-industry trade. The most plausible explanation of the phenomenon is the existence of product differentiation. Some French consumers buy Volks-wagens and some German consumers buy Renaults because there is a perceived difference between the different brands of cars. This explanation has to be supplemented by the existence of economies of scale: Volkswagen cannot produce varieties of cars to satisfy every segment of the market, because there would be cost disadvantages to the production of so many varieties. However, product differentiation almost surely implies imperfect competition: if a Renault 5 is seen by consumers as different from a VW Golf, then there is a downward-sloping demand curve for the Renault 5, and Renault has market power which it can exploit.

There is another major feature of world trade that casts doubt on the applicability of the traditional theory: the role of large firms. Many goods prominent in international trade, such as cars, consumer electronic products and steel, are the products of firms which have such large market shares. For example, almost 80 per cent of the cars sold in the European Community (EC) in 1988 were produced by six firms; while in Italy and France, over 60 per cent of the cars sold were produced by one and two firms, respectively. Even if we ignore product differentiation, it is difficult to believe that firms have no market power in such markets. Furthermore, an increasing share of international economic activity is accounted for by multinational corporations (MNCs) (see Graham and Krugman, 1991, for more information). The usual explanation for the existence of the MNC includes the presence of 'firm-specific advantages', stocks of knowledge or sunk capital that give the multinational an advantage over local competitors. Again, such firms should have market power.

Finally, the existence and survival of large firms suggest that economies of scale matter. Economies of scale were central to Adam Smith's explanation of specialization. However, as formal models of international specialization were developed, Smith's fundamental insight dropped out of view. The intimate connection between scale economies and imperfect competition was doubtless a major part of the explanation for this. It is possible, as we shall see in section 3.3, to have models in which scale economies coexist with perfect competition; but if scale economies are internal to the firm and are not exhausted at low levels of output, we cannot expect firms also to be perfectly competitive. A firm facing a downward-sloping average cost curve and a horizontal demand curve will expand indefinitely until it no longer perceives itself as having no market power.

Faced with these facts, it is not surprising that the literature on international trade under imperfect competition has grown so rapidly since 1979 – the surprise might be that imperfect competition was so neglected in the trade literature of earlier decades. This survey aims to cover only some central themes of the literature rather than being comprehensive. The next section presents a general framework in which to study the relation between trade and competition, and section 3.3 uses that framework to explore two effects of trade – on domestic competition and on product variety – on which traditional models are necessarily silent, but which it is plausible to suppose are important in reality. Section 3.4 is an apparent diversion from the main themes of the chapter, in that it studies models in which there is perfect competition, but there is a close relation between models of external economies and models of imperfect competition. Sections 3.5 and 3.6 return to the theme of the connection between trade and competition by analysing the effects of trade restrictions on firm conduct in imperfectly competitive markets, and the competitive effects of economic integration. Much of the analysis of imperfect competition has been conducted in partial equilibrium models, whereas the traditional theory of international trade is inherently general equilibrium, so section 3.7 builds some bridges between the old and the new by introducing imperfect competition into the general equilibrium trade model. Section 3.8 surveys some work that aims to incorporate the MNC into trade theory, and the chapter concludes with an outline of some recent work on trade and growth. All remaining discussion of policy issues under imperfect competition is left to chapter 6.

3.2   PRICING UNDER IMPERFECT COMPETITION

There is only one way for competition to be perfect, it is often said, but many ways for it to be imperfect. The result is that it is much harder to give a clear structure to the analysis of imperfect competition, and the student may be discouraged by the seeming succession of one model after another. I do not intend here to give an exhaustive inventory or taxonomy of all of the models in the literature, but rather to outline a fairly general class of models from which many of the issues discussed in the literature can be derived as special cases.

In developing a general model of trade under imperfect competition, we need to have a representation of consumer choice that treats product differentiation. The most popular model in the literature is that of Dixit and Stiglitz (1977). There are n varieties of the same good, with prices $p_j, j = 1, \ldots, n$. The assumed structure of preferences is such that consumers make decisions in two steps, first determining their total expenditure on all the varieties of the good together, and second dividing that expenditure between varieties. Utility derived from consumption of all varieties of the differentiated product is given by the sub-utility function

$$X = \left[\sum_j x_j^{(\varepsilon - 1)/\varepsilon} \right]^{\varepsilon/(\varepsilon - 1)} \tag{3.1}$$

where $\varepsilon > 1$.

Expenditure on all varieties is then a constant elasticity function only of a price index $P = P(p_1, \ldots, p_n)$ of the individual variety prices, with demand elasticity denoted μ. Demand for variety x_j is a constant elasticity function of the price of the variety relative to the price index and of the price index itself:

$$x_j = a(p_j/P)^{-\varepsilon} p^{-m-\mu} \tag{3.2}$$

where ε, the elasticity of demand with respect to the price of the variety itself, is greater than the aggregate demand elasticity μ.

Now assume that each variety is produced by a separate firm, and that the producer of variety x_j makes its sales decision on the Cournot assumption that other firms' sales quantities are given. Firm j's marginal revenue is

$$mr_j = p(1 - 1/e_j) \tag{3.3a}$$

where

$$1/e_j = s_j(1/\mu) + (1 - s_j)(1/\varepsilon) \tag{3.3b}$$

s_j being the value of firm i's share of the market for all varieties of the good. Equation (3.3b) is intuitively appealing: the closer a firm is to monopoly over the good, the closer is the perceived elasticity of demand to the aggregate elasticity μ, while the smaller is the firm's market share, the less influence the aggregate demand elasticity has on its perceived demand curve.

A profit-maximizing firm will now equate its marginal cost to marginal revenue to give

$$mc_j = p_j(1 - 1/e_j) \tag{3.4}$$

It is the relationship between price and marginal cost shown in equation (3.4) that both distinguishes the analysis of imperfectly competitive trade from the conventional theory and lies at the heart of most of the analysis in the literature.

Equation (3.3b) is derived from the Cournot assumption, but to incorporate the Chamberlinian 'large group' assumption that each firm ignores the impact of its decisions on the market as a whole, one simply sets s_j to 0. Alternatively, the model can become one in which products are homogeneous: with perfect substitution between varieties ε becomes infinite and $1/e_j = s_j/\mu$. If we assume both 'large group' behaviour and product homogeneity, we have $1/e_j = 0$, so perfect competition is also a special case of the above model.

Although the title of this section refers to pricing, and equation (3.4) is the key relationship, completion of a model of imperfect competition also requires a specification of entry conditions. One possible assumption is that the number of firms (and therefore varieties) in the market is fixed, in which case firms may make non-zero profits. The alternative is to assume free entry of identical firms, with the equilibrium value of n determined by the zero-profit condition

$$ac_j = p_j \tag{3.5}$$

In a monopolistically competitive equilibrium in which both (3.4) and (3.5) are satisfied, average cost exceeds marginal cost, so there must be internal economies of scale, that is to say average cost must decline as the firm's output increases. The simplest cost function with this property has a fixed cost element and constant marginal cost: average cost declines as the fixed cost is spread over larger output.

Although the general model sketched above includes several important special cases, it is not all-inclusive and there are alternative models. The assumption of Cournot competition can be replaced with the Bertrand assumption that firms take rivals' prices as given rather than their sales quantities, and this alters equation (3.3b) above (see Smith and Venables, 1988). More significantly, there are alternative models of product differentiation. In the Dixit–Stiglitz approach, all varieties of the good enter the representative consumer's utility function and all varieties are consumed. Helpman and Krugman (1985) call this the 'love of variety' approach. The principal alternative is what they call the 'ideal variety' approach developed by Lancaster (1979), but with antecedents going back to Gorman (1980, but written in 1956). In this alternative approach, different varieties of a good have different characteristics, and the individual consumer chooses to buy the variety whose characteristics are closest to the individual's ideal. This approach has the advantage of being more intuitively reasonable than the Dixit–Stiglitz approach and the disadvantage of being technically harder to work with. Anderson, de Palma and Thisse (1989) have presented conditions under which a Dixit–Stiglitz representation is a valid aggregation of a model in which individual consumer choice is described by the characteristics approach: a key condition is that the dimension of the characteristics space be large enough so that all varieties are in direct competition with each other.

The Dixit–Stiglitz structure was used by Ethier (1982) to explore the implications of product differentiation among intermediate goods. Output of a manufactured good is modelled as derived from differentiated intermediate inputs, with the production function having the property of constant returns to scale for a given number of inputs, but increasing returns in the number of inputs. (If in the sub-utility function (3.1), all varieties are produced in the equal amount x, then $X = xn^{\varepsilon/(\varepsilon-1)}$ which displays increasing returns with respect to n, since $\varepsilon > 1$.) Ethier's interpretation of the Dixit–Stiglitz model plays an important role in the most notable recent work on the links between international trade and economic growth, discussed in section 3.9 below.

A further important dimension of the modelling of imperfect competition concerns the market area within which prices are set. One can suppose that national markets are 'segmented', so that firms set prices in each country independently of the prices set in other countries, as in Brander and Krugman (1983); or that prices are set in an 'integrated' world market, as in Markusen (1981). Some trade policy implications of the differences are explored by Markusen and Venables (1988), and Venables (1990) and Ben-Zvi and Helpman (1992) present multi-stage models in which capacity decisions are made by firms on a global basis, but output is then allocated to national markets in which independent pricing decisions can be made.

3.3 TRADE, PRODUCT VARIETY, AND COMPETITION

The conventional theory of international trade identifies gains from trade as deriving from the alignment of domestic prices with the rates of transformation available in the international market. With imperfect competition, there are two additional possible sources of trade gains – from changes in the variety of products available to consumers and in the behaviour of firms. In this section, I present some simple models which illustrate these effects.

Product Variety

The effects of product variety are most easily seen in the monopolistic competition version of the model outlined in the previous section, with free entry of identical firms and the large-group assumption implying $e_j = \varepsilon$. Consider two or more separate national markets described by this model. If a single large world market is formed by putting together the national markets, producers in each country will find it profitable to sell to foreign as well as home consumers, and we will observe intra-industry trade. Since $e_j = \varepsilon$, it follows from (3.4) that the price–cost mark-up is unaffected by the size of the market, and from (3.5) it follows that the output of each firm is unchanged. With price and firm size unchanging, the number of firms, and therefore the number of varieties on offer, is the only variable that can change as we change the market configuration. There are gains from trade to consumers in all countries, and they arise purely from the increased variety of goods available. This is the case presented by Krugman (1980). Dixit and Norman (1980, chapter 9, section 2) show that where different varieties have different cost functions it is possible that enlarging the market will lead to the disappearance of some varieties so valued by consumers that trade causes welfare losses. However, such cases seem exceptional: the presumption is that with product differentiation we have an additional and potentially important source of gains from trade in the widening of consumer choice.

Trade and Competition

Intuition suggests that there should be a second important effect of trade in the presence of imperfect competition, an effect from increased competition. As it happens, this effect is absent from the model I have just sketched, because neither firm scale nor price–cost margins change as the market enlarges. Krugman (1979) introduces a pro-competitive effect from trade into the Chamberlinian large-group model by assuming that the elasticity of demand falls as consumption rises. Alternatively, we can revert to the Cournot assumption under which the perceived demand becomes more elastic as the firm's market share diminishes. Now the opening up of trade will have a pro-competitive effect as each individual firm's share of the (enlarged) market falls.

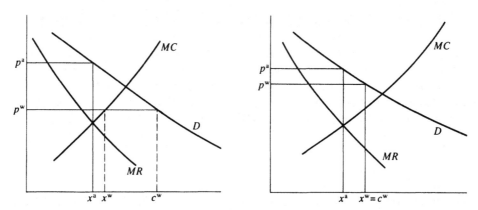

Figure 3.1 Trade with domestic monopoly

The pro-competitive effect of trade has long been understood and can be seen in the most simple models. A classic presentation is that of Bhagwati (1965), illustrated in figure 3.1. In autarky, a single home firm with an upward-sloping marginal cost curve has a monopoly and chooses the monopoly price and output p^a, x^a as shown in both panels of the diagram. If the rest of the world is perfectly competitive and the world price is p^w, then the domestic firm cannot charge a price above p^w. International trade has completely removed the home firm's monopoly power. The left panel of figure 3.1 shows the case where the world price is sufficiently low that the home firm's output supplies only part of the home market, with the rest being met by imports. In the right panel, the world price is so high that the home firm supplies all of the home market demand, but it still has to set the price p^w: even though it has the whole domestic market international trade has completely removed its market power. (In terms of equation (3.3b), even though $s = 1$, the firm is forced to behave as if $s = 0$; and since products are homogeneous, $\varepsilon = 0$.) This second case serves to make the important point that the disciplining effect of potential competition from imports may be as important as the effect of actual imports.

A second interesting model in which we see the pro-competitive effects of trade is the 'reciprocal dumping' model of Brander (1981) and Brander and Krugman (1983). Firms compete in Cournot fashion, and it is essential to the model that the two markets are segmented, so firms set prices independently in the different markets. In the simplest version, suppose that there are two countries, with a single firm in each selling a homogeneous good, both firms having the same constant marginal cost. In autarky, each firm is a monopolist, with price and sales shown on the left panel of figure 3.2 as p^a, x^a. When trade opens up, however, each firm will wish to enter the other's home market: with Cournot competition, starting from autarky each firm sees a residual demand curve in the foreign market that consists of the market demand curve less the incumbent firm's autarky output level x^a, and it is profitable to enter. The right panel of figure 3.2 shows the standard Cournot

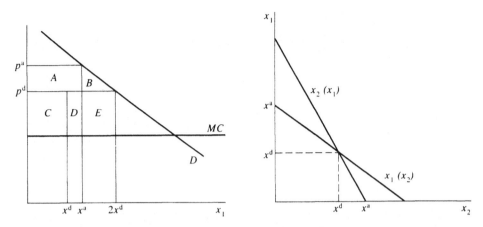

Figure 3.2 Reciprocal dumping

response function diagram for either of the national markets with the symmetrical free-trade duopoly equilibrium at x^d, x^d. The duopoly equilibrium has the lower price p^d shown in the left panel, and (3.3b) implies that with a constant elasticity demand function the price–cost margin will be halved as the home firm's share falls from 100 to 50 per cent. Consumers gain surplus corresponding to areas A and B in the left panel. The home firm loses profits shown by area $A + D$, but the foreign firm picks up profits given by $D + E$, and symmetrically the home firm is making an equal profit gain in the foreign market. There are gains from trade to the home firm and consumers taken together represented by $B + E$, resulting simply from the effect of trade in reducing the imperfect competition distortion between price and marginal cost.

Trade in this model is curiously pointless. There are no cost or variety gains to be obtained, and trade is generated solely by the existence of imperfect competition. The only effect of trade is the pro-competitive effect.

Figure 3.3 shows the reciprocal dumping model with international transport costs shown as t in the left panel. The consumer gain is $A + B$, the home firm loses profits in the home market of $A + D + G$ and gains profits in the foreign market of $D + E$, so the net gain to the home economy is $B + E - G$. The negative component G corresponds to the waste of resources involved in transporting identical goods in opposite directions across frontiers, and if transport costs are high enough, this cost can outweigh the pro-competitive gain to give an overall loss from trade.

This last result should be considered together with the result of Dixit and Norman reported above that trade can bring about welfare-reducing changes in product variety. There is a common element to the two results. In all models of imperfect competition we start off with distortions, most notably in the gap between prices and marginal costs but also possibly in the range of product variety. We have seen that trade under imperfect competition normally generates two powerful sources of welfare gain, from widening variety and increasing competition, but there may also be a worsening of the pre-existing

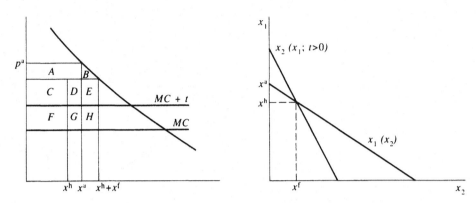

Figure 3.3 Reciprocal dumping with transport costs

distortions, and we therefore cannot in general guarantee that trade will be gainful, even though there is a strong presumption that it will be.

The central idea presented in this section, that international trade exerts a disciplining influence on domestic market power, has been explored in studies such as Caves (1980) and Geroski and Jacquemin (1981). Schmalansee (1989) reports a general finding in empirical studies that import competition does seem to exert a pro-competitive effect on pricing and profitability. Jacquemin and Sapir (1991) have made a start on investigating this issue in the context of the EC and found that the disciplining effect of import competition seemed to be associated with extra-EC rather than intra-EC trade. Sleuwagen and Yamawaki (1988) find evidence that integration in some sectors is shifting the locus of competition from the national to the European level.

3.4 TRADE AND EXTERNAL ECONOMIES

The previous section presented two aspects of the effects of trade in imperfectly competitive markets. In the monopolistic competition model, firms must have economies of scale, but we saw that gains from trade could come from increased variety without changes in the scale of production. In the homogeneous products oligopoly model, it is natural though not strictly necessary to suppose that firms have economies of scale, but the gains from trade came from competition effects rather than scale effects *per se*. If we wish to focus directly on the effects of trade on economies of scale, it is convenient to look at a model from which other considerations are absent, a model in which economies of scale coexist with perfect competition. This is possible if the economies of scale are external to the firm, and much of the early literature on scale economies and international trade focused on this case. Another case, considered in some detail in Helpman and Krugman (1985, chapter 4), is market contestability, where economies of scale lead to a single firm taking the whole market but the fear of 'hit and run' entry forces the firm to price at average cost.

Some of the issues can be illustrated in the simple example presented by Krugman (1987) where there is a single industry in which there are external economies, and these economies are national in the sense that a firm's costs depend on the scale of the industry in the country in which the firm is located (as opposed to international external economies, where firms' costs depend on the global scale of the industry). National external economies imply that there will be specialization in production of the increasing returns good, since costs will be lower when the industry is concentrated in one country. Specialization will tend to be to whichever location had the larger industry initially, for, other things being equal, it will tend to have an initial competitive advantage, and that advantage will grow as the industry expands. There will typically be multiple equilibria, with the final location of the specialized industry depending on the accidents of history. The market may choose an inefficient equilibrium; the increasing returns industry may end up located in a large country with an underlying comparative disadvantage in that industry if the cost advantage of the initial scale outweighs the under-lying comparative disadvantage.

It is often assumed that it is advantageous for a country to be the location of increasing returns industries. Krugman's analysis shows that this need not be the case. The benefits of specialization are reflected in lower prices of the increasing returns goods and these benefits can be obtained by all consumers of the goods. More precisely, if the pattern of overall trade is such as to bring about equalization of factor prices, prices of all goods will also be equalized and there will be no advantage to the country in which an increasing returns industry is located.

It is possible for trade to lead to welfare reductions, if the market chooses a 'wrong' specialization pattern. A very weak sufficient condition will rule this out; so long as increasing returns industries are 'on average' larger in the trade equilibrium than in autarky, trade will be beneficial to all countries. The general point is the same as the one made at the end of the previous section, and it is a point familiar in the analysis of gains from trade under perfect competition with market distortions; trade will be welfare-increasing so long as distortions are not increased by trade. As with competition and variety, there is a strong presumption, though not a guarantee, that scale economy effects will enhance the gains from trade and specialization.

3.5 COMPETITION AND TRADE RESTRICTIONS

The case illustrated in figure 3.1 of domestic monopoly disciplined by import competition was developed by Bhagwati as a prelude to a comparison of the effects of tariffs and quantitative restrictions (QRs) under monopoly. That comparison is made in figure 3.4. The tariff t raises the price of imports to $p^w + t$, but the domestic monopolist still faces a horizontal marginal revenue curve at this higher level of import price (up to the point where the marginal revenue curve intersects the domestic demand curve). So long as the tariff is

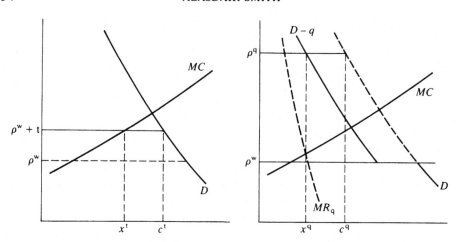

Figure 3.4 The non-equivalence of tariff and quota

not so large as to tempt the home firm to undercut the import price, the effect of the tariff is the same as in a competitive market. This is the case shown in the left panel of the figure. The right panel shows the 'equivalent' import quota, that is the quota set at the level of imports determined by the tariff in the left panel. Now, the domestic monopolist faces a downward-sloping residual demand curve given by the domestic demand curve with the import quota subtracted at price levels above p^w. The monopolist chooses a sales level at which the modified marginal revenue curve intersects the marginal cost curve, and we end up with a higher price and lower consumption than with the 'equivalent' tariff. The tariff and quota are not equivalent because the quota restores the monopolist's market power at the margin.

This idea, that QRs have an inherently anti-competitive effect, has been explored in more general models of imperfect competition, notably by Harris (1987) and Krishna (1989). There are, however, problems in modelling the anti-competitive effects of QRs in imperfectly competitive markets. In a Cournot model, firms in any case take rivals' sales as given so a QR has no effect on the nature of competition. In a Bertrand model firms take rivals' prices as given, and intuitively a QR will have an anti-competitive effect. I will be more tempted to raise my price if I think that you are constrained to keep your sales constant than if I think you will keep your price unchanged and so expand your sales.

However, Krishna's analysis uncovers a difficulty in the definition of equilibrium in the Bertrand model with a QR, a difficulty the nature and resolution of which are explained with admirable clarity by Krugman (1989). There is a single domestic firm and a single foreign firm and their products are imperfect substitutes. In the event that at a particular pair of prices, domestic consumers demand more foreign goods than the import quota allows, it is supposed that the price difference between the given foreign price and the market-clearing price for imports is collected by some middlemen,

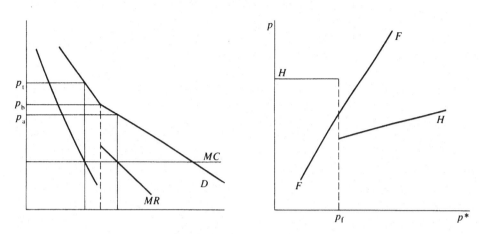

Figure 3.5 Mixed strategy equilibrium

and that it is the foreign firm's price which the home firm takes as given, so the home firm recognizes its ability to influence the consumer price of the imported variety. Now the home firm has two pricing options: to set a low price that will hold demand for imports below the quota limit, or to charge a high price, taking advantage of the quota.

The left panel of figure 3.5 (reproducing figure 20.5 of Krugman, 1989) shows the demand curve and marginal revenue curve of the home firm for a given foreign firm price. The quota becomes binding at the price p_b, so that the market price of imports rises as the home firm's price rises above p_b, while the price of imports is given by the price set by the foreign firm at domestic prices below p_b. Thus there is a kink in the home firm's perceived demand curve and a discontinuity in the marginal revenue curve. There are two locally profit-maximizing prices, p_t and p_a ('timid' and 'aggressive'), and which is the global maximum depends on the price charged by the foreign firm. The higher the price charged by the foreign firm, the higher is the domestic price p_b at which the kink appears, and the more attractive is the option of setting an aggresive price. The home firm's best response curve is thus a discontinuous one, shown as *HH* in the right panel of figure 3.4. The foreign firm's best response curve is shown as *FF* – as the home firm's price rises, the foreign firm, subject to the quota, raises its price. If the foreign firm's curve intersected the sloping section of *HH*, this would imply that the equilibrium was one in which the quota was too slack to have any effect, an uninteresting case. On the horizontal section of *HH*, the home firm is setting a high price, and the consumer price of imports is higher than the price set by the foreign firm, so the foreign firm can raise its profits by raising its price. Thus, if the quota is tight enough to have an effect, the outcome is a mixed strategy equilibrium in which the foreign firm sets the price p_f, in the belief that the probability that the home firm will set price p_a rather than p_t is such as to make this the optimal response, while the home firm faced with the price p_f is indifferent between the two prices p_a and p_t. In this mixed strategy equilibrium, the quota can be seen to have anti-competitive effects on prices and profits.

Smith and Venables (1991) exploit a particular feature of one set of QRs to provide an analysis of their effect within a Cournot model. Most of the restrictions on Japanese car imports into European countries take the form of restrictions on market share rather than on sales volume. Such a restriction will have an anti-competitive effect even with Cournot competition. I will be more reluctant to expand my sales if I realize that by increasing total market sales I am permitting you to sell more (while keeping your market share constant) than if I think that your sales quantity is given. In a numerical model of the European car market, Smith and Venables find the anti-competitive effect of QRs to be small but significant.

Messerlin (1990) has argued that another popular instrument of protection, anti-dumping action, will have an anti-competitive effect, as it encourages importers to enter into price-raising agreements with their aggrieved domestic competitors.

We now see both that there is some empirical support for the idea of imports as disciplining market power and that it should influence the choice of trade policy instruments. The policy implication is that trade policy should be considered as an element in domestic competition policy. Indeed, one can ask the question whether trade policy can substitute completely for domestic competition policy. This question is particularly relevant to discussion about the sequencing of microeconomic reform in Eastern and Central Europe. As formerly centrally planned economies privatize their state-owned enterprises they face the problem that state-owned industries typically have a very high degree of concentration; with each industrial sector dominated by a very small number of large enterprises. Will privatization replace technically inefficient state management with economically inefficient private monopoly? Should privatization await the development of effective instruments of domestic competition policy? The implication of our analysis is that the adoption of relatively free trade policy (as in Poland in 1990) can help to resolve this dilemma: import competition can discipline domestic monopoly.

However, the experience of the EC suggests that one should be very wary of relying too much on free trade as a substitute for competition policy. Tariff barriers have been completely removed on intra-EC trade, and even though there exist significant non-tariff barriers, intra-EC trade is surely more liberalized than virtually all other international trade. Yet the continued persistence of price differentials between national markets within the EC is notorious, and their implication is that intra-EC trade liberalization has not yet gone far enough to ensure a high degree of intra-EC competition. (See Cecchini et al., 1988, for a non-technical introduction both to the evidence of the non-completion of the single market and to the policy measures being undertaken in the single market programme.) Indeed, one can interpret the whole thrust of the single market '1992' programme as being to bring about the degree of competition which the removal of all tariff barriers has failed to achieve.

3.6 ECONOMIC INTEGRATION

Discussion of the 'gains from trade' may seem academic, in the sense that in the real world we never see economies moving from autarky to free trade. However, the analysis may be relevant to less dramatic changes. One such change is regional economic integration, where a group of countries remove barriers to trade within the group. Much attention has been devoted recently to studying and quantifying the effects of increased economic integration in imperfectly competitive markets. The seminal study is that of Cox and Harris (1985) on the effects of freeing trade between Canada and the USA. In a general equilibrium study which assumes a particularly strong link between domestic and international prices and assumes free entry of firms, they find that there are substantial gains to the Canadian economy from freer trade, fundamentally arising from the increased exploitation of economies of scale, as lower prices lead to exit of inefficiently small producers.

Smith and Venables (1988) study the effects of the EC's single market programme, in a way that focuses particular attention on the effects of integration on competition. A partial equilibrium model is applied to ten separate industries, with numerical parameters of the model chosen to reproduce a base data set as an equilibrium. The immediate effects of '1992', modelled as equivalent to a 2.5 per cent tariff reduction, are to increase intra-EC trade. This reduces the market shares of home firms and (see equation (3.3b)) therefore reduces prices. Consumers gain from this change, and firms lose, with modest net gains to the economy as a whole. Allowing firms to exit in response to the loss of profits (so as to satisfy equations like (3.5)) reduces the gains to consumers as firms' profits are restored, but in the end the combination of increased competition and increased scale of production gives lower prices and larger output levels, and modest overall welfare gains.

Smith and Venables assume that there is national market segmentation in the base equilibrium, and the analysis described in the previous paragraph maintains that assumption. However, they also consider the possibility of a change in firms' pricing behaviour, with the '1992' programme modelled as replacing segmented market pricing with market integration, interpreted as requiring firms to set the same prices for their sales in all EC markets (in addition to the 2.5 per cent reduction in tariff equivalents). This produces much bigger effects than the 2.5 per cent barrier reduction alone, and it is easy to see from equation (3.3b) why this should be. There are very substantial 'home market preferences' in intra-EC trade patterns, with the largest part of virtually every market being taken by domestic firms. Under the segmented markets assumption, this implies substantial price–cost mark-ups in concentrated industries. For example, pricing of cars in the Italian and French markets would reflect the fact that Fiat has over 50 per cent of the Italian market, while Peugeot and Renault each have about 30 per cent of the French market. Replace the assumption of market segmentation with an assumption that firms set EC-wide prices and now it is firms' shares of the EC market that enter into (3.3b). In the case of the car market, Fiat, Peugeot and Renault's pricing is supposed to reflect EC market shares in the range of 10–15 per cent. There is a strongly pro-competitive effect and Smith and Venables derive much larger estimates of the welfare effects on '1992' in this second scenario.

One can object to the modelling of such a change as a 'policy' change. Market segmentation implies the existence of barriers to arbitrage between national markets, and it needs to be explained what these barriers are and how '1992' is to remove them.

3.7 TRADE AND IMPERFECT COMPETITION IN GENERAL EQUILIBRIUM

The theory presented in chapter 2 is a general equilibrium theory; up to this point in this chapter we have been looking at partial equilibrium. To confront the question of whether the two theories are competitive or complementary, we have to introduce imperfect competition into our general equilibrium trade model. The key reference is Helpman and Krugman (1985, chapters 7 and 8), though earlier work is in Dixit and Norman (1980, chapter 9, section 3; reprinted as chapter 12 of Grossman, 1992) and in Helpman (1981).

Let there be two sectors, in one of which a homogeneous good Y, the numeraire, is produced under perfect competition. In the other sector, differentiated varieties of good X are produced under monopolistic competition, each firm in this sector producing a single variety. Each variety of good X is produced under the same conditions and has price p. The two factors K and L have prices w_K and w_L. Let x be output per firm of good X. Input coefficients for the competitive good are $a_{iY}(w_K, w_L)$ $(i = K, L)$, while the input coefficients for the monopolistically competitive sector depend on x as well as on factor prices: $a_{iX}(w_K, w_L, x)$ $(i = K, L)$, the last independent variable reflecting scale economies. Average and marginal cost of production of Y is given by the unit cost function

$$w_K a_{KY}(w_K, w_L) + w_L a_{LY}(w_K, w_L)$$

while the average cost of production of X is

$$c(w_K, w_L, x) = w_K a_{KX}(w_K, w_L, x) + w_L a_{LX}(w_K, w_L, x)$$

The equation of marginal cost to marginal revenue implies, with the large group assumption that $s_i = 0$ in equation (3.3b), that

$$c(w_K, w_L, x) + x c_x(w_K, w_L, x) = p(1 - 1/\varepsilon)$$

and substituting in the free entry condition that $p = c(w_K, w_L, x)$, we have

$$- c(w_K, w_L, x) / x c_x(w_K, w_L, x) = \varepsilon \qquad (3.6)$$

To this must be added the usual two pricing equations and two factor market equilibrium conditions:

$$1 = w_K a_{KY}(w_K, w_L) + w_L a_{LY}(w_K, w_L) \tag{3.7}$$

$$p = w_K a_{KX}(w_K, w_L, x) + w_L a_{LX}(w_K, w_L, x) \tag{3.8}$$

$$a_{KX}(w_K, w_L, x)X + a_{KY}(w_K, w_L)Y = K \tag{3.9}$$

$$a_{LX}(w_K, w_L, x)X + a_{LY}(w_K, w_L)Y = L \tag{3.10}$$

We have five equations which will determine the two factor prices, the level of output per firm in the differentiated product sector, and the level of outputs of the two goods (and thus the number of firms in the differentiated products sector, $n = X/x$) given goods prices p. Alternatively, treating these equations as describing an autarkic economy, or a world economy with factor price equalization (FPE), the addition of a goods demand equation will close the system.

One special case is of interest: the case of homothetic technology in the differentiated products sector. Then

$$c(w_K, w_L, x) = c(w_K, w_L)h(x)$$

$$\dot{c}_x(w_K, w_L, x) = c(w_K, w_L)h'(x)$$

and (3.6) reduces to $- h(x)/xh'(x) = \varepsilon$, which determines x independently of all the other variables in the system. Effectively, in this case we separate out the imperfect competition aspect of the model from the general equilibrium analysis, and determine the scale of imperfectly competitive firms from the interaction of scale economies and demand elasticity. Then the remaining four equations, with x given, are essentially the equations of the two-by-two

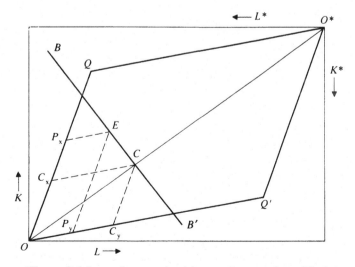

Figure 3.6 Imperfect competition and general equilibrium

Heckscher–Ohlin–Samuelson (HOS) model. In this case, competition and comparative advantage are independent of each other. The standard FPE theorem applies, for example. By contrast, in the more general model, factor price differences are compatible with equations (3.7)–(3.10) being satisfied in two countries, so long as each country has different levels of x. In general, free trade need not equalize marginal or average costs even when both sectors are active in both countries.

However, the concept of 'trade reproducing the integrated economy' (Dixit and Norman, 1980; Helpman and Krugman, 1985) is useful in analysing the case of FPE. Let equations (3.5)–(3.9) describe a two-country world in which technology and tastes are the same across countries and suppose that there is FPE, so that x is also the same in both countries. The international equilibrium is illustrated in figure 3.6 which reproduces Helpman and Krugman's figure 7.1.

The point E shows the endowments of two countries, home and foreign, measured from the respective origins O and O^*. The line BB' through E with slope $- w_L/w_K$ gives the national budget constraints. The budget line intersects the diagonal through the origins at C so that OC/O^*C gives the ratio of the sizes of the two countries. The slopes OQ and OQ' give the factor intensity ratios in the two sectors X and Y and are the same, because of FPE, as the slopes of O^*Q' and O^*Q. OQ (or O^*Q') represents factor employment in the X sector and OQ' (or O^*Q) represents factor employment in the Y sector. By choice of units, the lengths of these lines can be taken to measure sectoral output. Full employment of factors in the home country requires output OP_X of X and OP_Y of Y, so P_XQ of X and P_YQ' of Y are produced in the foreign country.

With identical homothetic preferences, consumption of each good will be divided between countries in the ratio of the national incomes, so OC_X of X and OC_Y of Y will be consumed in the home country. Since, however, each firm in sector X produces a differentiated product, the home country, although a net exporter of X, will import those varieties of good X produced by foreign firms.

Thus the equilibrium illustrated in figure 3.4 has both intra-industry and inter-industry trade, with the inter-industry trade pattern determined by relative factor endowments as in the standard HOS model. Indeed since point E represents the factor content of production and point C the factor content of consumption, the vector EC represents the factor content of trade, which is as predicted by the HO theorem.

The conclusion that much of the traditional analysis of inter-industry specialization survives the incorporation of scale economies and imperfect competition is also derived by Ethier (1982), in whose model, as we have seen, there are increasing returns with respect to the number of differentiated intermediate products. It is the fact that this form of increasing returns operates at the international level which leads to Ethier's result.

It should be fairly clear, in the light of the discussion in chapter 2, that straightforward modifications of the analysis above are needed to adapt it to the case of many goods and factors.

Helpman and Krugman (1985, chapter 8) discuss the empirical implications of the general equilibrium model with imperfect competition. The main observation is that relative country size has an effect on the volume of trade, additional to any effects arising from relative factor endowment differences. The volume of intra-industry trade is greatest between countries of similar size. This observation provides a justification for explaining the volume of trade by a gravity model, and Bergstrand (1989) derives a gravity equation from a model that includes factor proportions trade as well as intra-industry trade. Balassa and Bauwens (1988) investigate, using European data, the explanation of both inter-industry and intra-industry trade and find support for the idea that the former is explained by factor endowment differences and the latter by characteristics consistent with product differentiation being the main explanation of such trade.

3.8 MULTINATIONAL CORPORATIONS

The now standard textbook treatment of the MNC offers a three-part explanation of the existence of multinationals. Multinationals are to be explained by the *ownership* advantages enjoyed by the firm, the *location* advantages of foreign operation and the *internalization* advantages of keeping certain kinds of transactions within the firm – hence the 'OLI paradigm'. Thus foreign direct investment (FDI) by, say, Sony in the EC might be explained by the attractions to European consumers of the particular qualities of Sony's products, the need to produce some of these products in Europe to avoid protectionist barriers to imports from Japan or to encourage quicker corporate response to local market needs, and the difficulty of protecting the value to Sony of its brand name if it were to license to European firms the right to produce Sony-branded products.

Formal models of MNCs that incorporate such considerations and integrate them into the main body of trade theory have been developed by Markusen (1984), by Helpman (1984, 1985) (see also Helpman and Krugman, 1985, chapters 12 and 13) and by Ethier (1986). These models allow the spatial separation of 'headquarter services' such as management and R&D from production, and the different activities of the firm can be located in different countries depending on comparative advantage. Helpman thus derives predictions of the pattern of intra-firm as well as inter-industry and intra-industry trade. Ethier models the internalization motivation that leads the multinational to set up foreign subsidiaries rather than license its expertise to other firms.

Smith (1987), drawing on Hirsch (1976) and Horstmann and Markusen (1987), presents a simple oligopolistic model of the MNC in which FDI can play a 'strategic' role. An MNC faces the choice of competing in the host market either by exporting to it or investing in it. It faces a single potential domestic competitor in that market which decides whether or not to enter the market after the multinational decides whether or not to invest. For some parameters of the model, the potential multinational makes more profit as an exporter whether or not the home firm chooses to enter the market, but the home firm makes a profit only if the multinational is an exporter. By investing before the home firm makes its move, the multinational ensures that the home firm does not enter, and gains a profit level which is better than the profit level it would make if the home firm had entered. The firm is undertaking *strategic* direct investment. The point of this argument is to show that the location advantage need not be one associated purely with efficiency.

3.9 TRADE AND GROWTH

Grossman and Helpman (1991) (see also Grossman, 1992, chapters 17–19) have built an analysis of the links between trade, innovation and growth on the foundations of the Dixit–Stiglitz model. It is clear that an analysis of the economics of R&D involves imperfect competition, as a firm that has developed a new product will typically have some market power. Grossman and Helpman treat each new product as a differentiated product in a Dixit–Stiglitz framework, though with emphasis on the Ethier interpretation of that framework. R&D is, however, treated as a normal economic activity into which there is free entry. Given a starting-point where there are supernormal profits in R&D, free entry into R&D will reduce the rate of return and eventually the economy is driven to a stationary state in which there is no growth. But Grossman and Helpman then introduce the possibility that R&D contributes to the stock of generally available knowledge capital, a public good, as well as to the development of privately appropriable blueprints for new products. This then enables the economy to sustain a permanent rate of growth. The spillover effects of R&D prevent diminishing returns driving the economy back to a stationary state.

Grossman and Helpman offer an alternative model in which innovation consists of the development of superior versions of existing product varieties rather than a widening of the range of varieties, and find that this alternative model is in most (though not all) respects identical in its behaviour to the previous model.

International trade begins to play an interesting role in the Grossman–Helpman model when factor intensities are introduced into the story. R&D is supposed to require human capital as the only input into its production, and the impact of international trade on the rate of economic growth then depends on the effect of international trade on the availability of human capital for R&D. Trade may impede economic growth in a country that exports goods intensive in human capital as the exporting sector draws human capital away from research. With international spillovers of knowledge, the pattern of specialization is determined in essentially standard HO fashion (just as in Ethier's discussion of international scale economies – see section 3.7 above). A country rich in human capital specializes in R&D and in high-tech manufacturing and experiences a faster rate of growth of output, although rates of growth of consumption do not differ between countries in the long run. This last point is reminiscent of an observation made in section 3.4 above, that the benefits of a particular pattern of specialization are diffused through lower prices. When, however, knowledge spillovers are national, the pattern of specialization is one in which history may matter – a country with a head start in technology may maintain that lead. There are now several channels through which R&D may be affected by international trade. International diffusion of technical knowledge and reducing wasteful duplication of research efforts will both tend to raise economic growth. On the other hand, intense foreign competition with large or advanced countries, factor endowments that lead the country to specialize away from R&D, and policies that expand R&D activities in foreign countries will give trade a depressing effect on research.

NOTE

I am grateful for the comments of Michael Gasiorek and the editors.

REFERENCES

Anderson, Simon P., de Palma, André and Thisse, Jacques-François 1989: Demand for differentiated products, discrete choice models, and the characteristics approach. *Review of Economic Studies*, 56, 21–35.

Balassa, Bela and Bauwens, Luc 1988: The determinants of intra-European trade in manufactured goods. *European Economic Review*, 32, 1421–37.

Ben-Zvi, Samuel and Helpman, Elhanan 1992: Oligopoly in segmented markets. In Gene M. Grossman (ed.), *Imperfect Competition and International Trade*, Cambridge, Mass.: MIT Press, 31–53.

Bergstrand, Jeffrey H. 1989: The generalized gravity equation, monopolistic competition, and the factor-proportions theory of international trade. *Review of Economic Statistics*, 71, 143–53.

Bhagwati, Jagdish N. 1965: On the equivalence of tariffs and quotas. In Robert E. Baldwin et al., *Trade, Growth and the Balance of Payments*, Chicago: Rand-McNally, 53–67.

Bhagwati, Jagdish N. (ed.) 1987: *International Trade: selected readings*. Cambridge, Mass.: MIT Press.

Brander, James A. 1981: Intra-industry trade in identical commodities. *Journal of International Economics*, 11, 1–14.

Brander, James A. and Krugman, Paul R. 1983: A 'reciprocal dumping' model of international trade. *Journal of International Economics*, 15, 313–21, ch. 4 of Krugman (1990) and ch. 1 of Grossman (1992).

Caves, Richard E. 1980: Symposium on international trade and industrial organization. *Journal of Industrial Economics*, 29, 113–218.

Cecchini, Paolo with Catinat, Michel and Jacquemin, Alexis 1988: *The European Challenge 1992: the benefits of a single market*. Aldershot: Wildwood House.

Cox, David and Harris, Richard 1985: Trade liberalization and industrial organization. *Journal of Political Economy*, 93, 115–45.

Dixit, Avinash K. and Norman, V. 1980: *Theory of International Trade*. Cambridge: Cambridge University Press.

Dixit, Avinash K. and Stiglitz, Joseph E. 1977: Monopolistic competition and optimum product diversity. *American Economic Review*, 67, 297–308.

Ethier, W.J. 1982: National and international returns to scale in the modern theory of international trade. *American Economic Review*, 72, 950–9 and ch. 14 of Grossman (1992).

Ethier, W.J. 1986: The multinational firm. *Quarterly Journal of Economics* 101, 805–34 and ch. 16 of Grossman (1992).

Geroski, Paul and Jacquemin, Alexis 1981: Imports as a competitive discipline. *Recherches Économiques de Louvain*, 47, 197–208.

Gorman, W. M. 1980: A possible procedure for analysing quality differentials in the egg market. *Review of Economic Studies*, 47, 843–56.

Graham, Edward M. and Krugman, Paul R. 1991: *Foreign Direct Investment in the United States*, 2nd edn. Washington, DC: Institute for International Economics.

Greenaway, David and Milner, Chris 1986: *The Economics of Intra-Industry Trade*. Oxford: Basil Blackwell.

Grossman, Gene M. (ed.) 1992: *Imperfect Competition and International Trade*. Cambridge, Mass.: MIT Press.

Grossman, Gene M. and Helpman, Elhanan 1991: *Innovation and Growth in the Global Economy*. Cambridge, Mass.: MIT Press.

Hamilton, Carl and Winters, L. Alan 1992: Opening up international trade with Eastern Europe. *Economic Policy*, 14, 77–116.

Harris, Richard 1987: Why voluntary export restrictions are 'voluntary'. *Canadian Journal of Economics*, 18, 799–809.

Helpman, Elhanan 1981: International trade in the presence of product differentiation, economies of scale and monopolistic competition: a Chamberlin–Heckscher–Ohlin approach. *Journal of International Economics*, 11, 305–40, and ch. 13 of Grossman (1992).

Helpman, Elhanan 1984: A simple theory of international trade with multinational corporations. *Journal of Political Economy*, 92, 451–71 and ch. 29 of Bhagwati (1987).

Helpman, Elhanan 1985: Multinational corporations and trade structures. *Review of Economic Studies*, 52, 443–58 and ch. 15 of Grossman (1992).

Helpman, Elhanan and Krugman, Paul R. 1985: *Market Structure and Foreign Trade*. Cambridge, Mass.: MIT Press.

Hirsch, Seev 1976: An international trade and investment theory of the firm. *Oxford Economic Papers*, 28, 258–70.

Horstmann, Ignatius J. and Markusen, James R. 1987: Strategic investments and the development of multinationals. *International Economic Review*, 28, 109–21.

Jacquemin, Alexis and Sapir, André 1991: Competition and imports in the European market. In L. Alan Winters and Anthony J. Venables (eds), *European Integration: trade and industry*, Cambridge: Cambridge University Press for CEPR, 82–91.

Krishna, Kala 1989: Trade restrictions as facilitating practices. *Journal of International Economics*, 26, 251–70 and ch. 5 of Grossman (1992).

Krugman, Paul R. 1979: Increasing returns, monopolistic competition, and international trade. *Journal of International Economics*, 9, 469–79, ch. 9 of Bhagwati (1987) and ch. 1 of Krugman (1990).

Krugman, Paul R. 1980: Scale economies, product differentiation and the pattern of trade. *American Economic Review*, 70, 950–9, ch. 2 of Krugman (1990) and ch. 11 of Grossman (1992).

Krugman, Paul R. 1987: Increasing returns and the theory of international trade. In Truman F. Bewley (ed.), *Advances in Economic Theory*, Cambridge: Cambridge University Press, 301–28 and ch. 5 of Krugman (1990).

Krugman, Paul R. 1989: Industrial organization and international trade. In Richard Schmalansee and Robert D. Willig (eds), *Handbook of Industrial Organization*, vol. II, Amsterdam: Elsevier, ch. 20, and ch. 14 of Krugman (1990).

Krugman, Paul R. 1990: *Rethinking International Trade*. Cambridge, Mass.: MIT Press.

Lancaster, Kelvin 1979: *Variety, Equity and Efficiency*. New York: Columbia University Press.

Markusen, James R. 1981: Trade and the gains from trade with imperfect competition. *Journal of International Economics*, 11, 531–51 and ch. 3 of Grossman (1992).

Markusen, James R. 1984: Multinationals, multi-plant economies, and the gains from trade. *Journal of International Economics*, 16, 205–26, and ch. 28 of Bhagwati (1987).

Markusen, James R. and Venables, Anthony J. 1988: Trade policy with increasing returns and imperfect competition: contradictory results from competing assumptions. *Journal of International Economics*, 24, 299–316 and ch. 8 of Grossman (1992).

Messerlin, Patrick 1990: Anti-dumping regulations or pro-cartel law? The EC chemicals case. *The World Economy*, 13, 465–92.

Schmalansee, Richard 1989: Inter-industry studies of structure and performance. In Richard Schmalansee and Robert D. Willig (eds), *Handbook of Industrial Organization*, vol. II, Amsterdam: Elsevier, ch. 16.

Sleuwagen, Leo and Yamawaki, Hideki 1988: The formation of the European Common Market and changes in market structure and performance. *European Economic Review*, 32, 1451–75.

Smith, Alasdair and Venables, Anthony J. 1988: Completing the internal market in the European Community: some industry simulations. *European Economic Review*, 32, 1501–25.

Smith, Alasdair and Venables, Anthony J. 1991: Counting the cost of voluntary export restrictions in the European car market. In Elhanan Helpman and Assaf Razin (eds), *International Trade and Trade Policy*, Cambridge, Mass.: MIT Press, 187–220.

Smith, Alasdair 1987: Strategic investment, multinational corporations and trade policy. *European Economic Review*, 31, 89–96.

Venables, Anthony J. 1990: International capacity choice and national market games. *Journal of International Economics*, 29, 23–42.

4

TESTING TRADE THEORY

Edward E. Leamer

4.1 INTRODUCTION

A close look at the empirical work in international trade reveals that the methodological parable of hypothesis formulation, testing, rejecting and reformulation is a very misleading characterization of the intellectual life of international economists. An essay on 'testing trade theory' would be very short indeed, if it took the word 'testing' literally and if it dealt with reality rather than myth. Empirical work has had some impact on the way that economists think about the determinants of international trade, but the effects have not been great. Certainly no theory has been tested in the sense of placing it genuinely at risk and as a result all models that were ever contemplated survive empirical testing. Some models have been discarded, but not because of empirical findings.

It seems to me neither surprising nor inappropriate that all models survive empirical scrutiny. It is not surprising partly because our data are limited and noisy. But even with more data and more accurate data, we should not expect to refute any models. A model is a powerful device for organizing our thoughts; it is not literally true; indeed it derives its power from the very fact that it is not literally true. Thus there is no reason to test it. Instead of testing, we should be determining its accuracy and its usefulness. We should attempt to identify empirical circumstances in which the model is useful and other circumstances in which it is misleading.

Consider two variants of the law of one price: purchasing power parity (PPP) and factor price equalization (FPE). Purchasing power parity has been 'tested' incessantly, and often 'rejected'. Factor price equalization has not been tested: we know it is not so. But both theories are alive and well, in fact they seem equally healthy. What accounts for this? The 'testing' mentality of many of those who have studied PPP preordains their work to have little genuine impact. Economists know in advance of any organized study of the data that arbitrage is not perfect and instantaneous. Thus PPP is surely not exact. An empirical finding that PPP is not exact therefore cannot be at all upsetting. Studies of PPP that hope to leave an imprint should instead be determining the circumstances under which the model is adequately accurate, and the circumstances under which it is highly misleading. Rather than 'testing' they should be 'estimating': estimating the speed of arbitrage.

In great contrast to PPP, FPE has not been subject to 'testing'. It is not clear to me why there is such a difference in the intellectual history of these two models. Perhaps the reason is that FPE refers to indirect international arbitrage, through trade in goods rather than trade directly in factors. Perhaps empirical workers could not fool themselves into taking indirect arbitrage literally. In any case, when FPE has been studied, an 'estimation' attitude has been taken, not a 'testing' attitude. For example, Krueger (1978, p. 658) found that 'more than half of the difference between the United Nations estimates of per capita income of each of the less developed countries in the sample and the United States is explained by demographic variables alone'.

'Estimate, don't test' is one theme of this review. Empirical studies of trade theory have had relatively little impact because many researchers have had a 'testing' mentality. A second theme is 'theory before estimation'. Empirical studies have had relatively little impact because the theoretical foundations of the work are unclear.

If it feels like these two comments are pulling in opposite directions, indeed that is the case. I believe that an influential data analysis needs a clear theoretical foundation, but not one that is taken too literally. Adequately satisfying one of these requirements without badly violating the other is the art of data analysis.

A third, related, theme of this chapter is 'the three layers'. An influential research programme must include three layers of intellectual activity. First, a set of *issues* must be identified. Typically the issues in economics are policy problems, but there are also interesting scientific questions that can be pursued without any specific policy problem in mind. The second phase of a research programme is the formulation of a conceptual framework, or *theory*, for addressing the issues. The language in which the theory is formulated and communicated may be mathematics, but English is an alternative that is now too often overlooked. The third layer is the *data* layer which develops a correspondence between the important aspects of the theory and observable events. The tools of formal econometrics may be useful here, but tables and graphs can often be more persuasive.

We need some sensible balance between these three layers – issues, theory and data. But the theory layer is now much too thick in economics training and research. For example, think about how we discuss dimensionality questions in the context of the Heckscher–Ohlin (HO) model. We are required to learn that the production frontier has flats of dimension equal to the number of goods minus the number of factors. Thus, given certain product prices, the choice of output is indeterminate. But wait a minute: what issue is being addressed by this theoretical discussion? And how can we map the theory into observable phenomena? How do we actually go about counting factors and goods? And if not that, what observable phenomenon would make one think that there are flats on the production frontier? I am worried that this is an example of the pursuit of theory for its own sake. But economics is not a branch of mathematics, and though the question of dimensionality is intriguing, we have to insist on clear references to the issues and to the data.

The central issue of international economics is: how, if at all, should governments intervene in international commerce? It is easy to lose track of this issue and any other issue when one teaches and studies international economics. The teaching of international economics usually proceeds through four different models, each of which is extensively manipulated to derive many interesting conclusions. These models are:

1 the Ricardian model with a single labour input and with technological differences between countries;
2 the Ricardo–Viner model with a single mobile factor, labour, and a set of specific factors which are immobile across industries;
3 the HO model with at least two internally mobile factors and at least two commodities;
4 a variety of models with increasing returns to scale and market power at the level of the firm.

These models serve as vehicles for discussing the sources of international comparative advantage and the consequent effects that government interventions may have. The sources of comparative advantage are: (a) differences in technology, (b) differences in factor supplies, (c) economies of scale, (d) differences in tastes and (e) barriers to trade.

The myth of positive economics would make us expect to find in the literature some decisive empirical tests that have led the profession to discard one or more of these models. In fact, only two empirical findings seem to have had a major impact on the way that economists think. The first was Leontief's (1953) discovery that US imports were more capital intensive than US exports. This was widely regarded to be a great blow against the HO model, which was met by a variety of theoretical responses that either amplified or altered the HO model. The second major empirical finding was the extensive amount of 'intra-industry' trade catalogued by Grubel and Lloyd (1975). The extent of intra-industry trade is also regarded as a blow against the generality of the HO model and is at least partly responsible for the large theoretical literature on models with increasing returns to scale and product differentiation. Other than these two results, beliefs about the sources of international comparative advantage have not been greatly affected by any observations.

That seems a bit disappointing, which leads to the question: how can we do empirical work that is more influential? My answer has already been provided: we need balance between the three layers. The empirical work needs a solid base in economic theory. But the theory cannot be taken so seriously that we lose track of the issues. We must put real intellectual capital at risk.

It may seem obvious that empirical work should have a solid base in economic theory, but in fact it is usually extraordinarily difficult to translate a theoretical model into an empirical application. There are many examples of work in international economics in which the translation of the theory into an empirical exercise was casual and 'intuitive', and which later were discovered to have been fatally flawed.

It may also seem obvious that influential empirical work requires interesting and refutable hypotheses. But in fact a lot of time is wasted testing hypotheses that are surely false, a fact that is revealed whenever the data sets are large enough. The sharp hypotheses that are represented by each of the four models listed above, or each of the five sources of comparative advantage, are not sensibly tested. These models are only tools, each of which is appropriate in some circumstances and inappropriate in others. Empirical enterprises should therefore not attempt to test the validity of the theories. Instead, empirical work might identify the circumstances under which each of the tools is most appropriate, or measure the 'amount' of trade that is due to each of the sources. Neither of these tasks has been accomplished or often even attempted.

4.2 EMPIRICAL STUDIES OF THE RICARDIAN MODEL OF COMPARATIVE ADVANTAGE

A simple model of comparative advantage was offered by Ricardo in 1817. This familiar model includes two countries (England and Portugal), two goods (cloth and wine), a single input (labour) and constant ratios of output to input. The purpose of this model seems to lie primarily in the area of political philosophy, not economic science. Ricardo brilliantly makes the argument that both countries benefit from trade, even if one has an absolute productive advantage in both goods. Thus the imposition of trade barriers makes one and possibly both worse off. But it is difficult to detect anything genuinely empirical about this model. What are its testable propositions? Here are three:

1 *International trade is beneficial.* This proposition has been subjected to a great deal of theoretical scrutiny. Theorists have pointed out that some individuals may be made worse off if the ownership of productive factors is unequal and if factors are sector specific. Theorists have proposed many other models with features such as economies of scale, non-competitive market structures, etc. in which the proposition may not be true. But, to my knowledge, there has never been an attempt to test the very basic premise of economics that individuals and/or economies possess enough knowledge and skill to assure that 'voluntary' trades can only occur if both parties 'expect' to be made better off. Furthermore, I cannot imagine how this proposition might be tested. Surely this is a Lakatosian (1978) 'hard core' proposition that is protected from falsification by the undefinable word 'voluntary'.

2 *The observed terms of trade are bounded between the comparative labour cost ratios of the two countries.* This proposition is too closely associated with

the very simple one-factor, two-good, two-country model to be worthy of empirical scrutiny. And multidimensional generalizations of the Ricardian constant cost model, such as the one-factor many-good many-country model, are complex enough to make the link between the theory and the empirical work very difficult. It should thus not come as a surprise that (to my knowledge) there have been no studies of the relationships between relative prices of different commodities and relative labour costs. For that matter, if one were to do a serious study of the technological determinants of commodity prices, one would surely include more than just the labour input.

3 *A country exports the commodity in which it has a comparative labour cost advantage and imports the commodity in which it has a comparative disadvantage.* Again this proposition is too closely associated with the very simple model to be worthy of empirical scrutiny. But loose versions of this proposition were the first to be studied empirically. Before discussing these studies, we need to increase the dimensions of the Ricardian model, and also allow for imperfect substitutability between foreign and domestic goods.

Haberler (1933) and Viner (1937) generalize the simple Ricardian model to the case of two countries and many goods, producing the familiar 'chain of comparative advantage'. This chain is formed by ordering commodities by their relative comparative labour productivities in the two countries. Multiplying the inverse of these productivity ratios by the relative wage ratios in the two countries produces an ordered set of relative prices. One country produces the first subset of commodities with price ratios less than one, and the other country produces the second set of commodities with price ratios exceeding one. The borderline between these two sets of commodities depends on demand conditions, but the ordering does not.

The sharp implications of this theory concerning the extent of specialization can quickly be rejected by any data set. At even finely defined commodity categories, complete specialization is not the rule. Clearly the model needs amendment. The tradition, sometimes only implicit, is to treat goods produced by different countries as imperfect substitutes. This may be a casual way to deal with aggregation problems caused by the fact that only commodity aggregates are observed.

The following is a Ricardian model of price formation coupled with the assumption that goods produced by different countries are imperfect substitutes. Given that there is only labour input, we can use the labour productivity in industry k in country i and the prevailing wage to solve for the price of the commodity. Let Q_{ik} be the output of industry k in country i, L_{ik} the labour used in industry k in country i and q_{ik} the labour productivity $= Q_{ik}/L_{ik}$. If labour is uniform in quality, mobile across industries and the only input, then we can define

$$w_i = \text{the wage rate in country } i$$

and solve for the product price

$$p_{ik} = \text{wage}_i/(\text{output per man})_{ik} = w_i/q_{ik}$$

Further, assume that the relative demand for the commodity offered by countries i and i' satisfies the relationship

$$X_{ik}/X_{i'k} = f_k(p_{i'k}/p_{ik}) = f_k([q_{ik}/q_{i'k}]/[w_i/w_{i'}])$$

where X_{ik} = exports of commodity k by country i.

In words this last result asserts that export success depends on relative labour productivity. However, this is not enough to justify the cross-commodity comparisons that are now to be discussed because of the commodity subscript on the demand function f_k. It is necessary also to eliminate this commodity subscript by assuming that the elasticity of substitution between goods produced at different locations is the same for all goods $f_k = f$. This seems pretty doubtful.

The earliest study of the commodity composition of international trade by MacDougall (1951) implicitly uses this framework and explains the export performance of the USA relative to the UK in terms of the relative labour productivity. Using 1937 data MacDougall finds the export ratio $X_{ik}/X_{i'k} > 1$ whenever the US productivity advantage $q_{ik}/q_{i'k} > 2$ and notes that wage rates in the USA were approximately twice those in the UK. This seems supportive of the Ricardian model, but MacDougall notes that even in industries in which the UK has a strong comparative advantage, the UK share of the US market is small. He suggests that trade barriers may be the reason and finds that US tariffs did offset the UK's comparative cost advantage in many products.

Balassa (1963) extends the work of MacDougall and offers 'an empirical demonstration of the classical comparative cost theory'. Here are two of his results based on 1950 data on 28 manufacturing industries (standard errors in parentheses):

$$X_k = -53.3 + 0.721 P_k \qquad R^2 = 0.64$$
$$X_k = -181.2 + 0.691 P_k + 0.14 W_k \qquad R^2 = 0.81$$
$$ (0.167) \qquad (0.102)$$

where X_k = the export ratio $X_{ik}/X_{i'k}$, P_k = the productivity ratio $q_{ik}/q_{i'k}$ and W_k is the wage ratio: (US wage)$_k$/(UK wage)$_k$. Balassa's first result seems to support the comparative cost model in the sense that US export performance tends to be relatively good in industries in which it has a relatively large labour productivity. The second result is something of a mystery. Why should high wages lead to export success? This is very suggestive of a multi-factor model including human capital as one of the inputs.[1]

What have we learned from this? I think not too much. The regressions just described have not had a detectable impact on the collective consciousness of international economics. Why not? For the same reasons that much empirical work is limited in value. First, the Ricardian model is not sensibly interpreted literally when it is studied empirically, and the non-literal translations of the model seem to have a lot of loose ends. Second, the studies are done without referring adequately to the range of alternative hypotheses that might be considered. There must be any number of reasons why success in exporting is related to productivity. For these reasons there is little intellectual capital at risk when these regressions are estimated.

4.3 EMPIRICAL STUDIES OF THE RICARDO–VINER MODEL OF COMPARATIVE ADVANTAGE

When international economists think of the effects of tariffs, they often have the Ricardo–Viner model in mind. This model has a general mobile factor, say labour, that is used in all industries, and a set of specific factors each used in one sector only. One interpretation is that the specific factors represent the Ricardian technological differences. Viewed this way, the differences between the models are minor. Ricardo assumes a fixed marginal product of labour whereas the Ricardo–Viner model uses diminishing marginal products. Another interpretation of the model is that the specific factor is fixed in the short run, but not the long run. This second interpretation suggests a time series study based on a model with one set of equations that take capital in place as given and allocate the mobile factors across sectors and another set of equations that allocate new investment.

Although there have been studies of the Ricardian model, to my knowledge there have been no studies of the Ricardo–Viner model. This does not seem surprising if the specific factors are taken to be fixed over time. Then there is not enough of a conceptual difference between the Ricardian model and the Ricardo–Viner model to merit the attention of empirical workers. But a study of the effect of international events on the allocation of new investment could be based on the Ricardo–Viner model and could be very interesting.

4.4 EMPIRICAL STUDIES OF THE HECKSCHER–OHLIN MODEL

Economists generally regard the HO model to be superior to the Ricardian model for the intellectual reason that it offers a 'deeper' and more 'appealing' explanation of trade which does not have to resort to the 'gimmick' of technological differences. England trades cloth for wine with Portugal not because the technological knowledge of cloth production is unavailable in Portugal or because grape growing and wine production are a genetic mystery to the British, but rather because the Portuguese are relatively well supplied with land in a grape-growing climate and relatively poorly supplied with capital.

An elegant version of the HO general equilibrium model is based on the assumptions:

1 identical homothetic tastes;
2 constant returns to scale and identical technologies;
3 perfect competition in the goods and factor markets;
4 costless international exchange of commodities;
5 internationally immobile factors of production that can move costlessly among industries within a country;
6 equal numbers of goods and factors;
7 sufficient similarities in factor endowments that countries are all in the same 'cone of diversification'.

These assumptions imply that all countries have the same factor prices (FPE), and identical input/output ratios. These assumptions also imply that the vector of net exports is a linear function of the vector of factor supplies.

The production side of the general equilibrium model with equal numbers of goods and factors can be summarized by the system of equations

$$\mathbf{Q} = \mathbf{A}^{-1}\mathbf{V} \tag{4.1}$$

$$\mathbf{w} = \mathbf{A}'^{-1}\mathbf{p} \tag{4.2}$$

$$\mathbf{A} = \mathbf{A}(\mathbf{w}, t) \tag{4.3}$$

where $\mathbf{Q}$ is the vector of outputs, $\mathbf{V}$ is the vector of factor supplies, $\mathbf{A}$ is the input–output matrix with elements equal to the amount of a factor used to produce a unit of a good, $\mathbf{p}$ is the vector of commodity prices and $\mathbf{w}$ is the vector of factor returns. Equation (4.1), which translates factor supplies $\mathbf{V}$ into outputs $\mathbf{Q}$, is the inverted form of the factor market equilibrium conditions equating the supply of factors $\mathbf{V}$ to the demand for factors $\mathbf{AQ}$. Equation (4.2), which translates product prices into factor prices, is the inverted form of the zero profit conditions equating product prices $\mathbf{p}$ to production costs $\mathbf{A}'\mathbf{w}$. Equation (4.3) expresses the dependence of input intensities on factor prices $\mathbf{w}$ and on the state of technology t, $\mathbf{A}(\mathbf{w}, t)$ being the cost-minimizing choice of input intensities at time t. The assumption of constant returns to scale implies that $\mathbf{A}$ depends on the factor returns $\mathbf{w}$ but not on the scale of output $\mathbf{Q}$.

The consumption side of the model is neutralized by the assumption of identical homothetic tastes. Then, in the absence of barriers to trade, all individuals face the same commodity prices, and they consume in the same proportions:

$$\mathbf{C} = s\mathbf{C}_{\mathrm{w}} = s\mathbf{A}^{-1}\mathbf{V}_{\mathrm{w}} \tag{4.4}$$

where $\mathbf{C}$ is the consumption vector, $\mathbf{C}_{\mathrm{w}}$ is the world consumption vector, $\mathbf{V}_{\mathrm{w}}$ is the vector of world resource supplies and s is the consumption share. Thus trade is

$$\mathbf{T} = \mathbf{Q} - \mathbf{C} = \mathbf{A}^{-1}\mathbf{V} - s\mathbf{A}^{-1}\mathbf{V}_{\mathrm{w}} = \mathbf{A}^{-1}(\mathbf{V} - s\mathbf{V}_{\mathrm{w}}) \tag{4.5}$$

The consumption share s will depend on the level of output and also on the size of the trade balance, $B = \pi'\mathbf{T}$, where π is the vector of external prices which in the absence of trade barriers would equal the internal prices $\mathbf{p}$. Premultiplying (4.5) by the vector of prices π and then rearranging produces the consumption share

$$s = (\pi'\mathbf{A}^{-1}\mathbf{V} - B)/\pi'\mathbf{A}^{-1}\mathbf{V}_w = (\mathrm{GNP} - B)/\mathrm{GNP}_w \qquad (4.6)$$

This is often called the Heckscher–Ohlin–Vanek (HOV) model, referring to Vanek's (1968) use of the assumption of homothetic tastes. Using this HOV model, trade is a linear function of the endowments. The more basic HO proposition makes no reference to linearity and merely asserts that trade arises because of the unequal distribution of resources across countries. A pure HO model thus implies that if the ratios of resources were the same in all countries then there would be no trade. Several of the assumptions listed above can be altered without affecting this basic HO proposition. These assumptions only introduce non-linearities in the relationship between trade and factor supplies.

One rather silly assumption that cries out for change is equal numbers of commodities and factors. An alternative is that the number of commodities exceeds the number of factors. Then FPE need not occur, and if countries are sufficiently different in their relative factor supplies, they will have different factor prices and they will produce different subsets of commodities which use intensively their relatively cheap factors.

Factor Content Studies of the Heckscher–Ohlin Model

The first and by far the most influential study of the HO model was done by Leontief (1953) who found that US imports in 1947 were more capital intensive relative to labour than US exports. This empirical 'paradox' sparked a search of great breadth and intensity for a theory that could explain it. Among the explanations were labour skills, trade barriers, natural resource abundance, capital-biased consumption and technological differences.

Surprise! The Leontief finding is compatible with the USA being capital abundant (Leamer, 1980). This is a good illustration of the need for a clear conceptual framework when empirical work is being carried out since in its absence substantial mistakes can be made.

One suspicious step in Leontief's calculation is that he separately computes the factor content of exports and imports, whereas the HOV theory relates to net exports. The HOV theory implies that the factor content of trade satisfies the relationship $\mathbf{F} \equiv \mathbf{AT} = \mathbf{V} - s\mathbf{V}_w$, where the consumption share is $s = (\mathrm{GNP} - B)/\mathrm{GNP}_w$. From this set of equations we can separate the capital and labour content of trade:

$$\mathbf{F}_K = X_K - M_K = K - sK_w \qquad F_L = X_L - M_L = L - sL_w$$

where X and M refer to exports and imports respectively. Leamer (1980) shows that the Leontief finding, that exports are less capital intensive than imports, $X_K/X_L < M_K/M_L$, is compatible with capital abundance, $K/L > K_w/L_w$. Using

$$X_K = M_K + K - sK_w \quad \text{and} \quad X_L = M_L + L - sL_w$$

it is possible to write

$$X_K/X_L - M_K/M_L \propto \frac{K_w/L_w}{M_K/M_L}\left[\frac{K}{K_w} - s\right] - \left[\frac{L}{L_w} - s\right]$$

where the proportion symbol indicates that a positive number multiplies this expression to create an equality. This expression indicates that if capital is more abundant than labour and if the consumption share separates the abundance ratios, $K/K_w > s > L/L_w$, then exports must be more capital intensive than imports, $X_K/X_L > M_K/M_L$. (Under these conditions, both parts of the expression are positive.) But if the consumption share is small enough that $K/K_w > L/L_w > s$ and if imports are capital intensive, $(K_w/L_w)/(M_K/M_L) < 1$, then the last term can be sufficiently negative that imports are more capital intensive than exports even though the country is relatively capital abundant. For example, suppose there are two manufactures that are produced with capital and labour, and one agricultural product that uses land, labour and capital. If land is very abundant and if agriculture uses a lot of capital compared with labour, after allocating factors to agriculture the capital may be scarce compared with labour, and a capital-abundant country can import the most capital-intensive manufacture and export agricultural products and the labour-intensive manufacture. This cannot happen if there are only two factors, but a three-factor numerical example is given by Leamer (1980) and corrected by Heravi (1986).

A correct way to use the HOV theory to infer the relative abundance of factors from the factor content of trade refers to the factor content adjusted for the trade imbalance, $\mathbf{F}^A = \mathbf{AT} - \mathbf{V}_w B/\text{GNP}_w$. Using (4.5) and (4.6), this adjusted factor content is

$$\mathbf{F}^A = \mathbf{AT} - \mathbf{V}_w B/\text{GNP}_w = \mathbf{V} - (\text{GNP}_i/\text{GNP}_w)\mathbf{V}_w$$

Dividing each side by $(V_{wk})/(\text{GNP}_i/\text{GNP}_w)$ produces

$$Z_{ik} \equiv (\mathbf{F}^A{}_{ik}/V_{wk})/(\text{GNP}_i/\text{GNP}_w) = (V_{ik}/V_{wk})/(\text{GNP}_i/\text{GNP}_w) - 1 \quad (4.7)$$

The ratio of the resource share (V_{ik}/V_{wk}) to the GNP share $(\text{GNP}_i/\text{GNP}_w)$ of the right-hand side of this expression is a measure of the abundance of factor i. On the left-hand side of this expression is the exported share of the domestic supply adjusted for the trade imbalance. Thus the theory suggests there are two ways to measure factor abundance: directly by $(V_{ik}/V_{wk})/(\text{GNP}_i/\text{GNP}_w) - 1$ or through the adjusted factor content of trade $(\mathbf{F}^A{}_{ik}/V_{wk})/(\text{GNP}_i/\text{GNP}_w)$.

Measures of the adjusted factor content of trade Z_{ik} for the USA, the UK and Japan in 1967 using US factor intensities are reported in table 4.1.

Table 4.1 Ratio of adjusted net trade in factors to national endowment ($\times$ 100)

	USA	UK	Japan
Capital	0.08	− 12.86	− 5.47
Labour	− 0.25	0.63	0.10
Professional/technical	0.23	1.77	0.44
Manager	− 0.11	2.04	0.48
Clerical	− 0.19	1.37	0.33
Sales	− 1.10	1.30	− 0.05
Service	− 0.68	1.32	− 0.03
Agriculture	1.54	− 18.57	− 1.54
Production	− 0.34	1.11	1.18
Land			
Arable	19.45	− 313.42	− 341.42
Forest	− 23.82	− 2573.99	− 268.58
Pasture	− 1.63	− 91.89	− 1998.58

Source: Bowen, Leamer and Sveikauskus (1987)

The qualitative content of equation (4.7) has been studied in at least two ways: by examining the signs of the numbers Z_{ik} or their rank ordering. A Leontief type of study selects a country i and compares the numbers Z_{ik} for different factors k, say capital and labour. If $Z_K > Z_L$ where K and L refer to capital and labour, then trade reveals that the country is capital abundant compared to labour. Indeed that is Leamer's (1980) comment on Leontief: if you do the calculation right, then the USA is revealed to be relatively capital abundant. This is also true for the 1967 data reported in table 4.1 since the US capital number of 0.08 per cent exceeds the overall labour number of − 0.25%. According to the data in table 4.1, the USA is most abundant in arable land and most scarce in forest land.

It is also possible to make comparisons across countries. The UK is more scarce in capital than Japan which is more scarce than the USA. The UK is most abundant in labour, overall. Japan is scarcest in arable land.

A test of the HO theory compares the numbers in table 4.1 with direct measures of factor abundance. Tests of this form are what Bowen, Leamer and Sveikauskus (1987) call rank tests since they compare the rank order of factor abundance measured directly and through the factor content of trade.

It is also possible to perform 'sign' tests that compare the signs of the left and right of equation (4.7). This was first done by Brecher and Choudhri (1982) who mention that a feature of Leontief's data is that the net export of labour services is positive, even after adjusting for the trade imbalance. Using the right-hand side of (4.7), this implies that the US per capita GNP is less than world per capita GNP, which is impossible to square with the facts. Another way to describe sign tests is that they compare the resource abundance of one factor with an average of all the other factors since the GNP ratio is an earnings-weighted average of all the factor abundance ratios. By examining the signs in table 4.1 we infer that the USA was abundant in capital, professional workers and arable land and scarce in unskilled labour. Both the UK and Japan were scarce in capital and land and abundant in labour. Sign tests would compare these signs with the corresponding signs of direct measures of the factor abundance (4.7).

Bowen, Leamer and Sveikauskus (1987) in a study of 1967 data on 27 countries and 12 factors find about 35 per cent violations of the signs implied by (4.7) and about 50 per cent violations of the ranks. This seems disappointing, but what could be expected? In the absence of a clearly stated alternative theory, it seems impossible to determine just how many violations are enough to cast substantial doubt on the theory.

Remember, I think all three layers of an economic argument (issues, theory and data) need to be present if the argument is going to be genuinely persuasive. This research has a very clear theory and a close link between the theory and the data, but the issues have been forgotten.

Cross-commodity Comparisons

The HO model has often been studied empirically with cross-commodity comparisons implicitly based on the assumption that the export performance 'should' depend on the characteristics of the industry. Simple correlations were rather common early in the literature, but these gave way to multiple correlations in the 1970s.

For example, Keesing (1966) reports some simple correlations of export performance (US exports)/(group of 14 countries' exports) with skill intensities that are reported in table 4.2. These results are suggestive of human capital abundance in the USA because the largest positive correlations occur at the highest skill levels and because the unskilled labour share is actually negatively correlated with export performance.

Table 4.2 Keesing's (1966) simple correlations of labour share and export performance (US exports)/(group of 14 exports)

Skill groups	46 Industries	35 Industries[a]
I. Scientists and engineers	0.49	0.72
II. Technicians and draftsmen	0.37	0.55
III. Other professionals	0.41	0.58
IV. Managers	0.16	0.06
V. Machinists	0.22	0.37
VI. Other skilled manual workers	0.11	0.21
VII. Clerical and sales	0.35	0.44
VIII. Unskilled and semi-skilled	− 0.45	− 0.64

[a] Excluding natural resource industries.

A typical *multiple* regression is Baldwin's (1971) (reported incompletely):

$$X_k = -1.37(K/L)_k + \sum_f \beta_f p_{fk} - 421 s_k + 343 u_k \qquad R^2 = 0.44$$

where X_k is the US (adjusted) net exports of commodity k in 1962, $(K/L)_k$ the capital/labour ratio in industry k, p_{fk} the percentage of labour force in skill group f, s_k an index of scale economies and u_k = an index of the rate of unionization. One thing that might be concluded from this regression is that the negative sign on the capital intensity variable is suggestive of the Leontief paradox that the USA does not export goods that are capital intensive.

These simple correlations and multiple regressions raise a number of questions:

1 How should the export performance variable be scaled? Keesing scales by the exports of a comparison group of 14 countries. Baldwin uses the unscaled data, which seems a bit uncomfortable since all of his explanatory variables are scaled.
2 Is it more appropriate to use simple correlations or multiple regressions?
3 How should the 'importance' of a resource be inferred? By the size of the simple correlation? By the t-statistic in the multiple regressions?
4 Is it legitimate to exclude the natural resource industries?
5 Is it legitimate to include measures like the indices of scale and unionization?

These questions can only be answered with reference to a clear theoretical framework.

I have argued in several papers (Leamer and Bowen, 1981; Leamer, 1984, 1988), that cross-industry regressions generally have an unclear theoretical foundation. In deciding the kind of equation to estimate, the first important question is how to scale the dependent variable in a way that makes the cross-industry comparisons sensible. The absolute level of output or trade does not seem to be a very sensible dependent variable because some commodity groups form large shares of output and consumption whereas others form small shares. If no attempt is made to control for scale, any explanatory variable that is correlated with the size of the commodity group will pick up the scale effect. To put this another way, without some way to correct for the relative sizes of different commodity groups, the estimates will be highly sensitive to the level of aggregation. The scale effect has traditionally been controlled by dividing the dependent variable by some measure of market size. The ideal candidate would seem to be total world output. What seems to lie behind this normalization is the intuitive notion that a country's share of world output can be expected to depend on the input mix of the commodity: thus countries that are abundant in capital 'ought' to have larger shares of capital-intensive industries than of labour-intensive industries. But what seems intuitively clear is not always true. To explore this formally, let us focus on the production side of the HO model with equal numbers of factors and goods and with sufficient similarity of endowment supplies that all countries have the same factor prices and use the same input mixes.

Equation (4.1) then identifies a set of relationships between outputs, factor intensities and factor supplies. If data are collected for a single country only, then the endowment vector $\mathbf{V}$ is necessarily constant and (4.1) explains the level of production of each commodity as a function of the factor intensities $\mathbf{A}$. This equation suggests that the 'correct' variables to include in the equation are elements of the inverse of $\mathbf{A}$, not elements of $\mathbf{A}$. Usually, however, the dependent variable is not selected to be the level of output which can vary enormously if data are in monetary units and oddly if data are in other units. It is traditional to normalize by a variable that represents the 'size' of the commodity in world markets such as the level of the world's output of the commodity. By Cramer's rule, the share of the country output of commodity one is

$$Q_1/Q_{1w} = \det[\mathbf{V}, \mathbf{A}_2, \mathbf{A}_3, \ldots, \mathbf{A}_N]/\det[\mathbf{V}_w, \mathbf{A}_2, \mathbf{A}_3, \ldots, \mathbf{A}_N]$$

where $\mathbf{A}_j$ refers to a column of the matrix $\mathbf{A}$, Q_{1w} is the world output of commodity 1 and $\mathbf{V}_w$ is the world's vector of factor endowments. Note that this formula indicates that the share of world output of commodity one does not depend on $\mathbf{A}_1$, the input mix in industry one (Leamer, 1988)! This model thus suggests that it is entirely inappropriate to regress output shares on characteristics of industries.

Many cross-industry regression studies in the literature have not used the world shares as the dependent variable. Typically, the dependent variable is the trade-dependence ratio equal to the level of net exports as a share of domestic consumption. Exactly the same comment applies if the model (4.1)–(4.6) is used. Using Cramer's rule we can solve for the trade-dependence ratio for the first commodity as

$$T_1/C_1 = \det(\mathbf{V} - s\mathbf{V}_w, \mathbf{A}_2, \mathbf{A}_3, \ldots, \mathbf{A}_n)/\det(s\mathbf{V}_w, \mathbf{A}_2, \mathbf{A}_3, \ldots, \mathbf{A}_N)$$

The same result thus applies: the trade dependence ratio in industry 1 is altogether unrelated to the characteristics of that industry.

Another comment on cross-commodity regressions is offered by Leamer and Bowen (1981). It has been a tradition to regress trade on factor intensities and to assume that the signs of the coefficients reveal the relative abundance of factors. For example, a country that is relatively well endowed with capital is expected to have a positive coefficient on the capital variable when trade is regressed on a set of factor intensities. But as Leamer and Bowen (1981) observe, there is no assurance that this is true. The regression vector formed when the unscaled trade data $\mathbf{T}$ are regressed on the input intensities $\mathbf{A}$ is

$$(\mathbf{AA}')^{-1}\mathbf{AT} = (\mathbf{AA}')^{-1}(\mathbf{V} - s\mathbf{V}_w)$$

which has the same sign as $(\mathbf{V} - s\mathbf{V}_w)$ only under special circumstances.

Your 'intuition' about the correlation of trade and factor intensities may refer to the simple correlation, not the multiple correlation. The simple correlation between trade and the capital input, for example, is

$$\text{Corr}(\mathbf{T}, \mathbf{A}_K) = (\mathbf{T}'\mathbf{A}_K - \mathbf{1}'\mathbf{T}\mathbf{1}'\mathbf{A}_K/p)/\sqrt{(\mathbf{T}'\mathbf{T} - (\mathbf{1}'\mathbf{T})^2/p)}\sqrt{(\mathbf{A}'_K\mathbf{A}_K - (\mathbf{1}'\mathbf{A}_K)^2/p)}$$

$$= (K - sK_w)/p\sqrt{\text{Var}(\mathbf{T})}\sqrt{\text{Var}(\mathbf{A}_K)}$$

where $\mathbf{A}_K$ is the vector of capital requirements with one entry for each industry, p the number of industries and where I have used $\mathbf{T}'\mathbf{A}_K = K - sK_w$ and the trade balance restriction $\mathbf{1}'\mathbf{T} = 0$. Thus, if trade is balanced, $B = 0$, the sign of the simple correlation is the same as the sign of the excess factor supply $K - sK_w$. For example, a country that is well endowed in capital will have trade positively correlated with capital intensity. By this type of reasoning, the simple correlations in table 4.2 suggest that the USA was relatively abundant in all the skilled labour categories and relatively scarce in unskilled labour.

More than just the sign, it is natural to suspect that the simple correlation between trade and factor intensity is highest for the factor that is most 'important', scientists and engineers in table 4.2, for example. In theory, the absolute size of the correlation depends on the degree of 'peculiarity' of this resource supply $K/K_w - s$ and also on the term

$$K_w/\sqrt{\text{Var}(\mathbf{A}_K)} = 1/\text{Var}(\mathbf{A}_K/K_w)^{1/2}$$

The number $\mathbf{A}_{Kj}/K_w$ is the inverse of the amount of the output of commodity j that would be produced in the world if j used only capital. Thus the term $\text{Var}(\mathbf{A}_K/K_w)$ compares in a scale-free way the variability of resource use across industries. In that sense, the correlation is high if the supply of the resource is unusual and if the intensities are highly variable across industries.

Studies of the Heckscher–Ohlin Model Based on Cross-country Comparisons

Cross-country comparisons are another way to study the validity of the HO theorem. Studies of this type hold fixed the commodity and use the country as the experimental unit. Normally the tool of analysis is multiple regression with some measure of trade performance as the dependent variable and various characteristics of countries as the explanatory variable. Chenery (1960), Chenery and Taylor (1968) and Chenery and Syrquin (1975) were some of the earliest studies of this type, although these studies did not deal with details of the structure of trade but rather with more aggregate features of the economy like the ratio of gross imports to GNP. Leamer (1974) was one of the first to study commodity composition questions, contrasting the performance of three groups of variables as predictors of imports disaggregated by commodity; these groups are resistance (tariffs and distance), stage of development (GNP and population) and resource supplies (capital, labour, education and R&D). Leamer finds that the development group is generally most important in helping to predict import patterns.

The theory underlying many of these cross-section regressions is casual at best. This contrasts with Leamer (1984) which takes equation (4.5), the HOV model, $\mathbf{T} = \mathbf{A}^{-1}(\mathbf{V} - s\mathbf{V}_w)$, as the clearly stated foundation for running regressions of net exports on factor supplies. One function of such an estimation exercise implicitly is to infer the value of $\mathbf{A}^{-1}$ and to study how this changes over time. The question that is implicitly addressed is: 'What resource supplies determine comparative advantage?'

Some typical results from Leamer (1984) are reported in table 4.3. These are beta values from regressions of 4 commodity aggregates on 11 resource supplies. The data refer to trade and resource supplies of 60 countries in 1975. Incidentally, a beta coefficient is equal to the estimated coefficient times the ratio of the standard error of the explanatory variable divided by the standard error of the dependent variable. A beta coefficient answers the question: if the explanatory variable changes by a typical amount (one standard error), does the dependent variable change by a typical amount as well?

Table 4.3 Beta values of net export regressions

	Cereals	Labour-intensive manufactures	Capital-intensive manufactures	Machinery
Capital	− 0.17	0.08	0.78	0.49
Labour 1	0.74	− 1.13	− 1.8	− 0.39
Labour 2	− 0.55	0.93	0.85	0.18
Labour 3	− 0.15	0.08	0.37	0.02
Land 1	0.09	− 0.04	− 0.03	− 0.01
Land 2	0.03	− 0.02	− 0.01	0.0
Land 3	0.26	− 0.04	− 0.15	− 0.06
Land 4	0.05	− 0.15	− 0.10	− 0.11
Coal	0.03	− 0.14	− 0.09	− 0.02
Minerals	0.0	− 0.03	− 0.03	− 0.01
Oil	0.72	− 0.24	− 0.60	− 0.21

Labour is disaggregated by skill; land by climate.
Source: Leamer (1984)

Based on these beta values, comparative advantage in cereals is associated with abundance of highly skilled labour, land of type 3 and oil. Comparative advantage in the three manufactures is associated with supply of the moderately skilled workers and capital, and is negatively related to the supply of land.

Studies of the Heckscher–Ohlin Model Using Two-dimensional Data

Beginning with Leamer and Bowen (1981), I have often made the observation that the HO model links three separately observable phenomena: trade, resource supplies and technological input coefficients. A full test of the theory accordingly must begin with separate measures of all three of these concepts and must explore the extent to which the observed data violate the HO restrictions.

Hufbauer (1970) is a notable early study that employs measurements of all three concepts. Some typical results are reported in table 4.4. The countries in this list are ordered by measures of their capital per man with Canada being the most abundant in capital and Pakistan the least abundant. The capital per man in exports is compared with the capital per man in imports in the next two columns. It should be noted that the US data display the 'Leontief paradox' that imports are more capital intensive than exports. But this is not true for the other countries at the top of the list. Hufbauer reports that the capital per man (first column) has a correlation of 0.625 with the capital per man in exports (second column) and a correlation of − 0.353 with capital per man in imports (third column). This is regarded to be confirmatory of the HO model: capital-abundant countries tend to have capital-intensive exports and labour-intensive imports.

Table 4.4 Capital per man

	Abundance	Exports	Imports
Canada	8,850	17,529	11,051
USA	7,950	11,441	13,139
Norway	6,100	16,693	10,476
Sweden	5,400	12,873	11,373
Netherlands	4,750	11,768	11,706
. . .			
Korea	850	8,004	14,900
India	500	7,339	12,019
Pakistan	500	5,725	12,371

Source: Hufbauer(1970)

There are four comments that can be made about this study:

1 The study uses measures of all three concepts: factor supplies, trade and technological input intensities. As I have already mentioned, a full test of the HO model must surely make reference to all of these.
2 Hufbauer's analysis does not refer explicitly to any model. It separates imports from exports, which got Leontief in trouble.
3 I find it curious that the capital per man in exports varies greatly across countries in contrast to the capital per man in imports. I would not have expected this result based on my understanding of the HO model. What might account for it? Perhaps the model with more goods than factors can help. In the HO model with many goods and two inputs, countries concentrate production on just two of the goods and import all the rest. The two produced goods have similar capital intensities. In words, countries have a diversified import structure but a concentrated export structure.
4 Competing models and/or factors that might explain trade are 'tested' by comparing the size of the correlations that they produce. The list of theories is noticeably inclusive: factor proportions, human skills, scale economies, stage of production, technological gap, product cycle and preference similarity.

Bowen, Leamer and Sveikauskus (1987) also use measurements of all three concepts and link their work to a carefully formulated model, namely the

HOV model as captured by equation (4.7) which determines the adjusted factor content of trade as a function of resource supplies. Recognizing the impossibility of testing a theory without an alternative, these authors generalize the HOV model to allow (a) non-homothetic tastes characterized by linear Engel curves, (b) technological differences among countries that affect all technological coefficients proportionately and (c) various kinds of measurement errors. In the words of Bowen, Leamer and Sveikauskus (1987, p. 805): 'The data suggest errors in measurement in both trade and national factor supplies, and favor the hypothesis of neutral technological differences across countries. However, the form of the technological differences favored by the data involves a number of implausible estimates, including some in which factors yield strictly negative outputs. Thus, . . . The Heckscher–Ohlin model does poorly, but we do not have anything that does better.' But what are the issues? How does this help us design trade interventions?

Comment on the Studies of the Ricardian Model

I have argued above that the studies of the Ricardian model that regress measures of relative export performance on measures of relative labour productivities are only loosely connected with the Ricardian model. We can also ask if the Ricardian regressions make sense from the standpoint of the HO model. Clearly, the answer is no if the even HO model is used since it implies that labour productivities are the same in all countries. Cross-commodity empirical studies suggested by the HO model thus usually proceed as if this were so and use the input intensities from one country as explanatory variables rather than ratios of intensities from different countries. The HO regressions take the form $X_{ik}/X_{i'k} = f(q_{ik})$ where X_{ik} equal exports of commodity i by country k and q_{ik} is the corresponding labour productivity measured in one of the countries. This contrasts with the Ricardian equation which uses the *relative* labour productivities: $X_{ik}/X_{i'k} = f(q_{ik}/q_{i'k})$.

In a search to give the Ricardian regression some meaning from the standpoint of this version of the HO model, it seems natural to consider aggregation over goods or over factors. Aggregation is something that always needs to be considered since real data on commodities and factors necessarily refer to aggregates. In particular, differences in labour productivities may be a consequence of aggregation even though at the level of the commodity labour productivities are equal. The labour productivity within a commodity aggregate is equal to

$$\sum p_k Q_k / \sum L_k = \sum (p_k Q_k / L_k) L_k / \sum L_k$$

which is a weighted average of labour productivities with weights equal to the labour used in sector k. This aggregate labour productivity will thus be relatively high in countries with labour allocations concentrating on those industries within the aggregate with relatively high labour productivities. If the summation in this expression extends over all commodities, then the labour productivity is GNP per man which is an increasing function of the relative supplies of the non-labour factors. Those countries with relatively high GNP per man will therefore have relatively large allocations of labour to the industries with relatively high productivities. This can make the measured productivities for commodity aggregates different in the two countries even though they are identical at the level of individual commodities. Aggregates composed of commodities with uniform values of output per man will of course have the same level of aggregate output per man in both countries since the weights do not matter. But aggregates composed of commodities with variable labour productivities will tend to have high measured labour productivities in the capital-abundant country because it allocates relatively large shares of its work-force to the components with relatively high labour productivities.

This discussion of aggregation does not give a very sensible foundation to the Ricardian regressions since the proposition that the USA has a comparative advantage in those commodities with relatively high labour productivities amounts to the odd claim that the USA has a comparative advantage in the commodity aggregates composed of variable labour productivities.

As argued by Deardorff (1984), the uneven HO model can give greater content to the Ricardian regressions because factor prices are not necessarily equalized and labour productivities may differ across countries. The supply price of commodity k in country i depends on the factor return vector and the input vector by the zero profit condition (4.2): $p_{ik} = \Sigma_f w_{if} A_{ifk}$. The relative supply price of two different countries is thus

$$p_{ik}/p_{i'k} = \sum_f w_{if} A_{ifk} / \sum_f w_{i'f} A_{i'fk}$$

which depends on factor intensity differences and also factor return differences. This is not exactly expressible simply in terms of relative labour productivities even if there are only two factors, since other things matter, but differences in labour productivities do account for part of the differences in relative prices.[2]

4.5 EMPIRICAL STUDIES OF INTRA-INDUSTRY TRADE AND INCREASING RETURNS TO SCALE

The puzzling phenomenon of intra-industry trade has sparked a large theoretical literature dealing with differentiated goods produced with increasing returns to scale. Accompanying these theoretical pieces are a number of empirical studies of the determinants of intra-industry trade. This area of research has a special difficulty forming interesting empirical questions because the linkage of the theory and the data analyses of necessity is often casual. Here are some of the problems.

1 It is often difficult to find any variable that closely measures the hypothetical construct stipulated by the theory. For example, Loertscher and

Wolter (1980) measure 'the potential for large scale production' by value added per establishment. But it is not clear what this has to do with the fixed costs and differentiated products that are the bases for models of intra-industry trade. An industry that comprises much of GNP may be supplied by many very large establishments each producing at the efficient scale, and none the less have industry output exhibit constant returns to scale. A better variable might be value added per establishment relative to some measure of the total market of the good.

2 The theory consists of a set of separate models, each intended to capture one feature. There is ordinarily little attempt made theoretically to combine these models into one composite. They are combined empirically merely by inclusion of separate variables representing each model in a single linear regression equation. But in the absence of a clear combined theory, it may make more sense to look at simple correlations, rather than partial correlations, since there is no assurance that the other influences are properly controlled merely by dumping them into a regression.

3 Studies that combine data from many industries are especially suspect, since the theoretical underpinnings of these studies are often weak. Economists would distrust estimates of a price elasticity of demand based on observations of price and quantity collected from many industries. Some of this distrust should carry over to all cross-industry studies.

4 Null and alternative hypotheses are not often stated and are usually quite difficult to form. Hypotheses refer either to the opinion of economists or the uses to which the theory might be put. But because of measurement problems and theoretical doubtfulness, economists cannot have much in the way of well-formed opinions about the signs or sizes of the coefficients in these regressions. And the uses of these models seem pretty distant and unclear.

5 The counterfactuals that are implicit in the estimated regressions are often unclear. What exactly, for example, is meant by a change in value added per establishment? If you cannot answer that question, then how does this tell us anything about the role of scale economies in international trade?

6 It is sometimes difficult to determine whether a projected empirical regularity is due to the existence of economies of scale or more importantly to the assumption about the nature of tastes.

With all of these difficulties, it is not surprising that the impact that these empirical findings might have on our understanding of the role of economies of scale seems not much beyond a simple measurement of the amount of intra-industry trade for various commodity groups and countries: there seems like a lot of intra-industry trade, and the HO model does not seem capable of offering a very satisfying explanation of it.

An example of the kind of empirical work that has accompanied models of intra-industry trade is a study by Loertscher and Wolter (1980) who report:

> *Drawing* on the literature quoted above the following hypotheses *seem warranted*: (my italics)
> Intra-industry trade among countries is intense if
> (a) the average of their levels of development is high.
> (b) the difference in their levels of development is relatively small.
> (c) the average of their market sizes is large.
> (d) the difference in their sizes is small.
> (e) barriers to trade are low.
> Intra-industry trade in an industry is intense if
> (f) the potential for product differentiation is high and market entry in narrow product lines is impeded by significant barriers.
> (g) transaction costs are low.
> (h) the definition of an industry is comprehensive.

I have added the italics in this quotation to emphasize the casual link between the theory and the empirical work. The regression that Loertscher and Wolter compute explains a measure of intra-industry trade indexed by importer, exporter and commodity in terms of a set of variables selected to represent the various hypothetical determinants of intra-industry trade. One of their results is reported in table 4.5.

Table 4.5 Country- and industry-specific determinants of intra-industry trade. OECD countries, cross-section 1972/3

	Estimate	t^2-value
Country-specific variables		
Development stage differential	$-0.106 \ 10^{0}$	47.95
Average development stage	$0.259 \ 10^{-1}$	1.68
Market size differential	$-0.146 \ 10^{-5}$	82.71
Average market size	$0.296 \ 10^{-5}$	108.17
Distance	$-0.485 \ 10^{-4}$	44.52
Customs unions dummy	$0.382 \ 10^{0}$	64.89
Language group dummy	$0.171 \ 10^{0}$	6.43
Border trade dummy	$0.268 \ 10^{0}$	20.41
Cultural group dummy	$-0.423 \ 10^{-2}$	0.01
Industry-specific variables		
Product differentiation	$0.733 \ 10^{-3}$	0.45
Scale economies	$-0.311 \ 10^{-1}$	91.23
Transactions costs	$-0.225 \ 10^{-3}$	3.71
Level of aggregation	$0.137 \ 10^{-1}$	3.05
Product group	$0.112 \ 10^{0}$	5.56

Adjusted $R^2 = 0.070$, degrees of freedom = 6975.
Source: Loertscher and Wolter (1980)

From my perspective it is difficult to know what to make of a regression of this type. Most of the coefficients are very 'statistically significant', as might be expected with so large a sample size. The precision with which these coefficients are estimated is misleading, however, since the fit as measured by the R^2 is very low. One thing the low R^2 means is that the signs of the estimated coefficients are not resistant to measurement-error adjustments. In fact, I am pretty sure that any sign pattern of estimated coefficients would be possible if you assumed a little measurement error in a few of the variables. For the technical reasons, consult Klepper and Leamer (1984). Actually, the authors' reaction (p. 287) to the 'wrong' sign on the scale economies variable is indeed mismeasurement.

But the real difficulties of interpreting a regression of this type come from the very fuzzy link between the theory and the regression. Models do suggest that intra-industry trade is positively associated with scale economies. But no composite model has been presented which suggests that, controlling for all these other variables, the scale effect is positive. In the absence of a theory that tells what other things I should control, it is difficult to interpret a partial correlation which controls for a haphazardly selected group of other variables. Then it may make sense to look at the simple correlations.

Helpman's (1987) study of the effect of size dispersion on the amount of trade and the amount of intra-industry trade is noteworthy in its attempt to link more closely the theory and the empirical study. Neglecting Helpman's correction for trade imbalances, his size similarity index of a group I of industrial countries is defined to be a negative function of the variance of GNP shares:[3]

$$\text{SIM} = 1 - \sum (s_j)^2 = 1 - (1/n) - \text{Var}(s_j)$$

where s_j is the GNP share of country i in total GNP of group I. Total intra-group trade is

$$V_I = \sum_{i \neq j} X_{ij}$$

where X_{ij} is the value of exports from i to j. Helpman's model implies that the total trade increases with similarity:

$$V_I/\text{GNP}_I = (\text{GNP}_I/\text{GNP}_w) \times \text{SIM}$$

Helpman finds that for a group of 14 of the most industrialized countries both GNP similarity and trade intensity have increased more or less constantly from 1956 to 1981, giving the appearance that the model is supported.

One of the basic questions now arises: 'What is the theoretical basis for this empirical work?' To express it differently: what is being tested? Economies of scale appear to be central but, in fact, the result just described comes from the consumption side of the model, and makes no serious reference to the production side. In particular, suppose that we make the 'Armington' assumption that products are distinguished by location of production and make the further assumptions that tastes are identical and homothetic and that trade is balanced. Then purchases by country i of country j's product are equal to $(GDP_i/GDP_w) GDP_j = s_i s_j (GDP_l/GDP_w) GDP_l$ where $s_i = GDP_i/GDP_l$. Summing this over all importers and exporters produces the result

$$V_l = \sum_{i \neq j} s_i s_j (GDP_l/GDP_w) GDP_l = (1 - \sum_i s_i^2)(GDP_l/GDP_w)GDP_l$$

which is just the model that Helpman studies. If this model fits poorly, it is due to a failure of the proposition that all individuals consume the same share of total output of US wine, French wine, German cars, ... It need not have anything to do with the method of production or the nature of competition. The same result can be obtained by appending a different model of consumption on to the basic HO model of production.

Helpman also reports that his theory 'suggests' that: 'The share of intraindustry trade in bilateral trade flows should be larger for countries with similar incomes per capita. ... In order to examine the consistency of this hypothesis with the data', Helpman calculates bilateral intra-industry trade as

$$S_{ij} = 2 \sum_k \min(X_{ijk}, X_{jik})/\sum_i (X_{ijk} + X_{jik})$$

where k indexes commodities. For each of 12 different years this measure of intra-industry trade is explained in terms of three variables:

$$X_1 = \log |(GDP_i/POP_i) - (GDP_j/POP_j)|$$
$$X_2 = \min(\log(GDP_i), \log(GDP_j))$$
$$X_3 = \max(\log(GDP_i), \log(GDP_j))$$

The results for the extreme years are given in table 4.6.

Table 4.6 Regressions for intra-industry trade

	X_1	X_2	X_3	R^2
1970	− 0.044	0.055	− 0.014	0.266
	(− 3.141)	(4.153)	(− 1.105)	
1981	− 0.006	0.027	− 0.020	0.039
	(− 0.370)	(1.686)	(− 1.283)	

The t-values are in parentheses; $n = 14 \times 13/2 = 91$.
Source: Helpman (1987)

From these regressions we may conclude that intra-industry trade is more intense between countries that are similar either in terms of per capita GDPs or in terms of GDP itself, though this is more difficult to detect in the latter period. The conclusion regarding the effect of similarity in the levels of GDPs refers to the fact that the coefficient on the minimum GDP is positive and the coefficient on maximum GDP is negative and approximately the same absolute size. It also appears that the coefficient on the minimum GDP is the larger in absolute value, suggesting that country size as well as similarity contributes to intra-industry trade. A second regression reported by Helpman separates GDP size from GDP similarity and confirms that both seem to contribute positively to intra-industry trade.

This work has unearthed several interesting empirical regularities but there remains a great deal that could be done on the role of economies of scale in international relationships. For example, among the unanswered questions are: how much of total trade is due to economies of scale? How much of the gains from trade are due to economies of scale? What role do tastes have in determining the result? Why does the regression fit so poorly? Which industries are best described by models of imperfect competition? . . .

4.6 EMPIRICAL STUDIES OF THE EFFECT OF DEMAND

Trade is the difference between production and consumption. Most of the theoretical literature in international economics concentrates on the production side and often uses assumptions that neutralize demand as a determinant of the composition of trade. An early and notable exception is Linder (1961) who argues that differences in tastes is a deterrent to trade because of the costs of tailoring a product to fit local conditions. This is usually interpreted to mean that the intensity of bilateral trade decreases with differences in per capita income. The HO model, on the other hand, 'suggests' the reverse association because countries with substantially different per capita incomes are 'likely' to have different resource endowments, offer different baskets of goods for trade and therefore become trading partners.

Most of the theoretical work deals with the commodity composition of trade, not the partner composition. The Linder hypothesis has traditionally been interpreted in terms of its implications for partner composition by including a measure of similarity of per capita GNPs in 'gravity equations' that explain bilateral trade. The Linder hypothesis as it relates to the commodity composition has been studied recently by Hunter and Markusen (1988) who estimate a system of demand equations and study its implications for total trade. An interesting example of the gravity models is reported by Hoftyzer (1984) who presents a model that explains the bilateral trade of each of 11 importers using data for 58 exporters. His results for three of the importers are reported in table 4.7.

The Linder hypothesis is interpreted to mean that the dissimilarity of countries as measured by the difference in per capita incomes will lower the intensity of trade. In other words, the coefficient on $DIFF_y$ should be negative. Hoftyzer (1984) finds otherwise in the sense that for a few countries the estimated coefficient is negative, but for most it is positive. This contrasts with some more positive results by other authors, which Hoftyzer argues are due to their failure to control for border effects and membership in free trade associations and their failure to consider other functional forms which he does through the Box–Cox analysis. But I note that this finding is in conflict with Helpman's (1987) time series finding that the rapid growth of trade over the period 1960–90 was associated with a convergence of per capita incomes.

Table 4.7 Gravity equations: 1970 trade

Country	DIFF$_Y$	DIST	DIFF$_L$	ASSOC	COMMON	BORDER	R^2	λ
West Germany	0.01	− 4.65	− 0.29	− 0.22		0.56	0.55	0.001
	(0.01)	(5.00)	(0.06)	(0.55)		(1.45)		
Japan	− 2.18	− 11.52	− 1.40				0.13	0.3
	(0.08)	(2.70)	(0.12)					
USA	3.20	− 8.22	− 2.40			0.28	0.27	0.1
	(1.15)	(3.33)	(0.31)			(0.40)		

t – statistics in parentheses.
DIFF$_Y$ = absolute difference in income per capita.
DIST = great circle difference between economic centres.
DIFF$_L$ = absolute difference in land per capita.
ASSOC = common membership in free trade associations.
COMMON = commonwealth country.
BORDER = common border.
λ = Box–Cox parameter.

Source: Hoftyzer(1984)

It is again time to trot out our two questions for the last time. Does this work have a solid base in economic theory? No, not really. Are the hypotheses phrased in a way that puts intellectual capital at risk? Actually, I think so. Even though the theoretical foundation is murky, the finding of Hoftyzer (1984) seems to me to be unsettling to the Linder viewpoint. According to Hoftyzer (1984) trade may seem intense between similar countries, but that can be explained first by the fact that they are neighbours and/or members of free trade associations and second that, whatever relationship exists, it is not log-linear. This for me is a memorable result, affecting my understanding of the role of demand as a determinant of trade patterns.

Still we need to ask what exactly is being studied here. What is the counterfactual? Is the question as simple as determining the sign of the difference variable after accounting for a list of randomly selected other variables? That is an interesting question, but it seems like a very limited one. Maybe the deeper issues have to do with the gains from trade and the effects of trade policy on welfare. Are the gains from trade less if the trade is Linder trade as opposed to HO trade?

4.7 GROWTH AND OPENNESS

The phenomenal difference between the growth rates of the East Asian economies and the Latin American economies over the last several decades has stimulated a renewed interest in the determinants of economic growth. A prominent and important hypothesis is that these differences in growth rates can be explained by differences in the degree of openness to international commerce. Many suppose that the successful East Asian economies are open, and the unsuccessful Latin American economies are closed. But clear empirical support for this proposition is not easy to come by.

Cross-country Comparisons

Studies by Tyler (1981), Feder (1983), Kavoussi (1984), Balassa (1985) and Ram (1985) have examined the relationship between trade and growth in a cross-section of countries by regressing the rate of growth of GNP on the rate of growth of trade and the rate of growth of certain measurable inputs. Generally, the coefficient on the growth of trade is positive and 'statistically significant'. For example, Ram (1985) reports the following regression (t-values in parentheses):

$$\hat{Y} = -1.034 + 1.071\hat{L} + 0.130IY + 0.124\hat{X} \qquad R^2 = 0.46 \qquad n = 73$$
$$\quad\; (-1.15) \quad (3.41) \qquad (3.75) \qquad (4.01)$$

where the circumflex accent indicates the average annual rate of growth, Y is GDP, L labour force, X exports and IY the ratio of investment to GDP.

This kind of regression is based on the assumption that aggregate output is a log-linear function of capital, labour and technology, and that technology is a log-linear function of the level of exports. Criticisms of these findings abound.

First one might question whether the growth of GNP should be explained by the degree of openness or the growth thereof. In the regression just described, is it better to include the growth of exports or the initial ratio of exports to GNP? To seek a proper answer to this question it seems wise to model more carefully the dynamic relationship between GNP and openness. Traditional models of comparative advantage allow a one-time effect of liberalization, not a continuing effect on the growth rate. More recently, partly in response to the great differences in growth experiences of different countries, there has been an attempt to form models that do link the rate of growth with the degree of openness, not the change thereof. These models draw their dynamics from assumptions regarding economies of scale or the nature of technological change. But I am left with the impression that theory will not decisively answer this modelling question. I also suspect that the evidence embodied in aggregate data sets is unlikely to be decisive about the dynamic relationship between growth and openness.

Regardless of what model is adopted, the level of exports seems not a very good indicator of openness because much of the cross-country variation in the ratio of exports to GNP is due to differences in comparative advantage, not to government intervention in international transactions. This is more than just a measurement-error problem because these comparative-advantage components of the variation in export growth are unlikely to be exogenous to the process that determines GNP. For example, the discovery of gold in

California precipitated an economic boom affecting both the level of exports and the level of Californian GNP. This coincident boom in both GNP and exports obviously tells us nothing about the effect of openness on growth. A second problem with exports as a measure of openness is that exports may be high because of export promotion, rather than non-interference.

To explore and to combat these criticisms Edwards (1989, 1991) has experimented with many other measures of openness, including some from Leamer (1988) that attempt to control for differences in comparative advantage. The variety of ways that one can measure openness using trade data leaves the impression of an annoying degree of fragility in the inferences based on them.

The choice of measures of openness creates one set of concerns. The choice of economic model of aggregate output creates another. It seems appropriate at a minimum to consider at least two alternatives to the log-linear aggregate production function. One alternative is implied by the multi-product HO model with constant returns to scale at the level of the industry. This model implies that GNP is a linear function of the inputs with coefficients that depend on the product mix (the cone of specialization) and the level of technology: $GNP = \sum_i V_i w_i(V, t)$ where V_i is the supply of factor i, and w_i is the corresponding return which depends on factor supplies and technology. Stripped to its essentials, this model produces just another aggregate production function and openness is a source of growth if it somehow enhances the rate of dispersion or creation of technology. A more substantial conceptual difference occurs if the disaggregated model has some sectors with increasing returns to scale. Then openness can encourage growth because it creates a larger market.

These cross-country comparisons of growth performance have certainly increased our understanding of the determinants of growth and have added to the impression that growth is enhanced by openness, but much of the cross-country variation of aggregate growth rates remains unaccounted for. It appears that the processing of these kinds of cross-country aggregate data sets is suffering from diminishing returns. Perhaps much could be gained from the study of data disaggregated by industry, and by attempting to be explicit about estimating the rate of technological dispersion and the attainment of economies of scale.

Granger Causal Orderings

A number of studies have 'tested' to see if exports 'Granger cause' GNP growth. Readers of this work need to proceed with caution. It is an abuse of the language to refer to temporal orderings in terms of causation. For example, we know that weather forecasts precede the weather but few of us take this to be evidence that weathermen cause the weather. Studies of 'Granger causal orderings' of exports and GNP are not identifying causal directions but are only asking the question whether movements in exports tend to precede or follow movements in GNP. Studies of the temporal orderings of exports and GNP seem interesting on their face, but leave one wondering exactly how they relate to the growth and openness debate. Lal and Rajapatirana (1987) offer detailed criticisms and argue 'if a small country is developing efficiently in line with its comparative advantage, it will specialize and hence be compelled to turn to foreign markets for exports of goods that use its most abundant factor of production most intensively'. This may make it appear that GNP 'Granger causes' exports, but if the economy were closed the internal growth spurt would have been choked off due to lack of markets. This is just a version of the weather and weatherman story.

Cross-industry Comparisons

Most of the cross-industry studies have adopted the same casual conceptual framework as the aggregated studies. Some of these explain growth in output in terms of growth in inputs plus some measure of trade. Others study Granger temporal orderings. The one new wrinkle that is common in these disaggregated studies is the use of earnings shares to compute 'total factor productivities'. The logic for this computation is as follows. A typical production function can be written as $Q = f(K, L, t)$ where K is capital, L is labour and t is 'technology'. Differentiation of this function produces the relationship

$$dQ/Q = (f_K K/Q) \, dK/K + (f_L L/Q) \, dL/L + (f_t/Q) \, dt$$

where f_i refer to the marginal products and where the last term represents the effect of technological change on output. If the goods and factor markets were competitive and if the levels of the inputs of capital and labour were costlessly adjustable by the firms, then these inputs would be paid their marginal products and the expressions like $(f_L L/Q)$ would represent the input shares. Then we could write the growth in technology in terms of the growth in 'total factor productivity (TFP)':

$$dTFP/TFP = (f_t/Q) \, dt = dQ/Q - (f_K K/Q) \, dK/K - (f_L L/Q) \, dL/L$$

$$= dQ/Q - \theta_K \, dK/K - \theta_L \, dL/L$$

In words, the growth in TFP is measured as that part of the growth in output that is not accounted for by growth in inputs.

The tradition in this literature has been to explain the growth in TFP in terms of measures of openness, often imports and exports. The same concerns that were raised above about these measures of openness apply here as well. The substantial difference between these studies and the cross-country comparisons reviewed above is that these latter studies presume that input shares reveal marginal products.

I hope that you detected the liberal use of the subjunctive in the preceding paragraphs: there are lots of 'woulds' and 'weres' that reflect a high degree of scepticism about the computation of TFPs. Nelson (1981) is one source of criticism of these kinds of calculations. Here are some of my own. First of all there is the assumption that inputs are paid their marginal products. If you think that inputs are paid their marginal products, then it seems to me that you are obligated to tell us the time frame to which your thoughts apply. Is it minute by minute? Probably not. But the same reservations that make you doubt the relationship between compensation and marginal products minute by minute also apply to quarterly data and even to annual data. Second, what about technological change? Is it really only an accident or is technological improvement a consequence of an investment, probably in the form of a salary to some employees whose job it is to put in place the new technique. If it is the latter, then the growth accounting outlined above is conceptually incorrect. Another problem is that rapid development can effect substantial changes in the input shares. The formula above applies only to infinitesimal changes in the input mix unless the earnings shares are technologically fixed as in a Cobb–Douglas production function. There are also serious questions concerning the disaggregation of factors, particularly labour which surely embodies an amount of human capital that increases with development.

Any empirical exercise is subject to a barrage of criticisms that can be incapacitating to all but the most stout-hearted. The foregoing comments are not intended to produce this response. But wariness is suggested.

Studies of Major Liberalizations

One of the most influential arguments that link growth and openness has been the NBER multi-country project on 'trade regimes and economic development'. Krueger (1978) and Bhagwati (1978) co-ordinated studies of ten countries that had undergone major liberalizations. These studies gain credibility from the degree and kind of institutional knowledge that they reveal. Their ultimate appeal, however, probably comes from the readers' feeling that these observations come about as close to a controlled experiment as we are likely to get. Another study in the same genre is Edwards and Edwards (1987) which deals informatively with the Chilean liberalization from 1973 to 1983.

4.8 CONCLUSIONS

I want data to have a major effect on the way that international economists think. I am disappointed, but I am not defeated. I think we can do better. My principal piece of advice is: balance. We need to have balance between the three layers of economic reasoning – issues, theory and data. The theory layer has become so large that it sometimes appears as though there are no issues and no data. The data layer, when it is present, sometimes dangles without theory, and sometimes it takes the theory too seriously, and dangles without the issues. An influential piece of empirical work would take the theory just seriously enough and would make a clear reference to the issues. We can do it.

NOTES

Support from NSF grant SES-8708399 is gratefully acknowledged, as are the comments and assistance of Graeme Woodbridge and the comments of David Colander.

1 Bhagwati (1964) makes the comment that a critical step in the logic above is the linkage between relative product prices and relative labour productivities, but he finds no significant relation exists.

2 Deardorff's (1984) (loose) argument is based on the observation that countries with relatively high labour costs will use more capital-intensive techniques and have higher labour productivities. He notes that the responsiveness of labour productivities in the two-factor model satisfies $\mathrm{d}\log(Q/L)/\mathrm{d}\log(w/r) = \sigma\theta$ where σ is the elasticity of substitution between the capital and labour and θ the capital share. Thus if the elasticity of substitution were the same in all industries, differences in factor prices would cause the greatest differences in labour productivities in industries with the greatest share of capital. The looseness in the argument is the statement: 'Now suppose that the more capital abundant country has a comparative advantage in more capital intensive goods, as the Heckscher–Ohlin model predicts . . .' I am not sure that the HO model does make this prediction.

3 Helpman calls this a 'dispersion' index though it is a measure of how similar are the sizes of different countries.

REFERENCES

This bibliography is arranged to correspond to the sections in the chapter as indicated in the following outline. Some papers contain empirical analyses that overlap subjects in the text and their location in this bibliography is somewhat arbitrary. Surveys make up the first part of the bibliography and are associated with no special place in the text.

I Surveys and reviews
II Technology-based studies   (section 4.2)
    A Ricardian simple regressions
    B Ricardian multiple regressions
    C Product cycle models
III Studies of the Heckscher–Ohlin model   (section 4.4)
    A Factor content calculations
    B Cross-commodity studies – simple correlations
    C Cross-commodity studies – multiple regressions
    D Cross-country studies
    E Two-dimensional studies
    F Simulation studies
IV Models of imperfect competition   (section 4.5)
    A Studies of intra-industry trade
    B Cross-commodity studies of scale economies
    C Simulation studies
V Demand effects   (section 4.6)
    A Demand biases
    B Gravity models of bilateral flows

96 EDWARD W. LEAMER

I Surveys and reviews

Bowden, R. J. 1983: The conceptual basis of empirical studies of trade in manufactured commodities: a constructive critique. *Manchester School of Economics and Social Studies*, September, 51(3), 209–34.

Deardorff, A. V. 1984: Testing trade theories and predicting trade flows. In R. W. Jones and P. B. Kenen, *Handbook of International Economics*, vol. 1, Amsterdam: North-Holland, 467–517.

Kohler, W. 1988: Modeling Heckscher–Ohlin comparative advantage in regression equations: a critical survey. *Empirica*, 15(2), 263–93.

Leamer, E. E. and Stern, R. M. 1970: *Quantitative International Economics*. Boston: Allyn and Bacon.

Stern, R. M. 1975: Testing trade theories. In P. B. Kenen, (ed.), *International Trade and Finance: frontiers for research*, New York: Cambridge University Press, 3–49.

II Technology-based studies

A Ricardian simple regressions

MacDougall, G. D. A. 1951: British and American exports: a study suggested by the theory of comparative costs, Part I. *Economic Journal*, December, 61, 697–724.

MacDougall, G. D. A., Dowley, M., Fox, P. and Pugh, S. 1962: British and American productivity, prices and exports: an addendum. *Oxford Economic Papers*, October, 14, 297–304.

McGilvray, J. and Simpson, D. 1973: The commodity structure of Anglo-Irish trade. *Review of Economics and Statistics*, November, 55, 451–8.

Stern, R. M. 1962: British and American productivity and comparative costs in international trade. *Oxford Economic Papers*, October, 14, 131–42.

B Ricardian multiple regressions

Balassa, B. 1963: An empirical demonstration of classical comparative cost theory. *Review of Economics and Statistics*, August, 45, 231–8.

Bhagwati, J. 1964: The pure theory of international trade: a survey. *Economic Journal*, March, 74, 1–84.

C Product cycle models

Choudhri, E. U. 1979, The pattern of trade in individual products: a test of simple theories. *Weltwirtschaftliches Archiv*, 115, 81–98.

Hirsch, S. 1975: The product cycle model of international trade – a multi-country cross-section analysis. *Oxford Bulletin of Economics and Statistics*, 37, 305–17.

Soete, L. 1981: A general test of the technological gap theory. *Weltwirtschaftliches Archiv*, 117, 638–60.

Wells, L. T. Jr 1969: Test of a product cycle model of international trade: U.S. exports of consumer durables. *Quarterly Journal of Economics*, February, 82, 152–62.

III Studies of the Heckscher–Ohlin model

A Factor content calculations

Aw, B. Y. 1983: Trade imbalance and the Leontief paradox. *Weltwirtschaftliches Archiv*, 119(4), 734–8.

Baldwin, R. E. 1971: Determinants of the commodity structure of U.S. trade. *American Economic Review*, March, 61(1), 126–46.

Baldwin, R. E. 1979: Determinants of trade and foreign investment: further evidence. *Review of Economics and Statistics*, 61, February, 40–8.

Baruh, J. 1986: Factor proportions in Israel's manufacturing trade: 1965–82. *Journal of Development Economics*, November, 131–9.

Bhagwati, J. 1964: The pure theory of international trade: a survey. *Economic Journal*, March, 74, 1–84.

Bharadwaj, R. and Bhagwati, J. 1967: Human capital and the pattern of foreign trade: the Indian case. *Indian Economic Review*, October, 2, 117–42.

Brecher, R. A. and Choudhri, E. U. 1982: The Leontief paradox, continued. *Journal of Political Economy*, August, 90(4), 820–3.

Brecher, R. and Choudhri, E. U. 1984: New products and the factor content of international trade. *Journal of Political Economy*, October, 92(5), 965–71.

Casas, F. R. and Choi, E. K. 1984: Trade imbalance and the Leontief paradox. *Manchester School of Economics and Social Studies*, December, 52(4), 391–401.

Casas, F. R. and Choi, E. K. 1985: The Leontief paradox: continued or resolved? *Journal of Political Economy*, 93(3), 610–15.

Casas, F. R. and Choi, E. K. 1987: Trade imbalance, the factor proportions theory and the resource content of international trade. *Rivista Internazionale di Scienze Economiche e Commerciali*, 34(3), 213–30.

Clifton, D. S. Jr and Marxsen, W. B. 1984: An empirical investigation of the Heckscher–Ohlin theorem. *Canadian Journal of Economics*, February, 17(1), 32–8.

Deardorff, A. V. 1979: Weak links in the chain of comparative advantage. *Journal of International Economics*, 9, 197–209.

Fareed, A. E. 1972: Formal schooling and the human capital intensity of American foreign trade: a cost approach. *Economic Journal*, June, 82, 629–40.

Gift, R. and Marxsen, W. 1984: Aggregation and the factor content of trade: a comment. *Journal of Political Economy*, 92(5), 979–84.

Hamilton, C. and Svennsson, L. E. O. 1983: Should factor intensities be used in tests of the factor proportions hypothesis? *Weltwirtschaftliches Archiv*, 119(3), 453–63.

Hamilton, C. and Svennsson, L. E. O. 1984: Do countries factor endowments correspond to the factor contents in their bilateral trade flows. *Scandinavian Journal of Economics*, 86(1), 84–97.

Heller, P. S. 1976: Factor endowment change and comparative advantage: the case of Japan, 1956–1969. *Review of Economics and Statistics*, August, 58(1), 283–92.

Heravi, I. 1986: The Leontief paradox, reconsidered: correction. *Journal of Political Economy*, October, 94(5), 1120.

Holden, M. 1983: Empirical tests of the Heckscher–Ohlin model for South Africa – a reappraisal of the methodology. *South African Journal of Economics*, 51(2), 243–51.

Hong, W. 1987: Comparative statics application of the H–O model of factor proportions: Korean experience. *Weltwirtschaftliches Archiv*, 123(2), 309–24.

Keesing, D. B. 1965: Labor skills and international trade evaluating many trade flows with a single measuring device. *Review of Economics and Statistics*, August, 287–94.

Kenen, P. B. 1965: Nature, capital and trade. *Journal of Political Economy*, October, 73, 437–60.

Khanna, A. 1985: A note on the dynamic aspects of the H–O model: some empirical evidence. *World Development*, Oct./Nov., 13(10/11), 1171–4.

Kim, C. 1983: *Evolution of Comparative Advantage: the factor proportions theory in a dynamic perspective*. Tübingen: J. C. B. Mohr.

Leamer, E. E. 1980: The Leontief paradox reconsidered. *Journal of Political Economy*, June, 88, 495–503.

Leontief, W. W. 1953: Domestic production and foreign trade: the American capital position re-examined. *Proceedings of the American Philosophical Society*, September, 332–49.

Leontief, W. W. 1956: Factor proportions and the structure of American trade. *Review of Economics and Statistics*, November, 386–407.

Maskus, K. V. 1985: A test of the Heckscher–Ohlin–Vanek theorem: the Leontief commonplace. *Journal of International Economics*, November, 9, 201–12.

Mitchell, D. J. B. 1975: Recent changes in the labor content of U.S. trade. *Industrial and Labor Relations Review*, April, 355–69.

Roskamp, K. W. 1963: Factor proportions and foreign trade. *Weltwirtschaftliches Archiv*, 99, 319–26.

Roskamp, K. and McMeekin, G. 1968: Factor proportions, human capital and foreign trade: the case of West Germany re-considered', *Quarterly Journal of Economics*, February, 82, 152–60.

Stern, R. M. and Maskus, K. E. 1981: Determinants of the structure of U.S. foreign trade, 1958–76. *Journal of International Economics*, May, 11, 207–24.

Sviekauskus, L. 1983: Science and technology in United States foreign trade. *Economic Journal*, 93, 542–54.

Syrquin, M. and Urata, S. 1986: Sources of changes in factor intensity of trade. *Journal of Development Economics*, December, 24(2), 225–39.

Tatemota, M. and Ichimura, S. 1959: Factor proportions and foreign trade: the case of Japan. *Review of Economics and Statistics*, 41, 442–6.

Vanek, J. 1963: *The Natural Resource Content of United States Foreign Trade, 1870–1955*. Cambridge, Mass.: MIT Press.

Wahl, D. F. 1961: Capital and labor requirements for Canada's foreign trade. *Canadian Journal of Economics*, August, 27, 349–58.

Weiser, L. A. 1968: Changing factor requirements of United States foreign trade. *Review of Economics and Statistics*, August, 356–60.

Williams, J. R. 1970: The resource content in international trade. *Canadian Journal of Economics*, February, 3, 111–22.

B   Cross-commodity studies – simple correlations

Gruber, W., Mehta, D. and Vernon, R. 1967: The R&D factor in international investment in the United States industries. *Journal of Political Economy*, February, 75, 20–37.

Keesing, D. B. 1966: Labor skills and comparative advantage. *American Economic Review*, May, 56(2), 249–58.

Keesing, D. B. 1967: The impact of research and development on United States trade. *Journal of Political Economy*, February, 75, 38–48.

C Cross-commodity studies – multiple regressions

Anderson, J. E. 1981: Cross-section tests of the Heckscher–Ohlin theorem: comment. *American Economic Review*, December, 71, 1037–9.

Aw, B. Y. 1981: An empirical test of the Heckscher–Ohlin theorem using ASEAN data. *Malayan Economic Review*, April, 26(1), 25–38.

Aw, B. Y. 1983: The interpretation of cross-section regression tests of the Heckscher–Ohlin theorem with many goods and factors. *Journal of International Economics*, February, 14(1/2), 163–7.

Baldwin, R. E. 1971: Determinants of the commodity structure of U.S. trade. *American Economic Review*, March, 61, 126–46.

Baldwin, R. E. 1979: Determinants of trade and foreign investment: further evidence. *Review of Economics and Statistics*, 61, February, 40–8.

Baldwin, R. E. and Hilton, R. S. 1984: A technique for indicating comparative costs and predicting changes in trade ratios. *Review of Economics and Statistics*, February, 66(1), 105–10.

Baruh, J. 1986: Factor proportions in Israel's manufacturing trade: 1965–82. *Journal of Development Economics*, November, 131–9.

Baum, C. and Coe, D. 1978: A logit analysis of the factor content of West German foreign trade. *Weltwirtschaftliches Archiv*, 114, 328–38.

Branson, W. H. 1971: U.S. comparative advantage: some further results. *Brookings Papers on Economic Activity*, no. 3, 754–9.

Branson, W. H. and Junz, H. B. 1971: Trends in U.S. trade and comparative costs. *Brookings Papers on Economic Activity*, no. 2, 285–345.

Branson, W. H. and Monoyios, N. 1977: Factor inputs in U.S. trade. *Journal of International Economics*, May, 7, 111–31.

Brecher, R. A. and Choudhri, E. E. 1988: The factor content of consumption in Canada and the United States: a two-country test of the Heckscher–Ohlin–Vanek model. In R. C. Feenstra *Empirical Methods for International Trade*, Cambridge, Mass.: MIT Press, 5–17.

Choudhri, E. U. 1979: The pattern of trade in individual products: a test of simple theories. *Weltwirtschaftliches Archiv*, 115, 81–98.

Crafts, N. F. R. and Thomas, M. 1986: Comparative advantage in U.K. manufacturing trade 1910–1935. *Economic Journal*, September, 96(383), 629–45.

Deardorff, A. V. 1982: The general validity of the Heckscher–Ohlin theorem. *American Economic Review*, September, 72(4), 683–94.

Forstner, H. 1984: The changing pattern of international trade in manufactures: a logit analysis. *Weltwirtschaftliches Archiv*, 120(1), 1–17.

Forstner, H. 1985: A note on the general validity of the Heckscher–Ohlin theorem. *American Economic Review*, September, 75(4), 844–9.

Gavelin, L. 1983: Determinants of the structure of Swedish foreign trade in manufactures, 1968–1979. *Scandinavian Journal of Economics*, 85(4), 485–98.

Gruber, W. H. and Vernon, R. 1970: The technology factor in a world trade matrix. In R. Vernon (ed.), *The Technology Factor in International Trade*, New York: Columbia University Press, 145–231.

Harkness, J. 1978: Factor abundance and comparative advantage. *American Economic Review*, December, 68, 784–800.

Harkness, J. P. 1983: The factor proportions model with many nations, goods and factors: theory and evidence. *Review of Economics and Statistics*, May, 65(2), 298–305.

Harkness, J. and Kyle, J. K. 1975: Factors influencing United States comparative advantage. *Journal of International Economics*, May, 5, 153–65.

Helpman, E. 1984: The factor content of foreign trade. *Economic Journal*, 94, 84–94.

Katrak, H. 1973: Human skills, R&D and scale economies in the United Kingdom and the United States. *Oxford Economic Papers*, 25(3), 337–60.

Kellman, M. and Laudau, D. 1984: The nature of Japan's comparative advantage, 1965–80. *World Development*, April, 12(4), 433–8.

Kim, C. 1983: *Evolution of Comparative Advantage: the factor proportions theory in a dynamic perspective*. Tübingen: J. C. B. Mohr.

Lane, J. 1985: An empirical estimate of the effects of labor market distortions on the factor content of U.S. trade. *Journal of International Economics*, 18, 187–93.

Leamer, E. E. and Bowen, H. P. 1981: Cross-section tests of the Heckscher–Ohlin theorem: comment. *American Economic Review*, December, 71, 1040–3.

Lee, Y. S. 1986: Changing export patterns in Korea, Taiwan, Japan. *Weltwirtschaftliches Archiv*, 122(1), 150–63.

Lowinger, T. C. 1975: The technology factor and the export performance of U.S. manufacturing. *Economic Inquiry*, June, 13, 221–36.

Maskus, K. E. 1983: Evidence on shifts in the determinants of the structure of U.S. manufacturing industries foreign trade, 1958–76. *Review of Economics and Statistics*, August, 65(3), 256–72.

Mouna Roque, F. 1984: Factor endowments, technology, and foreign trade. *South African Journal of Economics*, December, 52(4), 377–90.

Neary, J. P. and Schwienberger, A. C. 1986: Factor content functions and the theory of international trade. *Review of Economic Studies*, July, 56(3), 421–32.

Onida, F. 1987: Italian patterns of trade: some econometric cross section and cross country evidence. Paper presented at the conference on Trade Patterns and Policies in Southern Europe, Lisbon, June.

Sandilands, R. J. and Ling-Hui, T. 1986: Comparative advantage in a re-export economy: the case of Singapore. *Singapore Economic Review*, October 31(2), 34–56.

Staiger, R. W. 1986: Measurement of the factor-content of foreign trade with intermediate goods. *Journal of International Economics*, November, 21(3/4), 361–8.

Stern, R. M. 1976: Some evidence on the factor content of West Germany's foreign trade. *Journal of Political Economy*, February, 84, 131–41.

Stern, R. M. and Maskus, K. E. 1981: Determinants of the structure of U.S. foreign trade, 1958–76. *Journal of International Economics*, May, 11, 207–24.

Urata, S. 1983: Factor inputs and Japanese manufacturing trade structure. *Review of Economics and Statistics*, November, 65(4), 678–84.

D Cross-country studies

Acquino, A. 1981: Changes over time in the pattern of comparative advantage in manufactured goods, an empirical analysis for the period 1962–1974. *European Economic Review*, 15, 41–62.

Arad, R. W. and Hirsch, S. 1981: Determination of trade flows and the choice of trade partners: reconciling the H–O and the Burenstam-Linder models of international trade. *Weltwirtschaftliches Archiv*, 117(2), 276–97.

Bowen, H. P. 1983: Changes in the international distribution of resources and their impact on U.S. comparative advantage. *Review of Economics and Statistics*, 65, 402–14.

Chenery, H. B. 1960: Patterns of industrial growth. *American Economic Review*, September, I, 624–54.

Chenery, H. B. and Syrquin, M. 1975: *Patterns of Development, 1950–1970*. London: Oxford University Press.

Chenery, H. B. and Taylor, L. 1968: Development patterns: among countries and over time. *Review of Economics and Statistics*, November, 50(4), 391–416.

Keesing, D. B. 1968: Population and industrial development: some empirical evidence from trade patterns. *American Economic Review*, June, 58(3), 448–55.

Keesing, D. B. and Sherk, D. R. 1971: Population density in patterns of trade and development. *American Economic Review*, December, 61(5), 956–61.

Kim, C. 1983: *Evolution of Comparative Advantage: the factor proportions theory in a dynamic perspective.* Tübingen: J. C. B. Mohr.

Leamer, E. E. 1974: The commodity composition of international trade in manufactures: an empirical analysis. *Oxford Economic Papers*, 26(3), 350–74.

Leamer, E. E. 1984: *Sources of Comparative Advantage, Theory and Evidence.* Cambridge, Mass.: MIT Press.

Onida, F. 1987: Italian patterns of trade: some econometric cross section and cross country evidence. Paper presented at the Conference on Trade Patterns and Policies in Southern Europe, Lisbon, June.

Tamor, K. L. 1987: An empirical examination of the factor endowments hypothesis. *Canadian Journal of Economics*, May, 20(2), 387–98.

E   Two-dimensional studies

Balassa, B. 1979: The changing pattern of comparative advantage in manufactured goods. *Review of Economics and Statistics*, 61, May, 259–66.

Balassa, B. 1986: Comparative advantage in manufactured goods: a reappraisal. *Review of Economics and Statistics*, May, 68(2), 315–19.

Bowen, H. P., Leamer, E. E. and Sviekauskus, L. 1987: Multicountry, multifactor tests of the factor abundance theory. *American Economic Review*, 77(5), December, 402–14.

Hufbauer, G. C. 1970: The impact of national characteristics and technology on the commodity composition of trade in manufactured goods. In R. Vernon (ed.), *The Technology Factor in International Trade*, New York: Columbia University Press, 145–231.

F   Simulation studies

Hartigan, J. C. and Tower, E. 1986: The Leontief question: a Cobb Douglas approach to simulating the distribution of U.S. income in autarky. *Weltwirtschaftliches Archiv*, 122(2), 677–89.

Staiger, R. W., Deardorff, A. V. and Stern, R. M. 1987: An evaluation of factor endowments and protection as determinants of Japanese and American foreign trade. *Canadian Journal of Economics*, August, 449–63.

IV   Models of imperfect competition

A   Studies of intra-industry trade

Balassa, B. 1986: The determinants of intra-industry specialization in U.S. trade. *Oxford Economic Papers*, July, 38(2), 220–33.

Balassa, B. and Bauwens, L. 1987: Intra-industry specialization in a multi-country and multi-industry framework. *Economic Journal*, December, 97(388), 923–39.

Bergstrand, J. 1983: Measurement and determinants of intra-industry trade. In P. K. M. Tharakan, (ed.), *Intra-Industry Trade: empirical and methodological aspects*, Amsterdam: North-Holland.

Davies, R. 1975: Product differentiation and the structure of United Kingdom trade. *Bulletin of Economic Research*, May, 27–41.

Greenaway, D. and Milner, C. 1984: A cross-section analysis of intra-industry trade in the U.K. *European Economic Review*, August, 25(3), 319–44.

Grubel, H. G. and Lloyd, P. J. 1975: *Intra Industry Trade*. London: Macmillan.

Havrylyshyn, O. and Civan, E. 1983: Intra-industry trade and the stage of development: a regression analysis of industrial and developing countries. In P. K. M. Tharakan, (ed.), *Intra-Industry Trade: empirical and methodological aspects*, Amsterdam: North-Holland.

Helpman, E. 1987: Imperfect competition and international trade: evidence from fourteen industrialised countries. *Journal of the Japanese and International Economies*, 1, June, 62–81.

Hitiris, T. and Bedrossian, A. 1987: Import penetration, export competitiveness and the pattern of U.K. intra-industry trade: a note. *Applied Economics*, February, 19(2), 215–20.

Loertscher, R. and Wolter, F. 1980: Determinants of intra-industry trade: among countries and across countries. *Weltwirtschaftliches Archiv*, 116, 280–93.

Lundberg, L. 1982: Intra-industry trade: the case of Sweden. *Weltwirtschaftliches Archiv*, 118, 302–16.

Marvel, H. P. and Ray, E. J. 1987: Intraindustry trade: sources and effects on protection. *Journal of Political Economy*, 95, 1278–91.

Owen, N. 1983: *Economies of Scale, Competitiveness, and Trade Patterns within the European Community*. Oxford: Clarendon Press.

Toh, K. 1982: A cross-section analysis of intra-industry trade in U.S. manufacturing industries. *Weltwirtschaftliches Archiv*, 118, 281–301.

B   Cross-commodity studies of scale economies

Choudhri, E. U. 1979: The pattern of trade in individual products: a test of simple theories. *Weltwirtschaftliches Archiv*, 115, 81–98.

Gavelin, L. 1983: Determinants of the structure of Swedish foreign trade in manufactures, 1968–1979. *Scandinavian Journal of Economics*, 85(4), 485–98.

Lee, Y. S. 1986: Changing export patterns in Korea, Taiwan, Japan. *Weltwirtschaftliches Archiv*, 122(1), 150–63.

Mouna Roque, F. 1984: Factor endowments, technology, and foreign trade. *South African Journal of Economics*, December, 52(4), 377–90.

Onida, F. 1987: Italian patterns of trade: some econometric cross section and cross country evidence. Paper presented at the Conference on trade Patterns and Policies in Southern Europe, Lisbon, June.

C   Simulation studies

Baldwin, R. E. and Krugman, P. R. 1988: Market access and international competition: a simulation study of 16K random access memories. In R. C. Feenstra, *Empirical Methods for International Trade*, Cambridge, Mass.: MIT Press.

Dixit, A. 1988: Optimal trade and industrial policies for the US automobile industry. In R. C. Feenstra, *Empirical Methods for International Trade*, Cambridge, Mass.: MIT Press.

Harris, R. G. 1984: Applied general equilibrium analysis of small open economies with scale economies and imperfect competition. *American Economic Review*, 74(5), 1016–32.

Harris, R. G. 1986: Market structure and trade liberalization: a general equilibrium assessment. In T. N. Srinivasan and J. Whalley, *General Equilibrium Trade Policy Modeling*, Cambridge, Mass.: MIT Press.

V Demand effects

A Demand biases

Arad, R. W. and Hirsch, S. 1981: Determination of trade flows and the choice of trade partners: reconciling the H–O and the Burenstam-Linder models of international trade. *Weltwirtschaftliches Archiv*, 117(2), 276–97.

Bowden, R. J. 1986: An empirical model of bilateral trade in manufactured commodities. *Manchester School of Economics and Social Studies*, September, 54(3), 255–82.

Ellis, C. M. 1983: An alternative interpretation and empirical test of the Linder hypothesis. *Quarterly Journal of Business and Economics*, Autumn, 24(4), 53–62.

Fortune, J. N. 1979: Income distribution and Linder's trade thesis. *Southern Economic Journal*, 46, 158–67.

Greytak, D. and McHugh, R. 1977; Linder's trade thesis: an empirical examination. *Southern Economic Journal*, 43, 1386–9.

Hirsch, S. and Baruch, L. 1973: Trade and per capita income differentials: a test of the Burenstam-Linder hypothesis. *World Development*, September, 1, 11–17.

Hoftyzer, J. 1975: Empirical verification of Linder's trade thesis: comment. *Southern Economic Journal*, April, 41, 694–8.

Hoftyzer, J. 1984: A further analysis of the Linder trade thesis. *Quarterly Review of Economics and Business*, Summer, 24(2), 57–90.

Hunter, L. C. and Markusen, J. R. 1988: Per capita income as a determinant of trade. In R. C. Feenstra, *Empirical Methods for International Trade*, Cambridge, Mass.: MIT Press, 89–109.

Kennedy, T. E. and McHugh, R. 1980: An intertemporal test and rejection of the Linder hypothesis. *Southern Economic Journal*, January, 46, 898–903.

Kennedy, T. E. and McHugh, R. 1983: Taste similarity and trade intensity: a test of the Linder hypothesis for United States exports. *Weltwirtschaftliches Archiv*, 119(1), 84–96.

Klieman, E. and Kop, Y. 1984: Who trades with whom – the income pattern of international trade. *Weltwirtschaftliches Archiv*, 120(3), 499–521.

Kohlagen, S. W. 1977: Income distribution and 'representative demand' in international trade flows – an empirical test of Linder's hypothesis. *Southern Economic Journal*, July, 44, 167–72.

Linnemann, H. 1966: *An Econometric Study of International Trade Flows*. Amsterdam: North-Holland.

Qureshi, U. A., French, G. L. and Sailors, J. W. 1980: Linder's trade thesis: a further examination. *Southern Economic Journal*, 46, 933–6.

Sailors, J. W., Qureshi, U. A. and Cross, E. M. 1973: Empirical verification of Linder's trade thesis. *Southern Economic Journal*, 40, 262–8.

Thursby, J. G. and Thursby, M. C. 1987: Bilateral trade flows, the Linder hypothesis and exchange rate risk. *Review of Economics and Statistics*, August, 69(3), 488–95.

B Gravity models of bilateral flows

Bergstrand, J. H. 1985: The gravity equation in international trade: some microeconomic foundations and empirical evidence. *Review of Economics and Statistics*, August, 67(3), 474–81.

104 EDWARD W. LEAMER

Bowden, R. J. 1986: An empirical model of bilateral trade in manufactured commodities. *Manchester School of Economics and Social Studies*, September, 54(3), 255–82.
Ellis, C. M. 1983: An alternative interpretation and empirical test of the Linder hypothesis. *Quarterly Journal of Business and Economics*, Autumn, 22(4), 53–62.
Gruber, W. H. and Vernon, R. 1970: The technology factor in a world trade matrix. In R. Vernon (ed.), *The Technology Factor in International Trade*, New York: Columbia University Press, 145–231.
Linnemann, H. 1966: *An Econometric Study of International Trade Flows*. Amsterdam: North-Holland.
Thursby, J. G. and Thursby, M. C. 1987: Bilateral trade flows, the Linder hypothesis and exchange rate risk. *Review of Economics and Statistics*, August, 69(3), 488–95.

VI Growth and openness

A Cross-country comparisons

Balassa, Bela 1978: Exports and economic growth: further evidence. *Journal of Development Economics*, 5, 181–9.
Balassa, Bela 1985: Exports, policy choices and economic growth in development countries after the 1973 oil shock. *Journal of Development Economics*, 18, 23–35.
Edwards, S. 1989: Openness, outward orientation, trade liberalization and economic performance in developing countries. Working Paper, UCLA.
Feder, G. 1983: On exports and economic growth. *Journal of Development Economics*, 12, 59–73.
Fishlow, A. 1985: *The State of Latin American Economics in Inter-American Development Bank, Economic and Social Progress in Latin America: annual report*, Washington, DC.
Fishlow, A. 1990: The Latin American state. *Journal of Economic Perspective*, 4, 61–74.
Kavoussi, R. M. 1984: Export expansion and economic growth: further empirical evidence. *Journal of Development Economics*, 14, 241–50.
Kravis, I. B. 1970: Trade as a handmaiden of growth – similarities between the 19th and 20th centuries. *Economic Journal*, 80, 850–72.
Lal, D. and Rajapatirana, S. 1987: Foreign trade regimes and economic growth in developing countries. *The World Bank Research Observer*, 2, 189–217.
Michaely, M. 1977: Exports and growth: an empirical investigation. *Journal of Development Economics*, 4, 49–53.
Ram, R. 1985: Exports and economic change: some additional evidence. *Economic Development and Cultural Change*, 33, 415–25.
Riedel, J. 1984: Trade as the engine of growth in developing countries, revisited. *Economic Journal*, 94, 56–73.
Tyler, W. 1981: Growth and export expansion in developing countries: some empirical evidence. *Journal of Development Economics*, 9, 337–49.
Williamson, R. B. 1978: The role of exports and foreign capital in Latin American economic growth. *Southern Economic Journal*, 45, 410–12.

B Intertemporal comparisons

1 Granger Causal Orderings of Export Growth and GNP Growth
Chow, P. C. Y. 1987: Causality between export growth and industrial development: empirical evidence from the NICs. *Journal of Development Economics*, 26, 55–63.

Darrat, A. F. 1986: Trade and development: the Asian experience. *Cato Journal*, 6, 695–700.

Jung, W. S. and Marshall, P. J. 1985: Exports, growth and causality in developing countries. *Journal of Development Economics*, 18, 1–12.

2 Event studies of major liberalizations (Chile, New Zealand)

Bhagwati, J. 1978: *Foreign Trade Regimes and Economic Development: anatomy and consequences of exchange control regimes*. Cambridge, Mass.: Ballinger.

Edwards, S. and Edwards, A. 1987: *Monetarism and Liberalization: the Chilean experiment*. Cambridge, Mass.: Ballinger.

Krueger, A. 1978: *Foreign Trade Regimes and Economic Development: liberalization attempts and consequences*. Cambridge, Mass.: Ballinger.

Krueger, A. 1981: Export-led growth reconsidered. In Wontack Hong and L. Krause (eds), *Trade and Growth of the Advanced Developing Countries in the Pacific Basin*.

C Cross-industry comparisons

Chen, T. and Tang, D. 1990: Export performance and productivity growth: the case of Taiwan. *Economic Development and Cultural Change*, 38, 577–85.

Dollar, D. and Sokoloff, K. forthcoming: Patterns of productivity growth in South Korea manufacturing industries, 1963–1979. *Journal of Development Economics*.

Krueger, A. and Tuncer, B. 1982: Growth of factor productivity in Turkish manufacturing industries. *Journal of Development Economics*, 11, 307–25.

Nelson, R. 1981: Research on productivity growth and differences. *Journal of Economic Literature*, XIX, 1029–64.

Nichimizu, M. and Robinson, S. 1984: Trade policies and productivity change in semi-industrialized countries. *Journal of Development Economics*, 16, 177–206.

Page, J. M. and Nishimizu, M. 1986: Productivity change in Egyptian public sector industries after 'The Opening', 1973–1979. *Journal of Development Economics*, 20, 53–73.

VII Additional references

A General references

Haberler, G. 1933: *The Theory of International Trade*, translated by A. Stonier and F. Benham. London: W. Hodge, 1936.

Klepper, Stephen and Leamer, Edward E. 1984: Consistent sets of estimates for regression with all variables measured with error. *Econometrica*, 52 (January), 163–83.

Lakatos, Imre 1978: *The Methodology of Scientific Research Programmes*. Cambridge: Cambridge University Press.

Linder, Stephan Burenstam 1961: *An Essay on Trade and Transformation*. New York: John Wiley & Sons.

Vanek, J. 1968: The factor proportions theory: the *N*-factor case. *Kyklos*, (October), 21(4), 749–56.

Viner, J. M. 1937: *Studies in the Theory of International Trade*. New York: Harper.

B Effects of trade barriers

1 Regression studies
Aitken, N. D. 1973: The effect of the EEC and EFTA on European trade: a temporal cross-section analysis. *American Economic Review*, 63, 881–92.

Balassa, B. 1966: Tariff reductions and trade in manufactures among industrial countries. *American Economic Review*, 56, June, 466–73.

Boadway, R. and Treddenick, J. 1978: A general equilibrium computation of the effects of the Canadian tariff structure. *Canadian Journal of Economics*, 11, 424–46.

Leamer, E. E. 1988: Cross-section estimation of the effects of trade barriers. In R. C. Feenstra, *Empirical Methods for International Trade*, Cambridge, Mass.: MIT Press, 51–82.

2 Simulation studies

Brown, F. and Whalley, J. 1980: General equilibrium evaluations of tariff-cutting proposals in the Tokyo Round and comparisons to more extensive liberalization of world trade. *Economic Journal*, 90, December, 838–66.

Deardorff, A. V. and Stern, R. M. 1981: A disaggregated model of world production and trade: an estimate of the impact of the Tokyo Round. *Journal of Policy Modelling*, 3, 127–52.

Deardorff, A. V. and Stern, R. M. 1986: The structure and sample results of the Michigan computational model of world trade and production. In T. N. Srinivasan, and J. Whalley, *General Equilibrium Trade Policy Modeling*, Cambridge, Mass.: MIT Press.

Dixon, P. B., Parmenter, B. R. and Rimmer, R. J. 1986: ORANI projections of the short-run effects of a 50% across-the-board cut in protection using alternative data bases. In T. N. Srinivasan and J. Whalley, *General Equilibrium Trade Policy Modeling*, Cambridge, Mass.: MIT Press.

Grais, W., De Melo, J. and Urata, S. 1986: A general equilibrium estimation of the effects of reductions in tariffs and quantitative restrictions in Turkey in 1978. In T. N. Srinivasan and J. Whalley, *General Equilibrium Trade Policy Modeling*, Cambridge, Mass.: MIT Press.

Harrison, G. W. 1986: A general equilibrium analysis of tariff reductions. In T. N. Srinivasan and J. Whalley, *General Equilibrium Trade Policy Modeling*, Cambridge, Mass.: MIT Press.

Keyzer, M. A. 1986: Short-run impact of trade liberalization measures on the economy of Bangladesh: exercises in comparative statics for the year 1977. In T. N. Srinivasan and J. Whalley, *General Equilibrium Trade Policy Modeling*, Cambridge, Mass.: MIT Press.

Mercenier, J. and Waelbroeck, J. 1986: Effect of a 50% tariff cut in the Varuna model. In T. N. Srinivasan and J. Whalley, *General Equilibrium Trade Policy Modeling*, Cambridge, Mass.: MIT Press.

Miller, M. H. and Spencer, J. E. 1977: The static economic effects of the U.K. joining the EEC: a general equilibrium approach. *Review of Economic Studies*, 44, 71–93.

Spencer, J. E. 1986: Trade liberalization through tariff cuts and the European Economic Community: a general equilibrium evaluation. In T. N. Srinivasan and J. Whalley, *General Equilibrium Trade Policy Modeling*, Cambridge, Mass.: MIT Press.

Whalley, J. 1986: Impacts of a 50% tariff reduction in an eight-region global trade model. In T. N. Srinivasan and J. Whalley, *General Equilibrium Trade Policy Modeling*, Cambridge, Mass.: MIT Press.

5

THE THEORY OF PROTECTION

James E. Anderson

5.1 INTRODUCTION

This chapter surveys the theory of protection. It follows the masterly example of Dixit (1985) in treating protection with the dual methods of modern public finance theory. A policy accounting system is developed in which the level of technical analysis is reduced to a supply and demand diagram. More importantly, the dual approach to protection provides the framework for empirical analysis of the cost of protection.

No attempt is made to be comprehensive. The primary objective is to develop flexible and powerful tools and show how they have successfully handled a number of important practical problems. The reader should note, besides Dixit, the excellent and comprehensive surveys of Corden (1974, 1982), and the full-length book treatment of Vousden (1990). The latter two authors use primal methods in the tradition of Meade's trade geometry (1952), which involve details and special assumptions about production and consumption structure that are unnecessary for most purposes in the analysis of protection.

The analysis gives quotas equal billing with tariffs, in contrast to Dixit and most other treatments of protection. Recent theoretical developments which analyse quotas with tariffs and tariffs with quotas are incorporated. The shift in emphasis is warranted, since non-tariff barriers have become the principal means of protection in developed countries (average tariff levels have fallen to less than 5 per cent), and quotas have significantly different effects from tariffs.

The basic model of this chapter is of a representative consumer/producer (agent) in a trading environment with trade distortions – quotas, tariffs and subsidies. The main problem of the theory of protection is to account for the effect of trade distortions on economic efficiency. Economic efficiency is defined in terms of the welfare of the representative agent, and distributive issues are submerged. (See Dixit and Norman, 1980, and Dixit, 1985 for a treatment of Paretian efficiency and trade in the many-agent case, in which distributive objectives are achieved with domestic tax/subsidy policies.) The analysis is static except in the last section.[1] The economy is perfectly competitive (in contrast to chapter 7), which means the agent is a fully informed price-taker in all markets. The technology has constant returns to scale.[2] Save where explicitly noted, the economy is assumed to be small; that is, to face fixed foreign prices.

The government returns its net revenues from trade distortion to the agent. The usual convention is to suppose that the rebate is in a lump sum equal to the full amount of the revenue. Here, it is assumed that some revenue is wasted. Below, a number of variants of waste are described within a common framework linking internationally shared quota rent, rent-seeking, tariff-revenue-seeking, smuggling and bureaucratic costs. Alternatively, the rebate could be in the form of a government-supplied good. The wastage here is that the government may not produce that quantity of the good which has a value to the agent exactly equal to the value of net revenues collected to pay for producing the good.

Trade policy is assumed to be exogenously set by the government. The presumption is that the government is benevolent, and will act to advance the welfare of the representative agent. This structure is in contrast to the political economy model reviewed in chapter 6, which assumes that agents rationally spend economic resources to influence the government, so that the level of trade distortions becomes endogenous. Both models of government capture elements of reality.[3] The two methods can be related by noting that even if the political economy view is adopted, the methods of this chapter apply to accounting for the effects of a shift in the political equilibrium.[4]

Rules for government intervention follow from the trade distortions accounting system based on the preceding structure of the economy and the government. Policy reform analysis starts from an initial position which is not optimal, and examines directions of welfare-improving changes in policy. The prior existence of trade distortions which may not be optimal is explained by changed conditions or error. In any case, the nature of the optimal distortion is a proper subject of study. Trade intervention can be justified as a means of correcting a distortion (a gap between marginal cost and marginal benefit), collecting revenue or redistributing income. Trade intervention can also be justified by a benevolent government as resulting from 'non-economic' constraints exogenously placed on the government agency by the political process. These constraints are protective, requiring the government to raise income, employment, output or some combination of these in various sectors of the economy. The trade intervention can be in the form of a quota (on imports or exports, or a 'voluntary' export quota) or a tariff (on imports or exports), or a subsidy on exports or imports, as well as more complex forms which combine elements of these. The main analysis here will be of the effect on welfare of imports quotas and tariffs. It makes no essential difference whether the imports are for final consumption or intermediate input use, nor does it matter whether the import has a domestically supplied perfect substitute. Optimal policy analysis examines how best to trade off the welfare loss of trade intervention against the gain from achieving protective purposes.

In the last section of this chapter, I survey some recent developments in the theory of protection which involve sequential decisions. Here, my choice of topics (inclusions and omissions) is idiosyncratic. The common theme linking these developments is that the government actions need not come first in the sequence, and that agents' expectations of government policy matter. The optimal time profile of trade reform – once-and-for-all vs gradual – is the first topic. Administered protection (for example, escape clause or antidumping policy) is the second topic. Since it yields protection based on a standing rule, the sequence is reversed: agents can anticipate protection. The last topic is time consistency: agents anticipate government policies which will be 'optimal' for the government in the future, which are generally not those which would be optimal today. In the absence of commitment by the government, suboptimal policies are the result.

5.2 THE DUAL METHOD

The model comprises two elements, the external budget constraint and the structure of supply and demand. A simple trade policy accounting system is developed using only these elements. The essentials boil down to a familiar supply and demand diagram analysis of tax incidence. Dual methods give a deep foundation to supply and demand, and provide a means of evaluating multidimensional trade restriction systems. The insights of the theory of protection do not, however, require a thorough knowledge of duality.

The fundamental resource requirement of a trading economy is that imports must be paid for. The three possible sources of funds are foreign exchange earnings from exports, earnings from the distortion of trade, and international transfers. Changes in trade distortions in effect make more or less foreign exchange available on balance, and thus change real income. The analysis which follows details the two separate elements of this linkage: how changes in distortions make more or less foreign exchange available, and how changes in foreign exchange change real income.

5.2.1 The External Budget Constraint

The external budget constraint of a static economy requires that there be no net transfer from or to foreigners: the net value of trade in goods and services plus any quota rent transferred to foreigners must be equal to zero in terms of foreign prices. International trade in factor services is suppressed here for simplicity, except for the section where it is treated explicitly. Since export trade will not be restricted (except as a special case), it is convenient to use exports as the numeraire (the unit of valuation), so that all prices are in terms of export units rather than currency units. There is an imported good subject to a quota of Q units. Its domestic price is p and its foreign price is p^*. The fraction ω of quota rent accrues to foreigners. There is another imported good not under quota, but subject to a specific tariff of t per unit.[5] The quantity of this import is Z, its domestic price is π and its foreign price is π^*. Finally, there is an export good not subject to restriction (except as a special case). The quantity of exports is X, and the foreign and domestic price of exports is unity, by the numeraire choice. The value of government imports is equal to G. The consolidated (public plus private) budget constraint is

$$p^*Q + \pi^*Z - X + G + \omega Q[p - p^*] = 0$$

Now modify the external budget constraint as follows: (1) Subtract the transferred quota rent, $\omega Q[p - p^*]$, from both sides of the equation. (2) Add the sum of tariff revenue and quota rent to both sides of the equation. (3) Subtract the value of government imports, G, equal to the tariff revenue retained by the government, αtZ, from both sides of the equation.[6] (4) On the left-hand side, reduce terms involving Q to pQ, and reduce terms involving Z to πZ, first substituting $\pi - \pi^*$ for t. On the right-hand side, combine the terms in tariff revenue and quota rent. Then the external budget constraint becomes

$$pQ + \pi Z - X = (1 - \alpha)tZ + (1 - \omega)[p - p^*]Q \qquad (5.1)$$

That is, net trade expenditure by the private sector, evaluated at domestic prices, is equal to retained quota rent plus returned tariff revenue. The right-hand side of equation (5.1) is the net revenue returned to the private sector. The gross tariff revenue is tZ, and α per cent of tariff revenue is assumed to be lost to bureaucratic costs, leaving a return to the private sector of $(1 - \alpha)tZ$.[7] The gross quota rent is $Q[p - p^*]$, and ω per cent of quota rent is lost to foreigners or to bureaucratic costs, leaving a return to the private sector of $(1 - \omega)[p - p^*]Q$. Assume for now that α and ω are constants (endogenous determination of α and ω is taken up in the section on revenue waste).

5.2.2 The Trade Expenditure Function

Dual methods treat the trade balance, the left-hand side of (5.1), as selected by the optimal behaviour of a representative agent. This is expressed as the trade expenditure function, which in turn is the difference between two underlying elements, the consumer's expenditure function and the gross domestic product (GDP) function. The consumer's expenditure function relates the value of consumption spending to the prices the consumer faces, and the level of utility enjoyed by the consumer. The GDP function relates the value of national product to the prices received (for outputs) or paid (for imported inputs in elastic supply) by producers, and the fixed factor endowments. This section reviews the consumer's expenditure and GDP functions separately, then combines them in the main tool, the trade expenditure function.

Consumption structure

As a consumer, the representative agent seeks to choose a consumption bundle so as to minimize expenditure at given prices while maintaining a target level of utility. Putting the problem in this dual fashion is equivalent to the older primal problem which describes the consumer as choosing a consumption bundle so as to maximize utility subject to the budget constraint, but it is much handier as a basis for empirical work. It also, as here, has advantages in theory. The minimum expenditure needed to support a reference level of utility u is equal to the expenditure function $e(p, \pi, u)$, where p and π refer as before to the domestic prices of the quota-constrained and unconstrained imports, and where the exported good has a price of unity and is thus suppressed in the argument list. $e_u du$ is the measure of real income change in terms of exports. (The convention adopted here and used subsequently is that subscripts denote partial differentiation.)

The most important property of the expenditure function is that its derivatives with respect to prices are the compensated (utility-constant) demand functions. Thus for example $e_\pi(p, \pi, u)$ is the demand function for the non-quota-constrained imported good.

This property follows from the assumption of minimizing behaviour. The reasoning is as follows. Expenditure is equal to the sum of the price times the quantity demanded for each good. The change in consumer expenditure as π changes infinitesimally comprises two parts, the initial quantity consumed of the non-quota-constrained good, Z, times $d\pi$; and the value of the change in the consumption bundle (the sum of the changes in the quantity demanded of all goods times the original prices). The second part, however, is equal to zero: at a constant level of u and the prices π and p, no change in the consumption bundle can be found which lowers the level of expenditure, and no change will be made which raises the level of expenditure, all due to the minimum value property of e.

Production structure

As a producer, the representative agent allocates resources so as to maximize the value of his output (national product) for given domestic prices, and subject to given factor supplies and the technology.[8] This is implied by competitive behaviour in an economy with no distortions save those in trade.[9] Note that the prices of domestic factors of production, which depend on resource allocation patterns, are subsumed in this account: they depend on the allocation, which depends on the maximizing behaviour and its parameters, the prices and the fixed factor supplies. The maximized value of national product is equal to the GDP (or revenue) function: $r(p, \pi, K, L)$, where K and L represent fixed aggregate supplies of factors of production. (There is no special reason to name the factors, or to have just two.)

The most important property of r is as follows: r_p is equal to the supply function of the import-competing good if there is domestic production of a perfect substitute for the import; it is equal to minus the imported input demand function if the good is an intermediate input into production; and it is equal to zero if the import is for final consumption only. As in the consumer case, this property is based on the assumption of optimizing

ANDERSON

behaviour: levels of production and imported input demand shift about as a result of the price change, but no change can alter the value of national product at constant prices.

It deserves emphasis that $r_p(p, \pi, K, L)$ is a general equilibrium supply (or input demand) function. Behind the scenes, industries expand and contract, labour and capital move from industry to industry, and factor prices shift, all being subsumed in the slope of the supply function, r_{pp}.

The Trade Expenditure Function

The basic formal building block for the welfare analysis of protection is the *trade expenditure function*, which is defined as the expenditure function minus the GDP function. Its value is equal to the net trade expenditure, $pQ + \pi Z - X$. It inherits all the properties of the expenditure and GDP functions, so its derivatives with respect to prices give the import demand functions (demand minus domestic supply, if any). In using relative prices, the price of exports has always been set at unity and hence not made explicit in the argument list of the expenditure and GDP functions. Nevertheless, $-X$ is equal to the partial derivative of the trade expenditure function with respect to the price of exports (the minus sign being needed to convert the excess demand, which is the derivative, into a positive quantity of exports). The trade expenditure function is formally written as

$$E(p, \pi, u; K, L) = e(p, \pi, u) - r(p, \pi, K, L) \tag{5.2}$$

$$= pQ + \pi Z - X$$

(For most of the discussion, the factor supplies K and L play no role, so they will be suppressed henceforth except where necessary.)

The derivatives of E with respect to price are the compensated (utility-constant) import demand functions. Formally

$$Q = E_p(p, \pi, u) \tag{5.3}$$

$$Z = E_\pi(p, \pi, u) \tag{5.4}$$

The tremendous economy of thought represented by (5.3) and (5.4) deserves emphasis. Behind the scenes, a change in p or π causes factors to shift between industries, factor prices to change, all built into the slopes of the import demand functions. Note that it need not be specified whether imports are non-competitive, have domestic perfect substitutes or are intermediate inputs.

As for the effect of changes in u, $E_u du$ is equal to $e_u du$, the measure of real income change in terms of the export good. Since trade expenditure is equal to $pQ + \pi Z - X$, the real income change, $E_u du$, must equal $p dQ + \pi dZ - dX$, where the differentials are understood to be due to a change in u at constant prices.

One final step is necessary before proceeding to the formal accounting for the cost of protection. The quota-constrained import has an exogenous quantity, Q, and an endogenous domestic price p, which adjusts to clear the market, given π and u. Equation (5.3) can be used to obtain the compensated-equilibrium value of p as a function of Q, π and u. Denote this solution, the compensated inverse import demand function, as

$$p = p(Q, \pi, u) \tag{5.5}$$

Substitute (5.5) into (5.4), and the quota-constrained demand function for the tariff-ridden import is

$$Z = Z(Q, \pi, u) = E_\pi(p(Q, \pi, u), \pi, u) \tag{5.6}$$

Equations (5.5) and (5.6) express the endogenous variables p and Z as functions of the exogenous trade policy variables and the reference level of utility.

5.3 THE TRADE POLICY ACCOUNTING FRAMEWORK

The main problem of the theory of protection is to evaluate the welfare consequences of changes in quota or tariff policies. For small changes, the change in the external budget constraint (5.1) implies[10]

$$p\mathrm{d}Q + Q\mathrm{d}p + \pi\mathrm{d}Z + Z\mathrm{d}\pi - \mathrm{d}X = (1 - \alpha)(t\mathrm{d}Z + Z\mathrm{d}t) +$$
$$(1 - \omega)([p - p^*]\mathrm{d}Q + Q[\mathrm{d}p - \mathrm{d}p^*])$$

The small country assumption means that p^* and π^* are constant (endogenous foreign prices receive an explicit treatment as a special case below). Then $\mathrm{d}\pi$ is equal to $\mathrm{d}t$, and $\mathrm{d}p^*$ is equal to zero. Collecting like terms, the system of accounting for change implies

$$p\mathrm{d}Q + \pi\mathrm{d}Z - \mathrm{d}X = -\alpha Z\mathrm{d}t + (1 - \alpha)t\mathrm{d}Z + (1 - \omega)[p - p^*]\mathrm{d}Q - \omega Q\mathrm{d}p \tag{5.7}$$

The left-hand side of (5.7) is the change in net trade expenditure at the initial (i.e. constant) prices. It might arise if a gift of foreign exchange enabled more net expenditure at constant prices.

The right-hand side of (5.7) is the net foreign exchange effect of the change in trade policy. (Foreign exchange is measured here in units of the export good.) The first term, $-\alpha Z\mathrm{d}t$, is the change in tariff revenue, given the trade volume, times the rate at which tariff revenue is wasted. The fourth term on the right, $-\omega Q\mathrm{d}p$, is the change in quota rent, given the trade volume, times the rent transfer rate. These terms disappear if α and ω equal zero (no waste). The middle two terms account for the net effect of volume changes (net of revenue loss for tariffs and net of quota rent loss for quotas). Both reflect a general principle in the analysis of distortions: real income varies with the size of the distortion times the change in the level of the distorted activity. The second term, $(1 - \alpha)t\,dZ$, is the distortion t (the gap between domestic marginal value of Z, π and the foreign marginal value, π^*) times the change in the level of trade in the distorted activity, dZ, all times the rate at which revenue is returned to the representative agent. The third term, $(1 - \omega)[p - p^*]\,dQ$, is the distortion $p - p^*$ times the change in the level of trade in the distorted activity, dQ, all times the rate at which rent is retained. The second and third terms disappear if α and ω are equal to one (full waste).

5.3.1 Accounting with Exogenous Waste

Net foreign exchange effect

Accounting for the net foreign exchange effect of trade policy uses the structure of supply and demand to link the changes in Z and p on the right-hand side of (5.7) to the exogenous changes in t and Q, while controlling for the simultaneous change in equilibrium utility u. Substituting from (5.2), (5.5) and (5.6), the external budget constraint (5.1) is rewritten in terms of exogenous variables, the trade instruments Q and t, and the level of utility u

$$E(p(Q, \pi^* + t, u), \pi^* + t, u) = (1 - \alpha)tZ(Q, \pi^* + t, u) + (1 - \omega)$$
$$[p(Q, \pi^* + t, u) - p^*]Q \qquad (5.1')$$

The accounting system totally differentiates equation (5.1'), and isolates terms in du on the left and terms in dQ and dt on the right. The utility-constant change in Z to be used on the right-hand side is equal to $Z_Q dQ + Z_\pi dt$, while the utility-constant change in p is equal to $p_Q dQ + p_\pi dt$.

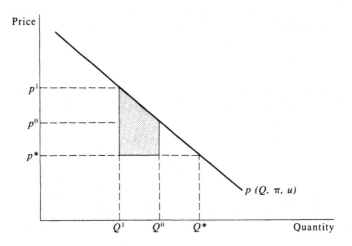

Figure 5.1 Welfare cost of a quota change

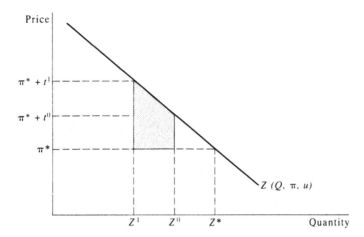

Figure 5.2 Welfare cost of a tariff change

The cases of ω and α equal to zero are familiar to many readers. For a quota change with no tariff, the right-hand side of (5.7) is equal to $[p - p^*]dQ$. For a tariff with no quota, the right-hand side of (5.7) is equal to $tZ_\pi dt$, where Z_π is the slope of the import demand curve. Figures 5.1 and 5.2 depict the net foreign exchange effect of a discrete change in a quota and a tariff, the terms

$$\int_{Q^0}^{Q^1} [p(Q, \pi^* + t, u) - p^*]dQ \text{ and } \int_{t^0}^{t^1} tZ_\pi(Q, \pi^* + t, u)dt$$

as the shaded areas. This is the method used in practice for numerous cost-of-protection studies. All that is required is an import demand elasticity or slope, usually assumed constant in the relevant range.

If ω is greater than zero, the formula for evaluating a quota alone, based on the right-hand side of (5.7), involves cumulating $((1 - \omega)[p - p^*] - \omega Q p_Q)dQ$. If α is greater than zero, the formula for evaluating a tariff alone involves cumulating $(-\alpha Z + (1 - \alpha)tZ_\pi)dt$. The loss term in the tariff case is illustrated by figure 5.3. The loss is equal to areas $B + A$ (equal to the shaded area on figure 5.2), plus α times the change in tariff revenue, $t^1Z^1 - t^0Z^0$, equal to $C - A$. Alternatively, the loss is B plus α per cent of the added tariff revenue at constant volume, C, plus the net revenue lost on the volume change, $(1 - \alpha)A$. The quota case is obtained by relabelling the price and quantity axes, and replacing α with ω as the loss ratio.

With more than one instrument of trade restriction, the terms in dZ and dp at constant u which appear on the right-hand side of (5.7) are $Z_\pi dt + Z_Q dQ$ and $p_\pi dt + p_Q dQ$, respectively. (An increase in π should ordinarily increase the pressure against the quota constraint, raising p, so p_π should be positive. An increase in Q should lower the price of a substitute for Z, hence Z_Q should be negative. For more details see Anderson and Neary, 1992.) For clarity, the

116   JAMES E. ANDERSON

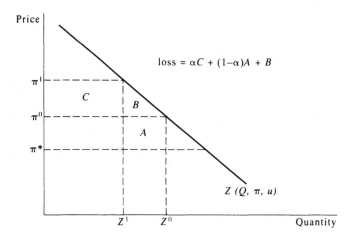

Figure 5.3 Welfare cost of a tariff increase with revenue loss

terms should be regrouped in terms of the instruments. The collection of terms multiplying dQ at constant u is called the shadow price of quotas, ρ. The collection of terms multiplying dt is called the marginal cost of tariffs, χ. Formally

$$\rho = (1 - \omega)[p - p^*] - \omega Q p_Q + (1 - \alpha)t Z_Q \tag{5.8}$$

$$\chi = -\alpha Z + (1 - \alpha)t Z_\pi - \omega Q p_\pi \tag{5.9}$$

The evaluation of a quota change, incorporating the cross-effect on tariff revenue, $(1 - \alpha)t Z_Q$, proceeds by integrating ρdQ. The evaluation of a tariff change, incorporating the cross-effect on rent transferred to foreigners, proceeds by integrating χdt. The picture of this evaluation adds to the loss on figure 5.3 an area derived from the effect of the change in π in the other market, $\int Q p_\pi$. The effect of discrete changes in both instruments simultaneously is evaluated with a contour integral which accumulates $\rho dQ + \chi dt$.[11]

Real income effect

It remains to account for the income effect of the foreign exchange made available by the trade policy change. To separate the change in endogenous u from the exogenous t and Q, that portion of the changes in Z and p due to the change in utility is deducted from both sides of (5.7). It is handy to define Z_I as equal to Z_u/E_u, and p_I as equal to p_u/E_u. These are interpreted as the effect of an increase in trade expenditure on Z and p respectively. (Formally, differentiate (5.1) using (5.5) and (5.6), collect terms in du on the left-hand side and use (5.8) and (5.9) on the right-hand side of the equation.) This yields

$$(1 - (1 - \alpha)t Z_I + \omega Q p_I)E_u du = \rho dQ + \chi dt \tag{5.10}$$

Solving for the real income change due to the trade policy,

$$E_u du = \frac{1}{(1 - (1 - \alpha)tZ_l + \omega Qp_l)}(\rho dQ + \chi dt) \qquad (5.10')$$

The coefficient on the right-hand side of (5.10′) is interpreted as the shadow price of foreign exchange, the marginal rate of transformation of foreign exchange into domestic real income. The shadow price of foreign exchange is ordinarily positive,[12] and in an undistorted economy it is unity.

The right-hand side of (5.10) represents the amount of foreign exchange (in terms of export goods) which could be deducted from the economy after the shift to the new trade policy, while maintaining a constant real income, $E_u du = 0$. In other words, it is the compensating variation in foreign exchange using the terminology invented by Hicks. The right-hand side of (5.10′) is the measure in terms of export goods of the real income change experienced due to the change in policy, known as the money metric utility change.

The conceptual distinction between measures based on (5.10) and measures based on (5.10′) is fundamental. The compensating variation assumes a constant utility is maintained by deducting from income the amount on the right-hand side of (5.10). The equivalent variation measure on the right-hand side of (5.10′) is a measure (in terms of the export good) of the utility change actually enjoyed. Compensating variation concept (5.10) is used more than money metric concept (5.10′) because the latter requires more information.[13]

The equivalent variation is in principle superior, since multiple changes evaluated using (5.10) need not have the same ranking as those same changes evaluated using (5.10′). That is, if using (5.10), reform A has a larger gain than reform B, which has a larger gain than reform C; it need not be true that reform A gains more utility than reform B which gains more utility than reform C. This well-known transitivity problem (see for example Chipman and Moore, 1980) disappears if income elasticities are all unity (preferences are homothetic) and is unimportant if real income changes are small. If income elasticities differ significantly from unity (which is likely in a detailed study of protection), and if the trade reforms create large real income changes (which is likely in highly distorted economies), intransitivity may be an important practical problem. Unfortunately, these conditions also present difficult problems for the analysis of protection using (5.10′), since many elasticities must be estimated or assumed convincingly enough to extrapolate the behaviour of demand and supply out of the range of previous experience.

5.3.2 Endogenous Revenue Loss

The foregoing assumes constant and exogenous fractions of tariff revenue and of quota rent are lost to foreigners. This section looks more deeply into the loss ratios and their endogenous determination.

Anderson and Neary (1992) interpret ω as the fraction of quota rent lost to foreigners because of the licence allocation system, which tends to create bargaining situations in which international rent sharing is expected. They show that the equilibrium rent share ω is constant with respect to the size of the rent in the special case where the Nash bargaining solution is assumed in a model with constant elasticities of intertemporal substitution and no bargaining costs. An alternative interpretation of ω, due to Krueger (1974), is that domestic agents waste (from a social point of view) a fraction of the quota rent in rent-seeking activity. Krueger assumed that ω was equal to one.

Krueger's insight was extended to tariff revenues by Bhagwati and Srinivasan (1980). Most analysts feel that quota rent-seeking is more significant in practice, but revenue-seeking probably also exists. An earlier parallel development by Bhagwati and Hansen (1973) allowed for foreign exchange to be used up in smuggling activity. A unified approach to accounting for any of these activities (directly unproductive or DUP activities according to Bhagwati, 1982) is to interpret the coefficients α and ω as representing the fraction of foreign exchange destroyed in the competition for revenues. The share parameters α and ω can also be interpreted as reflecting bureaucratic costs.

An added complication can arise when the lost rent or revenue is spent on domestic primary factor services, since the volume of trade of *tariff-ridden* goods will shift due to the change in factor supplies available for productive activities. This insight was developed in the context of smuggling activity by Sheikh (1974) and extended to tariff revenue-seeking by Bhagwati and Srinivasan (1980). The complication disappears if quotas are the only type of distortion, because the level of the distorted activity is fixed.[14]

The welfare implications of trade policy changes in the presence of revenue- or rent-seeking which uses domestic resources are readily treated with dual methods, spelled out in the next subsection. The final subsection extends the accounting method to the case of changes in quotas in the presence of smuggling.

Rent- and revenue-seeking with domestic resources

If rent- or revenue-seeking is competitive, then the value of domestic resources committed to the pursuit of quota rent or tariff revenue is equal to the lost rent or revenue. The first case assumes that α and ω are institutionally fixed, so that the total rent sought is limited. The second case sets out an endogenously determined loss share.

Suppose that there are rent- and revenue-seeking technologies. $f(k, l)$ is the amount of quota rent secured by employing domestic capital and labour in the amounts k and l. Entry into rent-seeking occurs until $f(k, l)$ is equal to $\omega Q[p - p^*]$. $g(k', l')$ is the amount of tariff revenue secured by employing domestic capital and labour in the amounts k' and l'. Entry into revenue-seeking occurs until $g(k', l')$ is equal to $\alpha t Z$. The GDP function now refers to the value of productive activity, not including rent- or revenue-seeking. Capital and labour are hired competitively at prices r_K and r_L, the value of marginal national product of a rise in the factor endowments K and L respectively.

Competitive seeking will employ factor proportions such that their value of marginal product is equal to their price. With constant returns to scale, the values $f()$ and $g()$ will always go to the institutionally fixed levels: no unexploited opportunities remain. The total value of resources wasted in rent-seeking activity at the limit is thus

$$r_K k + r_L l = \omega Q[p - p^*]$$

The resource waste in tariff revenue-seeking is

$$r_K k' + r_L l' = \alpha t Z$$

The first task is to show that when a quota is the only distortion, the previous analysis of the shadow price of quotas requires no modification when rent-seeking uses domestic resources. The net foreign exchange effect of an increase in the quota is equal to $p - p^*$ minus the marginal effect of the quota increase on resources lost to rent-seeking. This cost is equal to $\omega([p - p^*] + Qp_Q)$, which are the terms involving ω in the formula for the shadow price of quotas. Equation (5.8) still defines the shadow price of the quota.

Second, the effect of an increase in the level of seeking, as represented by an increase in ω, is straightforwardly welfare-decreasing, since it loses more resources to rent-seeking at the rate $Q[p - p^*]$. But third, when a tariff is also present, a qualification must be entered. An increase in the level of resources devoted to rent-seeking will alter the level of tariff-distorted activity. If an increase in the level of resources devoted to rent-seeking raises the level of tariff-distorted trade, this effect could conceivably outweigh the direct effect of an increase in rent-seeking, and make an increase in ω be welfare-improving.[15] This linkage also adds a term to the shadow price of quotas equal to $-tZ_K \, dk/dQ - tZ_L \, dl/dQ$. The sign of this term depends on the Rybczynski structure explained in chapter 2.

Tariff revenue-seeking with domestic resources follows the same decomposition, with a revenue-seeking loss effect of a tariff change equal to $\alpha(Z + tZ_\pi)$, plus the indirect effect via $tZ_K dk'/dt + tZ_L dl'/dt$. The marginal cost of a tariff is the old term on the right-hand side of (5.9), $-\alpha Z + (1 - \alpha)tZ_\pi$, minus the indirect effect $tZ_K dk'/dt + tZ_L dl'/dt$.

Now consider shares ω and α which are are endogenously determined. To allow an endogenous share less than one, the seeking technologies must be subject to diminishing returns to the variable factors capital and labour (plausibly associated with lobbyists crowding each other out in bidding for the attention of a fixed number of bureaucrats). The equilibrium level of rent-seeking is then determined by the equilibrium levels of capital and labour, $\hat{k}$ and $\hat{l}$, which satisfy the value of marginal product conditions: $f_k(\hat{k}, \hat{l}) = r_K$ and $f_l(\hat{k}, \hat{l}) = r_L$, with a similar determination of the level of revenue-seeking. Note that the equilibrium level of waste, $f(\hat{k}, \hat{l})$, is not directly dependent on the level of the trade distortion. Then if prices of capital and labour are invariant to t or Q, seeking activity is independent of marginal changes in the quota or tariff. At the margin, there is no change in the resources devoted to seeking. Under this assumption, the shadow price of quotas and the marginal cost of tariffs are defined by (5.8) and (5.9) with ω and α equal to zero.

Indirectly, of course, factor prices usually are dependent on trade policy in the general equilibrium. However, constancy of factor prices might be plausible in a partial equilibrium setting of limited trade reform. If factor prices are variable, the level of seeking changes, and the shadow price of quotas is modified by deducting the marginal increase or decrease in resources spent on seeking due to the change in the quota. (An explicit model of this marginal cost can be worked out using the dual methods of this chapter, but it is of secondary importance for present purposes.)

Smuggling

The analysis of smuggling follows a closely related line of reasoning. The tariff evasion costs may absorb foreign exchange or domestic factors, with the same formal effect as in revenue-seeking. For quotas, the issue is slightly complicated by the increase in the level of trade due to smuggling (in contrast, the domestic price of Z is invariant to smuggling so long as evasion is less than 100 per cent of the market). A model of enforcement must be added to link the formal quota $\bar{Q}$ to the total trade volume, with the simplest story being that total trade Q is equal to $(1 + \bar{\omega})\bar{Q}$. This means that for every licensed import unit, it is possible to smuggle $\bar{\omega}$ units. If smuggling requires only external resources, then the shadow price of quotas, where these are the only distortion, can be reduced to[16]

$$\rho = [p - p^*] - \bar{\omega}\bar{Q}p_Q$$

5.4 THE THEORY OF DISTORTIONS

The theory of distortions uses the preceding structure to lay out prescriptions for optimal and second-best policy. A distortion is a gap between marginal social benefit and marginal social cost in some activity. The gap provides an opportunity for efficiency-improving government policy. Bhagwati (1971) provides a useful four-way division of distortions, followed here, first into international vs domestic distortions and then into economic vs 'non-economic' distortions. The most important result is the principle of targeting: the best instrument is the one which directly acts on the distortion. This suggests that second-best instruments can be ranked in terms of their undesirable side-effects, and indeed such rankings are sometimes possible. The formulae for the optimal setting of first- or second-best instruments are often instructive, so a few are reviewed here. For simplicity, the parameters α and ω are set equal to zero.

5.4.1 International Distortions

An important distortion arises when a country's volume of trade has an effect on its terms of trade. For simplicity, assume here that there is only one imported good.[17] The distortion is equal to the difference between the marginal benefit of another unit of imports (the domestic price, p) and the marginal cost (the foreign price p^* plus the trade volume times the foreign price increase due to the increase in volume, Qp_Q^*). At free trade, the foreign and domestic prices are equal, and the distortion is equal to $-Qp_Q^*$, which is less than zero. The optimal policy is to reduce imports with a quota such that marginal benefit and marginal cost are equal. This is equivalent to a tariff at the *ad valorem* rate

$$\frac{p - p^*}{p^*} = \frac{Qp_Q^*}{p^*}$$

the well-known optimal tariff formula. This illustrates the principle of targeting: the optimal tariff or quota is best because it acts directly on the distortion.

A related case arises when some domestic factors are owned by foreigners, due to international investment or guest workers. An additional unit of foreign investment has marginal benefit equal to the domestic service price of capital, s (equal to r_K), while it has marginal cost equal to the service price paid to foreigners, s^*, plus the terms of trade effect $K_{s^*K^*}^*$, where K^* denotes foreign capital operated in the domestic economy. The optimal investment tax and investment quotas are defined along the lines of the preceding paragraph.[18] A significant extension allows for the premium $s - s^*$ to be internationally shared, with the fraction μ going to foreigners. Investment licences are often likely to be allocated in a manner which induces bargaining.[19] Then even if the domestic economy is small (s^* is fixed), the optimal foreign investment quota is defined by

$$(1 - \mu)[s - s^*] + \mu K^* s_{K^*} = 0$$

The desirability of such trade and investment policy is greatly limited by the likelihood of retaliation, which may help explain the lack of it. See Dixit (1985) for a review of game-theoretic models of trade policy. Common sense suggests that retaliation by other than economic means is also a potent restraint on trade policy.

A 'non-economic' international distortion arises in the case of sanctions. If a good is imported from a country whose exports are undesirable for some international political reason (e.g. Iraqi oil) then the government is faced with a constraint that trade must not exceed Q. A quota equal to Q is first-best, and is equivalent to a tariff equal to $p(Q, \pi, u) - p^*$ where u is the level of utility associated with the trade volume Q.

A deeper model of the 'non-economic' constraint may, however, suggest a more appropriate target, and hence a better instrument. International externalities are a good example. At this writing, environmentalists in the USA are lobbying against the proposed free trade agreement with Mexico on the grounds that Mexican pollution is positively linked to its trade with the USA. A trade policy may be a feasible means of shifting a foreign nation's level of pollution, but less efficient than an approach based on international regulation of common property resources, such as the recently proposed carbon emissions licences. See Markusen (1975) for a discussion.

5.4.2 Domestic Distortions

The main reasons for protection are domestic. Many arguments have been advanced for protection to achieve domestic goals set by benevolent governments (see Bhagwati and Srinivasan, 1980 and Bhagwati, 1971 for a full treatment). Here, unemployment and government revenue are used to illustrate the analysis. The principle of targeting applies. Trade distortion is inferior to an instrument which acts directly on the target, for example, wage subsidies for employment, and lump-sum taxes to raise revenue.

Sectoral employment target

Suppose that the level of employment in a particular sector must hit a target level. The first-best policy is a subsidy to employment in the sector. Formally, in an otherwise undistorted economy the net foreign exchange impact of a small rise in the sectoral employment target is $v\,dl$, where v is the gap between the value of marginal product of sectoral labour and the opportunity cost.[20] v is equal to minus the social premium on sectoral employment, the latter being the subsidy which must be paid to sectoral labour to induce the change. Behind the scenes, the necessary revenue is raised with a non-distorting tax.

In contrast, a tariff (with α equal to zero, full revenue retention) to achieve the same increase in employment has a net foreign exchange impact of $tZ_\pi dt + v\,dl$ where dt is understood to satisfy the employment target. The tariff must be inferior.[21] This additive property of the marginal evaluation of multiple distortions is extremely handy and formalizes the reasoning behind the principle of targeting: direct instruments remove the side-effect terms.

Revenue

A classic public economics problem is to raise government revenue with the minimum amount of welfare loss. The principle of targeting implies that the direct method of a lump-sum tax is best. Unfortunately, this is infeasible, so a ranking of distortionary tax instruments is necessary. Historically, many countries have relied on tariff revenue to finance a substantial portion of their government expenditure, with a declining ratio of tariff to tax revenue as development occurred.

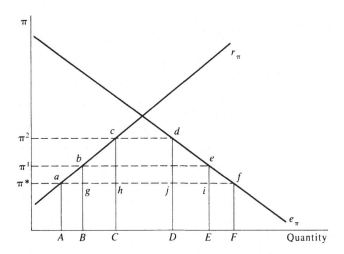

Figure 5.4 Tariffs and domestic distortions

Diamond and Mirrlees (1971) show that *consumption taxation* is a distortionary instrument which strictly dominates any tax system which distorts productive efficiency. This includes taxation of imported inputs and of imports for final consumption which are perfect substitutes for domestic production. Figure 5.4 illustrates their proposition for the latter case. The import demand $Z(p, \pi, K, L, u)$ is the horizontal difference between the general equilibrium supply function $r_\pi(p, \pi, K, L)$ and the compensated demand function $e_\pi(p, \pi, u)$. A tariff of t^2, equal to $\pi^2 - \pi^*$, raises revenue of $t^2 Z^2$, equal to the area *cdjh*. A consumption tax equal to $\pi^1 - \pi^*$ raises an amount of revenue $\pi^1 e i \pi^*$, assumed to be equal to $t^2 Z^2$. The tariff causes a deadweight loss equal to the area of triangle *ahc* plus the area of triangle *fjd*. The consumption tax causes a deadweight loss equal to the area of triangle *efi*. Triangle *efi* is smaller than *ahc* + *fjd* for two reasons. First, the deadweight loss implied by producing at a point other than *A* is avoided. Second, the tariff effectively subsidizes domestic production, and this subsidy must be made up with a still higher tax on trade.

The general reasoning is that a tariff imposes an avoidable inefficiency by taxing foreign and domestic products differentially. It pays to preserve production efficiency, while distorting only the margin between consumption and production.[22] If the tariff is on an imported input into production as opposed to final domestic output, a similar issue arises. A tax on all inputs at the same rate is equivalent to the consumption tax, so with only one input being taxed, the tax must be higher. In addition, the imported input tax creates inefficiency in production since the value of marginal product of the input exceeds its foreign price.

While the reasoning here applies only to the two-good case, its essence holds in higher dimensions. See Dixit (1985) for details. (Only one tax was analysed, but the homogeneity of demand and supply structures means that the tax structure is determined only in relative terms. The conventional way to present the tax model is to set the consumption, production and trade taxes on the numeraire good, exports, equal to zero.)

5.4.3 Non-equivalences among trade distortions

There is a variety of types of trade distortion, so relations among them are of some importance. The simplest type of relation is an equivalence, and a prominent early result was Lerner symmetry, establishing an equivalence between import and export taxes. Mundell symmetry relates trade taxes to domestic production and consumption taxes. A rich strand of literature studies situations under which a tariff and a quota are or are not equivalent. All the equivalence results are convenient benchmarks against which to assess the practical non-equivalences.

Lerner symmetry

The no-money-illusion property of demand and supply structures means that only relative prices matter to the welfare cost of trade distortions. Due to the external budget constraint, however, both domestic and international prices matter. A trade policy (a set of tariffs or quotas) forces a wedge between domestic and international prices. The Lerner symmetry proposition is that any pair of policies which produce the same domestic and international relative prices are equivalent. The usual interpretation is that a uniform *ad valorem* tariff on imports of τ per cent is equivalent to a uniform *ad valorem* tax on exports of τ per cent.[23] Directly extending this, a uniform tariff of τ per cent plus a uniform export subsidy of τ per cent restores the equality of domestic and international relative prices, or free trade. This logic has been used to advocate export promotion schemes in highly protectionist developing countries. But many other equivalences can be established, such as a tariff on one import equal to τ per cent is equivalent to a uniform tax on exports of τ per cent plus a uniform subsidy on other imports of τ per cent. Based on the previous analysis, the assumptions needed for Lerner symmetry are that the economy is initially undistorted and that revenue is fully redistributed in non-distortionary fashion. It bears emphasizing that all relative prices are acted on in Lerner symmetry.

Another equivalence is due to Mundell (1968). Noting that with international trade, consumption and production prices are acted on independently by consumption and production taxes, he argued that an import tariff was equivalent to a consumption tax plus a production subsidy, all at the same rate. Again, the assumption of no initial distortions and full redistribution in non-distortionary fashion is needed. The analysis of the superiority of a consumption tax over a tariff to raise revenue, based on figure 5.4, illustrates the logic. The tariff t^2 combines a tax on consumption of t^2, causing deadweight loss *djf*, with a subsidy to production of t^2, causing deadweight loss *ach*. This proposition is important in leading to the second-best ranking of production subsidies over tariffs when greater domestic production is a goal. Lerner symmetry can be combined with Mundell symmetry to generate numerous other equivalences.

Tariff-quota non-equivalence

Full tariff-quota equivalence is defined to mean equivalent in all relevant economic dimensions. Figures 5.1 and 5.2, when interpreted to apply to the same imported good, illustrate a tariff which is equivalent to a quota in volume, price and efficiency loss. The assumptions needed are that a single homogeneous product is restricted, that domestic and foreign suppliers are competitive, and that all quota rent and tariff revenue is returned to the representative consumer.

While pedagogically convenient, this equivalence proposition is misleading in practice, since the assumptions are not met. Relaxing any of the assumptions means that the tariff and quota can be equivalent in some dimensions, but not others. One important tactic here has been to define tariffs and quotas which are equivalent in trade volume, and compare the welfare loss of the two. This section sketches the main points, always under the assumption of no distortions other than those explicitly introduced. The main conclusion is that tariffs are generally preferable to quotas which restrict trade by the same amount. This proposition has been one of the most important conclusions of the theory of protection from a practical viewpoint, since the World Bank in the 1980s has made loans to client countries conditional on converting quotas into tariffs, apparently with considerable effect.

Anderson (1988) details the relative inefficiency of quotas when heterogeneity is recognized. Normally, quota constraints apply to a product group such as crude oil. But crude oil is in fact many products of differing chemical composition which might command different prices. In terms of the model of this chapter, Q and Z have the same units (barrels of oil) and are subject to an aggregate constraint. In such a case, the initial quota allocations are made according to historic market shares of firms, each of which for simplicity should be thought of as trading in one product. Trade in licences is frequently prohibited. The licence premia (the gap between foreign price and domestic price) then generally differ across the individual products. If there is trade in licences, a reallocation of licences will arise such that the premia in each use are equal, while still meeting the aggregate quota on the group. The gains from trade proposition of chapter 2 implies this reallocation raises welfare. This uniform premium is fully equivalent to a uniform tariff on the group, so the tariff is superior to any quota allocation save one. The tariff and quota are generally not equivalent.

A similar proposition is proved for tariffs equivalent in average volume to a fixed quota under uncertainty. The reasoning is that a fixed quota will have a different quota premium $p - p^*$ for each value of p^* and each position of the inverse demand curve $p(Q, \ldots)$, i.e. for each state of nature. A tariff will enforce a uniform premium, which could be achieved by an (infeasible)

market in state-contingent quota licences. Anderson (1988) presents empirical
studies showing that this arbitrage inefficiency of the quota adds substantially
to the deadweight loss of the tariff for both heterogeneity and uncertainty.

Figure 5.3 and the section on revenue loss show how non-equivalence arises
with less than full return of revenues. The classic case is where α is equal to
zero, the tariff results in a full return, while ω is equal to one, as with a
voluntary export restraint (VER) when all rent is retained by the foreigner. It
can be shown that if α and ω are equal and not necessarily zero, and the sole
distortion is either a quota or a tariff, equivalence still holds. Usually, though,
quotas are so narrowly allocated that they create bargaining situations in
which rent must be shared, whether it is a VER or not. In contrast, the tariff
should return a higher portion of the revenue. The quota which is equal to the
volume of trade under the tariff is less efficient under these assumptions,
provided there is no domestic resource used up in association with the loss.
ω can be reinterpreted as due to rent-seeking, and here, too, the judgement of
the profession has been that ω is likely to exceed α. In the presence of some
tariffs elsewhere in the economy, both forms of seeking create an indirect effect
whereby the new distortion has an effect on the level of tariff-distorted trade
via diversion of resources into rent- or revenue-seeking. Whether this is larger
for a new quota restriction than for a new tariff restriction is problematic.

Bhagwati (1965) showed how domestic monopoly makes a tariff superior to
a quota. A tariff allows foreign market discipline to be applied to the potential
monopolist, whereas a quota permits the exercise of domestic monopoly power
in the residual market. This insight has been elaborated in oligopoly models,
starting with Itoh and Ono (1982). The difference in instruments alters the
nature of the game between firms, with quotas serving as a 'facilitating
practice' (Krishna, 1989) which can improve profits of foreign and domestic
firms at the expense of consumers. These models are reviewed in chapter 7.

If the catalogue of 'other distortions' is extended indefinitely (some examples are imperfect asset markets, monopoly power in trade, revenue targets
and employment targets), a variety of possibilities open up, including some in
which a quota dominates a tariff. See Anderson (1988) for a review, and a
judgement that the qualifications may be disregarded for most purposes.

Other types of restriction

Specific tariffs (i.e. a fixed levy per unit of the imported good) have been used
above for the generic tariff, but *ad valorem* tariffs (a fixed proportion of the
foreign price of the imported good) are equally common. The two are
equivalent if the foreign price is unchanging, but otherwise not. Revenue-
seeking creates another non-equivalence, since importers facing an *ad valorem*
tariff can evade a portion of the tariff by underinvoicing, showing a foreign
price less than that actually paid.

Foreign exchange constraints on groups of goods create a quota which is
equivalent to an *ad valorem* tariff if foreign exchange licences are traded. If
not, the previous remarks on tariff and quota non-equivalence apply to *ad
valorem* tariff and foreign exchange quota non-equivalence.

An interesting type of policy is one in which the tariff is set as a function of an endogenous variable. The 'tariff-quota' is a function under which the rate of duty steps upward at a critical volume of trade. Anderson and Young (1982) rationalized tariff-quotas as optimal if the 'non-economic' constraint combined a mean volume restriction with a restriction on the expectation of imports above a critical level. Variable levies are another type of policy which sets the duty such that the foreign price is brought up to a target price. These are used by the EC as part of its agricultural policy.

Quality regulation is not primarily discriminatory between foreign and domestic firms. Nevertheless, there is a potential for its exploitation in a protectionist manner, and allegations of this behaviour are common. In its simplest form, a regulation such as the EC ban on beef containing certain hormones is equivalent to a prohibitive tariff or a zero quota on that type of beef. Conversely, a tariff or quota on a product group ordinarily induces changes in the average quality of the group. A specific tariff, or a quota allocated so that the quota licence premium is uniform across members of the group, will on average induce substitution towards the higher-priced varieties. This quality upgrading is due to the substitution effect, since the specific tariff raises low prices proportionately more than high prices (Falvey, 1979). In contrast, the *ad valorem* tariff preserves relative prices and induces no such substitution. Anderson (1988) argues that if protection is rationalized by non-economic objectives like sectoral employment or specific factor prices, under an intuitive and frequently used condition on preferences and techno-logy, the second-best policy is an *ad valorem* tariff.[24]

The last type of restriction considered here is the local content restriction. A car manufacturer is allowed to import parts free of duty so long as they do not exceed a certain fraction of a domestic measure, such as the quantity of like domestic parts, or the value of domestic parts, or the quantity or value of final output. The simplest form is the first, illustrated here by supposing that each car needs one engine, and that β per cent of cars produced are permitted to have imported engines. If p^* is the price of imported engines and p is the price of domestically produced engines, the average price of engines will be $p^a = \beta p^* + (1 - \beta)p$. If π is the price of cars, the constraint is formally written as

$$- r_p(p^a, \pi, K, L) = \beta r_\pi(p^a, \pi, K, L) \tag{5.11}$$

Equation (5.11) may be solved for the value of p^a, as defined above, which clears the market. The left-hand side of the equation is the demand for imported engines and the right-hand side is β times the supply of cars, using the properties of the GDP function. To see how this differs from a quota, compare equation (5.11) with the version of equation (5.3) relevant to an imported input, $Q = - r_p(p, \pi, K, L)$, to be solved for p. For second-best policy purposes, a local content scheme has an advantage over a simple quota because for a given level of domestic engine production (which for simplicity could be viewed as a target price p), it permits the domestic industry to purchase engines at a lower average price, hence allowing more trade and a lower efficiency loss.[25]

5.4.4 Multiple Trade Distortions: Structure of Protection Issues

Many important issues in the theory of protection concern the structure of multiple trade distortions. Real world policy acts in the presence of multiple distortions, usually changing only some of them. The most important problem of post-war international trade policy was to reduce the high tariff barriers of the inter-war period. Periodic rounds of GATT negotiations achieved great success among developed nations in this endeavour. The Kennedy and Tokyo Rounds used the principle of the uniform (across-the-board) cut as the basis for negotiations. More recently, less developed nations have liberalized trade by cutting high tariffs and converting quotas to tariffs while maintaining tariff revenue collections by keeping relatively constant average tariff levels. Are these likely to be welfare-improving? A related issue is: should liberalizations be all at once (an intertemporally uniform profile of tariffs) or staged? The theory of gradual or piecemeal reform derives principles for evaluating such questions.

What are the implications of cascaded tariff structures, in which tariffs on goods in intermediate stages of production are lower than those at finished good stages of production? The theory of effective protection was designed to provide an answer.

Gradual reform

Theorists came rather belatedly to the analysis of reform rules (Foster and Sonnenschein, 1970, Bertrand and Vanek, 1971, Bruno, 1972 and Hatta, 1977b are key contributions). The difficulty is that in starting from an initially distorted situation, there are a large number of cross-effects to evaluate. Two broad approaches came out of this literature. In the first, the uniform proportionate cut in tariffs turns out to be theoretically appealing, since welfare improvement is guaranteed regardless of the pattern of cross-effects.[26] The proof of this uniform radial cut proposition involves a straightforward but technical use of the properties of demand systems. See Dixit (1985) for a formal discussion.

The second proposition is the concertina cut rule: cut the highest *ad valorem* tariff first to the level of the next highest, then the pair of them to the level of the third highest and so on. Welfare is guaranteed to rise at each step if all goods are net substitutes (i.e. if the effect of an increase in the price of good i on the compensated excess demand for good j is positive). The concertina cut rule can be proved intuitively, as follows.[27] Suppose there are two tariffs, with the net foreign exchange effect of a policy change being $t_1 dZ_1 + t_2 dZ_2$, equal to $\tau_1 \pi_1^* dZ_1 + \tau_2 \pi_2^* dZ_2$. If all goods are net substitutes, a tariff cut must increase exports at constant utility (since it will then cause substitution away from consumption of exportables and substitution towards production of exportables); hence with balanced trade in terms of foreign prices, $\pi_1^* dZ_1 + \pi_2^* dZ_2 = dX > 0$. If the higher tariff is cut, this means $\tau_1 \pi_1^* dZ_1$

$+ \tau_2 \pi_2^* dZ_2 > 0$, hence welfare rises. While the net substitutes assumption might appear plausible, Lopez and Panagariya (1990) offer an important counter-example. If there are pure imported intermediate inputs, the net substitutes assumption necessarily fails. They provide counter-examples of welfare-decreasing concertina cuts in a model with imported intermediates. This is a serious limitation to the standard World Bank recommendation of cuts in extreme tariffs, especially since the preponderance of trade in protectionist less developed countries is on intermediate goods.

Attention has recently shifted to quota reform, in recognition of the growth of quotas as the main instrument of protection in developed countries. Corden and Falvey (1985) showed that if quotas are the only distortion and rent is fully retained, then all quota expansions are welfare-improving. Falvey (1988) extends the treatment to quota reform in the presence of tariffs. He also shows that the concertina and uniform radial cut propositions for tariff reform continue to hold in the presence of quotas. Anderson and Neary (1990) extend the quota reform treatment to the case of intermediate rent retention. Since the quota case is not covered in other survey treatments, it is worth developing here.

For the single quota case, the shadow price of quotas is, from equation (5.8) with no tariff,

$$\rho = (1 - \omega)[p - p^*] - \omega Q_{PQ} + tZ_Q$$

Corden and Falvey note that with no tariffs and no rent loss, $\rho = [p - p^*] > 0$. Moreover, this expression is the same in form for any number of quotas (simply subscript the prices and the shadow price) and rises in both Q_1 and Q_2 are welfare-improving. This can be generalized to quota reforms which allow some quota decreases (a relevant consideration in evaluating actual quota policy), since $\rho_1 dQ_1 + \rho_2 dQ_2$ is positive so long as the quota changes are on average positively associated with the unit quota rents. With tariffs in the model and no rent loss, Falvey (1988) develops the term tZ_Q for the many-good analogue, and shows that with all goods being net substitutes, ρ_i is positive if the percentage quota premium $[p_i - p_i^*]/p_i$ exceeds the largest explicit *ad valorem* equivalent tariff t_j/π_j. Then increases in any quota satisfying this condition are welfare-improving. Anderson and Neary (1990) develop the terms Q_{PQ} and tZ_Q for the many-good analogue and show that under the assumption of implicit separability of the trade expenditure function[28]

$$\rho_i = (1 - \omega)[p_i - p_i^*] - \frac{\omega}{\varepsilon} p_i - \tau p_i$$

where ε is the aggregate elasticity of demand for the quota-constrained product group and τ is the trade-weighted average *ad valorem* tariff on the tariff-ridden goods. Setting ω equal to zero for the moment, ρ_i is positive if the percentage quota premium exceeds the average *ad valorem* tariff. Anderson and Neary use this expression to note that a quota reform (which could include some quota decreases) is welfare-improving if the quota changes are positively associated with the unit rents and in addition (i) the foreign value of quota-constrained trade rises, and (ii) $\tau \leqslant -\omega/\varepsilon$, i.e. the average tariff rate is not greater than the rent loss fraction deflated by the elasticity of quota-constrained goods with respect to their own average price.

Effective protection

The theory of effective protection was developed in an attempt to characterize the protection given to an industry by the tariff system, recognizing that much of industrial output is sold to other industries as an intermediate input. Intuitively, an industry receives positive protection from a tariff on the good its output competes with, but negative protection from a tariff on goods competitive with inputs it must purchase. In light of this, it is perhaps no surprise that tariff structures are typically cascaded, with higher rates on more advanced stages of production.

The effective rate of protection is usually defined as the percentage increase in value added per unit of output due to the tariff system. Let τ_j be the *ad valorem* tariff rate for sector j and a_{ij} be the amount of product j required per unit of output of good i. Free trade value added per unit in industry i is equal to $v_i = \pi_i^* - \Sigma_j a_{ij}\pi_j^*$. With protection, the value added per unit is

$$v_i' = \pi_i(1 + \tau_i) - \sum_j a_{ij}\,\pi_j(1 + \tau_j)$$

The effective rate of protection is

$$\frac{v_i' - v_i}{v_i} = \frac{\tau_i - \displaystyle\sum_j a_{ij}^*\,\tau_j}{1 - \displaystyle\sum_j a_{ij}^*}$$

where a_{ij}^* is the input–output coefficient in value terms, $a_{ij}^* = a_{ij}\pi_j^*/\pi_i^*$. Usually, the formula uses the free trade input–output coefficients (which must be inferred from the observed distorted coefficients and an assumption about substitution possibilities, usually fixed coefficients). The effective rate is supposed to be associated with gross outputs or value added (industry payments to primary factors), but in some applications it is associated with the return to industry-specific primary factors.

The association of the effective rate of protection with industry interests is problematic for several reasons. First, suppose that there are no intermediate inputs, so that gross and net outputs coincide. In a general equilibrium supply model, a higher percentage tariff on the import which competes with the output of sector 1 than on the import which competes with the output of sector 2 does not mean that sector 1 expands output relative to free trade by more than sector 2. (Indeed, it is possible for one of the sectors to contract.) The simple ranking holds only under very special conditions on the general equilibrium supply structure. The most that can be said (with or without intermediate inputs) is that net outputs must be positively associated with prices (hence tariffs). Similarly, nothing can be said in general about the returns to specific factors in sectors 1 and 2 when the tariff on imports competing with 1 is larger than the tariff competing with 2. (See chapter 2 for a discussion of the relationship between goods prices and factor prices.) The link between a tariff system and either sectoral net outputs or specific factors must be calculated from a general equilibrium supply model.

The most favourable result for the effective rate of protection is due to Ethier (1977). He showed that if intermediate input requirements were fixed, it was possible to define a relationship between effective rates of protection and gross outputs which was the same as that between tariffs and net outputs: changes in tariffs (effective rates) and changes in net (gross) outputs must be positively associated. If substitution is possible between primary and inter-mediate inputs, in contrast, no such relation can be established. In particular, in a two-good case, it is possible for the relative effective rates and the relative output changes to be negatively associated. Two quite distinct analyses emerge, depending on whether the intermediate input is produced domestic-ally or not (Ethier, 1977). Separability in production with respect to the partition between primary and intermediate inputs reduces the ambiguity (Jones and Neary, 1984, section 3.1). Even so, the effective rate cannot give an answer that only a general equilibrium model can give.

For welfare results, the model of preceding sections makes clear that it is nominal tariffs which are of interest. Intermediate inputs needed no separate treatment, and were subsumed in the details of the technology leading to the GDP function. Imported inputs are treated in a formal way just like imports to final consumption in formulae (5.8) and (5.9).

Despite these negative results, much energy has been devoted to collecting the information necessary to measure effective rates of protection in a large number of countries and times. Has it been a waste? Effective rates of protection give a partial equilibrium index of the impact of protection on the ability of sectors to compete in factor markets with other industries. With fixed coefficients, they have the convenient property of a shorthand measure which 'on average' links gross outputs to the structure of protection in general equilibrium. Otherwise, the effort to collect the requisite information has probably been useful in its side-effects: producing consistent data on nominal tariff rates in concordance with domestic outputs, and developing input–output data. Both are required for computational general equilibrium methods.

5.5 SEQUENTIAL DECISION ISSUES

Recently, the theory of protection has taken seriously the sequential nature of decisions. The key idea is that current decisions are tied to agents' anticipation of future government policy. Three important implications flow from this. The first implication is that the policy which is optimal when agents do not anticipate government action differs from the policy which is optimal when they do anticipate. Section 5.5.1, for example, analyses the relative merits of once-and-for-all vs staged trade reform. The second implication is that government policy with anticipation can take the form of a rule, called administered protection, with the focus shifting to the effect of the rule on the current decisions of agents. Section 5.5.2 gives two practically important examples of administered protection, escape clause protection and anti-dumping.

The final implication can only be sketched here. An announced policy sequence which is optimal at the start of a government plan may not be credible, since it may not be in the government's interest to carry it out after the agents have made their current decisions. For example, in the second period of a two-period model, a tax on accumulated wealth is a non-distortionary means of raising revenue, so it dominates other forms of taxation at that date. In the first period, however, an anticipated tax on wealth in the second period discourages accumulation, so it is optimal for the government to announce a tax policy which is less punitive to accumulation. This will be believed only if a commitment mechanism can be found. Otherwise, the attention shifts to characterizing the tax policy which is 'time consistent'. See Staiger and Tabellini (1987) for some implications of this structure for the theory of protection.

5.5.1 The Time Profile of Reform

The desirability of once-and-for-all reform vs a diminishing tariff over time depends on the sequence of moves and on agents' expectations of government policy. Suppose that there are two periods, and two imports which represent the present and future. Discounting is incorporated in the structure of prices and tariffs. Both imports are restricted by a tariff with full return of the revenue. The first-period tariff is assumed to be fixed since it is too late to change it. The net foreign exchange effect of a marginal cut in t_2, from the right-hand side of (5.7), is equal to $t_1 dZ_1 + t_2 dZ_2$.

If the change in the future tariff level has not been anticipated, dZ_1 is equal to zero. In the absence of other distortions, immediate elimination of tariffs in the second period is the best policy, just as it is when the government has t_1 under control. If the cut in t_2 is anticipated, however, the anticipated level of the future tariff affects the present allocation of resources, so dZ_1 is not equal to zero. In the absence of adjustment costs, if present and future imports are substitutes, it can be shown that the best policy is a positive future tariff level t_2^*, though below the presently announced tariff level t_2. This is because a positive tariff in the future induces a somewhat higher level of unavoidably tariff-ridden trade in the present. Other things being equal, this is good.

But now complicate the story with adjustment costs. Adjustment costs (such as retraining or retooling) are popularly thought to provide a rationale for gradual reform. Without anticipation and in the absence of other distortions, however, it can be shown that immediate free trade (t_2 equal to zero) produces the optimal time path of adjustment.[29] Retraining and retooling take place according to the standard investment decision calculations, which are socially as well as privately optimal. But in the case where the agents anticipate the trade reform, $t_1 dZ_1$ is not generally equal to zero, and in addition, the social and private adjustment decisions differ. An interesting result is that too low a future tariff will induce too little present resource reallocation, as resources are induced to stay to enjoy the present period's more protected return. See Vousden (1990) for a more detailed discussion, following Leamer (1980).

5.5.2 Administered Protection

Administered protection covers a variety of rule-driven protection measures. The *escape clause* in US trade law allows industries injured by trade to receive relief with protection. Eaton and Grossman (1985) rationalize escape clause protection as providing insurance, so that firms facing risky terms of trade will produce a sufficient level of import-competing production. However, the desirability of such a policy is not known unless the underlying reason for the failure of the private insurance market is modelled. Dixit (1987) develops a model with *moral hazard* (the provision of insurance induces too little preventive action) as the reason for the failure of private insurance and shows that the optimal policy remains free trade, since protection induces too much production. Moreover, the usual principle of targeting applies: a direct insurance intervention would be superior.

Another prominent example of administered protection is anti-dumping. In US trade law, if foreign firms are discovered selling below foreign market price or average cost, the government is required to retaliate, either with anti-dumping duties or VERs. Here, the intervention rule modifies the current behaviour of foreign firms. Ethier (1982) shows that competitive foreign firms will dump in low-demand situations when layoffs incur a cost. Anti-dumping policies could be advantageous to the domestic economy if domestic firms have less contractual fixity of employment, because they shift more of the burden of adjustment to demand shocks back on to the foreigner. Anderson (1992) shows that competitive export firms dump when facing a prospective VER. More current exports gain more VER licences in the event of a VER, due to the custom of allocating licences in proportion to historic sales levels. Anderson (1992) shows that in these circumstances anti-dumping policy can be welfare-improving, since it shifts probabilistically from a future VER towards a future anti-dumping duty, which at least secures the revenue. (The reduced probability of free trade in the future and the reduced amount of dumping in the present do not offset this result.)

5.6 CONCLUSIONS

This chapter has surveyed the essential elements of the theory of protection. The dual approach used here allowed a very compact treatment of a wide range of issues in an accounting framework which is the basis for most empirical work on the evaluation of trade policy. The reader who learns the methods expounded here should be able to supply formal treatments of a number of issues not treated here, and covered in the more comprehensive surveys of Corden (1984) and Vousden (1990). Moreover, this chapter should provide an entry into the more advanced treatment of Dixit (1985).

A theme playing through the applications of the method in sections 5.3–5.5 is that the theory of protection is useful. In section 5.3 it provides the basis for a vast body of empirical work on the cost of protection and reform evaluation. In sections 5.4 and 5.5 it provides the basis for a number of practical propositions about trade policy.

Section 5.5 points the way to one of the major areas of current work in the theory of protection. Research which builds on agents' anticipations of policy and considers government commitment mechanisms may one day offer a theory of the trade policy institutional structure.

NOTES

I am grateful to Richard Tresch for his many helpful comments.
1 A standard reinterpretation of the model with many commodities allows one kind of intertemporal analysis. Commodities are dated, and net trade at any date need not be balanced while the present discounted value of trade must be. With perfect foresight, agents enter once-for-all contracts, and the formal analysis is equivalent to a static model. The same reinterpretation works for uncertainty, provided the set of markets is expanded to include contracts for all goods in all events – states of nature.
2 Diminishing returns can be accommodated by associating them with fixed factor supplies, if necessary with 'dummy' factors. See Dixit and Norman (1980) for an explanation. Increasing returns to scale are suppressed because they introduce several difficulties which complicate the analysis unnecessarily. First, the economy may be distorted, since in the absence of corrective tax/subsidy policy, marginal cost pricing is not efficient. Second, the fact that supply curves may slope downwards rather than upwards mars the usual association of a rise in output with a rise in the marginal cost of obtaining it. Third, scale economies are commonly associated with imperfect competition – the subject of chapter 3.
3 Baldwin (1985) notes that the executive branch of the US government appears to be less subject to narrow special interest group claims, and is much more internationalist than the legislative branch. Thus there appears to be scope for executive trade policy beyond serving special interests in a political equilibrium.
4 In principle, an endogenous trade policy approach is superior, since it explains shifts in policy. None the less, there are two good theoretical reasons to continue to use the exogenous policy approach. First, no single political economy model has achieved a dominant position. Second, the greater complexity added by endogenizing trade policy is a barrier to understanding the structure of various trade distortions and their interaction with each other and with classic public economics concerns.
5 The tariff could be *ad valorem* rather than specific, with the specific equivalent of the *ad valorem* tariff being $\tau\pi^*$, where τ is the *ad valorem* tariff rate.
6 The government retains some tariff revenue, reflecting bureaucratic costs or waste. It is assumed for the most part that such wasted revenue is spent by the

government on traded goods (the case where they are spent on domestic primary factors is covered in the section on rent-seeking).

7 If the redistribution of tariff revenue is regarded as coming from the supply of a good, such as public housing or transportation, the parameter α could represent a gap between the cost of the good, equal to the revenue, and the consumer's valuation of it. G is the difference between the total cost of the public good and the consumer's valuation of it. G/tZ is equal to α.

8 Factor supplies could be variable, allowing for labour–leisure choice, but this is an inessential complication.

9 The 'no distortions' assumption is potentially very troublesome, since it is so unrealistic. If the domestic distortions are in final goods markets (domestic taxes, monopoly power, externalities, scale economies of the multiplicative type) the analysis can easily be amended. Factor market distortions and a general treatment of scale economies are much more problematic. See Corden (1984) for a discussion of trade policy and factor market distortions.

10 This formulation assumes that trade policy does not alter α or ω.

11 Computing the contour integral is a technical matter. One point deserves mention, however. The use of compensated demand and inverse demand functions imposes symmetry conditions on χ and ρ which are necessary for the 'path independence' of the contour integral.

12 If all goods are normal, it can be shown that this expression is positive. Convert tZ_I to $\tau\pi Z_I$, where τ is equal to $t/(\pi^* + \tau)$. Note that normality of all goods means that πZ_I, the marginal propensity to spend on Z, is a positive fraction. Then $(1 - \alpha)\tau\pi Z_I$ is a positive fraction. With normality, p_I is positive. Then $(1 - (1 - \alpha)tZ_I + \omega Qp_I)$ must be positive. A positive value can also be based on an appeal to stability conditions.

To interpret the shadow price of foreign exchange, consider the effect of a transfer of one dollar. It permits net expenditure to rise by one dollar, which at constant prices means a rise in real income of one dollar: the shadow price of foreign exchange is equal to unity. With no distortions, this is the end of the story. But with trade distortions present, the rise in real income will change the burden of the distortion. With quotas, more quota rent is normally transferred abroad; while with tariffs, the distorted activity is normally expanded. This acts to lower (raise) the shadow price of foreign exchange.

13 A vast empirical literature uses variants of (5.10) in discrete form for studies of trade reform and of the cost of instituting protection in one sector in 'escape clause' (from GATT negotiated tariff bindings) cases. Here, elasticities are taken from detailed econometric estimates, at least in principle. There is a smaller but important literature using (5.10′) in computable general equilibrium (CGE) models. These 'solve' the information problem with extreme aggregation assumptions and severe restrictions on substitution effects which permit fully specified expenditure and GDP functions.

14 The literature has misleadingly linked the additional trade volume effect (tdZ, where dZ is due to the change in factor supplies available for productive use) to tariff revenue-seeking, whereas the phenomenon is due to either type of seeking in an economy with some tariffs.

15 The net effect is $-(r_K + tZ_K)dk - (r_L + tZ_L)dl$. The terms in brackets are the shadow price of capital and of labour respectively, i.e. the social value of another unit of capital and labour. A necessary condition for an increase in seeking to be welfare-improving is that the shadow price of at least one factor is negative.

16 The change in the quota results in net foreign exchange changing by $\rho = (1 + \bar{\omega})[p - p^*] - (\bar{\omega}(p - p^*) + \bar{\omega}\bar{Q}p_Q)$

where the second term is equal to the marginal change in revenue from smuggling.

17 The many-good optimal tariff analysis can be studied in Dixit (1985).

18 One complication is that in some production models, such as the Heckscher–Ohlin (HO) model, trade in goods is a perfect substitute for trade in factor services.

19 Only certain kinds of investment will be licensed, leading to a small number of foreign and domestic agents, where in the absence of quotas perfect competition reigned. Foreign direct investment is also associated with imperfect competition, which can be integrated with these models in some cases.

20 Formally, the sectoral employment level l is exogenous and enters the GDP function as $r(p, \pi, K, L - l, l)$. Then v is equal to $r_l - r_L$.

21 A host of studies of employment protection in the USA have been done in the 1970s and 1980s. A common convention for reporting the results is the cost per job saved, which is in essence $- t Z_\pi \mathrm{d}t / v \mathrm{d}l$, but for discrete changes. The models used provide a link between $\mathrm{d}l$ and $\mathrm{d}t$. The results range from two to more than ten times the average annual earnings in the job, which makes the extreme assumption that the worker's value when unemployed is equal to zero. See Baldwin, Mutti and Richardson (1980) for a seminal example.

22 A qualification must be entered. Diamond and Mirrlees prove their result for constant returns to scale technology. Diminishing returns can be converted to constant returns technology by inventing sector-specific dummy factors which receive the profits, with no effect on the conclusions. But increasing returns opens the door to several difficulties too complex to treat here.

23 This logic is very helpful in driving home the point that a contraction of imports implies a contraction of exports, so that special interests in the export sector should support free trade.

24 The condition is weak separability of preferences or technology with respect to the partition between the restricted product group and other goods.

25 For a target price p, equation (5.11) would be solved for the content ratio β which achieved the target. Of course, this need not be feasible: no trade might still not achieve the price p. The supposed advantages of local content schemes can disappear in more complex models. See Vousden (1990) for a discussion.

26 Kowalczyk (1989) has pointed out a qualification which arises when there are trade subsidies. It remains true that reductions in the wedges between foreign and domestic relative prices are welfare-improving, but this is not simply related to equiproportionate cuts in tariff and subsidy rates.

27 This proof is due to Lopez and Panagariya (1990).

28 This means the quota-constrained group of goods and the tariff-ridden group of goods have sub-expenditure function, i.e. have natural aggregates.

29 The argument is spelled out in Neary (1982), who goes on to analyse the second-best case for protection when wages are sticky. See also Mussa (1982).

REFERENCES

Anderson, J. E. 1988: *The Relative Inefficiency of Quotas.* Cambridge, Mass.: MIT Press.

Anderson, J. E. 1992: Domino dumping, I: Competitive exporters. *American Economic Review*, 82, 65–83.

Anderson, J. E. 1993: Domino dumping, II: Anti-dumping. *Journal of International Economics*, 35, 133–50.

Anderson, J. E. and Neary, J. P. 1990: Trade reform with quotas, partial rent retention and tariffs. *Econometrica*, 60, 57–76.

Anderson, J. E. and Young, L. 1982: The optimality of tariff-quotas under uncertainty. *Journal of International Economics*, 13, 337–52.

Baldwin, R. E. 1985: *The Political Economy of U.S. Import Policy*. Cambridge, Mass.: MIT Press.

Baldwin, R. E., Mutti, J. H. and Richardson, J. D. 1980: Welfare effects on the United States of a significant multilateral tariff reduction. *Journal of International Economics*, 10, 405–23.

Bertrand, T. J. and Vanek, J. 1971: The theory of tariffs, taxes and subsidies: some aspects of the second best. *American Economic Review*, 61, 925–31.

Bhagwati, J. N. 1965: On the equivalence of tariffs and quotas. In R. E. Baldwin et al., *Trade, Growth and the Balance of Payments: essays in honor of Gottfried Haberler*, Amsterdam: North-Holland, 53–67.

Bhagwati, J. N. 1971: The generalized theory of distortions and welfare. In J. Bhagwati et al., *Trade, Balance of Payments and Growth: essays in honor of Charles Kindleberger*, Amsterdam: North-Holland, 69–90.

Bhagwati, J. N. 1982: Directly unproductive profit-seeking (DUP) activities. *Journal of Political Economy*, 90, 988–1002.

Bhagwati, J. N. and Hansen, B. 1973: A theoretical analysis of smuggling. *Quarterly Journal of Economics*, 87, 172–87.

Bhagwati, J. N. and Srinivasan, T. N. 1980: Revenue-seeking: a generalization of the theory of tariffs. *Journal of Political Economy*, 88, 1069–87.

Bruno, M. 1972: Market distortions and gradual reform. *Review of Economic Studies*, 39, 373–83.

Chipman, J. S. and Moore, J. 1980: Compensating variation, consumer's surplus, and welfare. *American Economic Review*, 70, 933–49.

Corden, W. M. 1974: *Trade Policy and Economic Welfare*. Oxford: Clarendon Press.

Corden, W. M. 1984: The normative theory of international trade. In R. Jones and P. Kennen (eds), *Handbook of International Economics*, vol. 1, Amsterdam: North-Holland, 63–130.

Corden, W. M. and Falvey, R. E. 1985: Quotas and the second best. *Economics Letters*, 18, 67–70.

Diamond, P. A. and Mirrless, J. M. 1971: Optimal taxation and public production. *American Economic Review*, 61, 8–27 and 261–78.

Dixit, A. K. 1985: Tax policy in open economies. In A. Auerbach and M. Feldstein (eds), *Handbook of Public Economics*, vol. 1, Amsterdam: North-Holland.

Dixit, A. K. 1987: Trade and insurance with moral hazard. *Journal of International Economics*, 23, 201–20.

Dixit, A. K. and Norman, V. 1980: *Theory of International Trade*. Cambridge: Cambridge University Press.

Eaton, J. and Grossman, G. M. 1985: Tariffs as insurance: optimal commercial policy when domestic markets are incomplete. *Canadian Journal of Economics*, 18, 258–72.

Ethier, W. J. 1977: The theory of effective protection in general equilibrium: effective rate analogues of nominal rates. *Canadian Journal of Economics*, 10, 233–45.

Ethier, W. J. 1982: Dumping. *Journal of Political Economy*, 90, 487–506.

Falvey, R. E. 1979: The composition of trade within import-restricted product categories. *Journal of Political Economy*, 87, 1105–14.

Falvey, R. E. 1988: Tariffs, quotas, and piecemeal policy reform. *Journal of International Economics*, 25, 177–88.

Foster, E. and Sonnenschein, H. 1970: Price distortion and economic welfare. *Econometrica*, 38, 281–97.

Hatta, T. 1977a: A recommendation for a better tariff structure. *Econometrica*, 45, 1859–69.

Hatta, T. 1977b: A theory of piecemeal policy recommendations, *Review of Economic Studies*, 44, 1–21.

Itoh, M. and Ono, Y. 1982: Tariffs, quotas and market structure. *Quarterly Journal of Economics*, 96, 295–305.

Jones, R. W. and Neary, J. P. 1984: The positive theory of international trade. In R. W. Jones and P. B. Kenen (eds), *Handbook of International Economics*, vol. 1, Amsterdam: North-Holland.

Kowalczyk, C. 1989: Trade negotiations and world welfare. *American Economic Review*, 79, 552–59.

Krishna, K. 1989: Trade restrictions as facilitating practices. *Journal of International Economics*, 26, 251–70.

Krueger, A. O. 1974: The political economy of the rent-seeking society. *American Economic Review*, 64, 291–303.

Leamer, E. E. 1980: Welfare comparisons and the optimal staging of tariff reductions in a model with adjustment costs. *Journal of International Economics*, 10, 21–36.

Lopez, R. and Panagariya, A. 1990: *On the Theory of Piecemeal Tariff Reform: the case of pure imported intermediate inputs*. Washington, DC: World Bank.

Markusen, J. R. 1975: International externalities and optimal tax structures. *Journal of International Economics*, 4, 15–29.

Meade, J. E. 1952: *A Geometry of International Trade*. London: Allen & Unwin.

Mundell, R. A. 1968: *International Economics*. New York: Macmillan.

Mussa, M. 1982: Government policy and the adjustment process. In J. Bhagwati (ed.), *Import Competition and Response*, Chicago: University of Chicago Press for the NBER, 73–120.

Neary, J. P. 1982: Intersectoral capital mobility, wage stickiness, and the case for adjustment assistance. In J. Bhagwati (ed.), *Import Competition and Response*, Chicago: University of Chicago Press for the NBER, 39–67.

Sheikh, M. A. 1974: Smuggling, production and welfare. *Journal of International Economics*, 4, 355–64.

Staiger, R. W. and Tabellini, G. 1987: Discretionary trade policy and excessive protection. *American Economic Review*, 77, 823–37.

Vousden, N. 1990: *The Economics of Trade Protection*. Cambridge: Cambridge University Press.

6

THE POLITICAL ECONOMY OF TRADE POLICY

Stephen P. Magee

6.1 INTRODUCTION

This is a survey of the political economy of trade policy. For other reviews of work in this and related areas, see Baldwin (1986), Deardorff and Stern (1987), Hillman (1989), Inman (1985), Magee (1984), Magee, Brock and Young (1989), Mueller (1979), Nelson (1988), Sandler (1981) and Vousden (1990). The most interesting reading on this subject is the historical paper by Kurth (1979).

The material in sections 6.2 and 6.3 of this chapter is a condensed version of the work surveyed in Magee, Brock and Young (1989). Section 6.2 covers the early literature; section 6.3 covers issues in endogenous protection; and section 6.4 covers a sample of papers written or published in the period after 1988. Section 6.2 discusses alternative models of tariffs; the failure of economists to believe in free trade; cross-national determinants of national tariff levels; evidence on the fractions of economies devoted to rent-seeking; theories of lobbying, power and Arrow paradoxes; evidence on prisoners' dilemmas; the various types of country economic diseases, such as the Dutch disease; the political economy of country life cycles; and how the latter predicts why German protectionism helped Hitler into power.

Section 6.3 discusses endogenous policy theory, i.e. how the economy, lobbying and policies interact when all actors simultaneously pursue their own interests. Topics include tariffs as prices in political markets; a welfare impossibility theorem (why no policy improvements can be made); the difference between political efficiency and economic efficiency; how to estimate rent-seeking, even though it cannot be observed; the impossibility of Hotelling equilibria (why both parties will not choose the same policy); why perverse prisoners' dilemma lobbying equilibria emerge about 40 per cent of the time; how endogenous politics compensates for economic setbacks (endogenous politics provides implicit insurance against negative economic shocks); why endogenous politics causes increasing returns to factor endowments (the higher the capital–labour endowment ratio of a country, the higher the returns to capital and the lower the wages); why the general drop in protection since World War II (the ratio of the scarce factor, labour, has been steadily dropping relative to physical and human capital); the magnification paradox (why tariff rates drop while the fraction of resources devoted to protectionist lobbying increases); why Republican administrations in the

USA generate greater protection than Democratic ones; isoprotection curves (loci of inflation and unemployment rates along which equilibrium tariffs are constant); economic black holes (conditions with 100 per cent of resources devoted to redistributive battles; e.g. high-crime ghettos); and optimal obfuscation and the theory of the second-worst (since redistribution must be disguised from the redistributees, the equilibrium policy can be a second-worst one in terms of economic efficiency).

Section 6.4 covers recent work: why voluntary export restraints (VERs) are chosen rather than tariffs; why agricultural protection is so high in the advanced countries; recent measurements of rent-seeking; why so little is spent on lobbying relative to the benefits; estimates of the economic costs of lawyers; and why European unification will probably increase protection in the 1990s. Also included are several topics on public choice which have important implications for future research in international political economy: e.g. refinements of the definition of power; whether democracies are efficient or not; median voter versus the special-interest models of protection; analogies such as committees are to legislatures what farm teams are to baseball; endogenous real exchange rates; the political economy of strategic trade policy; time inconsistency and some political science questions.

6.2 EARLY WORK

This section covers work primarily before 1989. The political economy of trade policy grows out of pioneering work on collective action by Downs (1957), who noted that it is rational for voters to remain uninformed, and Olson (1965), who observed the exploitation of the organizers by the apathetic, i.e. those who lobby for protection will grant benefits to non-member free-riders in the industry who gain from protection but did not help obtain it. Another important strand was Stigler's (1970, 1971, 1972, 1974) work on the theory of regulation and Buchanan's (e.g. 1975) work on public choice. Buchanan provided some of the first conceptual linkages between political and economic activity and Stigler argued that self-interest will lead regulatees to co-opt regulators. Investments in politicians are just like any other investment: funds should flow to them so long as their risk-adjusted returns exceed those on other assets. Extensive coverage of Kurth's (1979) paper concludes this section.

Tullock (1967) spawned the work on rent-seeking in the 1970s and 1980s by observing that the entire area of consumers' surplus caused by tariffs might be wasted by groups attempting to capture the surplus. Krueger (1974) coined the term 'rent-seeking' to describe the process of wasted resources chasing politically created scarcities. To my knowledge, hers was the first international paper on endogenous lobbying.

The first papers on endogenous tariffs were by Brock and Magee (1975, 1978, 1980). They simultaneously solved the problem of optimal contributions by protectionist lobbies and the vote-maximizing tariff that the political parties would set. Findlay and Wellisz (1982) provided the first model of endogenous lobbying in general equilibrium. They had a Ricardo–Viner model of a developing country in which there is one mobile factor of production (labour) and two immobile factors: capital and land. Capital is employed in producing manufactured goods, the importable, while land is used in the production of the exportable good, agricultural products. Mayer (1984) followed with a model of tariffs with endogenous voters. He assumes that all parties will converge on the policy favoured by the median voter. Young and Magee (1986) had the first paper with both endogenous tariffs, endogenous lobbying and a full general equilibrium economic model. It was a $2 \times 2 \times 2 \times 2$ model in that it had two goods, two factors, two lobbies and two political parties and all displayed maximizing behaviour.

Work on endogenous policy theory generally is provided by Lindbeck (1975a, b, 1976, 1977, 1983, 1985a, b, 1986a, b) and by Magee, Brock and Young (1989), which summarized all of their work on endogenous policy from 1973 to 1989. Important empirical work on endogenous protection has been developed by Baldwin (1976, 1978, 1982a, b, 1986), Pincus (1975), Caves (1976) and Anderson (1980). Work is under way on trade policy in the new international economics framework by Helpman and Krugman (1985) and Krugman (1986) and the role of policy in computable general equilibrium (CGE) models by Whalley (1985) and other CGE theorists.

What is amusing is that many economists do not believe in the optimality of free trade. Frey et al. (1984) find that while 79 per cent of American economists believe that protection reduces welfare, the proportion is only 70 per cent in Germany, 47 per cent in Switzerland, 44 per cent in Austria and 27 per cent in France. It would be interesting to correlate these percentages with pre-EEC levels of protection by these countries.

Baldwin (1986) provides a survey of alternative approaches to tariff modelling in his review of trade policies in developed countries. While the special-interest model is the most popular model, he cites Caves's (1976) adding machine model, based on the voting strength of an industry; Cheh's (1974) adjustment assistance model, in which governments minimize short-run adjustment costs; the equity-concern model of Ball (1967), Constantopolous (1974), Fieleke (1976) and Baldwin (1982b), which fosters government concern for low-income workers; Ray (1981) and Lavergne's (1983) comparative cost model, which shows that tariffs can be explained by simple comparative disadvantage; Helleiner's (1977) international bargaining model, which suggests that developed country protection will be higher on imports from developing countries because the latter have high levels of protection; and Lavergne's (1983) status quo model which argues that protection today is correlated with the protection of yesterday. The latter has theoretical underpinnings in the conservative social welfare function of Corden (1974, (pp. 107–11), 1984). Feenstra and Bhagwati (1982) have a model of an efficient tariff. Lindbeck (1985a) argues that agricultural protection and rent controls have emerged from sudden drops in the income of certain groups. Gourevitch (1977) provides a historical comparison of tariffs in the late nineteenth century for the USA, Germany, France and the UK. He finds the following pattern of winners over losers across all the countries: producers over consumers, heavy industrialists over finished manufacturers, big farmers over small farmers and property owners over labourers; and substantial landowners and large-scale basic industry were consistent winners. For a good analysis of protection and the export–import bank in the USA, see Baron (1983).

Kindleberger (1986) provides evidence for the hegemonic theory of tariffs. According to the hegemonic theory, international trade was relatively open in portions of the nineteenth and twentieth centuries because of the existence of a large, stable nation more powerful than its rivals: the UK in the nineteenth century and the USA in much of the twentieth. According to this theory, this large state provided the public good of free trade. In fact, Kindleberger argues that the Great Depression was a partial consequence of the UK having relinquished its role but the USA dropping the ball by not having fully assumed its role as a hegemon. McKeown (1983) finds some empirical departures from the hegemonic theories of tariffs propounded by Kindleberger, Krasner (1976) and Keohane and Nye (1977). He finds that its predictive accuracy in explaining nineteenth-century tariff levels is poor.

Lindbeck (1985a) has organized redistributive policies into four groups: broad horizontal redistributions (labour to capital), life-cycle redistributions (social security), vertical redistributions (rich to poor) and fragmented horizontal redistributions (from general interests to special interests). He makes the important point that protection provides non-budget methods of redistribution, which explains why it is politically superior to production subsidies and consumption taxes.

Conybeare (1983) provides cross-national evidence on tariffs across 35 countries in 1971. He found that tariff rates were positively correlated across countries with indirect taxes (e.g. excise taxes) as a percentage of government revenue, the size of the central government as a percentage of total government and the instability of exports. Tariffs were negatively correlated with the commodity diversification of exports (and imports), GNP, GNP per capita, manufacturing as a percentage of GNP and government as a percentage of GNP.

What empirical evidence do we have about the proportion of country GNPs which are devoted to rent-seeking? Krueger (1974) found that 7 per cent of Indian GNP was absorbed in rent-seeking while 15 per cent of Turkish GNP was lost to rent-seeking over import licences alone. She indicated that with competitive rent-seeking, the entire value of the redistributive effect in tariff analysis can be wasted. Krueger indicated that the entire value of a rent-seeking individual's income could be wasted if the factor markets equate marginal returns between redistributive and productive activities. That is, in the traditional Corden (1957) diagram which decomposes the effect of a tariff change into the tariff revenue, the producer's surplus and the deadweight loss, the producer's surplus will be exhausted. Bhagwati (1980, 1982) correctly noted that the term 'rent-seeking' was not technically accurate in describing the process. But, like the variable gauge railroad problem, our system is stuck with the term 'rent seeking'.

Mohammed and Whalley (1984) indicate that redistributive activity might consume as much as 25–40 per cent of Indian GNP. Hamilton, Mohammad and Whalley (1984) have world-wide measurements of the rent-seeking costs of trade restrictions across countries. Ross (1984) finds that rent-seeking is approximately 38 per cent of GDP in Kenya. For papers on recent protectionism and potential harm to world welfare, see the series of papers by Salvatore (1985) et al. On the possibility that lobbying can increase welfare, see Bhagwati's (1980, 1982) work on directly unproductive activities (DUP). For a survey of rent-seeking, see Tollison (1982). On redistribution generally, Director's law states that public expenditures are for the benefit of the middle class but are funded by taxes levied on the rich and the poor (see Stigler, 1970).

Olson (1982) wrote an insightful and influential book suggesting that rent-seeking will rise with country age. The creeping economic sclerosis is based on lobby learning, redistributive conflict, growing webs of influence and political failure. Magee, Brock and Young (1989) argue that democracies are not economically efficient but they are politically efficient. While their black hole has empirical relevance in advanced countries only in ghettos, it indicates that diminishing returns to politics provides no theoretical protection from Olsonian sclerosis. What are the political implications of this economic black hole, of which wars, ghettos and sections of many developing countries are examples? Schumpeter's (1950) criterion for the success of an economic–political system is that it not create conditions which lead to an undemocratic regime, i.e. totalitarianism. Another possibility is Hirschman's (1970) idea that in deteriorating political and economic situations, the primary options are either 'exit' or 'voice'. Lindbeck (1985b) suggests the underground economy. Because of progressive taxation, the increased income coming from productive activity declines because of higher marginal tax rates. To compensate, individuals substitute away from redistribution prone sectors towards more efficient underground activities.

Olson (1965) examined lobbying, a subject closely tied to rent-seeking. He argued that lobby organization is easier with fewer numbers; in more concentrated industries; with more similar members; with greater external threats. Olson's work has been insightful and influential in subsequent research, although the political power of concentrated industries has been hard to demonstrate in many cross-section studies. Stigler (1970) and later Peltzman (1976) advanced the microfoundations of the self-interest model and provided evidence across US industries for its value in explaining regulation. Becker (1983) also argues that small groups will be successful in taxing larger groups for their subsidies. Taussig (1931) argued that special interests caused the proliferation of protection across industries and through time in the USA. H. P. Young (1978) models how a lobbyist should rationally allocate his funds most effectively among voters in a legislature. He notes that Republicans outspent Democrats by a ratio of approximately 2 to 1 in 1952, 1956 and 1968, all years in which they won the White House.

Free-riding is one of the major issues in lobbying. How can lobbies make all of the people contribute who gain from the activity? Marwell and Ames (1979) find that in experiments on graduate students, those majoring in economics were much more likely to free-ride in games than were those from any other subject area. Bauer, deSola Pool and Dexter (1963) conducted a survey in the 1950s which throws light on the profiles of individuals who were active in free trade and protectionist lobbies. They found that free traders are better educated, wealthier, more politically active and in the Republican Party while ultra-protectionists are more likely to be found in the Democratic Party.

How do writers measure power? H. P. Young (1978) shows that the US President is 88 times more powerful than a US representative or a senator since that is the number of them it would take to go from a majority to the two-thirds vote required in both chambers to override a Presidential veto. A rational lobby would be different between paying $88 million dollars to the President for a measure versus paying $1 million to each of 88 representatives and senators to override a Presidential veto.

How should voters be modelled? Downs (1957) assumes that voters are rationally ignorant. Anecdotal evidence for this is provided by Tullock (1979): the average US citizen does not even know which party controls Congress. McKenzie (1979) notes that philosophy majors are slightly better than economics majors in assessing the effects of government economic policy. Magee, Brock and Young's (1989) special-interest model follows the Downs assumption of rational ignorance. The theoretical alternative is the median voter model used by Mayer (1984); it assumes that voters are highly informed so that campaign contributions and political advertising are unnecessary. The Mayer approach has a conceptual flaw in that Aranson and Ordeshook (1981, p. 77) argue that the median voter hypothesis should not be applied in elections involving redistributive issues because of the absence of single-peaked preferences, and hence the presence of voting cycles.

With endogenous voter preferences, arrow paradoxes and voter cycling will always emerge on redistributive issues (Magee and Noe, 1989). They show that rational second- and third-choice voting by voters will always prevent a non-cyclical outcome. This is another reason for the difficulty of resolving redistributive fights, in general, and through voting, in particular. The basic idea is that on matters of redistribution, self-interested individuals will care little about their second and third choices and will alter those choices to block someone else from winning. If anyone unambiguously wins, the other two lose. Thus, second and third choices will be altered to guarantee the Arrow paradox outcome.

Why are tariffs used rather than more efficient policies? For interesting work on this, see Mayer and Riezman (1987). They note that political economy models cannot explain why tariffs are preferred as redistributive mechanisms over factor or production subsidies. They also argue that high-income groups may favour tariffs because this reduces their tax burden in a progressive tax system.

The prisoner's dilemma model is increasingly used to explain the presence of protection. Its simplest form is 2×2 game in which the best combined strategy is for both players to co-operate with the other player (e.g. free trade with no lobbying). However, if one lobby co-operates, then the best strategy for the other is to cheat (seek protection). Consequently, the equilibrium strategy is for both players to cheat (one lobby seeks protection while the other pursues pro-export policies). The prisoner's dilemma game is the only 2×2 game in which the pay-offs are such that the equilibrium strategy differs from Pareto-optimality. Messerlin (1981) was the first to apply the prisoner's dilemma game to tariffs. He did so in a bureaucratic model, using Niskanen's (1976) theory of bureaucracy. For an n-person prisoner's dilemma game using Olson's model of collective action, see Hardin (1971). Magee, Brock and Young (1989, chapter 10) review the experimental literature on prisoner's dilemma games and draw three implications for endogenous tariff theory. The first is based on the characteristics of the pay-offs themselves; the second describes the characteristics of the players; and the third pertains to the length of the game.

Two tournaments held by Axelrod (1980a, b) among game theorists and other experts were interesting in that the 'tit for tat' strategy beat all of the expert strategies entered in both tournaments, even though all players knew in advance that the tit for tat strategy was entered. Most of the other strategies could beat tit for tat head to head, but they compiled poorer scores against each other. Tit for tat is a model for successful political behaviour as well as life generally: it is co-operative, nice, tough and predictable. The tit for tat strategy is to co-operate on the first round of a many-round prisoner's dilemma game; it is nice in that it is never the first to defect; it rewards every co-operative move by an opponent with co-operation on the next round; it is tough in that every defection by an opponent results in its defection on the next round; and it is totally predictable. Axelrod also found that unpredictability leads to less co-operation. Thus, the typically random behaviour of consumer lobbies probably encourages protection.

There is some evidence in the literature for political compensation effects: the tendency for politics to compensate for unexpected negative shocks (see also the discussion of this in section 6.3). Hillman (1982) finds that a decline in the world price of a product has two consequences for the domestic political equilibrium. First, the political authorities may partially offset the decline by increased protection for the affected industry. This is consistent with a compensation effect. However, the decline in the world price may cause the domestic industry to become so politically weak that the domestic political authorities actually reduce the level of domestic production and hence accelerate the decline in the industry.

Some excellent evidence for the compensation effect is provided by McKeown (1983), who found that in the nineteenth and twentieth centuries, the major motivation for reductions in national tariffs was world prosperity. In contrast, increases in protection generally occurred during periods of world-wide depression. For an application of the relationship between terms of trade changes and rent-seeking, see Hamilton, Mohammed and Whalley (1984).

Mundell (1957) found that in the presence of a tariff, capital mobility could lead to factor price equalization (FPE) in an economy as would be the case with free trade. For a model in which various rigidities lead to greater FPE across countries with international factor mobility, see Neary (1985). With endogenous politics, Magee, Brock and Young (1989) show FPE cannot occur since the domestic political equilibrium is affected by a country's factor endowment. Thus the distribution of income is affected by factor endowments and hence by capital flows.

A variety of economic diseases plague contemporary economies. For an examination of the 'Dutch disease' (price increases in one sector causing contractions in other sectors), see Corden (1984) and Dornbusch and Frankel (1987). Brittan (1975) discusses the 'UK disease' (slow growth and high inflation). A closely related disease is stagflation (rising unemployment and inflation). Magee, Brock and Young's (1989) 'Brazilian vitality and the Indian disease', is the tendency for the capital stocks of capital-abundant countries to expand and the capital stocks of capital-poor countries to contract because of endogenous politics.

Baldwin (1986) analysed US trade policy, specifically, the vote on the 1973 Trade Bill: Democrats in both the House and the Senate were significantly more protectionist than were Republicans and protectionist labour union contributions were given primarily to those representatives who voted against the Act. Baldwin (1986) finds that both the President and Congress are more likely to adopt protectionist legislation just prior to an election. Baldwin (1985) has a good discussion of the trade policies of the Reagan administration's first term.

Kurth (1979) describes industry and country life cycles. Many advanced countries first had a textile industry, then a steel industry, and then one or more of the associated rail, shipping or car industries. He argues that the latecomers to the steel phase (Germany and Japan) had poorer outlets for steel so that the steel interests probably pushed them towards armaments and autocratic regimes. Textiles are interesting. Over the country life cycle they go from being an export industry early in the country's history to an import-competing industry. Thus, the current political influence of the textile industry is not related to its import-competing status: the industry was politically influential historically, even when it was an export industry.

On the subject of macroeconomic endogenous politics, consider the following outrageous but provocative idea suggested by Kurth's (1979) work. The ideas of Keynes were heavily promoted by special interests in the halls of government to push certain consumer and industrial goods. The economic success of cars, chemicals, electricals and other capital-intensive industries required a massive middle class with large spending power to support them. Furthermore, Keynesianism is implicitly anti-trade because of its focus on domestic spending. Lo, even Keynes was a handmaiden of the special interests.

Kurth (1979) presents other evidence that protectionist forces helped Hitler to power. He starts with the question: how do major powers market their steel? Kurth notes that the German steel industry was at a disadvantage relative to the UK after World War I because it did not have a strong consumer goods sector as did the UK, nor a domestic car industry (the UK was number two in the world), nor an overseas empire which consumed steel in the construction of railroads. The two best outlets for steel in Germany in the 1920s were exports to Eastern Europe and in the production of armaments. Thus, the steel industry in Germany in the 1920s supported the National People's Party which favoured rearmament, revision of the Treaty of Versailles and tariff barriers against steel imports from Western Europe.

Two other sectors emerged in Germany in the 1920s: chemicals and electricity. The chemical industry had a very strong interest in free trade because I.G. Farben was the world's largest chemical corporation and the largest corporation in all of Europe. Both the chemical and electrical industries wished to promote mass consumption and therefore these industries supported parties favouring social welfare, democratic politics and free trade. These industries joined with labour in opposition to the coalitions of the steel industry and the agriculturalists. A strategic mistake was made by I.G. Farben when it diverted most of its new capital investment in the 1920s into building enormous plants to produce gasoline from coal using a process known as hydrogenation. This was based on widespread forecasts, reminiscent of the 1970s, that world petroleum supplies would soon be exhausted.

The stock market crash in the USA and the beginning of the Great Depression, however, dealt a serious blow to the free trade policy of the German chemical and electrical industries because of the Smoot Hawley tariff and the rise in world tariff barriers. Suddenly, a coercive trade option (*Ostpolitik*) of the German steel industry became more attractive to chemicals and electricity. Furthermore, the depression induced declines in world oil prices in 1930–1 and the opening up of the vast east Texas oilfields in 1931 meant that Farben would face massive imports of cheap American oil. The only solution for Farben now was a strong protectionist government which would guarantee a market for its coal-based gasoline or a government which would actually buy the gasoline itself and consume it in large quantities for rearmament and military expansion.

In 1932, these developments caused the German chemical and electrical industries to switch from opposition to co-operation with the nationalistic and protectionist German steel and grain producers. The National People's Party was not popular enough to win the elections of 1932 so that first the steel industry and later the chemical and electrical industries shifted their financial lobbying support to a National Socialist Party under Hitler. In 1933, when the Nazis came to power, the foreign policy goals of the steel industry (rearmanent), the revision of the Versailles Treaty, high protection and the domination of Eastern Europe became the foreign policy of Germany under Hitler. QED. Protectionism helped Hitler ascend to power.

The tragedy of the commons (see Hardin, 1975) has an interesting implication for political economy. The government budget is similar to the common ground that was overgrazed by a city's cattle. The deterioration of the common stemmed from an absence of property rights. The same might be said of government budgets: the argument would suggest that excessive resources might be expended by lobbies over the budget because of an absence of rights. While this is an insightful theory, it does not square with the stylized fact that lobbying expenditures appear to be extremely small relative to the size of government budgets.

6.3 THE THEORY OF ENDOGENOUS PROTECTION

This section summarizes the work with which I am most familiar: Magee, Brock and Young's (1989) endogenous policy theory. It is a bridge between sections 6.2 and 6.4. Our theory can be used to explain endogenous authorship and even the structure of this chapter. First, some background. Wealth comes from two sources: production and predation. Production increases wealth while predation transfers wealth. Production is a co-operative effort in which direct actors may gain; predation is a non-co-operative effort in which the economic prey lose. In the words of parents, production is co-operative while predatory behaviour is selfish. Selfish individuals increase their welfare at the expense of good people.

Economic wealth can create political power and political power can create wealth. It is this mutual attraction between power and money that motivates redistributive activity. Endogenous policy theory attempts to explain how economies generate redistributive policies and the levels of lobbying resources which are expended as the well-organized work to exploit those who are not in lobbies. Theoretically, individuals and groups will devote resources to redistribution so long as the gains exceed the costs. Individuals will invest in both production and predation until the marginal returns from each are identical. At this point, an economic and redistributive equilibrium exists.

In an endogenous policy model, policies play the same role in politics that prices play in an economy: both are equilibrating variables which adjust until opposing redistributive forces are balanced. If, at this point, the textile lobby has a 20 per cent tariff while leather has only a 5 per cent tariff, then any attempt to increase either tariff will encounter greater opposition than support. These are the endogenous tariff levels for these industries.

The model used by Magee, Brock and Young to develop the results in the rest of this section is predominantly of the following sort: it is a $2 \times 2 \times 2 \times 2$ model with two goods, two factors, two lobbies and two political parties in which all display maximizing behaviour. The country is assumed to be a small, open advanced country which has two factors (capital and labour), two goods, two lobbies (one for capital and one for labour) and two parties (one for capital and one for labour). The country exports the capital-intensive good, which receives an export subsidy from the pro-capital party in exchange for campaign contributions from the capital lobby; the country imports the labour-intensive good, which receives protection from the pro-labour party in exchange for campaign contributions from the labour lobby. Goods and factor markets are perfectly competitive but influenced by the policies; lobbies channel resources to the parties to maximize the factor incomes of their memberships; parties choose levels of their policies to maximize their probabilities of election; and individual voters are rationally ignorant in accumulating insufficient information about the race, so that campaign contributions matter. The model is general but we typically use Cobb–Douglas production and utility functions and logit probability of election functions to get explicit values of the policies, the fractions of the factors devoted to lobbying and the probabilities of election of the political parties, and to perform comparative statics. Major work which we never plan to do is to generalize the functional forms. This work is best left to ambitious computable general equilibrium modellers.

There are at least four knotty welfare problems with endogenous policies: differential power, non-transparency, the waste-information trade-off and a new welfare impossibility theorem.

First, differential power questions raise difficult welfare when some of the actors are more powerful than others. One cannot add up the utils of all of the animals in the jungle to get aggregate welfare when the carnivores eat the herbivores, the herbivores eat the herbs, etc. When a lion eats a gazelle, does aggregate welfare go up or down? The lion is happier but the gazelle is not. While we might agree that the percentage decrement in gazelle welfare exceeds the increment to lion welfare, economists are not unanimous in condemning lion behaviour. There are redistributive food chains in the economy in which the protectionists prey on consumers, the doctors prey on patients, and taxpayers, and the lobbies, politicians and lawyers prey on everyone. Actually, the behaviour is technically parasitic rather than predatory, but 'prey' is a better term than 'parasitees'.

The differential power question is partially addressed in the literature on the economics of justice by Rawls (1971) and Nozick (1974). Simply put, Nozick believes that whatever you have at birth you can keep while Rawls believes that differential positive initial endowments are social goods which can be redistributed. I am not clear on whether they have the problem figured out. Nozick is clearly pro-lion while Rawls is pro-gazelle. I encourage readers who have the answer to this one to get their idea published and then call me, reversing the charges.

Second, consider the issue of non-transparency. By this we mean that in equilibrium, the redistributive effects of policies must not be obvious. Redistributive activity, like criminal behaviour, is most successful when undetected. On this subject, Justice Frankfurter said: 'There are two things which you do not want to see being made: laws and sausage.' Lobbies will not voluntarily disband because they would lose their gains from exploiting those who are not in lobbies. Thus, all welfare analysis of redistributive policies must accept the assumption that the policies being analysed are non-transparent to the exploitees, and hence probably economically inefficient.

Third, there is a waste-information trade-off. Lobbying is wasteful in a redistributive sense but the campaign contributions are used for advertising to elect parties and this has a value to voters because it provides information. Thus, welfare analysis needs to take both the negative waste and the positive information into account.

Fourth, with endogenous politics, there is a welfare impossibility theorem: it may be impossible to improve welfare. It is easy for economists to show that factor subsidies are superior to production subsidies which are superior to tariffs, etc. However, if that could be done, parties would already have done it. Since everyone, including economists, have their say when policies get selected, all of the efficiency considerations are built into the equilibrium values of the policies which are adopted. The welfare impossibility theorem grows out of Magee, Brock and Young's (1989) endogenous policy paradox, which states that there is no solution to the economic waste caused by competitive redistribution. Any change would put the system out of equilibrium. All of the power of all of the actors is fully revealed in the pre-existing political equilibrium. The thing which irks economists is that we just have very little political power.

Advanced countries have been coincidentally blessed by a congruence of the special interests who wrote the constitution and the general economic interest. If anything could be done, the welfare focus might be on constitution theory, particularly on how to get such a congruence of general and special interests. But remember that constitutions, too, are endogenous.

My current view is that the economic costs of lobbying and rent-seeking are just the transactions costs of running a democracy (Magee, 1990). Given this view, our job might be to analyse alternative constitutional set-ups to explain the variability in these transactions costs from, say, Switzerland to Bolivia. Lower lobbying costs are not necessarily good when there are offsetting information benefits. Utopian governments would maximize something akin to voter (consumers') surplus for their citizens. In general, transactions costs are to be reduced through efficiencies but with endogenous politics, they are a necessary cost of resolving redistributive conflict and cannot be just legislated away. For example, the legislature in Tennessee once repealed the law of gravity.

Too often, we forget to consider 'equilibrium' when thinking of government activities. We have tariffs and other puzzling policies precisely because they are politically efficient. In a competitive political system, policies will proliferate so long as they increase the probability of election of the party sponsoring the policy. In an efficient political system, there is no new policy which will increase the welfare (probability of election) of one of the parties. The list will include both welfare-increasing (Pareto) and welfare-reducing (redistributive) policies. Most intelligent people mistakenly think of governments as if they are never in equilibrium and that economically efficient policies are just around the corner.

Political parties are rational and politically efficient but the redistributive process, which is such an important part of political production functions, requires economic inefficiency. Bolivia has had more than 189 coups in the last 160 years. There are low barriers to entry or exit there: a perfectly competitive political market. In Japan, the same political party has been in power since 1945. This trade-off between economic and political efficiency requires more study. High levels of efficiency in political markets appear to retard efficiency in the economic markets and vice versa.

Magee, Brock and Young's (1989) simulations indicate that between 5 and 15 per cent of an economy's capital and labour is lost in rent-seeking in simulations across the many parameter values chosen for the model. This is an empirical upper limit since no free-riding was assumed within lobbies. However, the numbers fall in the range of empirical estimates discussed in section 6.2.

Should a protectionist lobby contribute to the party most likely to get elected or the one providing the highest protection? The theory says it should generally give to the one giving the highest protection. The worst thing that could happen is that the other party would get elected, so the protectionists should try to get the high-tariff party elected.

Should the protectionist lobby give to both parties or only one in a two-party race? The answer is 'only one'. This is the contribution specialization theorem. The protectionist lobby should give only to the protectionist party. See the reasoning in the previous paragraph. In the 1964, 1968 and 1972 Presidential races, 93, 86 and 92 per cent of the contributors respectively gave to one party.

Why does the median voter or Hotelling equilibrium not hold (in both political parties quote identical positions) with lobbies present? Neither lobby should contribute any funds in the Hotelling case since the policy after the election will be the same regardless of which party is elected. For this reason, the Hotelling case cannot be an equilibrium. Magee, Brock and Young present a tightly reasoned set of arguments that rule out lobbies influencing how high either party will set its tariff (if the lobbies could directly control the parties, free trade would always emerge in these static models, which is too counterfactual a result). The empirical implication of this point, as yet untested, is that parties across countries will not take identical positions on the issue of protection.

Stolper–Samuelson (SS) predict that capital and labour from a given industry will lobby on opposite sides of the free trade–protection issue while the Ricardo–Viner–Cairnes specific-factor model predicts that they will lobby on the same side. Magee (1980) used US data on industry lobbying for the Trade Reform Act of 1973 which indicated that for 19 out 21 industries, capital and labour lobbied on the same side (either for protection or for free trade), thus supporting a specific-factor approach. However, US trade acts only last for five years; because of this short time horizon, the results are necessarily biased in favour of the specific-factor model. In cross-section estimates of national tariff rates, Magee, Brock and Young (1989) found that their $2 \times 2 \times 2 \times 2$ model, using a long-run Heckscher–Ohlin–Samuelson (HOS) economic model, explained about 75 per cent of the variation in national tariff rates. The bottom line: specific-factor models are better at explaining short-run lobbying behaviour while long-run models are better at explaining cross-national levels of protection. For an economic reconciliation of short- and long-run models, see Mussa (1974). Magee and Choi (1991) apply vector autoregressive methods using data from 1900 to 1988 to test several international trade models. Among others, they find that special-interest tariffs are endogenous in three out of four tests and they find support for the SS theorem in one of two tests.

The book simulates the prisoner's dilemma approach to tariffs in their political–economic general equilibrium $2 \times 2 \times 2 \times 2$ set-up. Simulations indicated that the degenerate prisoner's dilemma equilibrium occurred about 40 per cent of the time. In these cases, both capital and labour were worse off lobbying than if neither lobbied. Both factors could not gain because tariffs reduce aggregate welfare in our assumed case of a small country. The prisoners' dilemma outcomes usually occurred when a country's capital–labour endowment ratio was about average, meaning that neither capital nor labour had a marked advantage in its economy relative to its trading partners. If a country had an extreme endowment ratio, then either capital or labour was able to dominate the other in politics and get even more from the political system with political lobbying than without, thereby avoiding the prisoner's dilemma. This occurred about 60 per cent of the time. In these cases the dominant factor exploits the other through the political system because it has more resources with which to lobby.

Magee, Brock and Young (1989) find a phenomenon called the compensation effect: whenever a factor's economic fortunes decline, it turns to politics for relief. An example is the effects of the decline in the US terms of manufacturing trade in the 1980s. Advances by the Japanese and other countries in cars, steel and textiles have reduced the world prices of US importables and thus increased the US terms of trade. Following the compensation principle, labour in importables increases its lobbying and receives more protection, particularly in senile industries. The pro-labour party (e.g. the Congressional Democrats) gains votes from having more lobbying money but loses because it must propose a higher tariff; the reverse pattern holds for the pro-capital Republicans. In the long run, all of the general equilibrium dirt settles, and the Democrats have fewer votes than before and the Republicans have more. To summarize: wages fall because of the initial decline in the terms of trade but there is a partial offset provided by the entire political process which cushions the blow.

One of the more unexpected results is the Magee–Young (1983) theorem that there are increasing returns to factor endowments: the more capital an economy has, the higher will be the returns to capital. Thus, if capital is already powerful in a country, politics makes it increasingly powerful through time. The intuition is that increased capital helps the pro-capital party get elected more often and when elected, it will provide a higher level of the policy which helps capital. Countries such as Brazil which are heavily endowed with capital will provide greater political protection to capital and this will lure in even more capital. The more capital advanced countries have, the better the legal systems appear to protect property rights: witness Germany and Japan. Since international capital will gravitate to countries where it is most protected, the result is political explanation for economic development. Data supports the theory's prediction of a bimodal distribution of world capital endowments: see Magee (1991).

Why has protection fallen generally since World War II in the USA and other developed countries? The answer is capital deepening. As capital has grown more rapidly, production labour has become a less important factor of production in the USA, its political influence has waned and, until recently, protection has declined. The number of US workers per unit of real capital today is about half what it was at the turn of the century. The pro-labour party is also suffering in Presidential races: US Democratic Presidential candidates have lost five out of the last seven elections. This is not driven by, but is consistent with, a story of increasing dominance by the abundant factor and the demise of the scarce factor. It illustrates endowment theory of protection.

The public furore over protectionism in the 1970s may be an example of the magnification paradox. The magnification paradox suggests that protection can fall while protectionist lobbying is rising. An increased magnification effect of product prices on factor prices causes both protectionist and pro-export forces to devote more economic resources to politics, but to come away with a lower equilibrium level of protection. Thus, the political noise level and the protection level can move in opposite directions. Magnification increases occur when the factor intensities of production in exportables and importables become more similar. There is anecdotal evidence that US factor intensities have become more similar in the last 40 years.

Magee's (1982) isoprotection curves can be drawn in the Phillips curve diagram and show combinations of unemployment and inflation which generate equal levels of equilibrium protection. Based on 1900–80 data, Magee, Brock and Young estimate the slope of these curves: every 1 percentage point increase in the US unemployment rate requires a 2 percentage point increase in the US inflation rate to keep the equilibrium level of protection constant. See also Magee and Young (1987).

Republican administrations generate greater protection while Democratic administrations generate freer trade. Republican presidents (such as Reagan) generate anti-labour macroeconomic policies which locate them on high isoprotection curves (high unemployment and low inflation); as a result, there is heavy protectionist pressures on Congress. Democratic administrations favour pro-labour policies such as low unemployment and high inflation. This pattern has definitely held in the post-war period for Republican presidents Eisenhower and Reagan with somewhat weaker results for Nixon and Ford. The reverse has been true for the macroeconomic and trade policies of Democratic presidents: Franklin Roosevelt, Kennedy, Johnson and Carter.

According to US tariff regressions, the three Presidential administrations in this century with the largest predicted increases in protection were all Republican Harding (with the Fordney–McCumber tariff, the largest increase of the century); Hoover (with Smoot–Hawley) and Reagan's first term. Reagan's first term had the third highest predicted increase in protection this century because of (1) an increase in the US manufacturing terms of trade index from 87 to 100; (2) a rise in the US unemployment rate from 6.4 to 8.5 per cent; and (3) a drop in the US inflation rate for producer prices from 9.7 per cent per annum to 4.2 per cent (all compared to the Carter administration). Historically, the Congress has been more protectionist than the Executive Branch. In the 1970s and 1980s, however, the Executive Branch has become increasingly protective of senile industries in its negotiation of voluntary export restraint (VER) agreements and in administrative protection (anti-dumping, etc.).

What are the upper limits on the proportion of resources which can be drawn out of economic activity and consumed in lobbying and political activity? Is there an economic black hole? One would expect theoretical limits on rent-seeking because of diminishing returns in production, consumption and voter responses (the marginal probability of election decreases with increases in resources and becomes more negative with increases in policies). With intermediate values of the degree of risk aversion, Magee, Brock and Young find an economic black hole: with high magnification, nearly 100 per cent of the economy can be devoted to lobbying in equilibrium. Thus, special-interest political activity can consume the entire economy. Empirical examples include wars and ghettos, in which redistributive activity is the only game in town.

The irony is that as the black hole is approached, the endogenous level of protection approaches zero. Both the lobbying ratios and the equilibrium policies are heavily driven by the magnification paradox. As the magnification parameter (the elasticity of factor rewards with respect to product prices) increases, the pay-off to lobbying increases and the tariff level required to facilitate a transfer decreases. Tariffs in countries with high magnification are more potent than those in countries with lower magnification. Magee (1990) labels the former Excedrin tariffs, because a smaller dose is needed, while the latter are aspirins. He estimates that the more potent Excedrin tariffs are more common in the advanced countries and elicit higher protectionist lobbying ratios there than the weaker aspirin tariffs in developing countries. The high levels of rent-seeking observed in developing countries may be explained by greater political competition, less informed voters, younger governments or different political production functions.

The book provides an empirical test of their endowment theory of tariffs across 58 countries, using data from the mid-1970s. They find, as predicted, that tariffs decrease with increases in a country's endowment of both physical capital and human capital. Second, there is evidence that skilled labour in all countries gains from less protection. This suggests a talent theory of comparative advantage. The less talented factors of production in every country compete with imports while the most talented compete on world markets through exports. This idea is explored further in Magee (1989). To date, the definitive empirical work on national comparative advantages is Leamer (1984). Third, an equation for the ratio of imports to GNP allowed a calculation of overprotection. They found that the most overprotected economies were

India, Turkey and Japan. Out of the 70 countries analysed, the analysis indicated that Japan was the third most heavily protected market in the world. This concludes the review of Magee, Brock and Young (1989).

6.4 RECENT WORK

This section is a non-exhaustive sampling of largely unpublished papers which have come across my desk, mostly from the period 1989–91. Important empirical evidence on protection is provided in an exhaustive study by Michaely, Papageorgiou and Choksi (1991). They provide the following stylized facts on the economics of protection and growth in developing countries from 1950 to 1985:

1 Severe trade restrictions significantly retard the subsequent growth of GDP.
2 Slow growth countries adopt trade liberalization to get out of the doldrums.
3 The stronger the liberalization of trade, the faster the subsequent GDP growth.
4 Large countries are less likely to pursue sustained trade liberalization.
5 Sustained liberalization is associated with political stability.
6 Sustained liberalization is associated with improved trade balances. The results are an impressive endorsement of free trade.

Tullock (1988) has posed an underdissipation puzzle on the question of rent-seeking: why is so little expended, relative to the benefits, on everything from protectionist lobbying to police protection? For example, in the USA less than 1/1000 of the value of the US budget appears to be spent on lobbying annually. On the tariff question, complete dissipation would involve lobbying expenditures equal to the entire area of producers surplus created by the tariff in the Corden diagram. This area is probably over $30 billion whereas the total amount of lobbying annually in the USA for the entire federal budget is less than $1 billion. Olson (1965) suggested that protectionist underdissipation is explained by free-riding by members of the protectionist lobby. Hillman and Riley (1989) show that asymmetric valuations of the object of the rent-seeking can lead to underdissipation. Ursprung (1989) finds that if the sought-after prize is a public good, then total rent-seeking will not exceed the average stake of an individual rent-seeker. Hillman (1989) gives the following sufficient conditions for complete dissipation: constant returns, symmetric information, risk-neutral contenders and identical valuation of the prize.

What is the relationship between rent-seeking and the size of government? Cowen, Glazer and McMillan (1989) find that rent-seeking which benefits public officials motivates them to increase the size of government. Although there are resources wasted in the pursuit of rents, there may be benefits if the government adopts beneficial projects that would not otherwise have been implemented. Coughlin, Mueller and Murrell (1990) argue that rent-seeking directed at increasing a group's public good expenditures increases the size of government, while rent-seeking directed at shifting the burden of taxes to other groups probably does not affect the size of government. Godek (1986) found that tariffs decrease with the share of government in GNP while quotas increase. He concludes from this that government activities are a substitute for tariffs but not for quotas.

It is difficult to measure rent-seeking directly. Laband (1990) estimates that the actual cost of transfer-seeking constitutes about half of US GNP in 1985 and argues that previous estimates of the costs of rent-seeking have substantially underestimated those costs. Choi and Magee (1991) simulate rent-seeking over trade policy in the USA between 1958 and 1987. They estimate no change in rent-seeking by capital over this period but a doubling of rent-seeking by American labour. Dougan (1991) spoofs the entire rent-seeking literature, arguing that rent-seeking probably exceeds total income in many countries including the USA. He says that a hereditary monarchy would be superior to all other forms of government. Magee (1990b) simulates the rent-seeking which would have been required to produce the actual tariffs observed in 21 countries. He found that the upper limit on rent-seeking over trade policy is only about 1–2 per cent of GNP and argues that the economic cost of rent-seeking is simply the transactions cost of running democracy.

A continuing puzzle is why VERs and inefficient policies are used to perform redistributions rather than more efficient ones. Since a tariff equals an equivalent consumption tax and production subsidy, the same redistribution benefits to producers or factors could be obtained by the production subsidy alone. This would avoid the social cost of the consumption deadweight loss and part of the voter antagonism. In fact, VERs and tariffs are counter-examples to the Wittman (1989) thesis that democracies are efficient.

There are several answers to why there are tariffs rather than production subsidies. One is that tariffs are easier to collect than other taxes and provide the major source of revenue for young countries. A second is Mayer and Riezman's (1990) distribution of tax revenue argument. In a progressive tax system, a person's tax share is higher than his income share. In this case, tariffs reduce the individual's direct tax burden while subsidies raise it. The subsidy is borne by a small group of upper-income people while the cost of the tariff, in terms of lost consumer surplus, is spread across the whole population. Thus, high-income individuals would favour tariffs over the more efficient production subsidy. Since we observe tariffs more than subsidies, the result appears to favour theoretically a special-interest over a median voter approach. A third argument for tariffs is Mayer and Riezman's (1990) large-country argument: through a terms of trade effect, all people whose income shares decline with more protection of the import industry prefer tariffs to subsidies. A fourth is Wilson's (1990) argument that constitutional limitations may force polities into inefficient forms of taxation. But there can be welfare gains if the politicians are also induced to reduce their provision of transfers. Thus, a switch from production subsidies to tariffs as the form of protection may reduce the level of excess burden and make both politicians better off. A fifth argument is Hillman's (1989) transparency argument and the optimal obfuscation argument in section 6.3 that governments prefer tariffs to subsidies because the welfare-reducing effects of tariffs are less transparent to individuals.

Coates (1990) notes that distorted trade policies are the cost that must be incurred for candidates to signal voters via campaign advertising. Voters accept a loss on tariffs but identify candidates closely aligned with their preferences on more important issues.

The contrast between median voter vs special-interest endogenous policy models has already been discussed. Congleton (1989) models these two approaches and shows how campaign contributions pull candidates away from the median voter positions. Thus, candidates face a trade-off between positions which maximize campaign funds and positions which would be immediately popular but garner smaller contributions. When prospective donors are distributed symmetrically about the median voter, any move by one candidate to attract funds from an interest group induces other interest groups to make reciprocal increases to the opposition. In this case, the optimal strategy for both candidates is to adopt the median voter's position. If financial support is not symmetrically distributed, candidates may be pulled away from each other's position and away from the median voter positions. Successful policy positions tend to be between the more forthcoming group's ideal point and the median voter initial position.

Crain, Tollison and Deaton (1990) develop some interesting analogies. They build on Stigler (1971) and argue that interest groups are analogous to firms and all interest groups are analogous to the industry. Political influence through lobbying can thus be analysed within a framework of the optimal scale and number of interest groups. They allow the entry and exit of interest groups in the interest group industry, as well as adjustments in the size of individual interest groups. Structural characteristics of the market for legislation and the costs of procuring influence have obvious parallels to firm costs. Legislatures are factor markets that furnish representation or influence over policy outcomes for political coalitions. Representation, or legislative influence, is a specialized input purchased by interest groups within the coalition industry. This characterization offers a straightforward way to examine scale adjustments within individual coalitions, as well as the number of coalitions in the industry. Changes in the price of influence are like changes in wages and they lead to larger or smaller coalitions and more or less coalitions. The empirical findings indicate that the predictions of the model hold up in explaining variations in the size of labour union coalitions as well as variations in the number of competing coalitions across states in the USA.

Crain (1990) has another analogy: committees are to legislatures what farm teams are to professional baseball organizations. The committee system is a filtering mechanism that identifies and sorts party members on the basis of conformity or loyalty to the party policy positions. Party members signal their loyalty to the leadership through their voting record, with more conformity leading to more influential committee assignments. This signal is constrained by the voting record being public to both voters and interest groups. The result is a bias in policy outcomes towards the preferences of the party leadership and away from constituent interests. Ditto for farm teams.

Why does agriculture have so much protection in the advanced countries? Balisacan and Roumasset (1987) provides a creative analysis. In the early stages of economic development, agricultural producers are typically large numbers of small subsistence farmers. This means that agriculturalists are disadvantaged in forming coalitions because of high organization (transportation and communication) costs. Urban consumers have high stakes in cheap-food agricultural policy because food constitutes a high proportion of their budgets. Industrialists want cheap food because this holds down subsistence wages. Thus, the balance of political power favours urban consumers and industrialists over farmers in low-income countries.

As countries become more advanced, manufacturing becomes more capital intensive and profits become less sensitive to wages and the price of food. The share of food in total consumer expenditures declines so that political pressure from urban consumers and industrialists also declines. With fewer and larger farmers, industry concentration increases and transportation and communication costs fall so that agricultural incomes are increasingly sensitive to price. With political sensitivity up and their coalition costs down, agriculturalists grow in political power relative to consumer groups and hence get greater protection from imports. QED.

What does the recent literature have to say about power? Hirshleifer (1989a) argues that power is the ability to achieve one's ends in the presence of rivals. He has contenders engaging in redistributive conflict and found that the poorer side tends to have a comparative advantage in conflictual activity. While the conflict process dissipates income in aggregate, it also brings about a more equal distribution of the remaining income. In contrast, under a hierarchical protocol, outcomes are more unequal with conflict. Skaperdas (1990) has a similar result: more powerful agents possess less valuable initial resources, the latter being valued by their marginal productivity.

Endogenous politics gives a new slant on the old question: does trade expansion increase or decrease income inequality? Fischer (1991), for example, found that trade expansion reduces equality in Latin America but does the reverse in South-East Asia. Choi (1991a, b) incorporates a political sector with two lobbies and two political parties into a Ricardo–Viner economy with two fixed and one mobile factor of production. This fixed factor model also displays the Magee–Young (1983) theorem of increasing returns to factor endowments. Thus, a higher endowment of capital leads to increased success of the pro-capital party, greater inequality and policies which are more favourable to capital owners. Balash (1992) found support for the view that pro-capital parties are more successful in countries with higher capital endowments.

Are democracies efficient? Some fraction of the time they are and the rest they are not. Without empirical evidence on these fractions, this is a quasi-religious question. Among others, efficient government advocates include Becker, Wittman, Glazer and McMillan, O'Flaherty and Coughlin. Becker (1983) argues that competition in political markets will drive the actors to minimize deadweight losses because policies that harm other groups induce opposition. Legislators or special-interest groups have an incentive to find policies that help a large majority of the citizenry. Wittman (1989) argues that democracy is economically efficient because US political parties, candidate reputations and government structure adapt to solve principal–agent problems. Glazer and McMillan (1990) view politics as a positive-sum instead of a zero-sum game, and allow legislators to choose between co-operative and non-co-operative strategies. They find equilibria in which all players choose co-operative policies, in contrast to policies which focus on redistribution.

O'Flaherty (1990) argues that democracy is efficient and popular because elections are not so much a way of reconciling conflicting preferences as of aggregating information. Democracy is a principal–agent problem with many principals. His most interesting argument is that majority rule uniquely minimizes the sum of type 1 errors (neglecting a deserving agent) and type 2 errors (rewarding an undeserving agent), and thus is a good way to aggregate information. For a survey of majority rule and election models, see Coughlin (1990). He suggests that important topics for future research are campaign contributions, violation of campaign promises, and the application of probabilistic voting models to questions of redistribution, taxes, shirking and the size of government.

Are democracies inefficient? Mills (1986) suggests a theft theory of democracy in which the government extracts surpluses from the predominantly agricultural population and uses such surpluses to benefit government insiders. Grossman and Suk Jae Noh (1990) extends this kleptocracy, in which the incumbent ruler's concern about his survival probability and time consistency constrain him to pursue benevolent policies. This is because the incumbent's survival probability and his collection of future tax revenues depend on current taxes, so that the equilibrium tax rate can be lower than at the peak of the Laffer curve.

Olson (1990) investigates rent-seeking by the government itself. He finds that an autocratic government which attempts to collect taxes for its own purposes will lower income and actually lower tax collections at each tax rate (compared to what would have happened under a democracy). The interesting part of this result is that the attempt of an autocracy to maximize the tax rate actually leads it to collect less in total taxes.

An interesting area of current and future research is endogenous explanations of real exchange rates. Work on the political business cycle would come close, but it needs a more monetary bent. For example, van der Ploeg (1989) argues that the incumbent political party chooses its exchange rate policy to maximize votes at the forthcoming election. Popularity at the polls depends on the government's track record on achieving high levels of output and real consumer wages. An appreciation of the exchange rate immediately cuts inflation, raises the value in domestic prices of net exports and therefore boosts real income and aggregate demand, but it takes time for the neo-classical substitution effects to build up and therefore in the long run net exports deteriorate and output falls. The consequences of this J-curve effect in the balance of trade for the political business cycle are as follows. Immediately upon entering office a government depreciates the exchange rate, which can be viewed as an investment in improving competitiveness, and thereafter gradually appreciates the exchange rate. A policy of real appreciation on election eve is sensible from a political point of view, because it cuts inflation, boosts real income and increases votes, while the undesirable effects on net exports, output and employment are typically felt later. Overvaluation of the exchange rate certainly gave short-term political support for Pinochet in Chile, Martinez de Hoz in Argentina and Thatcher in the UK. An alternative approach to the real exchange rate question is suggested by Havrilesky's (1988, 1989a, b) public choice model of monetary policy. He found a bias towards inflation because of the redistributive benefits to debtor groups from monetary surprises.

A useful analogy would be to expand the analysis of political efficiency using the traditional categories in industrial organization: conduct, structure and performance. A move in that direction is provided by Grier, Munger and Roberts (1992), who have a new slant on the Olson (1965) question of whether greater industry concentration retards or promotes political activity. They model the decision of firms on whether to establish political action committees, PACs. Their empirical results indicate that concentration both helps and hurts political activity, but over different ranges of concentration.

We consider here several political science issues: majorities, the judiciary, incumbency, seniority and constituent service. There is an old controversy between Stigler (1972) that large majorities are valuable versus Riker's (1962) view that a party should seek a minimum winning coalition. The question boils down to whether incumbents should collect large campaign chests and maximize the size of their votes or just go for 51 per cent.

Crain, Shughart and Tollison (1988) argue that the size of the majority is an important enforcement mechanism in political transactions. Without enforcement mechanisms, agreements between interest groups and legislators would be worthless. Interest groups are not likely to expend resources to secure the passage of legislation if laws are easily altered. The judicial branch acts as a third-party enforcer of agreements struck between legislatures and interest groups. This mechanism for enforcement is analogous to an explicit contract. Where explicit political contracts are inadequate or expensive, they examine the use of implicit or self-enforcing mechanisms. In contrast to third-party enforcement, implicit contracts are self-enforcing in that they rely on the on the threat of the termination of an interest group's wealth transfer to maintain the transactional relationship. The value of legislative control trades judicial independence against other relevant variables. Data across US states confirms the prediction: the more independent the judiciary, the less valuable are special-interest expenditures, and the smaller the majority held by the dominant party in the legislature.

McKelvey and Riezman (1992) ask why legislatures have seniority systems and why incumbent legislators tend to be re-elected by wide margins? The franking privilege, the specialized committee system, the norm of reciprocity, etc., are all ways that the Congress advances the re-election goals of its members. They build a theoretical model connecting the seniority system with the re-election goals of the legislators. They find that what drives incumbency is the recognition by voters that self-interested legislators with seniority will vote for a seniority system. If a sufficient number of the other legislators have seniority, then it is in the self-interest of a district to make sure that its legislator does also, since the legislature will undoubtedly impose a seniority system. If voters believe this, it becomes a self-fulfilling prophecy that the seniority system and an incumbency effect support each other in equilibrium.

Glazer and McMillan (1992) state that a legislator who devotes time and effort to drafting and promoting legislation which benefits others (as it must to win majority support) must inevitably spend less time campaigning, meeting with constituents and raising money. The latter indicate that the legislator's opportunity cost is not zero. Since all legislators who support a proposed policy benefit, then policy proposals have characteristics of a public good subject to the free-rider problem. Policy proposals have important opportunity costs in terms of a legislator's time, particularly forgone opportunities for constituency service.

Survey evidence by Cain, Ferejohn and Fiorina (1987, p. 39) indicates that one-quarter of the American public considers constituency service to be the most important role of their representatives. Johannes (1984, p. 188) also offers evidence that voters pressure congressmen to perform constituency service and provide district-oriented effort. He cites a CBS–*New York Times* poll which found that more people believe it important for a congressman to help people in their district who have a problem with the government than to work in Congress on bills of national interest. For a model of the trade-off between policy-induced campaign contributions and service-induced contributions, see Morton and Cameron (1991).

Denzau and Munger (1986) show that in contributing to members of legislatures, interest groups will seek out legislators whose voters are indifferent to the policy that the interest group seeks. Thus, disorganized voters do have their preferences over policies represented.

Roberts (1990) showed that the unexpected control of the US Senate by the Republican Party after the 1980 election was a good candidate for an event study. He found a systematic relationship between PAC contribution patterns and the stock market reaction to the 1980 Senate elections. Munger (1989a) used two-digit SIC industry classifications to show that committee assignments dictated the pattern of PAC contributions. Cox and Munger (1989) found that close elections stimulate more campaign contributions and these contributions increase voter turn-out. Promising work is under way by Starks at Texas applying the event-study methodology to international trade policies.

For an industry breakdown on major contributors in the 1988 Presidential election in the USA see Ferguson (1989). He found that both the investment banking and the computer industry were heavy contributors to both Bush and Dukakis. He found that large oil companies and utilities were also major contributors to Bush while media firms and real estate were major contributors to Dukkais. In other work, he argues that US multinational banks who were constrained by Iraq from recycling Kuwaiti petrodollars may have been bigger players in Bush's strategy to squash Saddam Hussein than the oil companies themselves.

What about the negative redistributive effects of lawyers? Laband and Sophocleus (1988) present a time-series regression of US GNP on the number of lawyers and bankers in the country. Their estimates imply that rent-seeking has reduced aggregate income by 45 per cent. Magee (1992, 1994) incorporates lawyers into a Barro endogenous growth equation for 54 countries to determine the optimal number of lawyers. He finds that the Europeans and most Far East countries have less than the optimal number while the USA has 40 per cent too many. Excessive numbers of lawyers create negative externalities just like pollution: the social cost is not the value of the chemicals dumped but the total harm which they cause. He found that the negative economic impact is over five times the rent-seeking expenditures themselves: there is less than $100 billion spent annually on all legal services in the USA but the loss to the economy of legal predation exceeds $500 billion. This translates into an annual GNP loss of about $1 million for every new American lawyer. These estimates are around 10 per cent of US GNP and are smaller than Laband's. For every 1000 white-collar workers, the USA has 38 lawyers, while Germany and Japan are near the optimum of 23.

On direct versus representative democracies, Lindbeck and Weibull (1989) find non-convergence (i.e. two parties would choose different platforms) under a representative democracy since there are personal dimensions to candidates while they obtain convergence under direct democracies (i.e. voting occurs only on the policies themselves).

Weck-Hannemann (1990b) has an interesting paper on protectionism in a direct democracy. He investigates two referenda in Switzerland on the issue of protection. One of them passed and one did not. Thus, even when citizens can decide directly on trade barriers, tariffs can still emerge. In Switzerland, he found public bureaucrats supporting tariffs over subsidies because they reduced the budget constraint for public employees. In addition, bureaucrats manipulated the agenda-setting process by combining a popular issue with protection. On the other vote the citizens of Switzerland showed some sophistication in their rejection of protection of agricultural products in 1986 because of a perceived excess supply of agricultural products.

Voluntary export restraints (VERs) are the biggest innovation in protectionist policy since World War II. They are a quantitative restriction on exports from an exporting to an importing country and allow the exporting country to capture all of the price increase caused by the restriction. Ethier (1991b) notes that over one-third of Japan's exports of manufactures to other industrial countries are subject to VERs. Because of this, the Europeans had to rethink the gains from trade in their dealings with the Japanese in their preparation for EC-1992. Trade with the Japanese brings the usual trade gains but a terms of trade loss and the loss of billions in tariff-equivalent revenue. For a good theoretical explanation of this process, see Hillman and Ursprung (1988). Das (1990) found that variables which increase the likelihood of protection due to increased lobbying by domestic firms may also increase foreign lobbying against protection. It is possible that the total level of protection may, in fact, fall. VERs have also expanded both because of increased foreign lobbying and because they are opaque to voters. For steel and cars, it is hard to imagine that these American industries could have come up with such ingenious VERs without help from the Japanese.

Up until the 1970s, international trade provided a constraint on market power by domestic labour unions and oligopolistic industries. However, the VER is reversing that result. The VER pulls foreign exporters into the lobbying process and they assist import-competing interests in obtaining protection. As Godek (1989) notes, VERs subsidize both foreign producers and domestic producers. Since both domestic and foreign lobbying resources are brought to bear for the VER, it has a higher tariff equivalent than the domestic lobby could obtain by itself.

Ethier (1991b) is correct that the Japanese were a major player in the VER innovation: they can produce policies even more efficiently than cars. Their redistributive intent is clear. The VER achieves higher levels of protection; the transfer of tariff equivalent revenue to Japanese exporters; there is reduced heat on American politicians from free traders; Japanese exporters use the VER to freeze out smaller rival firms and potential entrants; and Japanese wages fall in the short run relative to profits. The concern among American academics is that Japanese VERs illustrate economic brinksmanship: the Japanese civil service may be smart but not wise. Voters eventually understood VERs so that the Japanese may become scapegoats in a major economic downturn at the hands of American protectionists.

The welfare costs of these quantitative restrictions are high. Tarr (1989) used a computable general equilibrium (CGE) model to estimate the US welfare effects of the three most important VERs. He found that they have the following US tariff equivalents:

Textiles and apparel	40 per cent
Cars	23 per cent
Steel	7 per cent

The loss to US consumers he estimated at $21 billion, $14 billion of which is a direct transfer to foreign exporter profitability and a loss of US government revenue. These welfare losses are the same as those of a 25 per cent tariff on all US imports. US tariffs have not been that high since the 1930s; they were only 10.3 per cent in 1946. For an analysis of trade policy in the 1980s see Deardorff (1989). He found that the Reagan administration did not live up to its ideological free-trade rhetoric, but as critics claimed, was the most protectionist administration since Herbert Hoover.

Ethier (1991b) shows how VERs have become a prominent form of protection in the advanced countries during the 1970s and 1980s. Over 100 agreements now manage almost 10 per cent of world trade, including much of the world's trade in textiles and apparel. He analyses how VERs transfer tariff equivalent revenue to the exporting country. Ethier (1991a) says that VERs are the most prominent means by which national governments aid ageing industries suffering from import competition. An interesting aspect of any implicit social contract is that it is uncertain. He found that the circumstances which will result in an industry getting a VER are usually unclear. For a detailed study of the textile trade and the multi-fibre arrangement see Hamilton (1990b).

Interesting work has been done using financial event studies to quantify the wealth effects of American protection. Lenway, Rehbein and Starks (1990) found that protectionist American trigger price mechanisms introduced in 1977 provided positive cumulative abnormal stock returns to American firms of 2.6 percentage points after 12 days. The new steel VER introduced in 1982 yielded positive returns of 0.3 percentage points. Both results understate the true effects to the extent that the market anticipated the events. Rehbein and Starks (1991) found zero to negative effects on Japanese steel firms when American firms filed anti-dumping claims against them and negative effects of Reagan's new steel VER proposed in 1984. They verify that the negative effects were bigger for small Japanese firms, indicating that large Japanese firms use VERs to thwart smaller competitors.

The increased use of VERs over tariffs on international trade has allowed supplying nations to capture the quota rents through higher prices for their exports. A solution for this is for importing countries to auction import quotas. Since the government has limited information, quota auctions reveal the size of the protective effect of a quota and an open auction yields more revenue than either a discriminating or a uniform price auction. Since more information is conveyed in an open auction winner's curse discounting is lower.

Dinopoulos and Kreinin (1991) shows that the US VER on machine tools negotiated with Japan and Taiwan in 1986 had the usual economic effects: the import share from the restricted sources declined with some increase from the UK, a non-restricted source; prices rose; and rents were transferred to the supplying countries. The only surprise was an absence of quality upgrading. De Melo and Winters (1990) find that a VER diverts some of the exporting country's trade to other markets. They call this 'domino diversion' after Hamilton's 'domino effect', in which the fear of such diversion leads to the spread of protectionism. In addition, there is a decline in the demand for all factors, but particularly the intensive factor in the exporting industry.

On the subject of quantitative restrictions generally, Godek (1989) notes that non-tariff barriers cover between 30 and 50 per cent of world trade. In an earlier paper, Godek (1985) provides an interesting explanation for the presence of quotas and other quantitative restrictions. In an examination of approximately 300 US industries, he found that the ratio of quantitative restrictions increases as total protection increases. He concludes that quantitative restrictions are used to compensate foreigners and include them in the redistributive process. For a theoretical examination of the welfare effects of non-tariff barriers see Herberg (1988).

Greenaway (1989) found differences between volume and ratio VERs, the most important of which is that price fluctuations are greater under the former. Ennew, Greenaway and Reed (1990) showed that VERs and other quantitative restrictions in the UK have so changed the structure of British protection that now most nominal tariffs exceed effective tariffs. Greenaway's (1988) earlier paper showed that 40 per cent of British industries have negative effective rates of protection.

Cohen and Glazer (1990) investigate the time-inconsistency problem. In their view, recent research demonstrates that much of public policy can be fruitfully analysed as attempts to commit future governments. On this subject, see Kydland and Prescott (1977), who show that current decisions of economic agents depend on their expectations of future policies. The Reagan administration is alleged to have run budget deficits so as to reduce the ability of Democratic legislators or presidents to increase domestic spending in the future.

Staiger and Tabellini (1987) show that time-consistent equilibrium tariffs may dominate production subsidies. Thus, time consistency can have unexpected effects on the usual ordering of subsidies as superior to tariffs. Stahl and Turunen-Red (1993) find that in several finitely repeated tariff games free-trade agreements are likely to emerge. However, when political uncertainty is introduced, then free trade is much harder to sustain in a dynamic tariff game. Problems arise when voters believe that were the decision postponed, the future choice would not be identical to the one these voters would prefer. A person who votes to postpone the decision on whether to build a project does not commit government to any particular policy in future periods. But forcing government to build a project immediately can constrain government in future periods to provide the services generated by the project. The asymmetry between immediate construction of a project and deferring the decision leads to a bias in favour of immediate construction. Grossman and Suk Jae Noh (1990) are more optimistic on the ability of governments to solve the problem of time inconsistency with respect to tax rates. Because the ruler exercises sovereign power, an announcement about future tax rates can be credible only if expectations or tax announcements are time consistent. That is, only if the ruler will not be able to do better in the future than to validate this expectation or announcement. In particular, the time-consistency requirement restricts the equilibrium tax rate to be sufficiently high for the ruler to resist the temptation to set the actual tax rate higher than this expected rate. Their work suggests that equilibrium tax policies will be relatively benevolent because such a policy is both necessary and sufficient for a high survival probability.

World trade is evolving towards regional superblocs: Europe, the Americas and possibly the Far East. In this writer's opinion, a political entity as complicated as EC-1992 will require so much compromise that protectionism against outsiders might be the only glue which would hold it together. Willy de Clerq, when Commissioner for Foreign Relations in the European Commission, stated: 'We are not building a Single Market in order to turn it over to hungry foreigners' (Hamilton, 1990a). Statements like this sparked off fears that the 'new' Europe engaged in the 1992 programme will become a 'fortress Europe'. Economists are more optimistic. Kreinin (1991) feels that the 1992 initiative presents a window of opportunity for the EC to play an influential role in strengthening GATT.

For an application of seven different models of protection in the EC see Hamilton (1989). EC-1992 can be expected to have some of the usual gains from increased specialization, and possibly income convergences. Rassekh (1990) has found past convergence of GNP per capita among OECD countries (between 1950 and 1985). Convergence is usually explained by flows of technology from the high-income countries to the low-income countries. However, he found that countries with initially low incomes increased their trade openness faster than high-income economies. Apparently, international trade provided additional convergence by allocating resources more efficiently. Whether this would continue following EC-1992 remains to be seen.

The political economy of strategic trade policy is a popular and growing area for future study. Corden (1990) states that there are theories in the 'new international economics' which allow for oligopoly and strategic interactions among firms, and which introduces the idea that government policies, such as export subsidies or tariffs, may shift profits from a foreign firm to its domestic competitor, and that this may yield a national gain, at least provided the foreign government does not retaliate. Hence these theories have normative implications, with policy relevance. This profit-shifting concept originated with a series of papers by Brander and Spencer (1985).

The idea is that economies of scale could explain how Japanese protection of its domestic market would afford an advantage to its firms in foreign markets, i.e. industry protection should be positively correlated with industry export success. However, Dick (1993) tests and rejects this implication of the strategic trade policy model using data for over 200 four-digit traded US products: he found that high import protection is associated with lower shares of that product in world export markets. He provides alternative explanations, including political economy arguments.

Lindbeck (1989) notes that the moves towards industrial policies are merely veiled neo-protectionism and neo-mercantilism. He found that most of them have failed, both in countries with competent and incompetent regimes. If they are not the tools of special interests initially, they eventually become so.

On the question of country size, Kennan and Riezman (1988) argue that large countries gain from tariff wars, despite retaliation. They provide a potential explanation for the persistence of trade restrictions and the difficulty of obtaining free trade. McMillan (1990) has analysed section 301 of the 1974 Trade Act, which enables the President to retaliate against foreign countries' trade-restricting policies that reduce US exports.

Ray (1989) found that the pattern of protection in manufacturing in the USA has been consistent throughout most of the post-war period. In terms of commodity characteristics, US protection tends to be associated with consumer products, processed agricultural products and textiles. There is no evidence to suggest that those industries are likely to lose favour any time soon. Ray (1990) found that intra-industry trade contributes to the current bias in US protection against manufactured exports from developing countries. Interestingly, he found no evidence that US protection in manufacturing is associated with concentrated industries in which quasi-rents are substantial.

Lindbeck (1990) discusses vertical redistribution through the tax system in Sweden. He noted that total tax revenues were over 50 per cent of GNP and marginal tax rates were about 75 per cent for most income earners. While these high tax rates generate negative labour supply consequences, they are largely offset by a public sector provision of services to households. This effect is reflected in the high labour force participation rates of married women. For a paper on the economics of both horizontal and vertical redistributions, see Kristov, Lindert and McClelland (1992).

Hungerford (1990) finds that the addition of uncertainty and asymmetric information into a tariff game does not necessarily lead to non-co-operative (tariff-type) behaviour. However, the equilibrium strategy has the undesirable property of having retaliatory periods when neither country has defected. Cassing, McKeown and Ochs (1986) explain the countercyclical nature of trade barriers. They find that trade restrictions protect old regions as well as old industries. Panagariya and Rodrik (1991) use a political economy model to show that a uniform tariff rule would minimize the welfare costs of endogenously determined tariffs. Bennett and DiLorenzo (1984) show how unions and their employers obtain redistribution through protectionism. Frey and Gygi (1989) formulate efficiency conditions for international organizations. Moser (1988) found that GATT reduced tariffs and made them less dependent on cyclical pressures; however, GATT increased non-tariff protection. For an analysis of the effects of an underground economy, see the econometric study of Austria by Schneider, Hofreither and Neck (1988).

Gerard and Victoria Curzon (1989) have argued that the GATT system, as originally conceived, is unworkable because the rise of bilateralism has caused GATT to degenerate into sectorally managed trade.

6.5 CONCLUSIONS

Welfare implications? When policies are endogenous there are none. This would be like asking gazelles how they could increase national income in a lion–gazelle economy. See section 6.3.

NOTE

The author is indebted to Greg Hallman and Amy Jacoby for assistance in the preparation of this chapter.

REFERENCES

Anderson, Kym 1980: The political market for government assistance to Australian manufacturing industries. *Economic Record*, 56, 132–45.

Anderson, Kym 1989: Korea: a case of agricultural protection. *Food Price Policy in Asia*, 419, 109–53.

Aranson, Peter H. and Ordeshook, Peter C. 1981: Regulation, redistribution and public choice. *Public Choice*, 37, 69–100.

Axelrod, Robert 1980a: Effective choice in the prisoner's dilemma. *Journal of Conflict Resolution*, 24, 3–25.

Axelrod, Robert 1980b: More effective choice in the prisoner's dilemma. *Journal of Conflict Resolution*, 24, 379–403.

Balash, Peter C. 1992: *The Effects of Relative Factor Endowments Upon Economic Voting and Tariffs*. PhD Dissertation in Economics, University of Texas at Austin.

Baldwin, Robert E. 1976: *The Political Economy of US Postwar Trade Policy*. Bulletin no. 4, Centre for the Study of Financial Institutions, Graduate School of Business Administration, New York University.

Baldwin, Robert E. 1978: The economics of the GATT. In Peter Oppenheimer (ed.), *Issues in International Economics*, Stocksfield, England: Oriel Press, 82–93.

Baldwin, Robert E. 1982a: The inefficacy of trade policy. *Essays in International Finance*, 150, 1–26.

Baldwin, Robert E. 1982b: The political economy of protectionism. In Jagdish N. Bhagwati (ed.), *Import Competition and Response*, Chicago: University of Chicago Press, 263–86.

Baldwin, Robert E. 1985: Trade policies under the Reagan administration. University of Wisconsin, National Bureau of Economic Research, 10–33.

Baldwin, Robert E. 1986: *The Political Economy of U.S. Import Policy*. Cambridge, Mass.: MIT Press.

Baldwin, Robert E. (ed.), 1988: *Trade Policy Issues and Empirical Analysis*. Chicago: University of Chicago Press.

Balisacan, Arsenio M. and Roumasset, James A. 1987: Public choice of economic policy: the growth of agricultural protection. *Weltwirtschaftliches Archiv Review of World Economics*, 123, 232–48.

Ball, D. S. 1967: United States effective tariffs and labor's share. *Journal of Political Economy*, 75, 183–7.

Baron, D. P. 1983: *The Export–Import Bank*. New York: Academic Press.

Bauer, R. A., de Sola Pool Ithiel, and Dexter, Lewis A. 1963: *American Business and Public Policy: the politics of foreign trade*. New York: Atherton Press.

Becker, Gary 1983: A theory of competition among pressure groups for political influence. *Quarterly Journal of Economics*, 98, 371–400.

Bennett, James T. and DiLorenzo, Thomas J. 1984: Unions, politics, and protectionism. *Journal of Labor Research*, 5, 301–7.

Bhagwati, Jagdish N. 1980: Lobbying and welfare. *Journal of Public Economics*, 14, 355–63.

Bhagwati, Jagdish N. 1982: Directly unproductive, profit-seeking DUP activities. *Journal of Political Economy*, 90, 988–1002.

Brander, J. and Spencer, B. 1985: Export subsidies and international market share rivalry. *Journal of International Economics*, 18, 83–100.

Brittan, Samuel 1975: The economic contradictions of democracy. *British Journal of Political Science*, 5, 1.

Brock, William A. and Magee, Stephen P. 1975: The economics of pork-barrel politics. Report 7511, Center for Mathematical Studies in Business and Economics, University of Chicago.

Brock, William A. and Magee, Stephen P. 1978: The economics of special-interest politics: the case of the tariff. *American Economic Review*, 68, 246–50.

Brock, William A. and Magee, Stephen P. 1980: Tariff formation in a democracy. In John Black and Brian Hindley (eds), *Current Issues in Commercial Policy and Diplomacy*, New York: St Martin's Press, 1–9.

Buchanan, James M. 1975: *The Limits of Liberty: between anarchy and leviathan*. Chicago: University of Chicago Press.

Cain, B. E., Ferejohn, J. and Fiorina, M. 1987: *The Personal Vote, Constituency Service, and Electoral Independence*. Cambridge, Mass.: Harvard UP.

Cassing, J. H., McKeown, T. and Ochs, J. 1986: Regional demands for protection: an empirical analysis of the tariff cycle. Presented at the Conference on the Political Economy of Trade Policy, NBER.

Caves, Richard E. 1976: Economic models of political choice: Canada's tariff structure. *Canadian Journal of Economics*, 9, 278–300.

Cheh, J. H. 1974: United States concessions in the Kennedy Round and short-run labor adjustment costs. *Journal of International Economics*, 4, 323–40.

Choi, Nakgyoon 1991a: Essays in international trade: endogenous tariff theory. Unpublished Ph.D. dissertation, University of Texas at Austin.

Choi, Nakgyoon 1991b: A Ricardo–Viner model of endogenous tariffs. Mimeo, University of Texas at Austin.

Choi, Nakgyoon and Magee, Stephen P. 1991: Endogenous tariff estimates of rent seeking in the U.S.: 1958–1987. Mimeo, University of Texas at Austin.

Coates, Daniel Eric 1990: Essays on international trade policy. Ph.D. dissertation, Columbia University.

Cohen, Linda and Glazer, Amihai 1990: Commitment problems bias public policy. Mimeo, University of California at Irvine.

Congleton, Roger D. 1989: Campaign finances and political platforms: the economics of political controversy. *Public Choice*, 62, 101–18.

Constantopoulos, M. 1974: Labour protection in Western Europe. *European Economic Review*, 5, 313–28.

Conybeare, John A. C. 1983: Tariff protection in developed and developing countries: a cross-sectional and longitudinal analysis. *International Organization*, 37, 441–67.

Corden, W. Max 1957: The calculation of the cost of protection. *Economic Record*, 33, 29–51.

Corden, W. Max 1974: *Trade Policy and Economic Welfare*. Oxford: Oxford University Press.

Corden, W. Max 1984: Booming sector and Dutch disease economics: survey and consolidation. *Oxford Economic Papers*, 36, 359–88.

Corden, W. Max 1990: Strategic trade policy. How new? How sensible? Working Paper Series 396, The World Bank.

Coughlin, Peter J. 1990: Majority rule and election models. Mimeo, University of Maryland. Forthcoming, *Journal of Economic Surveys*.

Coughlin, Peter J., Mueller, Dennis C. and Murrell, Peter 1990: Electoral politics, interest groups, and the size of government. Mimeo, Department of Economics, University of Maryland.

Cowen Tyler, Glazer, Amihai, and McMillan, Henry 1989: Rent-seeking promotes the provision of public goods. Mimeo, University of California, Irvine.

Cox, Gary W. and Munger, Michael C. 1989: Closeness, expenditures, and turnout in the 1982 U.S. House elections. *American Political Science Review*, 83, 223–7.

Crain, W. Mark 1990: Legislative committees: a filtering theory. Mimeo, Fairfax, Va. Forthcoming in *Predicting Politics*.

Crain, W. Mark, Shughart, William F. II and Tollison, Robert D. 1988: Legislative majorities as nonsalvageable assets. *Southern Economic Journal*, 55, 303–14.

Crain, W. Mark, Tollison, Robert D. and Deaton, Thomas H. 1990: The price of influence in an interest-group economy. Mimeo, Center for Study of Public Choice, George Mason University.

Curzon, Gerard and Curzon, Victoria 1989: Non-discrimination and the rise of 'material' reciprocity. *The World Economy*, 12, 481–500.

Das, Satya P. 1990: Foreign lobbying and the political economy of protection. *Japan and the World Economy Journal*, May–June.

Deardorff, Alan V. 1989: Trade policy of the Reagan years. Mimeo, The University of Michigan.

Deardorff, Alan V. and Stern, Robert M. (eds) 1987: Current issues in trade policy: an overview. In *U.S. Trade Policies in a Changing World Economy*, Cambridge, Mass.: MIT Press, 15–68.

De Melo, Jaime and Winters, L. Alan 1990: Do exporters gain from VERs? Centre for Economic Policy Research, Discussion Paper 383.

Denzau, Arthur T. and Munger, Michael C. 1986: Legislators and interest groups: how unorganized interest get represented. *American Political Science Review*, 80, 89–106.

Dick, Andrew 1993: Does import protection act as export promotion?: Evidence from the United States. *American Economic Review*, 83: September.

Dinopoulos, Elias and Kreinin, Mordechaie E. 1991: The U.S. VER on machine tools: causes and effects. *Empirical Studies of Commercial Policy*. Chicago: University of Chicago Press.

Dornbusch, Rudiger and Frankel, Jeffrey A. 1987: Macroeconomics and protection. In Robert M. Stern (ed.), *U.S. Trade Policies in a Changing World Economy*, Cambridge, Mass.: MIT Press, 77–130.

Dougan, William R. 1991: The cost of rent seeking: is GNP negative? *Journal of Political Economy*, 99, 660–4.

Downs, Anthony 1957: *An Economic Theory of Democracy*. New York: Harper & Row.

Ennew, Christine, Greenaway, David and Reed, Geoffrey 1990: Further evidence of effective tariffs and effective protection in the U.K. *Oxford Bulletin of Economics and Statistics*, 100, 226.

Ethier, Wilfred J. 1991a: Voluntary export restraints. In Takayama, Ohyama and Ohta (eds), *Trade, Policy and International Adjustments*, San Diego: Academic Press, 3–18.

Ethier, Wilfred J. 1991b: The economics and political economy of managed trade. In Arye Hillman (ed.), *Markets and Politicians*, Boston: Kluwer Academic Press, 283–306.

Feenstra, Robert C. and Bhagwati, Jagdish N. 1982: Tariff seeking and the efficient tariff. In Jagdish N. Bhagwati (ed.), *Import Competition and Response*, Chicago: University of Chicago Press, 245–58.

Feenstra, Robert C., Lewis, Tracy R. and McMillan, John 1990: Designing policies to open trade. Working Paper WPS 3258, *National Bureau of Economic Research*, Feb.

Ferguson, Thomas 1989: By invitation only: party competition and industrial structure in the 1988 election. *Socialist Review*, 19, 73–103.

Fieleke, Norman S. 1976: The tariff structure for manufacturing industries in the United States: a test of some traditional explanations. *Columbia Journal of World Business*, 11, 98–104.

Findlay, Ronald J. and Wellisz, Stanislaw 1982: Endogenous tariffs, the political economy of trade restrictions and welfare. In Jagdish N. Bhagwati (ed.), *Import Competition and Response*, Chicago: University of Chicago Press, 223–38.

Fischer, Ronald 1991: Income distribution and the dynamics fixed factors model; theory and evidence. Mimeo, University of Virginia.

Frey, Bruno S. and Gygi, Beat 1990: The political economy of international organizations. *Aussenwirtschaft*, 45(3).

Frey, Bruno S., Pommerehne, Werner W., Schneider, Friedrich and Gilbert, Guy 1984: Consensus and dissension among economists: an empirical inquiry. *American Economic Review*, 74, 986–94.

Glazer, Amihai and McMillan, Henry 1990: Optimal coalition size when making proposals is costly. *Social Choice and Welfare*, 7: 4, 369–80.

Glazer, Amihai and McMillan, Henry 1992: Amend the old or address the new: broad-based legislation when proposing policies is costly. *Public Choice*, 74: 43–58.

Godek, Paul E. 1985: Industry structure and redistribution through trade restrictions. *Journal of Law and Economics*, 28, 687–703.

Godek, Paul E. 1986: The politically optimal tariff: levels of trade restrictions across developed countries. *Economic Inquiry*, 24, 587–93.

Godek, Paul E. 1989: Foreign firm profits and the political economy of international trade quotas. Mimeo, Economist Incorporated.

Gourevitch, Peter Alexis 1977: International trade, domestic coalitions and liberty: comparative responses to the crisis of 1873–1896. *Journal of Interdisciplinary History*, 8, 281–313.

Greenaway, David 1988: Effective tariff protection in the United Kingdom. *Oxford Bulletin of Economics and Statistics*, 50, 313–25.

Greenaway, David 1989: The non-equivalence restrictions: a further example. *Journal of Economic Studies*, 16, 61–5.

Grier, Kevin B., Munger, Michael C. and Roberts, Brian E. 1992: The industrial organization of corporate political participation. *Southern Economic Journal*, 57: 3, 727–38.

Grossman, Herschel I. and Noh, Suk Jae 1990: A theory of kleptocracy with probabilistic survival and reputation. *Economics and Politics*, 2, 157–71.

Hamilton Bob, Mohammad, Sharif and Whalley, John 1984: Rent seeking and the North–South terms of trade. Centre for the Study of International Economic Relations, Working Paper no. 8426C, Department of Economics, University of Western Ontario.

Hamilton, Carl B. 1989: The political economy of transient 'new' protectionism. *Review of World Economics*, 125, 522–46.

Hamilton, Carl B. 1990a: European Community external protection and 1992: voluntary export restraints applied to Pacific Asia. Seminar Paper no. 478, Institute for International Economic Studies, Stockholm University, September.

Hamilton, Carl B. (ed.) 1990b: *Textiles Trade and the Developing Countries: eliminating the multi-fibre arrangement in the 1990s*. Washington, DC. The International Bank for Reconstruction and Development – The World Bank.

Hardin, G. 1975: The tragedy of the commons. In D. Ackerman (ed.), *Economic Foundations of Property Law*, Boston: Little Brown.

Hardin, Russell 1971: Collective action as an agreeable *n*-prisoners' dilemma. *Behaviorial Science*, 16(5), 472–81.

Havrilesky, Thomas 1988: Electoral cycles in economic policy. *Challenge*, 31, 14–21.

Havrilesky, Thomas 1989a: A public choice perspective on the cycle in monetary regimes. *Cato Journal*.

Havrilesky, Thomas 1989b: Distributive conflict and monetary policy. *Contemporary Policy Issues*, 7, 50–61.

Havrilesky, Thomas 1990: A public choice perspective on the cycle in monetary regimes. *Cato Journal*, 9, 3, 709–18.

Helleiner, Gerald K. 1977: The political economy of Canada's tariff structure: an alternative model. *Canadian Journal of Economics*, 10, 318–36.

Helpman, Elhanan, and Krugman, Paul R. 1985: *Market Structure and Foreign Trade*. Cambridge, Mass.: MIT Press.

Herberg, Horst 1988: Welfare effects of non-tariff barriers for capital and labour: a general equilibrium analysis. Diskussionbeiträge aus dem Institut für Theoretische Volkswirtschaftslehre der Universität Kiel, Discussion Paper no. 79/88.

Hillman, Arye L. 1982: Declining industries and political-support protectionist motives. *American Economic Review*, 72, 1180–7.

Hillman, Arye 1989: *The Political Economy of Protection*. New York: Harwood Academic.

Hillman, Arye and Riley, J. G. 1989: Politically contested rents and transfers. *Economics and Politics*, 1, 17–40.

Hillman, Arye, and Ursprung, Heinrich 1988: Domestic politics, foreign interests and international trade policy. *American Economic Review*, 78, 729–45.

Hirschman, Albert O. 1970: *Exit, Voice and Loyalty*. Cambridge, Mass.: Harvard University Press.

Hirshleifer, Jack 1989a: The dimension of power as illustrated in a steady-state model of conflict. Mimeo, UCLA.

Hirshleifer, Jack 1989b: Conflict and rent-seeking success functions: ratio vs difference models of relative success. *Public Choice*, 63, 101–12.

Hungerford, Thomas L., 1990: GATT: a cooperative equilibrium in a noncooperative trading regime? Research Seminar in International Economics, Department of Economics, The University of Michigan, Seminar Discussion Paper no. 262, May.

Inman, R. P. 1985: Markets, government and the new political economy. In Alan Auerbach and Martin Feldstein, *Handbook of Public Economics*, sections I and II, Amsterdam: North-Holland, 647–777.

Johannes, John R. (ed.) 1984: *To Serve the People: Congress and Constituency Service*, University of Nebraska Press: Lincoln & Lincoln.

Kennan, John, and Riezman, Raymond, 1988: Do big countries win tariff wars? *International Economic Review*, 29, 81–4.

Keohane, Robert O. 1984: *After Hegemony*. New York: Princeton University Press.

Keohane, Robert O. and Nye, Joseph 1977: *Power and Interdependence*. Boston: Little Brown Publishing.

Kindleberger, Charles P. 1986: International public goods without international government. *American Economic Review*, 76, 1–13.

Krasner, Stephen D. 1976: State power and the structure of international trade. *World Politics*, 283, 317–47.

Kreinin, Mordechai E. 1991: EC-1992 and world trade and the trading system. In G. Yannopoulos (ed.), *Europe and America*, Manchester: Manchester University Press.

Kristov, Lorenzo, Lindert, Peter, and McClelland, Robert 1992: Pressure groups and redistribution. *Journal of Public Economics*, 48: 2, 135–63.

Krueger, Anne O. 1974: The political economy of the rent-seeking society. *American Economic Review*, 64, 291–303.

Krugman, Paul R. (ed.) 1986: *Strategic Trade Policy and the New International Economics*. Cambridge, Mass.: MIT Press.

Kurth, James R. 1979: The political consequences of the product cycle: industrial history and political outcomes. *International Organization*, 33, 1–34.

Kydland, F. E. and Prescott, E. C. 1977: Rules rather than discretion: the inconsistency of optimal plans. *Journal of Political Economy*, 85, 473–92.

Laband, D. and Sophocleus, J. 1988: The social cost of rent-seeking: first estimates. *Public Choice*, 58, 269–75.

Laband, David N. and Sophocleus, John P. 1992: An estimate of resource expenditures on transfer activity in the United States. *Quarterly Journal of Economics*, 107, 3, 959–83.

Lavergne, Real P. 1983: *The Political Economy of US Tariffs. An Empirical Analysis*. Toronto: Academic Press.

Leamer, Edward E. 1984: *Sources of International Comparative Advantage*. Cambridge, Mass.: MIT Press.

Lenway, Stefanie, Rehbein, Kathleen, and Starks, Laura T. 1990: The impact of protectionism on firm wealth: the experience of the steel industry. *Southern Economic Journal*, 56, April, 1079–93.

Lindbeck, Assar 1975a: Business cycles, politics and international economic dependence. *Skandinaviska Enskilda Banken Quarterly Review*, 53–68.

Lindbeck, Assar 1975b: Inequality and redistribution policy issues: principles and Swedish experience. Seminar Paper no. 44, Institute for International Economic Studies, University of Stockholm.

Lindbeck, Assar 1976: Stabilization policy in open economies with endogenous politicians. Seminar Paper no. 54, Institute for International Economic Studies, University of Stockholm.

Lindbeck, Assar 1977: *The Political Economy of the New Left: an outsider's view*. New York: Harper & Row.

Lindbeck, Assar 1983: Budget expansion and cost inflation. *American Economic Review*, 73, 285–90.

Lindbeck, Assar 1985a: Redistribution policy and expansion of the public sector. *Journal of Public Economics*, 28, 309–28.

Lindbeck, Assar 1985b: What is wrong with the Western European economies? *The World Economy*, 8, 153–70.

Lindbeck, Assar 1986a: Limits to the welfare state. *Challenge*, 28, 31–45.

Lindbeck, Assar 1986b: Public finance for market-oriented developing countries. Seminar Paper no. 348, Institute for International Economic Studies, University of Stockholm.

Lindbeck, Assar 1989: Policy autonomy vs policy coordination in the world economy. In Hans Tson Soderstrom (ed.), *One Global Market*, SNS: Center for Business and Policy Studies.

Lindbeck, Assar 1990: The Swedish experience. Seminar paper, Insitute for International Economic Studies, Stockholm.

Lindbeck, Assar, and Weilbull, Jorgen W. 1989: Political equilibrium in representative democracy. Seminar Paper no. 426, Institute for International Economic Studies, Stockholm.

McKelvey, Richard D. and Riezman, Raymond 1992: Seniority in legislatures. *American Political Science Review*, 86, 951–65.

McKenzie, Richard B. 1979: *The Political Economy of the Educational Process*. Boston: Martinus Nijhoff.

McKeown, Timothy J. 1983: Hegemonic stability theory and 19th century tariff levels in Europe. *International Organization*, 37, 73–91.

McMillan, John 1990: The economics of section 301: a game-theoretic guide. *Economics and Politics*, 2, 45–57.

Magee, Stephen P. 1980: Three simple tests of the Stolper–Samuelson theorem. In Peter Oppenheimer (ed.), *Issues in International Economics*, London: Oriel Press, 138–53.

Magee, Stephen P. 1982: The isoprotection curve: protection in the United States. Mimeo, University of Texas at Austin; for a published discussion, see Frey, Bruno S., 1984: *International Political Economics*. Oxford: Basil Blackwell, 56–8.

Magee, Stephen P. 1984: Endogenous tariff theory: a survey. In David C. Colander (ed.), *Neoclassical Political Economy*, Cambridge: Ballinger Press, 41–54.

Magee, Stephen P. 1989: The competence theory of comparative advantage. In David Avdretsch and Michael Claudon (eds), *The Internationalization of US Markets*. New York: NYU Press, 11–23.

Magee, Stephen P. 1990: International estimates of rent seeking as the economic cost of democracy and the excedrin tariff. Mimeo, University of Chicago, November.

Magee, Stephen P. 1991: Why there are developed countries: the bimodal distribution of world capital endowments. Mimeo, University of Texas at Austin.

Magee, Stephen P. 1992: The optimum number of lawyers: a reply to Epp. *Law and Social Enquiry*, 17, 667–93.

Magee, Stephen P. 1994: The Invisible Foot and the Waste of Nations: Lawyers as Negative Externalities. Forthcoming.

Magee, Stephen P., Brock, William A. and Young, Leslie 1989: *Black Hole Tariffs and Endogenous Policy Theory: political economy in general equilibrium*. New York: Cambridge University Press.

Magee, Stephen P. and Choi, Nakgyoon 1991: An empirical test of international trade theories, 1900–1988. Mimeo, University of Texas at Austin.

Magee, Stephen P. and Noe, Thomas 1989: Economic policy failure with endogenous voting. *Hong Kong Economic Papers*, 19, 9–12.

Magee, Stephen P. and Young, Leslie 1983: Multinationals, tariffs and capital flows with endogenous politicians. In C.P. Kindelberger and D. Audretsch (eds), *The Multinational Corporation in the 1980s*, Cambridge, Mass.: MIT Press, 21–37.

Magee, Stephen P. and Young, Leslie 1987: Endogenous protection in the United States, 1900–1984. In Robert M. Stern (ed.), *US Trade Policies in a Changing World Economy*, Cambridge, Mass.: MIT Press, 145–95.

Marwell, Gerald and Ames, R. 1979: Experiments on the provision of public goods I: Resources, interest, group size and the free rider problem. *American Journal of Sociology*, 84, 1335–60.

Mayer, Wolfgang 1984: Endogenous tariff formation. *American Economic Review*, 74, 970–85.

Mayer, Wolfgang, and Riezman, Raymond 1987: Tariff formation in political economy models. Conference on Political Economy, The World Bank, Washington, DC.

Mayer, Wolfgang, and Riezman, Raymond 1990: Voter preferences for trade policy instruments. *Economics and Politics*, 2, November, 259–74.

Messerlin, Patrick A. 1981: The political economy of protectionism: the bureaucratic case. *Weltwirtschaftliches Archiv*, 117, 469–95.

Michaely, Michael, Papageorgiou, Demetris, and Choksi, Armeane M. (eds) 1991: *Liberalizing Foreign Trade*: vol. 7, *Lessons of Experience in the Developing World*. Cambridge, Mass.: Basil Blackwell.

Mills, E.S. 1986: Positive theories of government. In *The Burden of Government*, Stanford: Hoover, ch. 9.

Mohammad, Sharif, and Whalley, John 1984: Rent seeking in India: its costs and policy significance. *Kyklos*, 37, 387–413.

Morton, Rebecca, and Cameron, Charles 1991: Elections and the theory of campaign contributions: a survey and critical analysis. Mimeo, Department of Economics and Finance, Nicholls State University.

Moser, Peter 1988: Does the GATT matter? The effect of the GATT on United States' trade policy. Mimeo, University of St Gallen.

Mueller, Dennis C. 1979: *Public Choice*. Cambridge: Cambridge University Press.

Mundell, Robert A. 1957: International trade and factor mobility. *American Economic Review*, 47, 321–35.

Munger, Michael 1989a: A simple test of the thesis that committee jurisdictions shape corporate PAC contributions. *Public Choice*, 62, 181–6.

Munger, Michael 1989b: Closeness, expenditures and turnout in the 1982 House elections. *American Political Science Review*, 83, 217–32.

Mussa, Michael 1974: Tariffs and the distribution of income: the importance of factor specificity, substitutability, and intensity in the short and long run. *Journal of Political Economy*, 82, 1191–203.

Nelson, Douglas 1988: Endogenous tariff theory: a critical survey. *American Journal of Political Science*, 32/3, 796–837.

Niskanen, W. 1976: Bureaucrats and politicians. *Journal of Law and Economics*, 19, 617–43.

Nozick, Robert 1974: *Anarchy, State and Utopia*. New York: Basic Books.

O'Flaherty, Brendan 1990: Why are there democracies? A principal agent answer. *Economics and Politics*, 2, 133–55.

Olson, Mancur 1965: *The Logic of Collective Action: public goods and the theory of groups*. Cambridge: Harvard University Press.

Olson, Mancur 1982: *The Rise and Decline of Nations: economic growth, stagflation and social rigidities*. New Haven: Yale University.

Olson, Mancur 1990: Autocracy, democracy, and prosperity. Mimeo, University of Maryland at College Park.

Panagariya, Arvind and Rodrick, Dani 1991: Political economy arguments for uniform tariff. Working Paper WPS 681, World Bank, May.

Peltzman, Sam 1976: Toward a more general theory of regulation. *Journal of Law and Economics*, 19, 211–40.

Pincus, J.J. 1975: Pressure groups and the pattern of tariffs. *Journal of Political Economy*, 85, 757–78.

Rassekh, Farhad 1990: The role of international trade in the convergence of per capita GDP in the OECD 1950–1985. Mimeo, Barney School of Business and Public Administration.

Rawls, John 1971: *A Theory of Justice*. Cambridge, Mass.: Harvard University Press.

Ray, Edward J. 1981: The determinants of tariff and nontariff trade restrictions in the United States. *Journal of Political Economy*, 89, 105–21.

Ray, Edward John 1989: Protection of manufacturers in the United States. Mimeo, Ohio State University.

Ray, Edward John 1990: U.S. protection and intra-industry trade: the message to developing countries. Mimeo, Ohio State University.

Rehbein, Kathleen and Starks, Laura T. 1991: Changes in U.S. trade policies: the wealth effects on Japanese steel firms. Mimeo, University of Texas at Austin.

Riker, W.H. 1962: *The Theory of Political Coalitions*. New Haven: Yale UP.

Roberts, Russell D. 1990: The tragicomedy of the commons. Mimeo, Olin School of Business, Washington University, November.

Ross, Victoria B. 1984: Rent-seeking in LDC import regimes: the case of Kenya. Discussion Papers in International Economics, no. 8408, Graduate Institute of International Studies, Geneva.

Salvatore, D. 1985: The new protectionism and the threat to world welfare: editor's introduction. *Journal of Policy Modeling*, 7, 1–22.

Sandler, Todd (ed.) 1981: *The Theory and Structures of International Political Economy*. Boulder, Colorado: Westview Press.

Schneider, Friedrich, Hofreither, Markus F. and Neck, Reinhard 1988: The consequences of a changing shadow economy for the 'Official' economy: some empirical results for Austria. Johannes Kepler Universität Linz, Arbeitspapier no. 8809.

Schumpeter, Joseph A. 1950: *Capitalism, Socialism, and Democracy*. New York: Harper & Brothers.

Skaperdas, Stergios 1990: Cooperation, conflict and power in the absence of property rights. Mimeo, Department of Economics, University of California, Irvine.

Stahl, Dale O. and Turunen-Red, Arja H. 1992: Seniority in legislatures. *European Journal of Political Economy*, forthcoming.

Staiger, Robert W. and Tabellini, Guido 1987: Discretionary trade policy and excessive protection. *The American Economic Review*, 77, 823–37.

Stigler, George J. 1970: Director's law of public income redistribution. *Journal of Law and Economics*, 13, 1–10.

Stigler, George J. 1971: The theory of economic regulation. *Bell Journal of Economics and Management Science*, 2, 3–21.

Stigler, George J. 1972: Economic competition and political competition. *Public Choice*, 13, 91–106.

Stigler, George J. 1974: Free riders and collective action: an appendix to theories of economic regulation. *Bell Journal of Economics and Management Science*, 5, 359–65.

Tarr, David 1989: *A General Equilibrium Analysis of the Welfare and Employment Effects of US Quotas in Textiles, Autos and Steel*. Washington: Federal Trade Commission.

Taussig, Frank W. 1931: *The Tariff History of the United States*, 8th edn. New York: G.P. Putnam and Sons.

Tollison, Robert D. 1982: Rent seeking: a survey. *Kyklos*, 35, 28–47.

Tullock, Gordon 1967: The welfare cost of tariffs, monopolies and theft. *Western Economic Journal*, 5, 224–32.

Tullock, Gordon 1979: Public choice in practice. In Clifford S. Russell (ed.), *Collective Decision Making: applications from public choice theory*. Baltimore: Johns Hopkins Press, 27–45.

Tullock, Gordon 1988: Future directions for rent seeking research. In C.K. Rowley, R.D. Tollison and G. Tullock (eds), *The Political Economy of Rent Seeking*, Boston: Kluwer, 465–80.

Ursprung, Heinrich W. 1989: Public goods, rent dissipation and candidate competition. Mimeo, University of Konstanz, July.

Van der Ploeg, Frederick 1989: The political economy of overvaluation. *The Economic Journal*, 99, September, 850–5.

Vousden, Neil 1990: *The Economics of Trade Protection*. New York: Cambridge University Press.

Weck-Hannemann, Hannelore 1990a: Protectionism between rent seeking and discretionary power: an institutional analysis. Mimeo, University of Konstanz.

Weck-Hannemann, Hannelore 1990b: Protectionism in direct democracy. *Journal of Institutional and Theoretical Economics*, 146, 389–418.

Whalley, John 1985: *Trade Liberalization among Major World Trading Areas*. Cambridge, Mass.: MIT Press.

Wilson, John 1990: Are efficiency improvements in government transfer policies self-defeating in political equilibrium? *Economics and Politics*, 2, November, 241–58.

Wittman, Donald 1989: Why democracies produce efficient results. *Journal of Political Economy*, 97, 1395–424.

Young, H.P. 1978: The allocation of funds in lobbying and campaigning. *Behavioral Science*, 23, 21–31.

Young, Leslie, and Magee, Stephen P. 1986: Endogenous protection, factor returns and resource allocation. *Review of Economic Studies*, 53, 407–19.

7

STRATEGIC TRADE POLICIES

Didier Laussel and Christian Montet

7.1 INTRODUCTION

The term 'strategic policy' can be used to characterize any governmental action in favour of a sector considered, rightly or wrongly, as strategic. This sector may be crucial for defence purposes like arms and other military equipment, it may provide strong positive externalities and spillovers for other industries, it may represent a lot of jobs and thus be politically very sensitive. A wide set of actions included under the headings of industrial policy and trade policy could then be considered as strategic.

In this chapter we will take a more restrictive and technical view of the term 'strategic', as it is used in game theory. We will focus our discussion on the policies involving agents conscious of their mutual interactions and behaving strategically in the sense that, in deciding which course of action to take, they take into account the possible effects on the other agents and the fact that the latter are expected to behave in the same way. Applications of game theory to international trade have been numerous in recent years and are still growing (see McMillan, 1986).

A very restrictive view would consider only the analysis of the interference of government policies with oligopolistic equilibria. This theory of strategic trade policy for oligopolies started with a series of articles by Brander and Spencer (1984a, b, 1985), and was continuously extended thereafter. We will also include in the study the interactions between governments when they define a policy of optimal tariff or other protectionist measures. Modern concepts of game theory, particularly dynamic games, fit well with observed actions and moves like tariff and subsidy wars and tacit co-operation for liberalization of trade. Since in international relations there are no institutions capable of making binding and enforceable arrangements, the analysis is generally conducted in terms of non-co-operative games.

The ideas and models we are going to discuss in this chapter have been increasingly recognized as a major advance in this branch of economics. They are certainly benefiting from the fact that game theory is currently fashionable. But it is clear that the concepts of game theory are particularly relevant in the area of trade policy where large agents, like multinational corporations (MNCs), governments of big countries or representatives of groups of countries, are powerful and are conscious of their mutual interactions. Obviously the results of the new theory and of its empirical counterparts are a major input in the current popular discussions about protection and subsidization of big businesses in the markets of semiconductors, cars, steel, aircraft, . . . and about various promises and threats concerning agriculture, services and other GATT issues.

Section 7.2 will study the basic models of strategic trade policy for oligopolies proposed by Brander and Spencer and their followers. Section 7.3 will develop several extensions including questions raised by multi-stage competition and entry strategies. The following two sections will be devoted to games between governments, first when agents are all price-takers (section 7.4) and then in the presence of oligopolies (section 7.5). In section 7.6, we will examine the major results obtained in empirical studies about strategic trade policy. A final section will present some concluding comments.

7.2 STRATEGIC POLICY FOR OLIGOPOLIES: BASIC ISSUES

The first meaning of 'strategic trade policy' is trade policy which takes account of interactions between domestic and foreign firms in an imperfectly competitive framework. Trade policy, which is here generally unilateral, is termed 'strategic' only because it is aimed at modifying the equilibrium of the game between firms. A famous example is the pioneering paper by Brander and Spencer (1985) in which a domestic government decides in a first stage upon a linear export subsidy and then, in a second stage, a domestic firm and a foreign firm compete in quantities (Cournot equilibrium) on a third market.

The same basic framework will be retained in what follows: (a) unilateral domestic government intervention through export taxes or subsidies; (b) a Nash equilibrium[1] between a foreign firm and a domestic one selling exclusively on a third market.

Strategic interactions between governments will be considered later (in sections 7.4 and 7.5). Restricting our attention to competition on third markets is necessary to isolate the strategic trade policy problem as defined above from problems of domestic distortions which are better dealt with by anti-trust policy or consumption subsidies. We will indicate in the following section how the results are modified when there are several domestic firms.

The analyses to be presented differ depending upon whether the two firms are incumbents (entry is blockaded or takes a long time) or potential entrants (entry is free), and on whether the two firms operate on prices, quantities or more sophisticated variables (such as supply functions or reaction functions). Consideration of entry is left for the following section.

Let us consider here the case where the domestic firm and the foreign firm are both incumbents and compete in quantities (the Brander and Spencer 1985 model). In the first stage the domestic government chooses unilaterally a constant export subsidy s per unit of output. Then, in the second stage, a Nash equilibrium in quantities between the two firms (Cournot equilibrium) takes place. For the sake of simplicity, let the two firms produce a homogeneous good. Assume that the inverse demand function is $p(Q)$ where Q is total industry output and $p'(Q)$ is negative. Suppose, moreover, that the two firms have the same total cost functions $C(Q)$ with $C'(Q) > 0$ and $C''(Q) \geq 0$. Finally, let $p'(Q) + Qp''(Q) \leq 0$. The Cournot equilibrium of the second stage of the game then satisfies the following first-order conditions (corresponding to the equalities of marginal revenues and marginal costs):

$$p(Q) + s + Q_1 p'(Q) - C'(Q_1) = 0 \qquad (7.1)$$

$$p(Q) + Q_2 p'(Q) - C'(Q_2) = 0 \qquad (7.2)$$

Given the above-mentioned assumptions the second-order conditions are statisfied and the reaction functions implicitly defined by (7.1) and (7.2) are downward sloping, i.e. the quantities are strategic substitutes according to Bulow, Geneakoplos and Klemperer's (1985) definition (the marginal profitability of one firm's output is a decreasing function of the other firm's output) and the Nash equilibrium values Q_1^* and Q_2^* are respectively increasing and decreasing functions of s.

In the first stage of the game the domestic government is assumed to choose s in order to maximize the domestic firm's profits net of export taxes or subsidies (implicit is the assumption that transfers between the households and the government are wholly in lump-sum form). The domestic firm's net profits may be written as

$$\Pi_1^N = \Pi_1(Q_1^*(s), Q_2^*(s), s) - sQ^*(s) \qquad (7.3)$$

where Π_1 denotes firm 1's profits including export subsidies.

The equilibrium condition for the first stage of the game is now

$$\frac{d\Pi_1^N}{ds} = \frac{\partial \Pi_1}{\partial Q_1} \frac{dQ_1^*}{ds} + \frac{\partial \Pi_1}{\partial Q_2} \frac{dQ_2^*}{ds} - s \frac{dQ_1^*}{ds} = 0 \qquad (7.4)$$

From the envelope theorem, the first term in the RHS of equation (7.4) equals zero (this is because Q_1^* is chosen in stage 2 in order to maximize Π_1). Equation (7.4) can equivalently be written as

$$p'(Q) Q_1^* R_2'(Q_1^*) - s = 0 \qquad (7.5)$$

where R_2' is the slope of the foreign firm's reaction function (implicitly equation (7.2) defines the foreign output Q_2 as a function of Q_1 which is called the 'reaction function' of the foreign firm). From (7.5) we conclude that if the two incumbent firms compete in quantities the domestic government should subsidize exports (in other words, the optimal level of s is positive) – this is a 'top dog' strategy according to Fudenberg and Tirole's (1984) 'animal terminology'. One way to look at this result is to consider the second term in the RHS of equation (7.4). This term may be called the strategic effect and, through a development of the comparative statics effects, it may be written as

$$\frac{\partial \Pi_1}{\partial Q_2} \cdot \frac{\partial^2 \Pi_1}{\partial Q_1 \partial s} \cdot \frac{\partial^2 \Pi_2}{\partial Q_1 \partial Q_2}$$

In this case, this strategic effect is positive because the first part is obviously negative, the second part is positive because, in Fudenberg and Tirole's terminology, subsidizing domestic exports make the domestic firm tough ($\partial^2 \Pi_1/\partial Q_1 \partial s > 0$) and the third part is negative because quantities are strategic substitutes ($\partial^2 \Pi_2/\partial Q_1 \partial Q_2 < 0$).

These results are illustrated by figure 7.1 where we have drawn in the (Q_1, Q_2) space the iso-profit curves of the domestic firm and the reaction function of the foreign firm. Note that successive iso-profit curves correspond to increasing profit levels as one approaches the Q_1 axis. $R_1(Q_2)$ is the domestic reaction function in the *laissez-faire* case where a Nash equilibrium occurs at point N where the two reaction functions intersect. The Stackelberg equilibrium point is where the foreign firm's reaction function is tangential to one iso-profit curve of the domestic firm, i.e. at S. The Stackelberg equilibrium is the equilibrium of a two-stage game in which the domestic firm would choose its output level in the first stage, before the foreign firm (the first mover is the leader and the second mover is the follower in such a game). Along NS domestic net profits increase as one moves from N to S. Subsidizing domestic exports shifts the domestic firm's reaction function outwards and moves the Cournot equilibrium down along R_2. Trade policy is optimal when the Nash equilibrium point coincides with point S where domestic net profits are at their maximum level given the foreign firm reaction function.

Eaton and Grossman (1986) have shown that when a domestic and a foreign incumbent produce imperfect substitutes and compete in prices, the

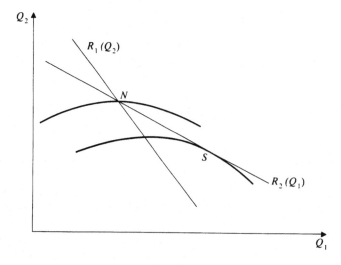

Figure 7.1 Iso-profit curves and reaction functions

strategic trade policy should be a 'puppy dog' one in order to soften competition. This is not surprising since prices are strategic complements according to the Bulow, Geneakoplos and Klemperer definition and the strategic effect may be shown to be negative. To see this let $D^i(p_1 \, p_2)$ be the demand function for firm i's output. Assume as usual that $D^1_1 < 0$, $D^2_2 < 0$, $D^1_2 = D^2_1 > 0$ and $D^1_1 D^2_2 - D^1_2 D^2_1 > 0$. The assumptions on the total cost functions are unchanged. Suppose finally that the marginal revenue of each of the two firms is a decreasing function of the firm's own price and an increasing function of the other firm's price. The Bertrand equilibrium at the second stage of the game satisfies the following first-order conditions:

$$D^1(p_1, p_2) + [p_1 + s - C'(D^1(p_1, p_2))]D^1_1(p_1, p_2) = 0 \qquad (7.6)$$

$$D^2(p_1, p_2) + [p_2 - C'(D^2(p_1, p_2))]D^2_2(p_1, p_2) = 0 \qquad (7.7)$$

Given the above assumptions, the second-order conditions are also satisfied and the reaction functions implicitly defined by the two above equations are upward sloping, i.e. the prices are strategic complements (the marginal profitability of a price increase for each firm is an increasing function of the other firm's price: this follows from the assumptions on the firms' marginal revenue and marginal cost functions). Moreover, the Nash equilibrium prices p^*_1 and p^*_2 are both decreasing functions of s.

In the first stage of the game the domestic government chooses s in order to maximize domestic profits net of taxes or subsidies:

$$\Pi^N_1 = \Pi_1(p^*_1(s), p^*_2(s), s) - sD^1(p^*_1(s), p^*_2(s)) \qquad (7.8)$$

Using the envelope theorem we obtain the first-order condition

$$\frac{d\Pi^N_1}{ds} = (p^*_1 - C')D^1_2 \frac{dp^*_2}{ds} - sD^1_1 \frac{dp^*_1}{ds} = 0 \qquad (7.9)$$

from which we deduce that the 'strategic effect' (i.e. the first term in the RHS of (7.9)) is negative and

$$(p^*_1 - C')D^1_2 R'_2(p^*_1) - sD^1_1 = 0 \qquad (7.10)$$

where R'_2 is the (positive) slope of firm 2's reaction function. From (7.10) we learn that if the two incumbents compete in prices while producing imperfect substitutes, the domestic government should tax exports. This result is illustrated by figure 7.2.

We have drawn the iso-profit curves of the domestic firm in the *laissez-faire* case as well as the reaction function of the foreign firm. Note that successive iso-profit curves correspond to increasing profit levels when they are further from the p_1 axis. The *laissez-faire* Nash equilibrium in prices (where each price is a best reply to the other firm's price) is at point N where the two reaction functions intersect. Given the foreign firm's reaction function, domestic net profits are at a maximum at point S, the Stackelberg equilibrium point, and increase along NS. But the domestic firm cannot credibly commit itself to a price corresponding to S since S does not lie on its reaction function. Taxing exports shifts the domestic firm's reaction function and raises domestic net profits since the Nash equilibrium point can move towards point S.

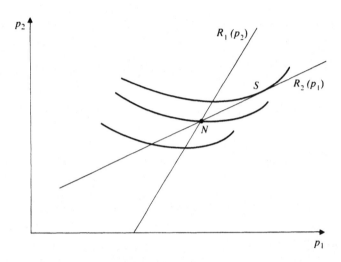

Figure 7.2 Competition in prices with imperfect substitutes

The reversal of results as to what an optimal trade policy should be is disturbing in the two incumbents' case but should not conceal that the foundations of such policy are the same: the domestic government aims to make the domestic firm the Stackelberg leader in the strategic variables space since the Nash equilibrium cum export taxes or subsidies coincides with this Stackelberg equilibrium point. Whereas the domestic firm cannot commit itself to a level of its strategic variable corresponding to this point which does not lie on its reaction function, the government is implicitly assumed to have the capacity to precommit itself to a tax (subsidy) function.

These same principles may be found in Laussel (1991) who tries to solve the problem of indeterminacy of the optimal trade policy in the two incumbents' case by solving the underlying problem of indeterminacy of the strategic variable in oligopoly (basically the problem is the indeterminacy of the Nash equilibrium in deterministic models when one does not arbitrarily restrict – as Cournot or Bertrand did – the set of admissible strategies).

As in Klemperer and Meyer (1989), it is assumed that the two firms produce a homogeneous good and that industry demand is subject to an exogenous random shock. Before the value of the shock is known, each firm chooses a supply function relating its quantity to its price, given the tax/ subsidy function initially chosen by the domestic government. Each firm's supply function traces out through its ex-post optimal points. In the linear case (linear demand function, linear marginal cost functions, linear–quadratic tax/subsidy function) a Nash equilibrium in supply functions is shown to exist and to be unique. The restriction to linear–quadratic subsidy functions is motivated both by technical reasons and by the fact that it is the simplest schedule that the domestic government may have an incentive to implement in this context (it has no incentive to use a linear schedule contrary to Brander and Spencer, 1985 or Eaton and Grossman, 1986). The unilateral use of this kind of schedule is aimed at inducing the domestic firm to behave as though it was the Stackelberg leader in the linear supply- functions space. As the supply-functions slopes are shown to be strategic complements, domestic government's optimal intervention induces the domestic firm to choose a steeper supply function than under *laissez-faire* so as to soften competition. This is done by selecting a tax/subsidy function such that the marginal tax rate is an increasing function of output and is zero in expected value: exports are subsidized at the margin for low realized values of industry demand and taxed at the margin for large ones in order to induce the domestic firm to choose a less price-elastic supply function. As in the price-competition case, unilateral intervention by the domestic government raises both firms' profits by softening competition instead of 'shifting' profits from the foreign firm towards the domestic one.

Notice that we constantly assumed in this section that the firms were selling on a third market. If we consider a larger framework of optimal policies for oligopolies including the correction of domestic distortions, then we must consider more than one policy instrument. A major problem is the hierarchy of policies in different market structures and according to the availability of policy instruments. A few studies have shown (Laussel and Montet, 1988; Krishna and Thursby, 1991) that the general principle of targeting of policies developed by Bhagwati (1971) and others can be applied with some qualifications in this context.

Trade policy may then have different objectives: in addition to a second-best role of correction of internal distortions, it has three distinct objectives: the traditional term of trade objective captured by the optimal tariff argument, rent-extracting of foreign rents in the domestic country and rent-shifting of foreign rents from foreign firms to domestic ones abroad. Under the assumptions of segmented markets and a fixed number of firms in each country one can show (see Laussel and Montet, 1988) that the principle of targeting is generally valid in a restrictive sense: the instruments of internal policy only affect the objectives of internal policy and the instruments of trade policy only affect the objectives of external policy. Furthermore, when one assumes that the marginal costs are constant, the two equilibria are independent and the principle of targeting is totally valid: each instrument affects only the objective to which it is directed.

When only some instruments are available, it is possible to define their best allocations to the various objectives. It is interesting to note that, in general, measures connected to anti-trust policy seem to be more effective than commercial policy, even from a single country point of view.

7.3 STRATEGIC POLICY FOR OLIGOPOLIES: MULTI-STAGE COMPETITION AND ENTRY

The analysis of strategic trade policy in the two incumbents' case may be extended in several ways. Instead of analysing competition between firms as a one-stage process where the strategic variables may be quantities, prices or supply functions, one may want to study two-stage games between firms in which the firms initially choose the level of a variable (capital stock, capacity of production, location, product quality or R&D expenditures) which becomes a parameter in the following stage of the game in which the firms compete in prices or in quantities (or other strategic variables). The overall game is then a three-stage one in which the domestic government determines its optimal policy before the game between the two firms begins. The analysis is modified in several respects: first, the domestic government can now intervene not only through export subsidies (or taxes) aimed at moving the Nash equilibrium in the last stage of the game but also through new instruments (like investment subsidies) which can affect directly the firms' initial choices (of capital stock for instance); second, export subsidies or taxes are designed to affect not only the last-stage equilibrium but also, through an announcement effect, the firms' choices in the previous stages of the game. On the one hand it is now possible to distinguish between commercial policy (export taxes or subsidies) and industrial policy (investment or R&D subsidies for instance) as parts of strategic trade policy. On the other hand, trade policy now aims at making the domestic firm behave as the Stackelberg leader (i.e. first mover) in the dynamic two-stage game with the foreign firm. It is well known that, in a dynamic game, there are time-inconsistency problems associated with the existence of a leader: the leader has an incentive to announce initially that it will choose some plan which it will have no incentive to implement later. It may, for instance, announce that it will produce large levels of output in the last stage of the game in order to deter investment by the follower in the previous stage of the game while it will have no incentive in this last stage to produce the announced level of output. Strategic trade policy may give credibility to these announcements through export subsidies for instance: the subgame perfect Nash equilibrium[2] of the two-stage game (such that there is a Nash equilibrium in the second stage given the first-period choices) is made, through the optimal domestic trade policy, to coincide with the time-inconsistent Stackelberg equilibrium of the same game under *laissez-faire*. The government is thus assumed once again to have the ability of precommitting itself in the domestic firm's place: this is the central assumption in all this literature. Note that considering dynamic games modifies the case for export subsidies (as opposed to export taxes) in a way which depends on the strategic substituability or complementarity of the new variables involved: considering strategic investment games is, for instance, likely to reinforce the case for a 'top dog' strategy of subsidizing exports (see Brander and Spencer, 1983 for instance) while the reverse may be true for strategic advertising games.

The case for export taxes is reinforced when there is more than one domestic firm: indeed the domestic firms do not account for the externalities which their output/price decisions create on the other domestic firms and hence tend to produce an output which is too large from the total net domestic profit maximization point of view. In the Cournot case, this effect has to be balanced against the strategic effect analysed above: it is stronger as the number of firms is larger. In the Bertrand case, the two effects are of the same sign and exports should be unambiguously taxed.

While strategic trade policy in the case of a game between potential entrants may have more spectacular effects than in the case of a game between incumbents, it has received less systematic attention (although see Dixit and Kyle, 1985). There do exist models with imperfect competition and free entry where the effects of tariffs, quotas, export subsidies . . . are analysed (see for instance Venables, 1985 or Horstman and Markusen, 1986). Here we adopt a different point of view: we restrict our attention to competition between potential entrants taking place exclusively on third markets, but we try to define optimal strategic trade policy for this case (instead of performing comparative statics exercises with respect to a variety of policy instruments).

The analysis of strategic trade policy in the case of competition between potential entrants requires at least the use of a three-stage game model. In the first stage the government decides on the levels of its policy instruments (export taxes or subsidies, entry-conditional lump-sum subsidies for instance). In the second stage, firms decide whether to enter and to sink a fixed cost or to stay out. Finally, in the third stage, the firms which have previously chosen to enter compete in prices, quantities or some other strategic variable.

Let us consider a highly simplified case where the potential entrants are on an equal footing (same cost functions for instance) and where under *laissez-faire* the profits of entrants are strictly negative when there are more than two firms in the industry. We shall not bother about the nature of the strategic variable used by the firms in the third stage of the game: an individual entrant's profit is always a function of the number of active firms in the industry. This function is non-increasing and even strictly decreasing in all cases except the case of Bertrand competition with homogeneous product and constant marginal cost. Under our assumptions the problem is reduced to a game between two players, a domestic firm and a foreign firm, each player having to choose either to enter (E) or to stay out (NE). The pay-off matrix of the game under *laissez-faire* is pictured in table 7.1, where F denotes the exogenous sunk cost and $\Pi(n)$ the gross profits as a function of the number n of entrants.

The firms' net profits are indicated for the four possible cases (the domestic firm's pay-off is given first). Assuming that $\Pi(1) - F$ is non-negative, only two distinct cases are of interest. First, if $\Pi(2) - F < 0$ (under duopoly, the firms' net profits are negative), there are under *laissez-faire* two symmetric Nash equilibria which are (E, NE) and (NE, E). This is because when the rival firm has chosen to enter it is better to stay out (duopoly entails losses to both firms) and when the rival has chosen to stay out it is better to enter (since monopoly net profits are strictly positive). Second, if $\Pi(2) - F \geqslant 0$, entry is a dominant strategy[3] for each firm (whatever the rival chooses to do, entering yields strictly positive profits and hence is better than to stay out) and (E, E) is the only equilibrium of the game. Note that we assume that for other potential entrants net profits would be negative in a duopolistic market in which they would compete with one of the two above firms.

Table 7.1 Pay off matrix with *laissez-faire*

		Foreign firm	
		E	NE
Domestic firm	E	$\Pi(2) - F, (2) - F$	$\Pi(1) - F, 0$
	NE	$0, \Pi(1) - F$	0,0

In the first case the optimal domestic policy is a lump-sum subsidy to the domestic firm of amount $F - \Pi(2) + \varepsilon$ conditional on the entry decision. Entry then becomes a dominant strategy for the domestic firm and (E, NE) the only Nash equilibrium of the game (see the modified pay-off matrix of the game in table 7.2). This case may then be called the 'strategic industrial policy case'. Note that this policy succeeds by making entry a dominant strategy for the domestic firm whereas under *laissez-faire* this firm cannot commit itself to enter the market; the burden of making this strategy credible falls once again on the government.

Table 7.2 Modified pay off matrix

		Foreign firm	
		E	NE
Domestic firm	E	$\varepsilon, \Pi(2) - F$	$\Pi(1) - \Pi(2) + \varepsilon, 0$
	NE	$0, \Pi(1) - F$	0,0

In the second case the only effective policy is a commercial policy but the government of the domestic country has first to choose whether it wants to deter the entry of the foreign firm or to accept it. This choice is of course only led by the net domestic profits associated with each of these strategies. When it is more profitable to accommodate entry by the foreign firm there is no entry game. In the entry-deterrence case the optimal commercial policy aims at making the foreign firm's profits negative in the event of entry. Note that this policy tries to modify the foreign firm's entry decision whereas the optimal policy in the first case was intended to modify the domestic firm's entry decision. Moreover this policy is here time-inconsistent: once the foreign firm has chosen to stay out of the market, the domestic government has no incentive to subsidize exports by a domestic firm which is now in a monopoly situation.

Of course, much more complex cases can be studied than the simple two-firm case above. For instance, let us assume that there are three potential entrants instead of two, one of them being a foreign firm, and suppose that while $\Pi(2) - F$ is non-negative, $\Pi(3) - F$ is negative. There are here three duopoly equilibria under *laissez-faire* which differ only from one another in the names of the active firms. The determination of the optimal strategic trade policy would require a careful analysis here. For instance, one may think of a combination of lump-sum entry subsidies to the domestic firms so as to make entry a dominant strategy for them and of export taxes aimed at softening competition between them. But this may make entry by the foreign firm profitable even if the domestic firms both enter. In any case the optimal policy is likely to be a rather complex combination of industrial and commercial policies.

Strategic trade policy, in the present meaning of these words, covers a very wide variety of situations, of which only a small number have been extensively studied. The entire field of oligopolistic competition is also the field of strategic trade policy! Accordingly, besides the commercial policy instruments like export taxes or subsidies, strategic trade policy may use many other policy tools (investment, R&D or entry subsidies for instance). However, the fundamentals of the public intervention are always the same: it is aimed at making the domestic firm(s) the equivalent of a Stackelberg leader in a *laissez-faire* situation. This may be obtained because the active government is assumed to be able to precommit itself to what the firm cannot do. This debatable assumption is at the heart of the strategic trade policy debate.

7.4 STRATEGIC INTERACTION BETWEEN GOVERNMENTS WHEN THE AGENTS ARE PRICE-TAKERS

A country may have some market power when all the other agents are price-takers. This situation has long been studied in international trade theory. It is well known that an optimal tariff can then improve the terms of trade and ultimately national welfare. But foreigners may also want to use this nationalistic policy. If the world consists of two large countries the argument applies to both of them and then each government's optimal action depends on the other's government action. Governments can behave strategically in the sense used in this chapter.

Since there is no supranational institution to enforce eventual contracts between the two countries (as it currently functions the GATT has not the power to make eventual agreements binding and enforceable), the question of optimal tariff and retaliation is best modelled as a non-co-operative game and the outcome can be described as a Nash equilibrium of the game. In general the interplay of the game is likely to be repeated over time so the governments will have the opportunity to develop more subtle strategic actions or what Schelling called strategic moves like threats and promises.

In a now classic article, Johnson (1954) studied the problem of optimal tariffs and retaliations. Although not in a game-theoretic model, he showed the 'prisoner's dilemma'[4] nature of the situation and the fact that both

188 DIDIER LAUSSEL AND CHRISTIAN MONTET

countries would gain from co-operation. Modern presentations (Dixit, 1987a; McMillan, 1986; Riezman, 1982, 1991) explicitly use game theory and develop various extensions of the analysis introducing dynamics and uncertainty.

Let us first introduce the static Nash equilibrium assuming that the world is composed of two countries whose governments have only one choice concerning trade: let it be free or putting a specified tariff on imports. This binary choice is sufficient to show the kind of prisoner's dilemma arising in this situation. If both governments choose a non-interventionist strategy the countries will enjoy the advantages of free trade. If both of them put a tariff on imports, in general their situation would deteriorate compared to the previous case. But the worst case would certainly be for a country to do nothing when the other one influences the terms of trade in its favour through the tariff policy.

Table 7.3 gives the pay-off matrix of this simple static game. This game has a dominant strategy equilibrium (which is also a Nash equilibrium). The choice of free trade is more efficient for both countries, but it is not an equilibrium of the non-co-operative game. If a preplay agreement were settled between the two governments, each would be interested in reneging on it, and could do so in the absence of a supranational institution with coercive power.

Table 7.3 Pay off matrix with a static game

		Country 2	
		Free	Opt
Country 1	Free	(8, 8)	(2, 10)
	Opt	(10, 2)	(4, 4)

Of course, the choice of strategies need not be so limited as in this extreme example. One can consider a more general situation where two countries produce two goods 1 and 2, country 1 exports good 1 and imports good 2, and countries can levy various tariffs on imports. Let us call t and t^* respectively the domestic and foreign *ad valorem* tariffs so that the national prices of the two goods are related by $p_2^1 = p_2^2(1 + t)$ and $p_1^2 = p_1^1(1 + t^*)$, with p_j^i the price of good j in country i. Each tariff can be positive or negative and take any value between -1 (imports would then be free) and t (prohibition of any import). The relative price on world markets is $p = p_2^2/p_1^1$. Let $M_i(p, t)$ denote country's i import demand as a function of the terms of trade and the tariff level; $i = 1, 2$. The trade balance condition is

$$pM_1(p, t) = M_2(p, t^*) \qquad (7.11)$$

This determines a function $p(t, t^*)$, which we assume to be continuous and differentiable. We assume that raising the tariff improves the terms of trade: $\partial p/\partial t < 0$, $\partial p/\partial t^* > 0$ (this is true if the Marshall–Lerner conditions hold[5] and if all tariff revenues are redistributed to consumers).

The pay-offs of the game are the values taken by the collective utility functions: $U = U(p, t)$, $U^* = U^*(p, t^*)$ which from (7.11) can be rewritten as functions of t and t^* only: $W(t, t^*)$ and $W^*(t, t^*)$. With the assumptions stated above each country is hurt by increases in the other country's tariff. We also assume that each country gains from a slight increase in its tariff starting from a zero tariff.

The functions W and W^* give welfare contours as illustrated on figure 7.1 (see McMillan, 1986 and Dixit, 1987a for a more detailed presentation).

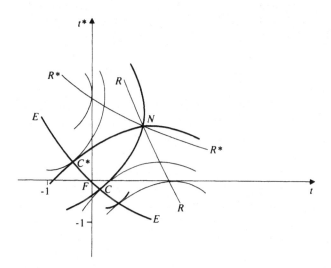

Figure 7.3 Nash equilibrium

Country 1's welfare increases as we move downwards and country 2's welfare increases when moving to the left. The locus of the maxima of these curves for country 1 – that is the points corresponding to $\partial W/\partial t = 0$ – is RR on figure 7.3. It is called the home country's reaction function (as Dixit argued, the term 'equilibrium locus' would be a better name since in a one-shot game there is not strictly such a thing as a reaction).

The corresponding locus for country 2 is R^*R^*. We assume here that they are negatively sloped and that they cross only once.

The intersection point N represents the Nash equilibrium of this game (in fact, autarky could be another Nash equilibrium, see Dixit, 1987a).

As in the case of the prisoner's dilemma, the equilibrium is not Pareto-efficient. Efficiency would require the same relative price in the two countries, that is

$$p_2^1/p_1^1 = p_2^2/p_1^2 \text{ or } p(1 + t) = p/(1 + t^*) \text{ or finally } t + t^* + tt^* = 0 \quad (7.12)$$

The locus of $t - t^*$ levels verifying condition (7.12) is the curve EE on figure 7.3. The points between C and C^* are preferred by both countries to the Nash equilibrium and in this case, the free trade solution lies on this segment (this is not always true; see, for instance, Kennan and Riezman, 1988 for a different case). The problem is that the countries cannot reach F or a point on CC^* without being constrained by an external force (like a powerful sort of GATT).

In the presentation above, the governments use *ad valorem* tariffs as their strategic instruments. Horwell (1966) has shown that the Nash equilibrium in specific tariffs between the two countries differs from the Nash equilibrium in *ad valorem* tariffs. More recently, Tower (1975) proved that the Nash equilibrium in quotas is yet another thing. The classical equivalence results cease to be valid when both governments are active. In this case, one encounters problems which are very much like the problem of divergence between Cournot and Bertrand equilibria in oligopoly (on these questions see Laussel, 1991). However, the above discussion remains qualitatively valid, whatever the strategic variables chosen by the governments.

Co-operation would certainly improve the situation for each country, but the question is then to know how this co-operation can be developed. Some authors have used co-operative game theory to show the advantages of various arrangements between countries. Mayer (1981) studies a co-ordinated reduction in tariff rates. The countries are searching for an equilibrium improving the situation of both parties. Free trade is one candidate, but as shown on figure 7.3, there are a lot of other policy combinations, where one country puts a tariff and the other country a subsidy, which satisfy the conditions of Pareto-efficiency for the two players. It is then a matter of bargaining between the negotiators to find the final outcome. Mayer suggests the use of formulae like the ones used in GATT negotiations: equal proportionate reductions, for example. Although these formulae are nice for practical and political reasons, and they have been used in practice, the basic difficulty is not solved since the various possible formulae have different effects on the countries' welfares and the bargaining problem is simply transferred to the choice of formulae.

Riezman (1982) uses the Nash solution for the bargaining problem. Under simple assumptions about the choices open to each country: either free trade or the optimal response to the other's tariff, and allowing mixed strategies, one can define a feasible set of outcomes in the space of countries' welfares. As in the original Nash model, the players use the non-co-operative equilibrium as a threat point.[6] Remember that both point N in figure 7.3 and autarky can serve as threat points (Dixit and Kyle, 1985 argue in favour of autarky as the more natural threat point). The solution is then characterized by the maximization of the product of the differences between the values of welfare with and without co-operation, for example:

$$(W - W_N)(W^* - W_N^*)$$

if N is taken as the threat point.

The Nash bargaining solution has also been applied by Chan (1988) to discuss the impact on the negotiation outcome due to different feasible utility-pay-off sets. He shows that a country's benefits are greater the more imbalanced the trading partner's commodity tastes and endowments.

As mentioned above, the bargaining outcome may imply that one country ends up subsidizing imports, which is hard to implement in practice. Also without binding agreements, a supranational force would be required to monitor the bargaining solution. This force does not exist in the present world and the prisoner's dilemma nature of the game may induce the countries to revert rapidly to the non-co-operative outcome.

Then it is worth considering the effect of the repetition of the game on the dynamic non-co-operative equilibrium. It is now well established in oligopoly theory and other applications of game theory that strategic moves such as threats and promises offer serious possibilities of tacit co-operation in dynamic games. The same logic is easily applicable to tariff games.

The complete developments along these lines use repeated games and supergames (infinite repetition of the stage game). But one may note that straightforward applications of conjectural variation models, despite the well-known weaknesses of this approach, give first interesting insights on the different possibilities of tacit co-operation related to the perception of the other player's relative aggressiveness. In the Jensen and Thursby model (1984), it is clear that higher conjectures about retaliations lead to lower equilibrium tariffs, just as in oligopoly the expectation of aggressive responses from rivals leads to a more collusive behaviour.

When the study is developed in a proper dynamic framework, the conditions of increased tacit co-operation can be formally defined. Consider first that the two governments expect an infinite repetition of the constituent game. The game consisting of all the repetitions is called a supergame. Each period's choices will depend on the history of the game and the memory of prior plays. A strategy in the supergame is a plan of actions for each period and it is natural to plan different actions according to the rival's prior plays.

Does this infinitely repeated game admit a perfect Nash equilibrium? There is an obvious solution: the repetition of the static Nash equilibrium. But there are other solutions, eventually more 'collusive'.

Let us revert again to the assumption that there are only two strategies in the stage game: free trade (F) and the static Nash equilibrium (N). A country may promise to be a free trader as long as the other country has not defected from the efficient solutions, and threaten to permanently revert to the Nash tariff-ridden equilibrium otherwise.

The threat is credible since after having observed a rival country's defection a reversion to the static Nash point constitutes a subgame Nash equilibrium. If the losses induced by the collapse of the 'colluding' behaviour are sufficiently high compared to the gains from a unilateral defection, the promise to be friendly is also credible. The intertwined threats and promises would then generate self-enforcing co-operative behaviour.

Let us briefly state the conditions under which the promises are credible. Each country is supposed to maximize the sum of its discounted total welfare. Let W^F denote the total welfare for one period in the case of free trade, W^d the welfare that could be obtained by unilateral defection and W^N the welfare which can be reached in the static Nash equilibrium. Consider a country contemplating the choice of remaining at free trade or defecting in order to get transitory benefits. If the two countries stay in free trade, the total welfare on the infinite horizon will be $W^F[1/(1 - \beta)]$ with β a positive discount factor $0 < \beta < 1$. If a country unilaterally defects it will obtain during the first period a welfare level $W^d > W^F$, and thereafter the sum of the W^N until infinity. So its total welfare would be $W^d + [\beta W^N/(1 - \beta)]$. It is clear that this country will remain a free trader if

$$\beta \geq [(W^d - W^F)/(W^d - W^N)] \tag{7.13}$$

or

$$(W^d - W^F) \leq (W^F - W^N)/r \tag{7.13'}$$

(with r, the rate of discount; $\beta = 1/1 + r$) that is, if the discounted future losses more than offset the immediate gains.

Condition (7.13) will be met if the transitory gains from defection are bounded ($W^d < \infty$), if the reversion to the static Nash equilibrium constitutes a true punishment ($W^N < W^F$), and β is high enough (close enough to unity).

One problem with the previous analysis is the multiplicity of equilibria of the supergame. In our presentation above we restricted the choices at each period to two actions: the static Nash equilibrium or the Pareto-efficient outcome (free trade). But there may be a lot of other tariff policies. A theorem of unknown origin, called the folk theorem, tells us that, for a discount factor close enough to one, any outcome between the static Nash point and free trade can be sustained as a perfect equilibrium of the supergame.[7] A preplay negotiation between the governments to find an agreement on the Pareto-efficient outcome(s) does not solve the multiplicity problem since it conveys the idea that the agents could renegotiate after a defection in order to avoid the mutually costly punishments. This possibility of renegotiations crucially undermines the credibility of the threats supporting the efficient outcome.

The adoption of one equilibrium among the set of possible candidates may lie on communication and behavioural rules like simple rules of thumb between players or the convergence to a focal point (Schelling, 1960), which in this case may be the free trade point. A great deal has still to be learnt from experimental economics and experimental games in this area.

It is also worth noting that the choice of an optimal punishment strategy along the lines suggested by Abreu (1988) for oligopoly theory could increase the likelihood of an outcome close to free trade. The idea is that to achieve free trade, for a given discount rate, the players must design the most severe punishment for defectors. Reversion to the static Nash equilibrium is in general not the most severe punishment and so is insufficient to sustain free trade. Fortunately here, as Dixit (1987a) noted, autarky could be used as a credible threat since it is also an equilibrium of the static game.

A second problem with the previous analysis is the assumption of an infinite repetition of the game. The governments may perceive their relations as limited in time. When the stage game is repeated only over a limited number of periods, it would seem that the only perfect equilibrium is the simple repetition of the static game Nash equilibrium. This result is easily deduced by checking each period equilibrium, starting by the last one and going back to the previous ones. At the last round there is no other credible action than the static Nash strategy. But a threat to punish defection at the penultimate round is then worthless and not credible. So the static Nash equilibrium will result also at this stage; and so on back to the first round.

On the other hand, some experiments conducted by Axelrod (1983) have shown that an efficient outcome may emerge from a non-co-operative finitely repeated game when agents adopt a 'tit-for-tat' strategy. Each agent simply reproduces what its rival did at the previous stage: defect if it defected, co-operate if it co-operated. Axelrod underpins the interesting properties of tit-for-tat with regard to communication and human relation: it is a simple, clear and forgiving strategy. Although it raises interesting questions about the relationships between formal game theory and experimental studies of human behaviour, this argument is not too serious in our case since there are two static Nash equilibria: the point called N (representing an equilibrium with trade and tariffs) and autarky. The mutual threat to play autarky at the last stage is credible. Each government understands that if it does not play nicely at the penultimate round, the other country will retaliate by choosing autarky at the end. A straightforward application of Benoît and Krishna (1985) would illustrate the possibilities of improvement in co-operation in the previous stages of the game.

Formal game theory and its various applications to oligopoly offer some other reasons why tacit co-operation may emerge from a repetition of the game with a finite horizon. In particular, the introduction of incomplete information can bring some level of collusion. This was first suggested by Dixit (1987a) who used the model of Kreps and Wilson (1982a) to describe governments playing Bayesian strategies to learn about the nature of the other government. A long phase of free trade may be rational before a collapse of the tacit co-ordination in the last phase of the play. Jensen and Thursby (1984) have also proposed a model of tacit co-operation due to incomplete information.

All these models can explain how countries are normally able to sustain a larger level of trade (freer trade) than with static Nash equilibrium tariffs. But they cannot explain why, in certain periods, there are reversals to a higher level of protection or why countries use special measures like voluntary export restraints (VERs) or orderly market arrangements. Bagwell and Staiger (1990) have studied a repeated game model in the presence of volatility in the trade volume. This trade war model, clearly inspired by the work of Rotemberg and Saloner (1986) on price wars in oligopoly, shows that episodes of 'special protection' might be viewed as part of a tacit agreement to sustain a level of trade higher than the static non-co-operative outcome. In a repeated game situation with volatile trade swings, increases in the volume of trade create incentives for each government to defect unilaterally from a collusive equilibrium. A limited level of protection called 'managed trade' is then required to lessen the effects of the increase in the trade volume and to sustain a level of tacit co-operation.

In another recent extension of the repeated game analysis, Riezman (1991) proposed a model focusing on the effects of uncertainty and of the observability of protectionist measures. If protection is not observable, the outcome depends on the trigger strategies[8] (see Friedman, 1971) used to punish eventual defections from the co-operative agreement. Countries can use an import trigger strategy. Cheating on the tacit agreement would then be detected by observing home imports since an increase in the foreign country's tariff rate would lead to a fall in home imports (given some restrictions on offer curve elasticities). So if home imports fall under some predetermined critical level, this might with some probability reveal foreign country cheating. A period of punishment (high tariffs) would then follow. Riezman shows that, in this case, some level of co-operation can be supported. But countries can also use a terms of trade trigger strategy, that is try to detect cheating by observing the terms of trade changes. When the terms of trade are too low, this might probabilistically indicate cheating and be followed by a reversion to a high tariff period. But in this case, tacit co-operation cannot occur. This is so because reversions to high tariffs are also triggered by terms of trade being too high (contrary to the case of oligopoly rivalry – see Green and Porter, 1984 – or to the case of import trigger strategy above, here each agent's cheating moves the observed variable in opposite directions). Each country has thus an incentive to cheat because from an individualistic point of view it reduces the probability of reversion to high tariffs. This result shows clearly the crucial importance of the choice of the mechanism used to induce co-operation.

Some other refinements of this approach may be expected in the near future. In the longer term, one may hope to have a better understanding of the emergence of focal points to solve the problem of the multiplicity of equilibria. One particular question of interest in our case is the study of the motivations for protection. In reality tariff wars rarely correspond to terms of trade objectives and it is more than doubtful that governments ever have optimal tariff objectives. Fortunately most of the previous analysis applies to situations where governments have other motivations like employment or responses to lobbying activities. A mixture of this theory of strategic protectionism and the political economy of trade policy could certainly constitute a promising approach (see Feenstra and Lewis, 1987). This more 'realistic' view of tariff conflicts and tacit co-operation requires a good understanding of the functioning and outcomes of games between governments when the other agents, essentially firms, have some market power.

7.5 STRATEGIC INTERACTIONS BETWEEN GOVERNMENTS IN THE PRESENCE OF OLIGOPOLY

In sections 7.2 and 7.3, 'strategic trade policy' was defined as unilateral government intervention in situations of strategic interaction between domestic and foreign firms. In section 7.4 it was defined as strategic interaction between governments in otherwise perfectly competitive situations. We want now to study cases where the game-theoretic elements are present at both levels: in the first stage there is a Nash equilibrium between the governments who decide upon the levels of some policy instruments knowing precisely how the second-stage Nash equilibrium between the firms depends upon their first-period policy choices.

For the sake of simplicity we shall assume as in sections 7.2 and 7.3 that only two firms (a domestic and a foreign one) compete exclusively on a third market. The fundamentals of the public intervention are obviously the same when both governments are active as when one of the two is committed to *laissez-faire*. The outcome of the overall game generally differs, however. Moreover it is now sensible to ask whether the countries lose or gain in a 'policy equilibrium' with respect to the *laissez-faire* situation. We shall now try to shed some light on these two issues, assuming that the two firms are on an equal footing (viz. they have the same cost functions, face symmetrical demand conditions . . .).

Things are simpler when both firms are incumbents. Assume that the governments are restricted to use linear subsidy (tax) schedules as is implicit in the existing literature (allowing them to use more general subsidy/tax functions would entail indeterminacy of the equilibrium of the policy game, at least in deterministic models). When firms compete in quantities, the policy equilibrium coincides with a kind of 'consistent conjectural variations' (CCV) equilibrium since each government knows the reaction function of the foreign firm in the second stage of the game and maximizes against this reaction function (remember that at a CCV equilibrium a firm has a guess about its rival's reaction function which happens to be correct around the equilibrium point). Firms' net profits (i.e. net of export subsidies) are lower than at the *laissez-faire* (Cournot) equilibrium. This is the classical prisoner's dilemma model which, more generally, occurs whenever the firms' variables are strategic substitutes according to the Bulow, Geneakoplos and Klemperer (1984) definition. Under the same assumption as in section 7.2, the second-order conditions for the firms' profit maximization are satisfied and the government of country i's choice of the unit export subsidy s is equivalent to the choice of an output level for the home firm, given s and the reaction function of the other firm. It is not difficult to check that firms produce a larger output at this kind of 'double Stackelberg equilibrium' than at the Cournot equilibrium and that their profits are accordingly lower. Indeed it is optimal for each government, given the policy chosen by the other, to induce its own firm to take a more aggressive stance whenever the firms' variables are strategic substitutes in order to benefit from the reaction of the other firm. Of course, the validity of these results is limited to the case where direct quantity controls are not available. Indeed, Cooper and Riezman (1989) have shown that there are strategic advantages associated with the use of direct quantity controls: the domestic firm is prevented from reacting to the policies of the foreign government since its reaction function is now rigid. In a deterministic model these controls clearly dominate export subsidies and lead to a policy equilibrium identical to the *laissez-faire*, Cournot, one. If, however, there is some demand uncertainty, Cooper and Riezman have shown that the strategic advantages of direct quantity controls have to be balanced against the losses from suboptimal adaptation to uncertainty.

When the firms compete in prices, the policy equilibrium is equivalent as above to a CCV equilibrium but here the firms' net profits are larger than at a *laissez-faire* equilibrium (which is here the usual Bertrand equilibrium). This 'spontaneous harmony' result occurs more generally when the firms' variables are strategic complements (see for instance the linear supply-function case in Laussel, 1991). Under the assumptions made in section 7.2, the government's choice of s_i amounts to choosing p_i knowing s_j and the reaction function of firm j. It is easy to show that the equilibrium prices are higher at this policy equilibrium than at the Bertrand equilibrium and that the firms' net profits are accordingly larger. It is indeed optimal for each government to induce its domestic firm to take a less aggressive stance in order to benefit from the rival's reaction which here goes in the right direction since the prices are strategic complements. Direct price controls, if available, are clearly dominated here by export taxes. Under price controls, the policy equilibrium will be identical to the Bertrand equilibrium, because a rigid reaction function prevents the domestic firm from raising its price in reaction to a price rise by the foreign firm. Moreover, under demand uncertainty, there are losses due to suboptimal adaptation to uncertainty which follow from direct price controls.

To conclude with the two incumbents' case, note that if one firm has an advantage over the other (such as a cost advantage, for instance) it is possible to obtain policy equilibria where the former gains while the latter loses when one compares net profits with their *laissez-faire* values.

When the firms are potential entrants and share the same characteristics, it is useful to establish the same distinction as in section 7.3 between two cases. In case I, where $\Pi(1) - F > 0$ and $\Pi(2) - F < 0$ under *laissez-faire*, the optimal unilateral public intervention was to grant the domestic firm an entry-conditional subsidy just sufficient to make entry a dominant strategy. When both governments are active, they neutralize each other and the policy equilibria coincide exactly with the *laissez-faire* ones. This is simply because the governments, on which the entry decision now actually falls, maximize the same pay-off functions as firms under *laissez-faire*. The game has the same equilibria (E, NE) and (NE, E) which differ simply by the name of the firm which enters the market.

In case II where $\Pi(2) - F > 0$, the game becomes very complex. Each government has to decide both upon an entry-conditional subsidy (or tax) and an export subsidy (or tax), knowing how the equilibrium of the subsequent game between the two firms depends upon its policy choices. Given the policy chosen by the foreign government, the domestic government has always to select either an entry deterrence or an accommodation strategy. Consequently, the reaction functions of the governments are discontinuous and there may be multiple equilibria as well as no equilibrium at all, even in otherwise very simple models. Games with more than two potential entrants are inextricably complex.

7.6 EMPIRICAL STUDIES OF STRATEGIC TRADE POLICIES

For several years an increasing number of studies have tried to shed some light on the empirical validity of strategic trade policy arguments. First, and although this may hardly be ranked under the heading of empirical studies, one may note that several major contributors to the theory of strategic trade have presented somewhat informal but very clever comments about how the theory fits with facts and institutions characterizing international trade and policies (see Krugman, 1984a, 1987a; Dixit, 1987b, and many contributions in Krugman, 1986). Most of these papers express some doubts about straightforward applications of the Brander and Spencer arguments. Krugman provides some evidence about the inefficiency of strategic targeting of industries in Europe or in Japan. Dixit emphasizes the inadequacies of the American institutions for developing credible strategic moves. More generally, these authors wonder if the monopolistic rents in the potential strategic sectors are large enough to justify taking the risk of commercial wars. None of the big industrial sectors targeted by governments in the world seems to obtain the high monopolistic rents which are supposed to be the heart of the conflict. It may happen that a large portion of these rents are hidden by relatively high wages or other inflated costs. But the argument about the weakness of rents seem to be a serious obstacle to the implementation of strategic trade policies for oligopolies.

Formal empirical research in this area has also been started in recent years, although, at this stage, not a single theoretical proposition has been properly tested in an econometric model. Empirical work consists essentially of computable equilibrium models, calibrated on actual data and used for various policy simulations. Partial equilibrium models have been used to study the potential effects of strategic policies for particular oligopolistic industries. General equilibrium models have been applied to the study of tariff and subsidy conflicts and tacit co-operation between countries. A detailed survey of this empirical literature can be found in Richardson (1989).

The diversity of results obtained in the theory of strategic trade policy for oligopolies (see section 7.1) required some attempts to quantify the magnitude of the effects of different policies and to assess the sensitivity of the outcomes to the assumptions concerning market structures and firm behaviour. The complexity of the models and the difficulty of obtaining reliable data were taken as justifications for the use of calibrated simulation models. An industry is chosen as being a good candidate for rent-shifting and other strategic purposes. A partial equilibrium model is carefully specified to get a good representation of the main characteristics of this industry. Then, the standard technique of computable general equilibrium (CGE) is used. Some parameters are taken from past econometric studies and calibration to real data gives the remaining parameters required to make the equilibrium of the model correspond to the observed figures in a base year. Various simulation exercises can then be developed. The purpose is not to test a model but more modestly to illustrate theoretical relations by using a real world example. It is hoped that if the model captures relatively well the characteristics of the industry and if the main parameters are not too sensitive to data imperfections the results could give good insights on the direction of the effects if not on their precise magnitude.

All the empirical studies developed along these lines use various specifications of oligopoly behaviour (often represented by the values of conjectural variation coefficients) with different specifications of demand functions, cost conditions, product differentiation strategies, and number of active governments.

In the pioneering work on the subject Dixit (1988) has chosen to study the US–Japan rivalry on the American car market. The analysis is conducted in a conjectural variation model of oligopoly with differentiated products: American cars and Japanese cars. There is no entry in the market, demand is linear, marginal costs are constant. The author examines the positive effects of the VERs decided in 1981 and finds that they encouraged collusion among firms. The normative analysis considers different optimal policies depending on the availability of the instruments: optimal tariff, optimal subsidy and optimal tariff-cum-subsidy. The assumption of linear demand functions is a priori favourable to a positive optimal tariff. But it is interesting to know how far from zero this tariff might be. Dixit finds that a positive tariff and production subsidies are desirable but that the corresponding gains in welfare would be relatively small. Laussel, Montet and Peguin-Feissolle (1988) adapted the model to the conditions of the European car market and studied the optimal policies of the Japanese government as well. The effects of optimal tariffs are also very small and the current quantitative restrictions appear to be nearly optimal for the Japanese.

Smith and Venables (1988, 1990) have studied strategic policies for various industries in the UK and in Europe. They introduce economies of scale, product differentiation and different entry conditions. When applied to the UK optimal trade policy, the model gives results similar to Dixit. When applied to post-1992 European integration, the model shows that the increase in welfare would be greater without a maintenance of national market segmentation and with free entry.

Baldwin and Krugman have introduced dynamic economies of scale and a few other original cost and demand conditions to study two interesting and politically sensitive cases: the semiconductor market (1988) and the wide-bodied aircraft market (1989). In the first model, assuming that the 16K RAM Japanese market has been closed to imports, it appears that this policy, through the learning effects, has had the export promotion consequences enlightened by theory (Krugman, 1984b). Unfortunately, the welfare effects are evidently negative for the USA but also for Japan. The second model shows that the subsidies given to Airbus have stimulated competitive pressures in this highly concentrated market: according to the simulations prices would have been 40 per cent higher with a Boeing monopoly than with the subsidized entry of Airbus. But again the net welfare effects are not positive. In Europe, the final outcome is a transfer from taxpayers to consumers with a slightly negative net effect. The policy is of course harmful for Boeing's equity owners. The only real benefits of the policy go to third countries whose consumers take advantage of lower prices without supporting the cost of the subsidies.

The results of these models must be regarded with great caution. Their authors themselves insist on the dependence on crude assumptions and limited observations. The robustness of the results has been explicitly discussed by several researchers. Krishna (1990) expresses scepticism about the use of calibrated models. She reconsidered Dixit's analysis with a different model, including product differentiation between cars of the same country. The optimal policy is then different from Dixit's results and the optimal policy in Dixit would now lower American welfare. On the other hand, Venables (1990) is more positive on the robustness issue. He studies the problem in a multi-country calibrated model for nine EC industries. Calibration and simulation exercises are done under alternative theories of trade policy. The author finds that the policy effects are not too sensitive to the type of equilibrium. But the effects of strategic trade policies are always relatively small.

Despite these words of caution about the interpretation of these calibrated exercises, one can obtain a set of common results enlightning the robustness and empirical relevance of strategic policy measures.

First, all these studies permit us to have an approximate idea of the relative size of the effects of strategic trade policy. The theory fits well with a set of observed facts in various oligopolistic industries. In general, they reveal that the policies may have significant effects on output and prices and important redistributive effects.

The most frequently cited result is certainly the relatively small size of the net effects on domestic welfare. In certain cases (Dixit, 1988; Smith and Venables, 1988, 1990; Laussel, Montet and Peguin-Feissolle, 1988) some level of protection plus subsidies to the industry are capable of increasing domestic welfare. In other cases, the suppression of obstacles to trade is the source of welfare gains (Baldwin and Krugman, 1988, 1989; Smith and Venables, 1988; Rodrik, 1988). The introduction of assumptions less favourable to the case of strategic policy, like foreigners' relations (Laussel, Montet and Peguin-Feissolle, 1988) or distortions due to the subsidy policy (Dixit, 1987b) lessen or eliminate the eventual gains. In general, the results are not in favour of straightforward applications of the theory.

The standard results about the hierarchy of trade and industrial policies (see Bhagwati, 1971 for the general theory and Laussel and Montet, 1988 for a discussion of the hierarchy of policies with imperfect competition) are generally verified. Trade policy is less efficient than a direct correction of the distortions, for example anti-trust policy.

Another major finding from these exercises is the importance of the conditions of entry (Venables and Smith, and Rodrik). The effects of imperfect competition and increasing returns to scale are significantly larger in the case where entry is possible.

All the works discussed above consider partial equilibrium of certain selected industries. The assumption is that the policy for the targeted industry will not have any significant effect on the allocation of resources in the other sectors. But if other industries are also characterized by imperfect competition and economies of scale, the protection of a particular sector may have significant negative effects on the others and lead to undesirable changes in welfare (see Dixit and Grossman, 1986 for a theoretical analysis). A complete assessment of the interactions between sectors requires a general equilibrium model which can also be quantified using the techniques of CGE modelling. Computable general equilibrium models are in general designed for applications of competitive analysis. This is still useful for the study of strategic policies between governments when agents are price-takers. A few CGE models have been constructed to study trade policy in the presence of imperfect competition and increasing returns. Cox and Harris (1984) and Harris (1984) examine the effects of trade liberalization in Canada, stressing the role of the assumptions concerning entry, increasing returns to scale and pricing behaviour by firms. Domestic goods are considered as imperfect substitutes for imports. Canadian firms are price-takers with respect to world prices, but have between themselves a relatively collusive behaviour corresponding to a mixture of a monopolistic competition outcomes and the focal pricing policy described by Eastman and Stykolt (1960). It is then clear that trade liberalization would reduce the prices for Canadian goods, reduce the number of firms and reduce their costs through a move down the average cost curves.

The authors study the effects of the elimination of tariffs and other barriers either unilaterally or in a multilateral agreement. The welfare gains may be as high as 4 per cent of the GNP for unilateral liberalization and 9 per cent of the GNP for multilateral agreement. Beyond the precise magnitude of the gains, the major idea is certainly their relative importance compared to similar studies using a competitive framework. Other works along these lines come to relatively less important gains when the assumption of focal pricing policy is not adopted and some other assumptions are modified. Brown and Stern (1988), for instance, get gains of 1.1 per cent of GNP for Canada and 0.1 per cent for the USA after a bilateral suppression of protectionism between the two countries.

All these works show the importance of the degree of collusion in pricing, the role of entry and the scale effects. Although one may expect a refinement of the methods used in this area, it is now possible to conclude that the results of CGE models are not favourable to strategic policy.

Despite their weaknesses, empirical studies of strategic policies have already been very useful in showing that intervention in favour of oligopolies can rarely bring high welfare gains if any and that general equilibrium considerations definitely confirm the advantages of free trade. Of course the analysis must now be developed in order to improve the robustness of the results. A serious improvement is required in terms of measurement and collection of data indispensable for studying imperfect competition phenomena: trade barriers, price–cost margins, etc. This information must then be treated in econometric studies allowing systematic testing of theories. Important progress has been made recently in the field of econometric studies of oligopoly (see Bresnahan, 1989). Importing these methods in the area of trade policy is desirable (see Levinsohn, 1991 for a first attempt).

7.7 CONCLUSIONS

Strategic trade policy is certainly an important achievement which has considerably modified the standard way of thinking about trade policy. The new theory and its empirical counterparts have shown that free trade can remain the best policy only after new important qualifications and that it cannot be obtained without an amount of tacit co-operation between governments. Many commentators have interpreted the theory as a source of arguments in favour of sophisticated protectionism and industrial policy. The theme of strategic interventionism has even become popular among businessmen and politicians, particularly as a reaction to Japanese successes in several key industries. But the theoretical and empirical results obtained at this stage may rather be used as a subtle defence of free trade. One can agree with the defenders of protectionism on the inadequacy of traditional views resulting from direct applications of purely competitive models. One can then agree on the necessity of including in the theory such factors as oligopolistic behaviour, increasing returns to scale, learning effects, strategic interactions between governments, etc. But one must stress that if optimal rules of government intervention can be obtained under assumptions featuring the previous factors, the foundations of interventionism are still disputable. Remember that the major results rest on the idea that the governments have more credibility than the firms for certain announced actions; is this really true? One may also note that the direction of desirable actions cannot be defined a priori, but only on a case-by-case basis. This raises the serious issue of the amount and quality of information needed by the government to define optimal policies (on this point see Grossman, 1986). Furthermore, interventionism always leads to lobbying activities and other pressures from interest groups. So in the end, for reasons such as insufficient information, complexity

of oligopoly behaviour, general equilibrium effects, risks of mutually destruct-
ive tariff or subsidy wars, lobbying activities, the best policy may remain free
trade. The defence of free trade is then more powerful than through dogmatic
repetitions of the good old arguments derived in perfectly competitive
frameworks.

The major achievement of the new theory may be to illuminate the
incentives that the governments face to protect domestic oligopolies and the
difficulties they encounter to get out of prisoner's dilemma in trade conflicts.
Understanding more precisely these aspects of trade policy and quantifying
them will improve the general capacity of institutions like the GATT to devise
new rules favourable to free trade. Ironically strategic trade theory may
happen to be the most powerful set of ideas to help promote freer trade in
the modern world.

NOTES

1 This chapter uses extensively basic concepts of non-co-operative game theory. We
   will recall some definitions, but for a good introduction to non-co-operative game
   theory see D. Kreps (1990) or J. Tirole (1988) and for a good survey of
   applications of game theory in international economics see McMillan (1986).
      A game is a situation in which each agent looks for maximizing her/his pay-off
   by choosing the best plan of actions, taking into account the interdependencies
   with the other players. A description of an agent's planned actions in all possible
   situations is called a strategy. A particular game is then defined by a set of players,
   a set of strategies for each player from which the agent will choose the one he/she
   considers the best, and a pay-off function for each agent.
      Loosely speaking, one can say that at a Nash equilibrium each agent does the
   best he/she can given the other agent's actions. More formally, a set of strategies
   is a Nash equilibrium if player i's choice is optimal given all the other players'
   choices, and the same is true for each player. At a Nash equilibrium the set of
   expectations concerning each agent's choice corresponds to the chosen actions and
   nobody wants to change his/her behaviour.
2 The concept of subgame perfect equilibrium allows us to get rid of non-credible
   strategies, that is announced strategies which would become irrational at the
   moment when implementation was supposed to occur. A perfect Nash equilibrium
   requires that the strategies chosen by the players be a Nash equilibrium in every
   subgame (in a multi-period game, the beginning of each period is also the
   beginning of a subgame), whatever actions have gone before.
3 One says that a player has a dominant strategy when this he/she has one optimal
   choice of strategy no matter what the other players do.
4 The prisoner's dilemma is a typical example of a game having a dominant strategy
   equilibrium, at which each player, playing rationally, ends up with a lower pay-off
   than if he/she had played a more co-operative strategy with his/her rival.
5 The sum of the elasticity of export demand and the elasticity of import demand
   exceeds one.
6 The threat point gives the credible outcome in case of disagreement between the
   players.
7 In fact any individually rational outcome can be maintained as a Nash equilibrium
   of the supergame denoting as individually rational any outcome which gives each

agent a pay-off no lower than the one it could obtain by its own actions [its minmax pay-off].

8 A trigger strategy implies acting collusively or 'co-operatively' if co-operation occurred in the previous period and turning to a punishment action if some defection occurs. In case of imperfect information, the punishment action is triggered by the observation of some events used to detect eventual cheating on the agreement.

REFERENCES

Abreu, D. 1988: On the theory of infinitely repeated games with discounting. *Econometrica*, 56, 383–96.

Axelrod, R. 1983: *The Evolution of Cooperation*. New York: Basic Books.

Bagwell, K. and Staiger, R. 1990: A theory of managed trade. *American Economic Review*, 80, 779–95.

Baldwin, R. and Krugman, P. 1988: Market access and international competition: a simulation study of 16K random access memories. In R. Feenstra (ed.), *Empirical Methods for International Trade*, Cambridge, Mass.: MIT Press, 171–97.

Baldwin, R. and Krugman, P. 1989: Industrial policy and international competition in wide-bodied aircraft. In R. Baldwin (ed.), *Trade Policy Issues and Empirical Analysis*, University of Chicago Press and NBER.

Benoît, J. P. and Krishna, V. 1985: Finitely repeated games. *Econometrica*, 53, 890–904.

Bhagwati, J. N. 1971: The generalized theory of distortions and welfare. In J. Bhagwati et al. (eds), *Trade, Balance of Payments and Growth*, Amsterdam: North-Holland, 69–90.

Brander, J. and Spencer, B. 1984a: Trade warfare: tariffs and certels. *Journal of International Economics*, 16, 227–42.

Brander, J. and Spencer, B. 1984: Tariff protection and imperfect competition. In H. Kierzkowski (ed.), *Monopolistic Competition and International Trade*, New York: Oxford University Press, 194–206.

Brander, J. and Spencer, B. 1985: Export subsidies and international market share rivalry. *Journal of International Economics*, 18, 83–91.

Bresnahan, T. 1989: Empirical studies of industries with market power. In R. Schmalensee and R. Willig (eds), *Handbook of Industrial Organization*, Amsterdam: North-Holland, 1011–57.

Brown, D. and Stern, R. 1988: Computable general equilibrium estimates of the gains from U.S.–Canadian trade liberalization. Paper presented at the Conference on The Economic Aspects of Regional Trading Arrangements, Lehigh University, Bethlehem, Pennsylvania.

Bulow, J., Geneakoplos, J. and Klemperer, P. 1985: Multimarket oligopoly: strategic substitutes and complements. *Journal of Political Economy*, 93, 488–511.

Chan, K. S. 1988: Trade negotiations in a Nash bargaining model. *Journal of International Economics*, 25, 353–63.

Cooper, R. and Riezman, R. 1989: Uncertainty and the choice of trade policy in oligopolistic industries. *Review of Economic Studies*, 56, 129–40.

Cox, D. and Harris, R. 1984: *Trade Industrial Policy and Canadian Manufacturing*. Toronto: University of Toronto Press.

Dixit, A. 1987a: Strategic aspects of trade policy. In T. Bewley (ed.), *Advances in Economic Theory: Fifth World Congress*, New York: Cambridge University Press, 329–62.

Dixit, A. 1987b: How should the United States respond to other countries' trade policies? In R. Stern (ed.), *U.S. Trade Policies in a Changing World Economy*, Cambridge, Mass.: MIT Press, 245–82.

Dixit, A. 1988: Optimal trade and industrial policies for the U.S. automobile industry. In R. Feenstra (ed.), *Empirical Methods for International Trade*, Cambridge, Mass.: MIT Press, 141–65.

Dixit, A. and Grossman, G. 1986: Targeted export promotion with several oligopolistic industries. *Journal of International Economics*, 21, 233–49.

Dixit, A. and Kyle, A. 1985: On the use of trade restrictions for entry promotion and deterrence. *American Economic Review*, 75, 139–52.

Eastman, H. and Stykolt, S. 1960: A model for the study of protected oligopolies. *Economic Journal*, 70, 336–47.

Eaton, J. and Grossman, G. 1986: Optimal trade and industrial policy under oligopoly. *Quarterly Journal of Economics*, 101, 383–406.

Feenstra, R. and Lewis, T. 1987: Negotiated trade restrictions with private political pressure. University of California-Davis Working Paper no. 290.

Friedman, J. W. 1971: A non-cooperative equilibrium for supergames. *Review of Economic Studies*, 38, 1–12.

Fudenberg, D. and Tirole, J. 1984: The fat-cat effect, the puppy-dog ploy and the lean and hungry look. *American Economic Review Paper and Proceedings*, 74, 361–6.

Green, E. and Porter, R. 1984: Noncooperative collusion under imperfect price information. *Econometrica*, 52, 87–100.

Harris, R. 1984: Applied general equilibrium analysis of small open economies with scale economies and imperfect competition. *American Economic Review*, 74, 1016–33.

Horstman, I. and Markusen, J. 1986: Up your average cost curve: inefficient entry and the new protectionism. *Journal of International Economics*, 20, 225–49.

Horwell, J. D. 1966: Optimum tariffs and tariff policy. *Review of Economic Studies*, 33, 147–58.

Jensen, R. and Thursby, M. 1984: Free trade: two non-cooperative approaches. Working paper, Ohio State University.

Johnson, H. G. 1954: Optimum tariffs and retaliation. *Review of Economic Studies*, 21, 142–53.

Kennan, J. and Riezman, R. 1988: Do big countries win tariff wars? *International Economic Review*, 29, 81–5.

Klemperer, P. and Meyer, P. 1989: Supply function equilibria in oligopoly under uncertainty. *Econometrica*, 57, 1243–77.

Kreps, D. 1990: *A Course in Microeconomic Theory*. New York: Harvester Wheatsheaf.

Kreps, D. and Wilson, R. 1982a: Reputation and imperfect information. *Journal of Economic Theory*, 27, 253–79.

Kreps, D. and Wilson, R. 1982b: Sequential equilibria. *Econometrica*, 50: 863–94.

Krishna, K. 1990: The non-optimality of optimal trade policies: the U.S. automobile industry revisited, 1979–1985. In P. Krugman and A. Smith (eds), *Empirical Studies of Strategic Trade Policies*, London: CEPR and NBER.

Krishna, K. and Thursby, M. 1991: Optimal policies with strategic distortions. *Journal of International Economics*, 31, 291–308.

Krugman, P. R. 1984a: The U.S. response to foreign industrial targeting. *Brookings Papers on Economic Activity*, 1, 77–131.

Krugman, P. R. 1984b: Import protection as export promotion: international competition in the presence of oligopoly and economies of scale. In H. Kierzkowski (ed.), *Monopolistic Competition and International Trade*, New York: Oxford University Press, 180–93.

Krugman, P. R. 1987a: Strategic sectors an international competition. In R. Stern (ed.), *U.S. Trade Policies in a Changing World Economy*, Cambridge, Mass.: MIT Press, 207–32.

Krugman, P. R. 1987b: Is free trade passé? *Journal of Economic Perspectives*, 1, 132–44.

Laussel, D. 1991: Strategic commercial policy revisited: a supply function equilibrium model. *American Economic Review*, 82, 84–99.

Laussel, D. and Montet, C. 1988: On the hierarchy of trade and industrial policy for oligopolistic industries. Mimeo, University of Aix-Marseille II, 23pp.

Laussel, D., Montet, C. and Peguin-Feissolle, A. 1988: Optimal trade policy under oligopoly: a calibrated model of the Europe–Japan rivalry in the EEC car market. *European Economic Review*, 32, 1547–66.

Levinsohn, J. 1991: Testing the imports-as-market-discipline hypothesis. Mimeo, Hoover Institution, Stanford, 23pp.

McMillan, J. 1986: *Game Theory in International Economics: vol. 1, Fundamentals of Pure and Applied Economics*, M. Kemp (ed.), London: Harwood.

Mayer, W. 1981: Theoretical considerations on negotiated tariff adjustments. *Oxford Economic Papers*, 33, 135–53.

Richardson, J. D. 1989: Empirical research on trade liberalization with imperfect competition: a survey. *OECD Economic Studies*, 12, 7–58.

Riezman, R. 1982: Tariff retaliation from a strategic viewpoint. *Southern Economic Journal*, 48, 583–93.

Riezman, R. 1991: Dynamic tariffs with asymmetric information. *Journal of International Economics*, 30, 267–84.

Rodrik, D. 1988: Imperfect competition, scale economies, and trade policy in developing countries. In R. E. Baldwin (ed.), *Trade Policy Issues and Empirical Analysis*, Chicago: University of Chicago Press, 109–37.

Rotemberg, J. and Saloner, G. 1986: A supergame-theoretic model of price wars during booms. *American Economic Review*, 76, 390–407.

Schelling, T. 1960: *The Strategy of Conflict*. Cambridge, Mass.: Harvard University Press.

Smith, A. and Venables, A. 1988: Completing the internal market in the European Community: some industry simulations. *European Economic Review*, 32, 1501–26.

Smith, A. and Venables, A. 1990: Trade and industrial policy: some simulations for EEC manufacturing. In P. Krugman and A. Smith (eds), *Empirical Studies of Strategic Trade Policies*, London: CEPR and NBER.

Spencer, B. and Brander, J. 1983: International R&D rivalry and industrial strategy. *Review of Economic Studies*, 50, 707–22.

Thursby, M. and Jensen, R. 1983: A conjectural variations approach to strategic tariff equilibria. *Journal of International Economics*, 14, 145–61.

Tirole, J. 1988: *The Theory of Industrial Organization*. Cambridge, Mass.: MIT Press.

Tower, E. 1975: The optimum quota and retaliation. *Review of Economic Studies*, 42, 623–30.

Venables, A. 1985: Trade and trade policy with imperfect competition: the case of identical products and free entry. *Journal of International Economics*, 19, 1–19.

Venables, A. 1990: Trade policy under imperfect competition: a numerical assessment. In P. Krugman and A. Smith (eds), *Empirical Studies of Strategic Trade Policies*, London: CEPR and NBER.

8

TRADE AND DEVELOPMENT: PROTECTION, SHOCKS AND LIBERALIZATION

Paul Collier and Jan Willem Gunning

8.1 INTRODUCTION

Trade policy essentially comes down to protection. We begin with three 'stylized facts' of protection and development. First, many developing countries (LDCs) have heavily protected import-substitute sectors. Whereas over the past 40 years protection levels have generally declined in developed countries (DCs) and are now at modest levels for most commodities, they have increased in many LDCs. For example, by the late 1980s the average nominal protection afforded to Kenyan manufacturing was in excess of 100 per cent. Second, high protection appears to have been deleterious to the rate of growth. Those LDCs which have had the least protected economies, most notably the East Asian group, have grown outstandingly fast, whereas the most heavily protected African and Latin American economies have often grown less rapidly than their populations. Although trade policies are unlikely fully to have accounted for these differences, they have probably played a substantial part. For example, Mundlak, Cavallo and Domenech (1990) using a simulation model of Argentina, demonstrate that had trade policy been similar to Australia and New Zealand, growth would also have been comparable. Third, despite the evident costliness of high protection, trade liberalization of heavily protected economies has proved surprisingly difficult. In several countries liberalization has been attempted but subsequently aborted.

Each of these three stylized facts raises a question. Why are many LDCs so much more heavily protected than DCs? Why has this protection apparently been so deleterious to growth? Why, if there are such large gains from liberalization, has it proved so difficult? Much of the literature on trade and development has attempted to address one or other of these questions.

This chapter cannot hope to provide a survey of this enormous literature and in fact it is very selective.[1] In section 8.2 we survey how the well-established theories have answered these questions. In section 8.3 we introduce some more recent theories which centre upon the nature and consequences of external shocks. Finally, in section 8.4 we review some of the recent work on trade liberalization.

8.2 STANDARD THEORIES OF PROTECTION

Standard theories of trade and development address mainly the second of our three questions, namely why protection has proved so damaging.

The basic analysis of the costs of protection, though much refined since, was largely developed by James Meade (1955) and Harry Johnson (1960). In their framework, protection takes the form only of tariffs. The costs arise through misallocations in production and consumption, depicted by the familiar triangles. The costs of protection increase much more rapidly than the rate of protection. As an approximation, they increase in the square of the tariff. Hence, the theory correctly predicts that heavily protected LDCs would suffer disproportionately high welfare losses. Qualitatively this is consistent with increasing protection (which we observe in many LDCs) causing slower growth. However, a serious problem with this theory as an account of why protection has been so damaging is that for plausible values of demand and supply elasticities, it yields costs of protection which are usually less than 1 or 2 per cent of GDP. Although this translates into huge sums, it is far too small to account for persistently slow GDP growth in highly protected economies. A major advance in the analysis of the costs of protection was made through the concept of rent-seeking. Krueger (1974) showed how resources might be devoted to the acquisition of import quotas. If private agents competed for these quotas then the value of the resources devoted to their acquisition (i.e. to rent-seeking) would equal the rental value of the quotas. Hence, the rents involved in quotas were not a transfer within the society but rather a deadweight loss. This fundamental insight was important because the value of rents in many LDCs, though not known accurately, was likely to be high. This was because the severe trade restrictions commonly imposed, often took the form of quotas. To return to our Kenyan example, the nominal rate of protection in manufacturing (112 per cent) was made up equally of tariffs and the 'implicit tariff' of quotas. In many LDCs the importance of quotas is even greater: in Zambia during the early 1980s the nominal rate of protection was around 200 per cent, but tariffs were very low, in the range 15–30 per cent. Various estimates of the value of the rentals on quotas have ranged between 7 and 15 per cent of GDP. On the assumption of competitive rent-seeking, this is also the cost of the deadweight loss incurred. These estimates are very much larger than the deadweight cost of tariffs. They therefore go much further than the traditional theory in accounting for the worse performance of protected economies. Nevertheless, the persistently slower growth of heavily protected economies has cumulatively amounted to larger losses of GDP than can readily be accounted for by rent-seeking. Further, the measures of the costs of rent-seeking proceed by valuing the rents and then assuming that rent-seeking is competitive. However, there are many mechanisms of patronage which are fundamentally uncompetitive and which, in the process, prevent rents from being dissipated by the costs of rent-seeking.

The 'new trade theory' of trade in differentiated products, although of little applicability as regards LDC production, nevertheless has important insights for the implications of protection for LDC consumption. The major discovery of this theory is that for those differentiated products for which there are some fixed costs of production, and hence economies of scale, trade confers welfare gains even between identical economies. LDC economies being very small (in the sense of low GDP rather than being price-takers), in autarky can only accommodate a very narrow range of differentiated products. Trade, by radically widening the range of choice, therefore substantially lowers the cost of living. That is, it lowers the cost of achieving a given level of utility.

The welfare gains come from two sources. Firstly, consumers are able to satisfy a 'taste for variety'; that is, the consumer may choose to consume several variants of the same good. Second, since consumers are heterogeneous with respect to tastes, a wider range of varieties yields a closer approximation of one or other of these varieties to the ideal variety of each of the heterogeneous consumers. Those gains from trade which stem from the widening of choice are therefore likely to be larger in LDC than in DC economies since the typical LDC is radically smaller relative to the world economy than the typical DC. Offsetting this scale effect, the demand for differentiated product is probably income elastic. The gains from trade, or conversely, the costs of protection, are likely to be particularly high when trade restrictions take the form of import quotas. Quotas, more than tariffs, can drastically narrow the range of choice.

The gains from wider choice are difficult to quantify. To do so properly requires the estimation of a detailed demand system on data gathered both before and after a trade liberalization. To date, this has not been attempted. A less data-intensive approach, measuring the effects of the Tanzanian liberalization of the mid-1980s (Collier and Gunning, 1990), suggests that the welfare gains from that liberalization may have been very large indeed. However, the results are sensitive to the specification of the elasticity of substitution which in that study was imposed rather than estimated. In highly repressed trade regimes, it seems quite likely that the welfare losses from narrowed choice may even exceed those generated by rent-seeking. The losses from narrowed choice are also inevitable, given quantitative trade restrictions, whereas the costs of rent-seeking are contingent upon whether the process is competitive.

If rent-seeking is more costly than tariffs, and choice restriction more costly than rent-seeking, it might appear that choice restriction is the most potent explanation for the poor performance of highly protected economies. However, even if choice restriction is very costly, it cannot account for any part of the slow growth of heavily protected countries. Growth is measured in terms of GDP, whereas the costs of choice restriction are measured in terms of utility: for a given GDP utility will be higher with the wider choice enabled by liberal trade.

To summarize, we began with a stylized fact that trade restrictions have been very damaging in LDCs. Two conventional theories, the costs of tariffs and the costs of rent-seeking, offered explanations as to why GDP would be lower in a protected economy. However, the scale of the loss, though serious, seemed not to account for the huge losses which trade restrictions appear to have cumulatively inflicted. The new theory on the costs of choice restriction, though it may well account for very large losses, conveys the dismal message that, high as the GDP losses from protection may be, they substantially understimate the full damage done.

Although the main focus of the standard theory of protection has been on its costs, some attention has been given to our first question, namely why many LDCs have such high levels of protection.

One line of inquiry is to identify the circumstances in which protection might actually be desirable. This is an unpromising explanation of LDC protection since, were the policy soundly based, highly protected economies would have tended to outperform rather than underperform less protected economies. Indeed, the often less than coherent protectionist sympathies of development economists have not survived rigorous scrutiny. The 'infant-industry argument' in its traditional form has been shown not to constitute a case for any sort of government intervention (Baldwin, 1969). In modified forms it can justify intervention, but not in the form of trade policy (see Corden, 1974). The more recent theory of strategic trade policy, which can conceivably justify an active trade policy for some DCs, describes interfirm bargaining games which are clearly inapplicable for LDCs. As Corden (1990) says, the theory 'has very little relevance for developing countries' (p. 28).

The principal area in which an active trade policy seems likely to be justified is the taxation of those exports in which LDCs have, individually or collectively, substantial market power. As a national strategy this can be costly except in the short term: for example, Zanzibar used to hold a near monopoly on cloves but due to over-restriction of supply new producers entered and Zanzibar now holds only around 10 per cent of the world market. As a cartel, however, the strategy of export taxation can be profitable for many years. The most celebrated example of this is OPEC; however, a far more long-lasting and profitable instance is the de Beers-led diamond cartel. Both of these cartels are natural resource based. It is rather harder to maintain a cartel for agricultural commodities because if the existing produ-cers succeed in making a crop highly profitable, others can rapidly enter. As it happens. in an uncoordinated way several of the beverage-producing nations have highly restrictive trade policies. Panagariya and Schiff (1991) used a model to explore the effect on the terms of trade of a production expansion of the main African cocoa producer, Ghana. The results suggest that African producers in aggregate face a demand curve with virtually unit elasticity, so that the benefits from simultaneous export expansion are small (although still positive). Trade restrictions, while not unilaterally optimal for any grower, may then appear not to have been costly in aggregate. However, although for some of the beverage producers (Ghana, Uganda) beverages dominate exports, export and import taxes are decisively not equivalent. By using import taxes such countries make it unprofitable for any new export activities to emerge, perpetuating their undiversified export base. This would be avoided were the trade taxation only imposed directly upon the product in which there is monopoly power. Thus, even when there is a good case for a restrictive trade policy, this does not constitute grounds for protection. A second reason for an active trade policy is if it is administratively much easier to raise revenue by taxing external trade than by other taxes. However, the ease of smuggling makes the administrative attraction of taxing trade illusory.

The main thrust of the research on explaining why LDCs have high protection therefore accepts the proposition that the policy is harmful, but concentrates upon its distributional consequences. It may be that although the average agent loses from protection, some identifiable groups gain. These groups then have an interest in lobbying for the policy of protection. Two approaches have been followed; the first has been concerned with earned incomes and the second with rents. Since protection changes relative commodity prices, it will also change relative factor prices. The first approach explores whether these price changes confer absolute gains upon some factor(s). If factors are fully mobile between sectors then (on the usual assumptions) the Stolper–Samuelson (SS) theorem indeed tells us that the factor used intensively in the import-competing sector benefits both relatively and absolutely from protection. Since the import-competing sector will be intensive in the scarce factor, which in most LDCs might be thought to be capital, this tells us that owners of capital are likely to be the beneficiaries of protectionism. To turn this into an explanation for high protection in LDCs requires the addition of some political process: capital owners, recognizing the general equilibrium implications of protection, lobby for it and their lobby carries the day against the countervailing labour lobby. It has long been recognized that this explanation fails at the first step: there is good evidence, at least for DCs (Magee, 1980), that labour and capital do not line up in opposing lobbies for trade policy, but rather see themselves as having a common industry-specific interest: car workers and car makers both want import controls on cars. Either this is because the hypothesized general equilibrium effects are too subtle to be understood as the basis for action, or, more radically, it is because they misdescribe the mapping from commodity to factor prices.

An alternative to the mobile factors model which underpins the SS theorem is the Ricardo–Viner model in which only labour is fully mobile whereas capital is sector-specific. This is a caricature of a more general process in which resource movement is costly. The Ricardo–Viner model generates different distributional consequences of protection from SS. The only unambiguous gainers are the sector-specific factors in the protected industry. The factors specific to the unprotected sector lose absolutely, while the mobile factor may lose or gain depending upon the pattern of its consumption. Since the sector-specific factors may well include human capital, this may explain why, within an industry, labour and capital appear to see themselves as having a common interest in protection.

These alternative models both stress changes in earned income as the motivation for protection, identifying different groups of factors as beneficiaries. What is missing is a theory of how these potential beneficiaries succeed in influencing policy. In this they face three problems. First, the group must overcome the problem facing any collective action, namely free-riding. Second, they must outcompete other lobbies. Third, the government (or whatever entity is setting trade policy) must be amenable to lobbying pressure. The first two of these problems have been addressed by Becker (1983). He considers the characteristics of beneficiaries which make successful collective action more or less feasible. How far can this approach explain LDC trade policy? A notable application of the interest group model to explain an important aspect of LDC trade policy was Bates (1981). However, Bates concentrated upon export taxation rather than import controls. He analysed why many African states had been able to raise taxation on agricultural exports to very high levels, arguing that it was because the rural population had become marginalized in the political contest. Although in the standard two-good analysis the general equilibrium consequences of export taxes and import taxes are formally equivalent (if government revenue is simply recycled), they are hardly politically equivalent. The owners of sector-specific factors in the import-competing sector seem vastly more likely to press for import restrictions (tariffs or quotas) than for an export tax. Bates's explanation for high taxes on agricultural exports was that the potential lobby against them, the rural population, was too weak politically to oppose the lobby for them, but the lobby for them was not another industry but rather the state itself. Far from being recycled in a distributionally neutral way to private agents, as assumed for tractability in many standard models, the revenue from trade taxes was the motive for the intervention.

This takes us to the second approach, to the political economy of protection, in which the focus is on the rents generated by trade policy. The rents accrue either as revenue to the government or as supranormal profits to whoever acquires the entitlements to trade at world prices. Analyses in which the government seeks revenue from trade policy for its own interests are instances of the more general concept of the 'predatory state' (Lal, 1989, chapter 13). In this framework the constraint upon the government is not pressure from opposing lobbies, but merely that if it is too greedy, raising export and import taxes too high, revenue will decline as it moves to the wrong side of the Laffer curve. Rimmer (1991) identifies just such a case for Ghana. By the early 1980s the amazingly high trade taxes which Bates had analysed in the 1970s were generating rapidly decreasing revenue. The state 'withered away' (Lal and Myint, 1992) as the revenue base eroded, so that the interest of the state changed from the maintenance to the dismantling of the control regime (see below).

The attraction of the predatory state account of trade policy is that it does appear to offer an explanation as to why LDCs are usually so much more protectionist than DCs. In DCs the political process is democratic (to varying degrees) and so state policy is strongly influenced by lobbies of groups of electors, or financiers of campaigns. The recent theory of 'black hole tariffs' (Magee, Brock and Young, 1989) exploits this feature. The state has little capacity to pursue its own, distinct interests. By contrast, in many LDCs there is no meaningful electoral process and the state can itself become the dominant interest group. However, a difficulty with the predatory state account of trade policy in LDCs is that it fails to explain why restrictions so often take the form of import quotas, which generate no government revenue, rather than tariffs. The only circumstances in which the two are revenue-equivalent is when the quota is either zero or auctioned. The zero quota is a special case in which the benefits accrue only to the domestic producer. For all other non-auctioned quotas, clearly, states which use them cannot be revenue-maximizing. One possibility is to explain non-zero import quotas in terms of lobbying by those agents who stand to benefit. The unique susceptibility of governments to a lobby in favour of import quotas might be explained in Becker's terms by the very large advantages conferred and the very small number of beneficiaries (making co-ordination easier). However, this encounters a further problem. The agents who benefit from non-zero import quotas are those on whom the licences are conferred, and this is the importers. Yet although collectively importers benefit from restricted trade, individually they have a powerful interest in lobbying for a more generous entitlement. In other words, the group which most benefits from quotas is quite likely to be the most persistent lobby for trade liberalization![2]

It seems then that the rents from quotas may often be inadvertent rather than the *raison d'être* for protection. We would then need to ask why protection takes the form of quotas. For this there are two candidates. The first takes us back to the Ricardo–Viner model and argues that the key beneficiaries are the owners of sector-specific capital in the import-competing sector. These beneficiaries then form the lobby for protection. There are three reasons why quotas are preferred over tariffs. First, a Becker argument again, they are more opaque: the tariff equivalent of quotas might be several hundred per cent on some items, a tariff rate impossible to legislate. Second, unlike tariffs, quotas eliminate competition at the margin and may facilitate cartelization of the market. The third reason is rooted in macroeconomic policy, a theme we will be exploring in section 8.3.

8.3 TRADE SHOCKS

Many LDCs are prone to trade shocks since their exports are undiversified and consist to a substantial extent of primary commodities. Commodity prices are extremely volatile; e.g. coefficients of variation for sugar, coffee and cocoa prices are 0.92, 0.42 and 0.51 respectively.[3] Changes in commodity prices tend to be asymmetric: positive shocks are more common than negative ones in the sense that the typical pattern is one of long troughs and sharp peaks. One reason for this is the fundamental asymmetry involved in storage: stocks cannot be negative and a stock-out will give rise to a sharp price increase.[4] The prevalence of positive shocks is fortunate since there are several asymmetries which make the welfare loss from a slump larger than the gain from a boom: there may, for example, be borrowing constraints in foreign financial markets and fixed capital formation is difficult to reverse.

Hence LDCs are periodically faced with large trade shocks due to changes in commodity prices. To illustrate: the beverage boom from which many coffee, tea and cocoa producing countries benefited in the late 1970s represented for one of those countries, Ivory Coast, a windfall with a present value of more than 80 per cent of one year's GDP. While this case is extreme, there are many examples of shocks in the range of 20–50 per cent of GDP (see Ghanem, 1991; Bevan, Collier and Gunning, 1990b).

These shocks are important in two ways. First, empirically trade shocks appear very difficult to handle: the loss from negative shocks seems much larger, and the gain from positive shocks much smaller than the terms of trade change itself would suggest (Roemer, 1985; Neary and van Wijnbergen, 1986; Gelb, 1988; Bevan, Collier and Gunning, 1990a, b). Shocks appear to pose special problems and this may help to explain the poor growth performance of many LDCs. Second, temporary negative shocks tend to trigger permanent increases in protection, particularly in the form of quotas. This provides an answer to the previous section's question.

The consequences of a trade shock depend on how it is perceived, on the way the control regime affects private agents' responses and on the policy response of the government. In the hypothetical case when there is no government a positive shock perceived as permanent raises wealth and will therefore lead to an increase in consumption expenditure. Some of this will be on non-tradables and this will tend to increase their price. This is the spending effect familiar from Dutch disease theory (cf. Corden and Neary, 1982; Corden, 1984; Neary and van Wijnbergen, 1986). There will also be substitution effects in production: the booming export sector and the non-tradables sector will bid mobile factors out of the production of importables. This change of resource allocation at the expense of non-booming tradables is, of course, optimal and in that sense (as has often been remarked) the Dutch disease is not a disease.

There are, however, two reasons for concern. First, the control regime may make the optimal response infeasible. The control regime may include price control or wage rigidities which prevent optimal adjustment to the shock. For example, if real wages are rigid in terms of importables, labour will not leave that sector so that the production of exportables and of non-tradables cannot expand. Conversely, if wages are fixed in terms of non-tradables then the product wage will rise in the importables sector while remaining constant for non-tradables. Hence labour is fired in one sector without being rehired elsewhere in the economy: the positive shock then causes unemployment (van Wijnbergen, 1984).

It is quite possible that the control regime is relatively innocuous in itself, but becomes very damaging in the face of shocks by preventing optimal factor relocation. The analysis of the public sector's role under trade shocks has recently therefore given less emphasis to the policy response to a shock and more to the pre-shock control regime.

The second reason for concern is that the shock, while perceived as permanent, may actually be temporary. The factor relocation may then have to be reversed and this can, of course, be costly. This seems to be the policy concern behind Dutch disease theory. While this suggests that the theory is based on a rather special case (all agents being modelled as incorrectly treating a temporary shock as permanent), it highlights the importance of the nature and perception of the shock.[5] Except in the rather special case of Dutch disease theory, part of the income increase will be seen as transient. Under most utility functions this provides an incentive to save in order to smooth consumption. In fact it may be optimal to save most of the windfall in which case the Dutch disease emphasis on the change in consumption spending is misplaced.

Private agents can save by acquiring claims on other agents, including the government. In aggregate, however, saving requires net acquisition of foreign assets or domestic real capital formation. In many LDCs the domestic rate of return exceeds the world deposit rate of interest. In these circumstances holding foreign assets can be optimal, but only temporarily. First, it offers an escape from diminishing returns. In a model with only tradable capital, savings will be invested domestically until the rate of return has fallen to the deposit rate of interest. From thereon windfall savings will be used for foreign asset acquisition. After the boom these foreign assets are repatriated. Second, once we allow for non-tradable capital ('construction') the price of capital goods becomes endogenous. This provides a disincentive to bunched investment. Foreign assets then offer the advantage of not eroding the real value of windfall savings: they can be held abroad and returned when capital prices have fallen. It may be optimal to continue investing domestically after the end of the commodity boom. Repatriated foreign assets are then used to stretch the investment boom.

With non-tradable capital the commodity boom is reflected in a temporary increase in the price and in the output of the construction sector, a construction boom. This happened for example in Kenya during the coffee boom of 1976–9. In Kenya the construction boom was reinforced by the control regime which included exchange control. This made it difficult for private agents to acquire foreign assets and thereby increased domestic investment out of windfall savings (Bevan, Collier and Gunning, 1987, 1990a).

It should be noted that there will be a construction boom even in the case of a permanent shock. If capital is sector specific then in the case of a boom the spending effect raises the marginal productivity of capital in the production of non-tradable consumption goods and when investment requires non-tradable capital goods this will be reflected in a construction boom.[6] (Note that in the case of a negative shock there also is an incentive to invest, but now in the importables sector.)

We can abstract from such wealth-induced investment by assuming that only tradables are consumed. This brings out the importance of the perception of the nature of the shock and of the country's access to a world capital market very clearly. For if the shock is seen as permanent there now is no reason to invest in response to it. If it is seen as temporary there will be windfall savings but no construction boom to the extent savings are invested abroad. However, if there is no access to a perfect world capital market so that in steady state equilibrium the domestic rate of return exceeds the deposit rate of interest, then part of the windfall savings will be invested domestically.

As in the static case, the resulting construction boom does not represent a disease provided the nature of the shock is correctly perceived and agents are free to adjust their portfolio of foreign and domestic assets.

These ideas can be illustrated with an optimization model, based on Bevan, Collier and Gunning (1990a). The model describes the problem faced by a developing country which has to adjust to a temporary positive trade shock, a commodity boom. The scope for smoothing consumption is limited since the country does not have access to a perfect capital market. Indeed, we will begin by describing a country with a closed capital account and then move to the more realistic case of an LDC which faces a borrowing constraint in the world capital market.

First consider the problem

$$\max_c \int_0^\infty u(c)e^{-\rho t}dt$$

subject to

$$\dot{k} = g(k) - c + b \qquad (8.1)$$

Here c denotes consumption, $u(c)$ the instantaneous utility function, ρ the time preference rate, $g(k) = f(k) - \delta k$ output net of depreciation and k the capital stock. We assume the functions f and u to be strictly concave. Boom income b is a positive constant during the period $[0, T)$ and is otherwise equal to zero. Initially the economy is in steady state equilibrium with the capital stock equal to k^* where $g'(k^*) = \rho$. The problem at time $t = 0$ is to choose an optimal consumption path taking into account that the boom will be over at time T.

Write λ for the costate variable corresponding to the capital stock k. Conditions for an optimum include

$$\dot{\lambda} = -g'\lambda \qquad (8.2)$$

$$e^{-\rho t}u' = \lambda \qquad (8.3)$$

Differentiating (8.3) with respect to time gives

$$\rho\lambda - e^{-\rho t}u''\dot{c} = g'\lambda$$

Hence $u''\dot{c} = (\rho - g')u'$ or

$$\dot{c}/c = \sigma(g' - \rho) \qquad (8.4)$$

where $\sigma = - u'/(u''c)$ is the intertemporal elasticity of substitution.[7] Note that $\dot{c} = 0$ implies $k = k^*$. This is shown as the vertical $\dot{c} = 0$ locus in figure 8.1. The Keynes–Ramsey rule implies that c falls (rises) to the right (left) of the locus, as indicated by the arrows.

The budget constraint (8.1) defines a $\dot{k} = 0$ locus.[8] For higher consumption levels the capital stock falls while below the locus net investment is positive. There are two paths which converge to the steady state equilibrium at A; these form the stable branch SS.

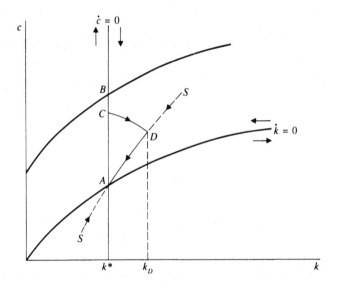

Figure 8.1 Adjustment with tradable capital, closed capital account

The initial equilibrium is at A where c and k are both constant. The trade shock ($b > 0$) shifts the $\dot{k} = 0$ locus upwards. If the boom were permanent, equilibrium would shift instantaneously to B: the extra income would simply be consumed. With a temporary boom consumption will not rise to the full extent. Adjustment starts at a point such as C. This lies below the new $\dot{k} = 0$ locus hence k increases and c falls along the path CD. When the boom ends the $\dot{k} = 0$ locus shifts back to its original position so that point D now lies above the locus. Hence after the boom the economy moves to the left in the diagram: the capital stock falls. Note that at time T the problem reduces to the standard Ramsey model with b in equation (8.1) equal to zero. Hence adjustment in the post-boom period is along the stable branch SS, from D back to A.

Adjustment to a temporary positive shock therefore involves two phases. During the first one the capital stock increases as part of the boom income is invested and in the post-boom period this investment is reversed, enabling a higher consumption level. Investment smoothes consumption: instead of following a step function consumption is permanently higher than before the shock, jumping up at time $t = 0$ and then declining monotonically towards its pre-shock level.

In this model the capital account is closed so that all domestic savings are invested domestically. Now consider an LDC which has access to a world capital market, but an imperfect one: it can hold foreign assets (a) but it cannot borrow ($a \geqslant 0$). The world interest rate is lower than the time preference rate ($\rho > r^*$) so that at A the domestic rate of return (g') exceeds the world interest rate: there is an incentive to borrow.

Suppose that with a closed capital account investment would proceed so far that the rate of return fell below r^*: k_D in figure 8.1 exceeds k^{**} where $g'(k^{**}) = r^*$. Then obviously foreign assets will be used because they offer the advantage of a higher rate of return. In this case non-human wealth (w) will be held in the form of domestic capital until $k = k^{**}$ and beyond that point in the form of foreign assets. This makes it possible to write this model with two assets in the same form as the single-asset Ramsey model. If we replace k by w and the function g by

$$h(w) = g[\min(w, k^{**})] + r\max(0, w - k^{**})$$

then the previous analysis applies. Hence in figure 8.2 wealth increases in the boom period (along CE) and then returns to its pre-boom level (along the stable branch from E to A). Initially all savings are invested domestically (CD) until k^{**} is reached. For the remainder of the boom period investment is in foreign assets (DE) and after the boom these assets are first repatriated (EF) before domestic investment is reversed (FA).

Clearly, in this model the possibility of temporarily holding foreign assets raises welfare: if the capital account is closed smoothing consumption is more costly because of the restricted asset choice.

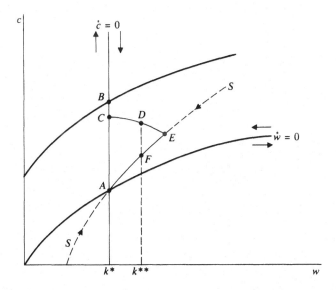

Figure 8.2 Adjustment with tradable capital, open capital account

In this model the same good can be used for consumption and investment. Now consider a two-sector economy, producing a tradable consumption good (t) and a non-tradable capital good (i) ('construction').[9] Both sectors produce under constant returns to scale using capital and labour and these factors are both intersectorally mobile. Labour is in fixed supply ($\bar{l}$). We assume the construction sector to be labour intensive.

In this case the model is

$$\max_{k_i, l_i} \int_0^\infty u(c)e^{-\rho t}dt$$

where $c = t(k - k_i, \bar{l} - l_i) + b$, subject to

$$\dot{k} = i(k_i, l_i) - \delta k \tag{8.5}$$

This gives

$$\dot{\lambda} = -e^{-\rho t}u't_k + \delta\lambda \tag{8.6}$$

$$t_k = pi_k \tag{8.7}$$

$$t_l = pi_l \tag{8.8}$$

where p is defined as $e^{\rho t}\lambda/u'$. The marginal productivity conditions (8.7) and (8.8) allow us to write output as a function of the aggregate capital stock and the relative price of capital goods: at an optimum $t = \tilde{t}(k, p)$ and $i = \tilde{i}(k, p)$ where because the tradable sector is capital intensive the partial derivatives satisfy

$$\tilde{t}(k, p)_k > 0 > \tilde{i}(k, p)_k$$

and

$$\tilde{t}(k, p)_p < 0 < \tilde{i}(k, p)_p$$

We assume that $\tilde{t}_{kp}$ is non-positive.

As before we derive an expression for the growth rate of consumption

$$\frac{\dot{c}}{c} = \frac{\tilde{t}_k + \dot{p} - (\rho + \delta)p}{p}\sigma \tag{8.9}$$

Note that if capital goods are tradable ($p = 1$ and hence $\dot{p} = 0$)) this reduces to the Ramsey equation.

The $\dot{k} = 0$ locus is again defined by $i = \delta k$. Substituting $i = \tilde{i}(k, p)$ and using $c = \tilde{t}(k, p) + b$ the slope of the locus is given by

$$\frac{\mathrm{d}c}{\mathrm{d}k} = \tilde{\imath}_k + (\delta - \tilde{\imath}_k)\tilde{\imath}_p / \tilde{\imath}_p$$

This is positive provided δ is sufficiently small.[10]

Substituting $\dot{c} = \tilde{\imath}_k \dot{k} + \tilde{\imath}_p \dot{p}$ in (8.9) gives the $\dot{c} = 0$ locus as[11]

$$\tilde{\imath}_k(1 - \dot{k}/\tilde{\imath}_p) = (\rho + \delta)p$$

The slope of this locus in (c, k) space is positive (given our assumption that the construction sector is labour intensive). Hence while in the one sector model the $\dot{c} = 0$ locus was vertical here the locus is upward sloping (figure 8.3).

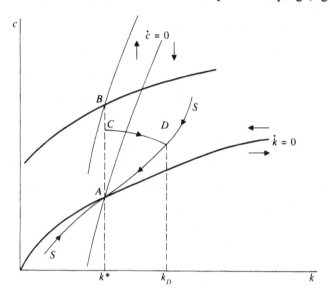

Figure 8.3 Adjustment with non-tradable capital, closed capital account

The boom shifts both the $\dot{k} = 0$ locus and the $\dot{c} = 0$ locus upwards. If the shock is permanent the new equilibrium is at B. In the case of a temporary shock adjustment is along CDA; as before, c declines throughout while the capital stock increases during the boom period and returns to its old value in the post-boom period.

The adjustment path is shown in figure 8.4 in (p, k) space. Here both loci are upward sloping but the $\dot{k} = 0$ locus is steeper than the $\dot{p} = 0$ locus. In the case of a closed capital account the price of construction jumps up at the beginning of the boom and then continues to rise during the boom period along AB.[12] This implies that the domestic rate of return $r = (\tilde{\imath}_k + \dot{p} - \delta p)/p$ falls. If r^* is reached it is again optimal to acquire foreign assets.

In figure 8.5 two possibilities are shown for the case of an open capital account. In the first case there is an initial phase of domestic investment until $r = r^*$; in the second case r drops to r^* instantaneously. Once foreign assets are held $r = r^*$ by arbitrage and hence the horizontal $\dot{p} = 0$ locus through F

220   PAUL COLLIER AND JAN WILLEM GUNNING

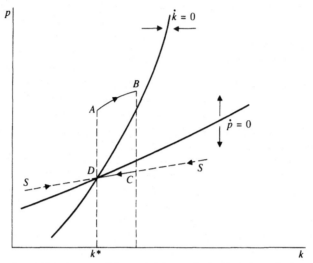

Figure 8.4 Adjustment with tradable capital, closed capital account

(where $\tilde{t}_k = (r^* + \delta)p$) is the relevant one. Hence p falls: in the first case starting in point C and in the second case immediately. Unlike in the previous model, in this model there can be simultaneously foreign and domestic investment.

Since $r^* < \rho$ it is not optimal to hold foreign assets permanently. Hence foreign assets will be drawn down. Eventually $a = 0$ and the $\dot{p} = 0$ locus shifts back to its original position. The final adjustment phase is then again along the stable branch, from E or G back to A.

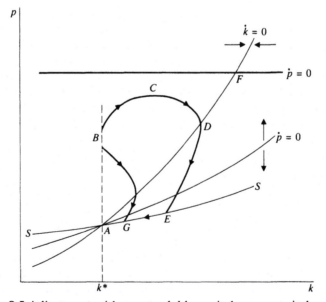

Figure 8.5 Adjustment with non-tradable capital, open capital account

In this model investment may continue after the boom, financed by drawing down foreign assets. Alternatively, repatriated foreign assets are used after the boom to finance a higher level of consumption as in the previous model.

In either case access to the world capital market raises welfare compared to the closed capital account model. It does so in two ways. First, as in the earlier model, domestic investment is subject to diminishing returns while the interest rate on foreign assets is constant. Second, it offers the possibility of postponing investment until the price of capital goods has fallen.

In an economy with a government, private agents are constrained by the control regime. This may isolate them from shocks, e.g. through stabilizing taxation. One reason for such a policy is a perceived asymmetry in information: governments correctly recognize the shock as permanent but private agents do not. If governments indeed have such an informational advantage this does not establish a case for stabilization but for information dissemination.[13]

In the unconstrained case private agents can freely lend and borrow abroad to smooth their consumption stream. In many LDCs exchange control makes this option illegal. However, private agents may be able to hold foreign assets indirectly by acquiring financial claims on the government which then effectively holds foreign assets on their behalf. This approach suffers from two defects. First, governments are likely to fail in such a custodial role. Second, many developing countries are characterized by financial repression so that financial assets offer very unattractive returns. For example, the choice of financial instruments available to smallholder producers of agricultural exports is often limited to currency and Post Office deposits with high transaction costs and negative real interest rates.

In addition there is an asymmetry: producers may be able to use the financial system to deposit their windfall savings but they are unable to borrow because of collateral problems. This leads to the savings problem analysed by Deaton (1990) where there is an incentive for precautionary saving since in the case of a negative shock consumption can be smoothed only by running down previously accumulated savings. An important effect of financial repression is that it limits the efficiency of precautionary saving by lowering the deposit interest rate.

International policy responses to trade shocks involve price stabilization schemes (which reduce exposure to shocks) and compensatory arrangements (which aim to mitigate the effects of shocks). Price stabilization has attracted enormous attention during the 1970s. The enthusiasm has waned for several reasons. The theoretical literature has emphasized that (except in the unlikely case of linear demand and supply curves) stabilization at the mean is not possible. Hence feasible stabilization affects the expected price. This 'transfer effect' may well be negative and substantial, outweighing the risk benefit to producers of stabilization. Secondly, buffer stocks are likely to be very costly and they are vulnerable to speculative attack (see Newbery and Stiglitz, 1981; Newbery, 1990; Gilbert, 1991; Herrmann, Burger and Smit, 1990). The UNCTAD Integrated Programme for Commodities produced only one new agreement (for natural rubber) and performance of commodity agreements has been poor in a number of instances, tin being the most spectacular one.[14]

The alternative international policy instrument involves compensatory arrangements, such as the ones operated by the IMF and the European Community (EC). These schemes allow a country to borrow when exports have fallen, thereby effectively tying aid to export price shortfalls. There are two practical problems. First, these schemes are fairly small, and second there is evidence that the timing of disbursements and repayments actually makes these schemes destabilizing (Herrmann, Burger and Smit, 1990). More fundamentally, it is not clear what informational advantage the IMF or the EC has which would make them particularly suitable for running this insurance scheme. Most importantly, compensatory arrangements give entitlements to governments. If the problem is perceived as instability of the income of producers it is not clear how loans to the government are passed on to producers.

Now consider national policy. Here it is useful to distinguish three approaches. The first one involves national stabilization: the government isolates domestic producers from the volatility of world prices through stabilizing taxation (typically a progressive export tax) or a domestic buffer stock operation. This approach has at least one theoretical disadvantage: there is no incentive for producers to increase production when world prices rise[15] and a practical one: the temptation to convert marketing boards designed for domestic stabilization into fiscal agents, has often proved difficult to resist.

Under the second approach producers are exposed to international price instability but they are offered financial assets which enable them to smooth consumption through (dis)saving. Financial reform is needed to make this attractive.

The third approach involves substitutes for missing markets. Just as a government can play a custodial role by enabling private agents to acquire foreign financial assets indirectly, it can enable them to reduce price risk by indirectly engaging in forward transactions. Marketing boards which guarantee to buy at pre-announced prices effectively offer farmers forward contracts. The board can then offset the price risk by using futures markets. As Gilbert (1991) points out, this arrangement either gives the board monopsony power or suffers from problems of enforcing the 'forward contract' since farmers will have an incentive to sell to private traders if the spot price at harvest time exceeds the board's price. This may be overcome if instead of offering a fixed price the board guarantees a floor price and offsets its risk position by buying exchange put options. This solves the enforcement problem and therefore does not require a monopsony: when the spot price exceeds the floor it does not matter to whom the farmer sells while if it falls below the floor the farmer will exercise his option on the board.[16] In the latter case the value of the option held by the board will just compensate it for the difference between the floor and the spot price.

The floor price options approach may be used to deal with negative shocks where it is difficult to devise instruments which allow peasant producers to borrow. Conversely, the option approach does not eliminate upward price risk and this asymmetry is not serious provided producers have access to financial assets with attractive returns. Hence a combination of financial reform and floor guarantees may be the best policy.

The government's policy response to a trade shock may involve a change of the protection afforded by trade policy. First, to the extent trade policy relies on quotas and these are not relaxed during a boom, protection increases. Imports subject to effective quotas are then non-tradable at the margin and the spending effect of a boom will force up their domestic price. In the absence of exchange rate adjustment this amounts to an increase in the tariff equivalent of the quota.

This may be very damaging. For example, if all imports are subject to binding value quotas then a boom results paradoxically in a fall of export volumes: since the value of imports cannot increase the export price increase is offset by a reduction in quantity. The trade policy then induces a highly inefficient response to an export price increase. In this case the damage is not done by a policy response to the trade shock (the government does not change its trade policy although that passivity makes the policy more restrictive) but by the control regime: the quotas already in force before the boom.

A more usual response is to vary trade policy in response to a trade shock (particularly in the case of a negative one), a policy rule termed endogenous trade policy. Governments are often reluctant to adjust the exchange rate. When a negative shock reduces real income and the fixed exchange rate policy maintains the domestic price of importables constant there is an excess money supply and hence a loss of reserves. The government reacts to this by tightening trade policy so that the price of importables rises in spite of the fixed exchange rate.

The macroeconomic policy then leads to protection. While this was not the objective it may be difficult to reverse. Hence the tightening of trade policy may become permanent; temporary shocks then leave a legacy of quotas. In LDCs restrictive trade policies can often be traced to macroeconomic crises rather than to lobbying for protection. For example, in Kenya a foreign exchange crisis in 1971 led to the adoption of quantitative restrictions on imports. Many of the import controls which were then introduced were maintained after the crisis.

This macroeconomic explanation for trade policy also helps explain the revealed preference for quotas. For the impact on the demand for foreign exchange of a tariff increase is uncertain while quotas (fixed in terms of foreign exchange values) provide an exact rationing instrument.

8.4 TRADE LIBERALIZATION ATTEMPTS

The general growth in protection in many LDCs over the past 40 years has been precisely counter to the liberalizing trend in DCs. There have, however, been numerous attempts at liberalization, some sustained and others aborted. An important distinction is between liberalizations which are unilateral decisions and those which are the outcome of bargains struck with other entities. We consider them in turn.

Suppose that the new government of an LDC inherits trade restrictions in the form of a mixture of tariffs and quotas which it wishes to dismantle. The choices it must make concern co-ordination, pace and sequence. Co-ordination refers to the other policy instruments which must be changed in order to maintain policy compatibility: that is, sustainable balance of payments and fiscal positions. Pace refers to the speed of policy change. Obviously, at one extreme all trade restrictions can be removed at once, subject to the maintenance of compatibility. For any slower pace the issue of sequence also arises: the choice as to which tariffs should be reduced first and whether quotas should be relaxed ahead of tariff reductions. A major new study on trade liberalizations, primarily in LDCs (Papageorgiou, Choksi and Michaely, 1990) appears to be somewhat dismissive of the co-ordination problem: 'the study regards exchange rate policy as falling outside the direct content of a trade liberalisation program. So the close association between strong programs and currency depreciation is not in this case a matter of definition: strong reformers tended, as a matter of fact, to depreciate their currencies when launching their trade reforms' (p. 19). This claim that the exchange rate is not central to liberalization, implies that there should be no systematic effects upon the balance of payments, and that the fiscal impact is generally favourable, in turn implying no need for offsetting tax changes. The study also argues strongly that large, rapid liberalization is more successful than gradual liberalization, in consequence dismissing issues of sequencing.

If liberalization is so unproblematic, why then do many liberalizations get aborted? One explanation rests upon the political economy of LDC liberalizations. Mostly they are not unilateral decisions but the outcome of bargaining with donor agencies, notably the World Bank (for example, Kenya in 1989) or the IMF (for example, Zambia in 1985). The bargain generally takes the form of aid in return for reform, the aid being described as covering the 'costs of adjustment'. The aid is therefore temporary.

The problem with such a bargain is that it is liable to be time inconsistent. If the government's preference ordering is

liberalization + aid > protection > liberalization without aid

then temporary aid is liable to produce only temporary liberalization (Mosley, 1987).

It may well be that Papageorgiou, Choksi and Michaely underplay the co-ordination problem. Although trade liberalization does not inevitably worsen the balance of payments, it seems likely to do so. Liberalization lowers the domestic price of importables, thereby reducing the demand for money. The resulting excess supply of money manifests itself as a payments deficit. To maintain payments balance, therefore, the demand for money must be maintained (or its supply reduced). One way to achieve this is by offsetting the reduction in importables prices brought about by trade liberalization with an exchange rate depreciation. The domestic price of importables is related to the exchange rate and trade restrictions through

$$P_d = P_w e(1 + t) \tag{8.10}$$

where P_d is the domestic price of the importable, P_w the international price (in dollars), e the exchange rate (units of domestic currency per dollar) and t the nominal rate of protection (tariffs plus the tariff equivalent of quotas).

Hence, it is quite possible so to co-ordinate trade liberalization and exchange rate policy that the domestic price of importables is unaltered. In this case the demand for money will not fall (indeed it will gradually grow as the liberalization increases real income) and so the balance of payments should not deteriorate. Often, however, LDC governments are resistant to exchange rate depreciation. This is where temporary aid is both appealing and dangerous. It is appealing because it offers the prospect of financing a payments deficit for an 'adjustment period'. As long as the government merely sells the aid-provided foreign exchange to its citizens rather than increasing its own expenditure, the aid directly reduces the money supply. Further, the liberalization gradually increases real income, and hence the demand for money. Ideally, between them these two effects are sufficiently powerful for temporary aid to obviate the need for exchange rate depreciation. More realistically, they may reduce that need. It seems then that by means of aid the government can reconcile a large and rapid trade liberalization with slow and deferred depreciation.

A fundamental problem with this strategy is that it is likely to induce destabilizing speculation on the part of private agents within the economy. Private agents know that for the duration of the aid imports are temporarily cheap. Post-aid, either the government plucks up the courage to depreciate the exchange rate or it aborts the trade liberalization. Private agents need not even form a view as to which of these outcomes is the more likely since, from (8.10), they have equivalent consequences for the domestic price of importables. If the anticipated increase in the price of importables exceeds the domestic interest rate, then private agents will choose to accumulate inventories of imports in preference to domestic financial assets. Now introduce some uncertainty among private agents as to whether, when it comes to the crunch, the government will depreciate the exchange rate or abort the liberalization. Note that this uncertainty arises largely because of the aid. Private agents cannot tell whether the government is genuinely committed to liberalization, has already decided to take the aid donors for a ride, or has simply welcomed the money and deferred the agony of decision. Although this is not important for the choice of whether to accumulate inventories of imports, it is extremely important for the choice of where to install fixed investment. If the liberalization is maintained then the best strategy will be to invest in the export sector which will benefit from the exchange rate depreciation. If, instead, the government aborts the liberalization, then the import-substitute sector will revert to being profitable. Since once capital is installed it is at best costly to shift it between sectors, the uncertainty as to policy creates a premium on keeping options open by delaying investment and acquiring financial assets (Dixit, 1989). These two private responses reinforce each other. If investment is deferred, the gains in real income from resource reallocation take longer to come through and so the post-aid exchange rate depreciation must be larger if it is to maintain policy compatibility. This, in turn, makes it less likely that the government will choose this option rather than abort the liberalization. Further, if investment is deferred, it becomes atypically easy to finance the accumulation of inventories of imports. Such inventories become the option-preserving asset which dominates both domestic financial assets and investment in fixed capital. However, in aggregate, inventory accumulation is socially costly in two ways. First, since the profits from such inventory holding arise from the anticipation of internal changes in relative prices, their source is a transfer within the society. In calculating the social rate of return these transfers net out, leaving a social return of zero. The social opportunity cost of foreign exchange tied up in zero-yielding assets in foreign exchange scarce economies is likely to be high. Second, and ultimately more important, inventory accumulation will accelerate reserve loss. This creates a confusing signal for the government that the liberalization appears to have radically deteriorated the balance of payments, hence needing a massive exchange rate depreciation if it is to be sustained. It also hastens the day of judgement, when the government must choose between depreciation and aborted liberalization. In turn, by advancing the time at which cheap imports will cease, inventory accumulation raises the rate of return on inventories: the same capital gain will accrue over a shorter period. Thus, unlike investment in fixed capital, investment in inventories is subject to increasing returns. The upshot of this is that aid-funded liberalizations are intrinsically precarious, liable to induce a crash in investment in real capital and a speculative flight into inventories which exhausts the reserves and panics the government into aborting the reform. Once the speculation starts, because returns are increasing, it is likely to be unstoppable.

The literature on the theory of liberalization is recent and a little confusing since it is couched in terms of the anticipation of the reversal of the liberalization. The fundamental advances were by Calvo (1987, 1988). Calvo showed that, given the exchange rate, if there was an anticipation of an increase in trade restrictions, rational agents would accumulate inventories as long as the return exceeded the interest rate. In the Calvo model the timing of the reversion to protection is exogenous: private agents simply believe that it will happen with a probability of unity. In some of the subsequent literature (Froot, 1988) the probability of reversion is endogenous to the terms of trade, which is introduced as a stochastic variable. However, in both cases the expectation concerns the reversal of the trade reform. However, as discussed above, the motivation for inventory accumulation is independent of whether the liberalization is aborted or validated by devaluation. The problem arises not out of the incredibility of trade liberalization being sustained but rather out of the temporary incompatibility of exchange rate and trade policies. It is the policy combination, not the trade liberalization, which is incredible. One or other policy must be modified and it does not matter to inventory holders which is chosen. The deferral of fixed investment arises directly out of neither policy incompatibility nor the incredibility of liberalization but rather from policy uncertainty. In the Calvo model, where it is known with certainty that the liberalization will be aborted, there is no such uncertainty. However, indirectly, policy uncertainty arises out of policy incompatibility since current policies are unsustainable and so the government is manifestly deferring its choices.

An effect analogous to temporary aid is if the economy experiences a favourable external shock which is perceived as temporary while the government is following an 'endogenous trade policy rule' as discussed in the previous section. Knowing the shock and the rule, private agents are then able to infer that the trade liberalization will be reversed and so have an incentive to accumulate inventories of imports.

Returning to the case in which aid can be used to enable abrupt liberalization with a deferral of exchange rate change, an alternative is that the pace of trade liberalization should be harmonized with that of exchange rate adjustment. If the latter can be large and abrupt then so too can the liberalization. In such a case there is probably little to be said for gradualism. Fernandez and Rodrik (1990) provide a political economy argument to support the empirical finding of Papageorgiou, Choksi and Michaely (1990) that large abrupt reforms are more likely to persist than gradualism. Suppose that those employed in the protected sector are unsure of the returns which their endowments would earn in the export sector. If they are not risk averse, they will base their comparison upon the mathematical expectation of the returns. However, this expected value may lie below actual returns in the protected sector, whereas with full information many agents may stand to gain. Lack of information prevents a lobby of potential beneficiaries from emerging. However, after the reform is fully completed, the same inertial factor works to preserve the liberalization. More generally, liberalization involves shifting some agents unwillingly into the export sector from the rest of the economy. Once they have been shifted, these agents acquire an interest in the maintenance of the reform; until they have been shifted they, and many more who run a risk of being shifted, have an interest in opposing it. If, however, the exchange rate change can only be gradual, then a further consideration arises as to the sequencing of the liberalization.[17]

Two broad features of sequencing have emerged. One is that tariff harmonization tends to precede general tariff reduction. The other is that quotas tend to get converted into tariffs. Together, these form a sequence: first quotas are converted to tariff equivalents, then tariff rates are harmonized and, finally, tariff rates are lowered.

The rationale for this sequence is that quotas are highly damaging and so should be removed first, while it is the dispersion of tariff rates as much as their average level which is costly. Hence, the economy can reap large gains from liberalization before it lowers the average level of protection and needs to adjust the exchange rate. However, the sequence is not without problems. First, quotas are sledom replaced by their full tariff equivalent. Partly, this is because the equivalent is not known with any precision and partly because the rate would sometimes be so high as to be politically embarassing. As a result, the removal of quotas requires an uncertain synchronized exchange rate adjustment for the maintenance of compatibility. Second, the whole sequence is liable to give rise to a temporary revenue boom. The conversion of quotas to tariffs will raise revenue, whereas the subsequent reduction of tariff rates is likely at some stage to lower revenue. The danger with engineering a temporary revenue boom is that, even if the government in some sense recognizes the trajectory, expenditure may rise semi-permanently.

Although a temporary revenue boom is an induced consequence only of a particular sequencing of trade reform, the optimism of Papageorgiou, Choksi and Michaely in respect of the fiscal consequences of trade liberalization has been more generally questioned. Pinto (1989) presents an influential model in which liberalization is necessarily damaging to the budget. This model rests upon quite special and implausible assumptions. Nevertheless, the central point about the consequence of liberalization for the budget is that even the sign of the impact is contingent upon magnitudes which are emprically quite difficult to discover. This adds to the air of policy uncertainty: not only are private agents unsure about the intentions of the government, they should be unsure about its technical capacity to forecast the fiscal and balance of payments implications of that policy which it chooses to implement.

Unilateral trade liberalization may, therefore, be quite precarious because of policy uncertainty. The participation of aid donors, though directly improving the fiscal and payments balances, may well accentuate speculation and policy uncertainty as discussed above. It is noteworthy that neither unilateralism nor donor conditionality have been the vehicles for DC liberalization. For DCs the driving force behind liberalization has been multilateral co-ordination whether through customs union or the GATT. There have been numerous attempts at customs union among LDCs. On the whole these have been either inconsequential or disastrous: the East African Community ended by its member states closing their borders. Since contiguous LDCs tend to have rather similar economic structures, the gains from intra-area trade are modest, while the diversion of trade is considerable. As a result it is quite probable that the net efficiency effects are negative whereas the intra-union distributional effects are powerful. Losers (namely those countries which are importing high-cost manufactures from other members rather than from the world market) are conscious of large losses, while beneficiaries cannot compensate losers and remain better off. The institution is therefore a recipe for political conflict.

Whereas the essence of customs union is reciprocity, LDCs in their trade bargaining with DCs have demanded non-reciprocal concessions. A classic example of this is the Lomé convention which confers partial access of 66 African, Caribbean and Pacific countries to the EC. This lack of reciprocity has had two damaging effects. First, it has severely limited LDC access to DC markets: DCs have only been willing to make unreciprocated concessions at the periphery of LDC comparative advantages. For example, the East Asian countries have highly restricted access to Europe for their manufactures, while Africa has restricted access for its agricultural produce. Second, and perhaps fundamentally, it has lowered the cost of protection for LDCs relative to DCs. The latter maintain near-free trade because they are trapped in a web of reciprocal threats of retaliation, the counterpart of the reciprocal promises which achieved their trade liberalizations. LDCs are highly protected because this did not trigger equivalent reprisals. They were effectively outside the two core bargaining processes, that between the members of the EC and that between the USA, Japan and the EC.[18] Perhaps this explains both why LDCs became highly protected and why their liberalization attempts have been so fraught compared with the remarkable liberalization achieved among DCs. Because the reprisal cost of protection is so much lower for LDCs, they are less locked in to any liberalization which is either unilateral or merely donor-conditioned. As we have seen, liberalizations in which there is a question mark over persistence are liable to be less successful as a result. Indeed, if investment collapses, they might be worse than no liberalization. Recently, therefore, economists have started to call for LDC liberalization to be done in the context of reciprocal concessions and threats of retaliation from DCs (Rodrik, 1989) as a way of locking in reform.

8.5 CONCLUSIONS

We started by posing the questions why should LDCs have become so heavily protected, and why, given that this was so damaging, should liberalization have been so fraught. On balance, we would favour the macroeconomic answers over the political economy answers, although the latter are probably more prevalent in the literature. Trade restrictions perhaps built up primarily because they were a simple answer to payments crises given fixed exchange rates rather than because of pressure from those groups which ex-post benefited. Payment crises in LDCs have been endemic because of their proneness to temporary trade shocks. The trade restrictions adopted during such crises have proved difficult to dismantle in part because the dynamics of uncoordinated changes in macroeconomic policy can, through speculation, easily lead to programme collapse.

NOTES

1   For a more comprehensive survey we refer to Bliss (1989).
2   We are indebted to Ron Findlay for this point.
3   Deaton (1990), table 2, monthly prices 1960–88 deflated by US consumer prices.
4   Deaton and Laroque (1992) solve a stock-holding model with intertemporal arbitrage in which stock-outs generate the observed price pattern.

5 Powell (1990) analyses commodity price forecasts and shows that for many agricultural commodities a boom is difficult to predict but that once a boom has started its duration can be predicted quite accurately. The coffee boom of 1976–9 was in this category.

6 If capital is mobile the outcome depends, of course, on relative factor intensities. In a three-sector model (tradables, non-tradable consumer goods and non-tradable capital goods) with a perfect world capital market a construction boom (in the sense of an increase in the output and the price of non-tradable capital) can occur only if construction is more capital intensive than tradables (van Wincoop, 1993). This seems implausible. Observed construction booms must therefore be explained in terms of capital market imperfections or factor immobility.

7 Equation (8.4) gives the Keynes–Ramsey rule: consumption increases (decreases) if the marginal productivity of capital exceeds (is less than) the rate of time preference. Cf. Blanchard and Fischer (1989, chapter 2) for a recent exposition of the Ramsey (1928) model.

8 The locus is upward sloping up to the point where $f' = \delta$.

9 We ignore tradable capital goods because they can be aggregated with tradable consumption goods and we assume that only tradables are consumed to abstract from the Dutch disease spending effect.

10 For a large δ the positive effect of a capital stock increase on consumption may be more than offset by the increase in replacement demand for capital goods.

11 Note that in equilibrium ($\dot{k} = 0$) this equates the return to one unit of tradables invested domestically (the marginal productivity minus the depreciation rate: $\tilde{\iota}_k/p - \delta$) to its opportunity cost in terms of forgone consumption, ρ.

12 The price p must rise since $\dot{c} = \tilde{\iota}_k \dot{k} + \tilde{\iota}_p \dot{p}$ and c falls while k increases. At time T the price drops. This ensures a jump in the production of tradables so that consumption does not drop at the end of the boom. At T, r jumps up so that the rental price rp is continuous. The post-boom adjustment path is along CD.

13 This was done during the coffee boom in Kenya where coffee growers were informed through the co-operatives that the shock was temporary.

14 See Gilbert (1987) and Winters and Sapsford (1990) for evaluations of commodity agreements and Anderson and Gilbert (1988) for the case of tin.

15 Gilbert (1991) emphasizes that this efficiency loss is more serious in the case of annual crops than in the case of minerals or tree crops.

16 The options approach has two disadvantages. With returns random and borrowing impossible the seriousness of a price fall depends on whether the producer has run down his assets. Hence options values differ between producers depending on asset positions. If a market for options existed then heterogeneity would be reflected in not all producers buying options. In a peasant economy where a floor price is used as a substitute for a missing options market, there does not seem to be good mechanism by which liquidity-constrained producers can communicate the higher value they place on the option implied by the floor price. Hence the options approach involves two inefficiencies. First, since the board cannot be well informed on peasants' asset positions, the floor price it sets is in a sense arbitrary. Second, too much coverage is provided since the approach ignores the heterogeneity of producers. When the spot price falls below the floor price all producers are protected, including those for whom the option value is low.

17 This is sequencing within trade reform rather than sequencing within economic reform as in Kowalczyk (1989).

18 This is partly the result of the preferential treatment accorded to LDCs under GATT rules.

REFERENCES

Anderson, R. W. and Gilbert, C. L. 1988: Commodity agreements and commodity markets: lessons from tin. *Economic Journal*, 98, 1–15.

Baldwin, R. E. 1969: The case against infant-industry tariff protection. *Journal of Political Economy*, 77, 295–305.

Bates, R. H. 1981: *Markets and States in Tropical Africa*. Berkeley: University of California Press.

Becker, G. S. 1983: A theory of competition among pressure groups for political influence. *Quarterly Journal of Economics*, 98, 371–400.

Bevan, D. L., Collier, P. and Gunning, J. W. 1987: Consequences of a commodity boom in a controlled economy: accumulation and redistribution in Kenya, 1975–1983. *World Bank Economic Review*, 1, 489–513.

Bevan, D. L., Collier, P. and Gunning, J. W. 1990a: *Controlled Open Economies*. Oxford: Clarendon Press.

Bevan, D. L., Collier, P. and Gunning, J. W. 1990b: African trade shocks: consequences and policy responses. Mimeo, Centre for the Study of African Economies, Oxford.

Blanchard, O. J. and Fischer, S. 1989: *Lectures on Macroeconomics*. Cambridge, Mass.: MIT Press.

Bliss, C. 1989: Trade and development. In H. Chenery and T. N. Srinivasan (eds), *Handbook of Development Economics*, Amsterdam: North-Holland, 1187–240.

Calvo, G. A. 1987: On the costs of temporary policy. *Journal of Development Economics*, 27, 245–61.

Calvo, G. 1988: Costly trade liberalizations: durable goods and capital mobility. *IMF Staff Papers*, 35, 461–73.

Collier, P. and Gunning, J. W. 1990: Real incomes and supply response in rural Tanzania during adjustment, 1983–88. Mimeo, Centre for the Study of African Economies, Oxford.

Corden, W. M. 1974: *Trade Policy and Economic Welfare*, Oxford: Clarendon Press.

Corden, W. M. 1984: Booming sector and Dutch disease economics: survey and consolidation. *Oxford Economic Papers*, 36, 359–80.

Corden, W. M. 1990: Strategic trade policy: how new? How sensible? World Bank, Country Economics Department Working Paper 396.

Corden, W. M. and Neary, J. P. 1982: Booming sector and de-industrialisation in a small open economy. *Economic Journal*, 92, 825–48.

Deaton, A. 1990: Saving in developing countries: theory and review. In *Proceedings of the World Bank Annual Conference on Development Economics 1989*, Supplement to the *World Bank Economic Review* and the *World Bank Research Observer*, 61–96.

Deaton, A. and Laroque, G. 1992: On the behaviour of commodity prices. *Review of Economic Studies*, 59, 1–23.

Dixit, A. 1989: Intersectoral capital reallocation under price uncertainty. *Journal of International Economics*, 26, 309–25.

Fernandez, R. and Rodrik, D. 1990: Why is trade reform so unpopular? On the status quo bias in policy reforms. NBER Working Paper no. 3269.

Froot, K. A. 1988: Credibility, real interest rates, and the optimal speed of trade liberalization. *Journal of International Economics*, 25, 71–93.

Gelb, A. and associates 1988: *Oil Windfalls: blessing or curse?* New York: Oxford University Press.

Ghanem, H. 1991: The Ivorian cocoa and coffee boom of 1976–79: the end of a miracle? Mimeo, World Bank.

232   PAUL COLLIER AND JAN WILLEM GUNNING

Gilbert, C. L. 1987: International commodity agreements: design and performance. *World Development*, 15, 591–616.

Gilbert, C. L. 1991: Domestic price stabilization schemes for developing countries. Mimeo, Queen Mary and Westfield College, University of London.

Herrmann, R., Burger, K. and Smit, H. P. 1990: Commodity policy: price stabilization versus financing. In L. A. Winters and D. Sapsford (eds), *Primary Commodity Prices: economic models and policy*, Cambridge: Cambridge University Press, 240–302.

Johnson, H. G. 1960: The cost of protection and the scientific tariff. *Journal of Political Economy*, 68, 327–45.

Kowalczyk, C. 1989: Trade negotiations and world welfare. *American Economic Review*, 79, 552–9.

Krueger, Anne O. 1974: The political economy of the rent-seeking society. *American Economic Review*, 64, 291–303.

Lal, D. 1989: *The Hindu Equilibrium*. Oxford: Clarendon Press.

Lal, D. and Myint, H. 1992: *The Political Economy of Poverty, Equity and Growth in Developing Countries*. Oxford: Oxford University Press.

Magee, S. P. 1980: Three simple tests of the Stolper–Samuelson theorem. In P. Oppenheimer (ed.), *Issues in International Economics*, London: Oriel Press, 138–53.

Magee, S. P., Brock, W. A. and Young, L. 1989: *Black Hole Tariffs and Endogenous Policy Theory*. Cambridge: Cambridge University Press.

Meade, J. 1955: *Trade and Welfare*. London: Oxford University Press.

Mosley, P. 1987: Conditionality as bargaining process: structural adjustment lending, 1980–86. *Essays in International Finance* no. 168, Princeton.

Mundlak, Y., Cavallo, D. and Domenech, R. 1990: Effects of macroeconomic policies on sectoral prices. *World Bank Economic Review*, 4, 55–79.

Neary, J. P. and van Wijnbergen, S. (eds) 1986: *Natural Resources and the Macro-economy*. Oxford: Basil Blackwell.

Newbery, D. M. 1990: Commodity price stabilization. In M. Scott and D. Lal (eds), *Public Policy and Economic Development*, Oxford: Clarendon Press, 80–108.

Newbery, D. M. G. and Stiglitz, J. E. 1981: *The Theory of Commodity Price Stabilisation. A Study in the Economics of Risk*. Oxford: Clarendon Press.

Panagariya, A. and Schiff, M. 1990: Commodity exports and real income in Africa: a preliminary analysis. Paper presented at the Africa Economic Issues Conference, Nairobi, 4–7 June.

Papageorgiou, D., Choksi, A. M. and Michaely, M. 1990: *Liberalizing Foreign Trade in Developing Countries: the lessons of experience*. Washington, DC: World Bank.

Pinto, B. 1989: Black market premia, exchange rate unification and inflation in sub-Saharan Africa. *World Bank Economic Review*, 3, 321–38.

Powell, A. 1990: The cost of commodity price uncertainty. Mimeo, Nuffield College, Oxford.

Ramsey, F. P. 1928: A mathematical theory of saving. *Economic Journal*, 38, 543–59.

Rimmer, D. 1991: *The Political Economy of Poverty, Equity and Growth in Ghana*. London: Pergamon.

Rodrik, D. 1989: Credibility of trade reform: a policy maker's guide. *The World Economy*, 12, 1–16.

Roemer, M. 1985: Dutch disease in developing countries: swallowing bitter medicine. In M. Lundahl (ed.), *The Primary Sector in Economic Development*, London: Croom Helm, 234–51.

van Wijnbergen, S. 1984: Inflation, employment and the Dutch disease in oil-exporting countries: a short-run disequilibrium analysis. *Quarterly Journal of Economics*, 99, 233–50.

van Wincoop, E. 1991: Structural adjustment and the construction sector. *European Economic Review*, 37, 177–201.

Winters, L. A. and Sapsford, D. (eds) 1990: *Primary Commodity Prices: economic models and policy*. Cambridge: Cambridge University Press.

9

INTERNATIONAL ECONOMIC INTEGRATION

Robert C. Hine

9.1 INTRODUCTION

'International economic integration' describes both a state of affairs and a process. As a state, it refers to a fusion of formerly separate national economies. More usefully, as a process it signifies the gradual elimination of economic frontiers between countries, an 'economic frontier' being 'any demarcation over which mobilities of goods, services and factors of production are relatively low' (Pelkmans, 1984). In one sense integration is a global phenomenon, as the network of international trade and foreign direct investment intensifies, encouraged by multilateral agencies like the GATT and spearheaded by the activities of multinational companies (MNCs). In this chapter, however, international economic integration is more narrowly defined as the attempt by governments to link together the economies of two or more countries through the removal of economic frontiers under specific integration schemes, such as the European Communities (EC) or the North American Free Trade Area (NAFTA). Dismantling economic frontiers like tariffs and immigration controls has the general economic aim of raising living standards in the participating countries, but a political purpose of fostering peaceful relations among the participants may also be important, indeed on occasions paramount.

Reflecting differences of purpose, integration schemes vary in scope and ambition. Following Balassa (1961), several stages or levels of integration may be distinguished:

1 In a *free trade area* (FTA) the member countries remove tariffs and quotas on imports on their partners' goods, but retain their own restrictions on imports from non-member countries; since this could lead to goods from outside the area entering a high-tariff country via a lower-tariff member, thereby undermining the effectiveness of the high tariff (*trade deflection*), rules of origin confine tariff-free treatment within the FTA to goods largely or wholly produced in the FTA.
2 A *customs union* (CU) goes further than an FTA in that member countries apply a common external tariff on goods from outside the CU; this simplifies the treatment of goods within the CU – regardless of origin all goods circulate free of tariffs and quotas.
3 A *common market* is a CU in which there is also the free movement of factors of production – labour and capital.

4 In an *economic and monetary union* (EMU) there is a single currency and monetary policy, and major economic policies are co-ordinated.

This classification, though useful analytically, corresponds only partially to economic reailty. Since non-tariff barriers are now more important trade impediments than tariffs a CU which fails to liberalize beyond tariffs and quotas will remain fragmented along national lines. This is why the EC launched its 1992 programme to create a single European market. Also it may be questioned whether FTAs, CUs or common markets are now viable if they do not include some degree of policy co-operation or co-ordination, particularly in relation to competition policy. Indeed it is arguable that integration schemes are inherently unstable, obliging the member countries constantly to take further measures or risk failure. This is because interest groups who lose one form of national protection (e.g. tariffs) will lobby governments for an alternative (e.g. state subsidies).

There are numerous integration schemes world-wide. On the whole those involving developing countries have had relatively little impact (Langhammer, 1992). This chapter will therefore focus primarily on integration schemes involving developed countries and particularly on the most advanced one, the EC. The survey is in three parts. The first deals with the theory of economic integration, particularly CU theory; quantitative studies of integration are the subject of the second part; the chapter concludes with a review of policy aspects of integration.

9.2 THE THEORY OF ECONOMIC INTEGRATION

Integration schemes affect the economies of the member countries through three main channels (Brown and Stern, 1989):

1 *Intersectoral specialization effects*, as tariff adjustments lead to a once-for-all ('static') reallocation of a country's resources among sectors.
2 *Rationalization effects* as production is reorganized to take advantage of economies of scale and is spurred to greater efficiency by a sharper competitive environment; where there are external economies of scale, integration may stimulate a higher growth rate by increasing the return to capital thereby inducing greater capital formation (Baldwin, 1992); such 'dynamic' effects are in principle sustained.
3 *Macroeconomic effects* as increased trade affects economic variables such as growth and inflation.

Until recently most theoretical work on integration focused almost exclusively on the static specialization effects (1), even though it was widely accepted that the dynamic aspects (2) were potentially more important. The static analysis has been developed mainly through the theory of CUs. This survey will review Vinerian CU theory, the economic rationale for CU formation and some recent developments in CU theory; it will conclude with a brief discussion of factor market integration.

9.2.1 The Theory of Customs Unions[1]

9.2.1.1 Viner's analysis

The formation of a CU may be expected to increase trade between the member countries since it involves the removal of customs barriers on their mutual trade. Three questions then arise: will this increased trade be to the economic benefit of the individual member countries? To the union as a whole? To the world? Until Viner (1950) the answer of most economists to these questions would have been an unqualified 'yes'. Their reasoning was supposedly based on the classical theory of comparative advantage. It may be summarized as follows: (a)free trade maximizes welfare while the imposition of tariffs reduces it, (b) the creation of a CU involves the elimination of tariffs and is therefore a step towards free trade, and (c) thus the creation of a CU increases welfare, even though it may not maximize it.

In *The Customs Union Issue* (1950), Jacob Viner[2] showed that this argument was not generally correct. Viner accepted that CU formation would increase trade between the member countries but he argued that whether or not this was desirable depended on the source of increased trade. Viner identified two possible cases: trade creation and trade diversion. *Trade creation* involves a shift in domestic consumption from a high-cost domestic source to a lower-cost partner source, as a result of the abolition of tariffs on intra-union trade. *Trade diversion* involves a shift in domestic consumption from a low-cost world source to a higher-cost partner source, as a result of the elimination of tariffs on imports from the partner.

Viner argued that the closure of (high-cost) home industries through trade creation would be advantageous for the home country because it would release resources for use in industries where the home country had a comparative advantage. The partner country would gain or at least not lose from its new exports to the home country, and therefore the union as a whole would be better off. By contrast, trade diversion would be damaging to the home country because of the switch to a higher-cost source of imports (worsening the home country's terms of trade). The partner country would, in Viner's analysis, derive no benefit from this – the higher price would be needed to meet its higher costs – and therefore the union as a whole would be worse off. Viner concluded that a welfare assessment of the effects of CU formation depended on the balance between trade creation and trade diversion: a predominantly trade-creating union would be desirable, while a predominantly trade-diverting union would be damaging[3].

Viner was vague about the assumptions underlying his analysis – as Meade (1955) observed, Viner's analysis is most suitable under (a) constant costs of production and (b) perfectly inelastic demand. Meade, Gehrels (1956) and Lipsey (1960) pointed out that relaxing the demand assumption opened up the possibility of a further source of gain – a *consumption effect*. The removal of tariffs on imports from the partner country may lead to a fall in prices paid by the home consumer, and, if demand is not completely inelastic, to a rise in quantity consumed. This consumption effect is beneficial to the extent that price relatives in the home country now reflect more accurately opportunity costs on the world market. The associated increase in imports was described by Meade (1955) as 'trade expansion'. As Johnson (1960) argued, both trade creation and trade diversion may have consumption as well as production effects. It is even possible that, contrary to Viner's view, a purely trade-diverting CU could increase welfare if the consumption gain exceeded the terms of trade loss (Lipsey, 1960).

Viner provided a key insight into the effect of CU formation: since a CU may be trade creating and/or trade diverting it is not possible to generalize about the economic desirability of CUs – each must be assessed individually. Following Lipsey and Lancaster (1956–7), CUs came to be regarded as a good illustration of the theory of second-best: where two or more obstacles exist to the achievement of a Pareto-optimal position, the removal of only one or some of them does not necessarily improve welfare.

9.2.1.2 Customs union theory: the standard analysis

Many of the important findings of CU theory were first demonstrated in a partial equilibrium (PE) framework despite its limitations as a vehicle for CU analysis. As Lipsey (1960) and others have emphasized, whereas the PE approach would be valid for a small change in one tariff, CU formation may involve large changes in many tariffs. Consequently, the PE approach ignores potentially important feedback effects between sectors, but it has the merit of providing a simple framework for analysing some of the key issues in CU formation and most CU theory is set within either a PE or a two-good general equilbrium framework.

As a branch of international trade theory CU theory shares the standard assumptions of that theory, to which CU-specific assumptions are added (see e.g. Pelkmans, 1984, p. 8). Thus mainstream CU analysis focuses on a world of three countries, two of which – the home and partner countries – form a CU, the rest of the world (RoW) being excluded. The home country being small faces a completely elastic partner and RoW supply. It is assumed that the tariff in the home country – taken to be an importer – becomes the common external tariff of the union, and that there are no other trade restrictions. Production of the homogeneous good in the home country is under rising marginal costs and perfect competition prevails throughout. There are no externalities. Welfare effects are analysed in relation to three groups: consumers and producers (whose welfare is reflected, respectively, in consumers' surplus and producers' surplus) and taxpayers (who receive tariff revenues). Net welfare effects can be assessed by assuming that a system of compensation is possible.

Consider the case where the home country (H) initially applies a non-preferential tariff p_1p_3 (figure 9.1), securing a price in H of p_3. A CU formed

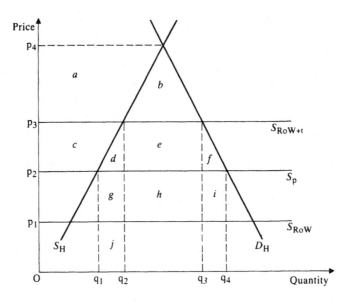

Figure 9.1 Customs union effects when the partner country and the rest of the world are large

between H and P gives consumers in H access to tariff-free imports from P, lowering H's price to p_2. Consequently, production of q_1q_2 in H is displaced by lower-cost production in P and consumption increases by q_3q_4. Imports rise to q_1q_4 and now come exclusively from the partner country. The extra trade – imports of $q_1q_2 + q_3q_4$ – represents trade creation. Imports of q_2q_3 from RoW are switched away to P, a higher cost source of supply – this is the trade diversion.

How do these changes affect welfare in H? All imports now come from a tariff-free source – P – hence taxpayers will lose the tariff revenue of $(e + h)$. The lower price will increase the welfare of consumers, measured by the gain in consumers' surplus of $(c + d + e + f)$, but will leave producers worse off by area (c) – the fall in producers' surplus. The net effect in H can be expressed as: $(d + f) - (h)$ which is, in general, indeterminate. The components (d) and (f) correspond to the trade creation gain, with (d) the production effect as high-cost production in H is replaced at the margin by lower-cost production in P, and (f) the consumption effect as the distorting effect of tariffs on consumers in H is reduced. Area (h) is the trade diversion loss, reflecting the deterioration in H's terms of trade as imports are shifted to a higher-cost source.

This assessment of the welfare effects of CU formation is based on the (arbitrary) assumption that the initial tariff in the home country is p_1p_3. Suppose instead that the pre-union tariff is p_1p_4, the minimum prohibitive tariff. CU formation can result only in trade creation, and there is a net welfare gain of $(b + d + e + f)$. Similarly, if the RoW supply price had exceeded that of P, only trade creation could arise from CU formation. Alternatively, with an initial tariff in the home country of p_1p_2 the CU is purely trade diverting, producing a welfare loss for H of $(g + h + i)$.

These examples illustrate the basic Viner proposition that we cannot make any general statement about the economic desirability of CUs. As later analysts demonstrated, this conclusion depends critically on the underlying assumptions. In particular, the assumptions that (a) the union members are too small to affect their terms of trade with RoW and (b) that the level of the common external tariff is set at the previous level of the national tariffs (i.e. there is a given tariff rate) are particularly significant. We will consider the implications of relaxing them in section 9.2.1.4. Before doing so, we will remain with the 'small union case' and explore the controversy over whether or not a small country can gain anything from membership of a CU that it cannot obtain unilaterally from a non-preferential tariff policy.

9.2.1.3 Is there an economic rationale for a small country to join a CU?

The standard analysis shows that in some circumstances CU formation could be welfare-improving for a small country. The welfare gains are associated with trade creation. The question arises: is there an alternative trade policy, not involving trade discrimination, which could secure the benefits of trade creation, without exposing a country to the losses of trade diversion? Cooper and Massell (1965) argued that not only is there such a policy, but that there is always a non-preferential policy which is superior to CU membership even if the CU is only trade creating. If correct, this suggests that there is no economic rationale for CU formation – CUs must be established for political or other non-economic reasons.

The Cooper and Massell argument can be explored within the framework of figure 9.1. The key to the analysis is that there exists a non-preferential tariff which produces the same price level in H as would occur if that country formed a CU with P. This tariff is p_1p_2 and, applied non-preferentially, results in a price in H of p_2, the market-clearing price in the CU.[4] It is the 'appropriate' tariff in the sense that it sustains the same level of production in the home country as would a CU. Therefore, whatever the rationale for protection, for the home producers and consumers there is no difference between CU membership and the application of the 'appropriate' non-preferential tariff. To the extent that prices fall, the two options will have an identical trade creation effect. Attention must thus focus on the effect on taxpayers. In a CU, H will receive no tariff revenues because its imports come entirely from P and they are tariff-free. By contrast, with the appropriate non-preferential tariff of p_1p_2, imports will always come from the lower-cost RoW source and taxpayers will receive tariff revenue of $(g + h + i)$. Therefore, taking the interests of producers, consumers and taxpayers together, joining a CU must be inferior to adopting the appropriate non-preferential tariff. In trade creation/trade diversion terms, the non-preferential tariff is superior because:

1 In the absence of trade discrimination in favour of a higher-cost supplier, there can be no trade diversion.
2 The gains from trade creation can be maximized by ensuring that this new trade comes from the lowest-cost supplier (RoW) and not just from a lower-cost one (the partner country).

These results lead to the very important conclusion that either CUs are formed for entirely non-economic reasons, or the standard analysis makes assumptions which are so inappropriate that the economic rationale for CU formation is lost.

Cooper and Massell concentrated on the importing country's possible interest in CU membership. Wonnacott and Wonnacott (1981) argue that this is unsatisfactory since CU formation is motivated more by *potential export advantages*. Their crucial modification to the standard analysis is the assumption that the RoW applies a tariff. They accept that it is logically consistent to argue that as the RoW is 'large' it is indifferent to its trade with the other countries and will not therefore apply a tariff. However, the Wonnacotts suggest that (a) although in relation to the focus good the RoW is large, this need not be the case for all goods – a tariff on the focus good might then serve as a bargaining counter, and (b) the standard analysis assumes that the RoW is large in order to abstract from terms of trade effects, even though the large country assumption may not be fully warranted in practice; there seems no good reason, in a tariff-ridden world, to compound the unreality by assuming that the RoW applies no tariff. The effect of assuming that the RoW applies a tariff is to create two world prices: a world import price (p_m) at which imports may be purchased, and a world export price (p_x) which will be received on exports to RoW and which will be below p_m by the amount of the RoW tariff. The gap between p_m and p_x may be further widened by transport costs: since CUs are typically formed between neighbouring countries, transport costs are likely to be greater with RoW than between the union members.

Consider a CU formed where the RoW applies a tariff and, unlike previously, assume that P is not large in relation to H. With (non-preferential) tariffs in H and RoW, P is prevented from fully exploiting its comparative advantage in the focus good. Forming a CU will help to remedy this by opening up H's market: RoW and P supply H at price p_m. In figure 9.2, which represents H and P 'back to back', the net welfare gain to P from its new exports q_5q_6 is the producers' surplus gain of $(i + j)$ less consumers' surplus loss of (j). In a tariff-ridden world, P cannot secure these gains unilaterally. CU formation provides a framework for reciprocal access to export markets. Importers do not lose from this process since the price paid for imports is no higher than the world import price (p_m) – in figure 9.2, H has a net trade creation gain of (l).

The Wonnacotts' analysis has been criticized as overly simple: by taking out the RoW through its tariff it is an argument for free trade rather than autarky (El-Agraa, 1984). However, Hamilton and Whalley (1985) in a simulation study of world trade 'confirm the implication [of the Wonnacotts] that the gain from reducing a partner's tariff is typically a much more important consideration in evaluating potential benefits from a CU than the traditional concerns of trade creation and trade diversion'. Berglas (1983) has claimed that the Cooper and Massell critique still applies on condition that (a) the direction of trade flows is not affected by CU formation, and (b) all three countries participate in international trade. The Wonnacotts argue that (b) must be stronger – it must apply to every good.

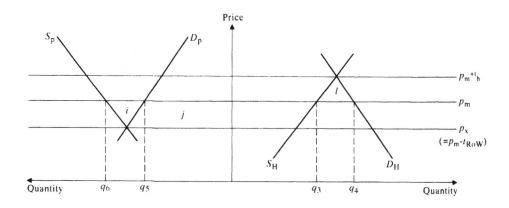

Figure 9.2 Customs union formation when the rest of the world applies a tariff

Viner was aware of the argument that the creation of a CU by increasing the size of the 'home' market might enable economies of scale to be more fully exploited, but was doubtful of its empirical importance. Corden (1972a) formalized the cost reduction effect of CU formation in the presence of economies of scale. He assumes that both H and P have a single actual or potential producer who faces a declining average cost curve (AC_1). In figure 9.3, the RoW applies a tariff p_1p_2, and AC_1 reaches a minimum above the world export price (ruling out unsubsidized exports pre-CU) beyond the size of the national market. Pre-CU, production is possible only with the protection of a tariff p_2p_4. Consider two situations. In case A, each country supports its own production pre-CU with a tariff of p_2p_4 such that the producer can realize a price equal to average costs. CU formation allows one producer – say H's producer – to supply the whole market and thereby reduce its average costs. With an unchanged tariff, the price would remain at p_4, and union consumption would be q_{11}. Average costs on q_{11} would be p_3 and excess profits of $(r + s)$ would accrue to the producer while consumers and taxpayers would be unaffected. The net gain to H is $(r + s)$. In P, production ends but there is no producer surplus loss given the downward-sloping cost curve; nor are consumers or taxpayers affected. With a zero welfare effect in P, the union must gain because of the cost reduction effect in H.

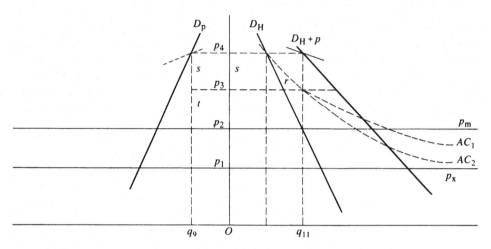

Figure 9.3 Customs union formation in the presence of economies of scale

In case B, suppose that only H had a producer pre-CU. P receives tariff revenue on its imports of q_9. CU formation has the same effect on H as in case A – a gain of $(r + s)$ – but in P there is now a loss of tariff revenue $(s + t)$ as imports are switched from the RoW to H (trade diversion). For the member countries together, the welfare effect of CU formation is indeterminate $(r - t)$. Hence exploiting economies of scale more fully could be a motivation for CU formation, but this depends on the balance between the cost reduction effect and trade diversion. The balance is more likely to be favourable where the number of producers declines and where economies of scale are pronounced. In favourable cases (e.g. with average cost curve AC_2), costs could be lowered sufficiently so that no common external tariff would be required.

Thus far we have not questioned the purpose of tariffs. If we accept the view that economic welfare consists in the individual consumption of goods and services, then tariffs appear irrational. Trade creation which undermines their effectiveness leads to a welfare improvement. Johnson (1965) offered an alternative view, and a further rationale for CU formation. Suppose that an externality exists in that the electorate values industrial production not just for the private benefits from the goods produced but also from the mere presence of industrial activity (e.g. for reasons of prestige). The free-trade level of production would be suboptimal and the first-best policy would be to use a subsidy, which does not distort consumption, to expand production. If, however, it is assumed that subsidies are ruled out, an importing country could use a tariff to stimulate production such that at the margin the excess private production and consumption costs just equalled the collective gain from industrial production.

The welfare effect on such a country of joining a trade-creating CU would clearly be negative, since it would eliminate production on which the collective gain was greater than the private loss. Consider, however, an exporting country with a similar collective preference for industrial production, again ruling out the use of a subsidy. If this country could join a trade-diverting CU it would not only secure a private welfare gain (the increase in producers' surplus would outweigh the loss in consumers' surplus) but also a collective gain on the increased production. These gains could exceed the trade diversion loss of its union partner: a trade-diverting CU could be welfare increasing for the union as a whole in the presence of an externality.

This section has considered whether a small country can gain anything from CU membership that it cannot achieve with a non-preferential trade policy. The answer is yes – if one is willing to modify certain of the assumptions made in the standard analysis. Two general comments are warranted. First, the arguments examined are all exercises in second-best. Given the wide range of intervention measures that are employed in developed countries, the concentration on tariffs as the instrument of protection appears inappropriate. Second, if tariffs are taken to be arbitrary interferences with free trade, then CU formation appears of interest only in a tariff-bargaining context. Alternatively, if tariffs are taken to reflect accurately externalities associated with production, then the welfare implications of trade creation need to be reconsidered.

By dropping the small-country assumption a further source of gain from CU membership is opened up: acting together CU members may be able to improve their terms of trade with third countries (see e.g. Mundell, 1964; Arndt, 1968). Trade diversion reduces imports from the RoW, driving down their supply price. Assuming that the balance of payments comprises only trade, exports to the RoW fall and their price increases. The union's terms of trade are improved and this could offset the specialization loss through reduced trade. As Mundell (1964) observes, there is a presumption that the terms of trade of both members of a CU will benefit, though if the RoW retaliates then it is no longer certain that the CU members will gain. Terms of trade issues and the response of non-member countries are taken up in the next section.

9.2.1.4 Given tariffs, optimal tariffs and trade diversion

The standard analysis (section 9.2.1.2) demonstrates that, assuming a given tariff, it is not possible to generalize about the welfare effects of CU formation; the outcome depends on the relative incidence of trade creation and trade diversion. In the period following the publication of Viner's book, analysts therefore focused on identifying the circumstances in which a CU was most likely to be welfare increasing, that is, on the conditions most conducive to trade creation rather than trade diversion (see e.g. Hazelwood, 1987).

To increase the chances of trade creation, there should be:

1 an extensive overlap among the union members in activities protected by the tariff;
2 wide differences between the member countries in the costs of producing the protected commodities.

To minimize the likelihood of trade diversion, there should be:

1 many union members, so that there are few countries whose trade could be diverted;
2 initially a low level of trade relative to production; and
3 a high proportion of pre-union trade conducted with future partners in the CU. In short, CUs should be formed among countries whose economies are currently competitive but potentially complementary.

This line of argument is based on a passive approach to external trade by the CU: the CU maintains the previous national tariff rate as the rate for the common external tariff. This has some merit for demonstrating the potential effects of CU formation but the given tariff assumption does not seem appropriate for judging the desirability of CU membership. It is true that with a given tariff there are some circumstances in which a country could lose from joining a (trade-diverting) CU, but as Krugman (1991) points out, this is true of many economic policies and 'policy concerns based on the possibility of widespread stupidity by governments may be realistic but not very interesting'. If a CU sets its common external tariff optimally then membership must always be beneficial. Of course in practice governments are unlikely to adjust tariffs optimally, but as Krugman further observes, this reduces concern over CU formation to a fear that governments will make mistakes.

The argument that a CU is always potentially beneficial to its member countries has been elegantly made by Kemp and Wan (1976). It may be illustrated by considering the case where a CU is formed by two countries that by coincidence have the same tariff rate which is maintained as the CU's external tariff rate. The expansion of trade between the member countries represents a mixture of trade creation and trade diversion and, as discussed in section 9.2.1.2 above, the welfare consequences will in general be ambiguous. Kemp and Wan argue, however, that the member countries can be certain of gaining if they set an appropriate external tariff rate. To do this they must reduce the tariff rate so that trade with non-member countries is kept at the pre-union level, thereby ruling out trade diversion. At the new, lower, tariff rate the offer to non-member countries is unchanged and consequently the terms of trade with the outside world do not alter. With no trade diversion and unchanged terms of trade with non-members, but with trade creation between the members, CU formation must benefit the members. If the CU sets a different tariff rate from that described, this must be because it offers a yet higher welfare. Thus Kemp and Wan's analysis demonstrates that potentially a CU is always beneficial.

From a non-member country perspective, Kemp and Wan, and also Vanek (1965) and Ohyama (1972), have shown that CU formation need not be damaging provided that a CU's external tariff is set at a rate which avoids trade diversion. If this principle could be applied to all CUs, there would be an incentive for CUs to form and to amalgamate, culminating eventually in global free trade. However, in the absence of an internationally enforceable rule to prevent trade diversion, a CU is likely to set its external tariffs at a higher level in order to take advantage of the greater size of the union and thereby to secure improved terms of trade. This could prompt non-member countries to respond by themselves forming CUs. Without co-operation, external tariffs are then likely to be increased, reducing trade between the CUs. Krugman (1991) has considered how the number of regional trading blocs (each based on a CU) into which the world is divided might affect world welfare. He finds that as the number of trading blocs decreases so also does world welfare because of mutual trade diversion, reaching a low point with three blocs; a single bloc (global free trade) is of course optimal. As Krugman acknowledges, these results may not be very robust. In particular, if trading blocs are formed by 'natural' trading partners (between whom transport costs are low) the welfare outcome may be much more favourable.

9.2.1.5 Dynamic effects of customs unions

Thus far, we have focused on the static effects of CU formation but dynamic effects, defined by Kreinin (1974) as 'changes in the growth rate resulting from expansion in the size of the market and the attendant addition of productive resources', are potentially more significant because of their cumulative nature. Dynamic effects are particularly associated with an increase in competitive pressures following the removal of trade barriers, and with increased scale. Increased competition reduces monopoly rents and stimulates managerial efficiency. However, until recently a satisfactory framework for analysing these effects was lacking. The development by trade theorists of models incorporating imperfect competition opens new possibilities. Two types of model have emerged, one based on monopolistic competition and the other on an oligopolistic market structure. Their application to CU problems, though still in its infancy, is beginning to produce some interesting results.

In their pioneering monopolistically competitive model, Ethier and Horn (1984) assume that two countries forming a CU each produce (a) a range of differentiated manufactured goods under economies of scale and (b) food under constant costs. The RoW produces only food (in a fixed quantity) which it exchanges for manufactured goods. Consumers have a love of variety, consuming a little of each available variety of the manufactured good. The model assumes a high degree of symmetry and Ethier and Horn comment on two experiments they conduct with their model. First, they consider the impact of a slight increase in the common external tariff on food imports. They conclude that the CU will produce fewer varieties of the differentiated goods as resources are sucked into increased CU food production, although output of each of the remaining varieties will be unchanged. The shift in demand by the CU away from food turns the terms of trade in favour of the CU. They conclude that the direction of the net change in benefit for any member of the CU is ambiguous. It is more likely to be positive: (a) the more sensitive the terms of trade are to changes in product variety; (b) the less the evaluation of variety; and (c) the larger the share of

RoW in world income. The RoW loses both from the terms of trade effect and the reduction in product variety. Second, they consider the effects of erecting a marginal internal barrier to trade in the CU, with each member trying to protect its own manufacturing. Each union member will divert spending from its partner's manufactures to its own. The number of varieties, and hence manufactures production, will as before decrease: the attempt to protect manufacturing has the opposite effect of shifting resources into agriculture. Again, the effect on the welfare of each CU member is ambiguous, as is the effect on the non-member(s) whose consumption of manufactures increases but comprises fewer varieties.

Modelling integration effects under oligopoly is notably exemplified by Smith and Venables's (1988) contribution. They examine how national trade barriers influence the behaviour of oligopolistic firms in particular industries. Firms decide how many varieties, and how much, of a product to sell in each market in alternatively Cournot or Bertrand games with their rivals. Their decisions are based on equating perceived marginal revenue with marginal cost in each market, where the slope of each firm's perceived demand curve depends on the number of product varieties on offer and the firm's share of the market. In order to study the effect of the EC's single market programme, Smith and Venables calibrated their model to each of ten important industry markets. They thus incorporated actual industry data in their model so as to reproduce approximately the current situation in each of the markets. The next step was to rerun the simulation on the assumptions that (a) trade barriers within the EC were removed, reducing costs by 2.5 per cent but that (b) firms continue to treat each national market separately – the segmentation variant. The final step was to impose full integration on the simulation so that prices net of transport costs are equalized across the EC. From the simulations, welfare effects of 1992 were obtained for the sample industries.

Krugman and Venables (1990) have used both monopolistic competition and oligopoly structures in examining a neglected issue in CU analysis: the economic geography of CUs, in particular the relationship between a central and a peripheral country. Their model explores a fundamental ambiguity in the integration of a low-wage, small (peripheral) country and a high-wage, large (central) country: The removal of trade barriers makes it more attractive to move production out to the low-wage periphery, but at the same time the cost disadvantage of serving both countries from production in the centre is diminished. The extent of barrier removal (integration) is shown to be critical: while the complete removal of obstacles to trade always raises the competitiveness of the periphery, their partial elimination may in principle have a perverse effect.

Another promising avenue for understanding the dynamic effects of integration is provided by the fast developing work on endogenous growth models. Rivera-Batiz and Romer (1991) have examined how pure scale effects from integration could affect both the level and growth of output in a pair of similar economies. Technological progress is represented by the invention of new types of capital goods. Integration which permits a freer flow of ideas and a greater spillover of knowledge could speed up growth, but only under certain specifications of the production function for the designs of new capital goods. Rivera-Batiz and Romer suggest that the fundamental gain from integration is that the fixed cost of a new design need be incurred only once instead of twice in separate economies. This can be ensured by allowing a free flow of goods and, under certain specifications of the model, a free flow of ideas.

9.2.1.6 CU Theory: Limited progress, new directions

Following Viner's fundamental breakthrough, CU theory has made only limited progress. Pomfret (1986) may be somewhat extreme in labelling CU theory as 'one of the most disappointing branches of postwar economics', but as Kowalczyk (1990) argues, 'too much effort has gone into establishing what remains a quite small number of results'. Venables (1991) too considers that attempts to build on Viner's foundation have not been particularly successful, leading to 'a plethora of cases generating rather few insights'. Analysts have offered several possible explanations for the slow progress of CU theory. Beyond the inevitable complexity of second-best analysis, these include: (a) preoccupation with an inappropriate terminology, (b) focus on non-marginal rather than marginal tariff adjustments and (c) the assumption of a prespecified or constant pattern of trade.

Terminology. A chief criticism of Viner's trade creation/trade diversion dichotomy is that outside his analytical framework the terms are open to differing interpretations and their welfare implications are no longer clear-cut. Indeed it can be argued that the continued use of these terms has held back analytical developments (see Kowalczyk, 1990). There has certainly been no shortage of alternative terminologies (e.g. Collier, 1979) but none has gained general acceptance. Rather than abandoning the Vinerian terms, Ethier and Horn (1984) have argued for supplementing them with an additional one: trade modification. Where two countries remove a tariff on a good traded only between themselves, this may reduce imports of a substitute good supplied by the third country, even though tariffs on this good have not changed. This is similar to, but conceptually distinct from, trade diversion. Analogously, imports of third-country goods which are complementary to the liberalized good would increase.[5]

Non-marginal changes. Perhaps influenced by GATT rules on CUs which require the complete elimination of tariffs and quotas on trade between CU members, CU analysts have focused on non-marginal tariff changes. Yet in practice CUs are often formed progressively over a relatively long-time period and are incomplete because of non-tariff trade barriers. This suggests that a consideration of partial preferences and marginal tariff adjustments may have something useful to say. Indeed, Ethier and Horn (1984) have shown that partial trade preferences may be superior to the GATT alternatives of zero or complete discrimination. Consider first a situation of non-discriminatory world trade and suppose that a subset of countries make a marginal reduction of tariffs on their mutual trade. Provided that their total trade increases, their welfare must also be improved since the cost of the additional imports will be less than their contribution to welfare by approximately the amount of the tariff. Secondly, consider the consequences of introducing a small tariff on trade between the members of a CU. Again, as long as trade with the RoW increases, the movement towards partial preferences will improve welfare. Free trade between CU members implies that a marginal import from a partner country yields a welfare gain equivalent to the welfare reduction due to the exports required in payment. The loss of this trade at the margin has a zero first-order welfare effect, but a marginal import from the RoW has a positive welfare effect because with the tariff the welfare gain the import produces is greater than the sacrifice necessary to pay for it. In principle, therefore, partial preferences could lead to welfare gains. In practice these gains might be difficult to realize because the powerful influence of producer pressure groups is likely to mean that partial preferences would be introduced to foster trade diversion rather than trade creation, thereby failing to meet Ethier and Horn's condition for welfare improvement.

Trade patterns. Venables (1991) argues that CU theory has been held back by the need to specify the pattern of trade between countries. With 3 commodities and the minimum 3 countries, there are 11 possible patterns of trade, and the consequences of CU formation are sensitive to the assumed trade pattern (for a survey of 3×3 CU theory see Lloyd, 1982). Moreover, in 3×3 or higher dimension models it is difficult analytically to allow trade patterns to change, in notable contrast to Viner's concept of trade diversion. A promising alternative approach is to work with a continuum of products (see e.g. Appleyard, Conway and Field, 1989), thus not requiring trade patterns to be prespecified and allowing them to change. Using this approach with three countries, Venables (1991) locates product types on a particular representation of three-dimensional space, the unit simplex. Production is under constant returns to scale, but with a different technology in each country, i, reflected in the (single) factor requirement per unit of output (α_i in figure 9.4). The equilibrium source of supply then partitions the simplex into three regions corresponding to the three sources of supply – home, partner and RoW (see figure 9.4). Each country consumes all product types and the size and shape of the regions depend on relative production costs, and on the trade policy pursued.

This representation not only permits a convenient graphical representation but also provides a framework in which the key findings of CU theory can be clearly articulated in what is inevitably a complex second-best environment. In particular, the interrelationship between internal and external tariffs is explored and optimal policies characterized. Thus it is established, for example, that if the internal or the external tariff is set above its optimal value, then the second-best response is to raise the value of the other tariffs.

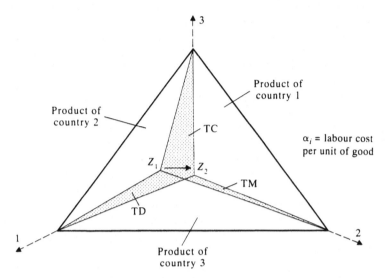

Figure 9.4 Simplex for country 1 showing sources of product types and impact of joining a CU with country 2

Given the recent developments noted in this and the preceding section, it may be fair to conclude this review of CU theory on a moderately optimistic note. In particular, the incorporation of imperfect competition and product differentiation into CU theory offers the prospect of a better understanding of integration in the contemporary economic environment.

9.2.2 Factor Market Integration

It is a well-known proposition of international trade theory that trade can act as a substitute for factor mobility and under certain circumstances can lead to a convergence of factor prices (wage rates and interest rates) between countries (the factor price equalization theorem). However, the assumptions underlying the analysis are highly restrictive (e.g. no trade barriers or transport costs, incomplete specialization, common technology, perfect competition in perfect markets, perfect mobility of factors within markets, homogeneous factors, no factor intensity reversals) and moreover the analysis is static. In a real world which is constantly changing and in which the assumptions noted are unlikely to be fully realized it is unsurprising that factor prices remain uneven. There is, however, a second, more direct, way in which international economic integration could promote convergence of factor prices: through the elimination of restrictions on factor movements (e.g. ending immigration controls). Consider the case shown in figure 9.5 which relates to the labour markets in two countries, A and B. Their combined labour force is $O_a O_b$ with $O_a C$ being the labour force in A, and $O_b C$ being B's labour force. In addition to labour it is assumed that there is a fixed bundle of other resources in each country so that as employment in

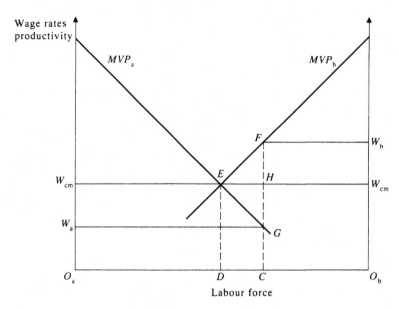

Figure 9.5 Forming a common market for labour between two countries, A and B

each country increases the marginal productivity of labour diminishes (along MVP_a in A and MVP_b in B). In a perfectly competitive market wage rates would be determined by the productivity of labour at the margin, hence they would be OW_a in A and OW_b in B. Suppose now that the two countries agree to create a common market for labour, allowing labour to move freely between them. Labour in A will be attracted to B by the higher wage rate there. As labour migrates to B, productivity at the margin will rise in A and fall in B. When CD labour has migrated to B, productivity at the margin will be equalized at $O_a W_{cm}$, and hence this will be the wage rate throughout the common market. In country A there will be a loss of output through emigration of $DEGC$, but in B the extra labour will generate additional output of $DEFC$, so that creating the common market results in an overall gain in the combined output of A and B of EFG.

Beyond the efficiency gain from the creation of the common market for labour, there will be important redistributional effects. The original labour force in B will suffer a decline in wage rates, from $O_b W_b$ to $O_b W_{cm}$, their total loss of wages being $HFW_b W_{cm'}$. By contrast, the owners of other resources in B will be better off by $EFW_b W_{cm'}$. The positions are reversed in A. The wage rate of the original labour force (including the migrants) rises from $O_a W_a$ to $O_a W_{cm}$, and their total wages increase by $W_a W_{cm} HG$. Owners of the non-labour resources, however, are worse off by $W_a W_{cm} EG$. Creating the common market thus leads to migration, a convergence of wage rates and a redistribution of income between labour and the owners of non-labour resources. The redistributional effects could, of course, be modified by government taxes and subsidies.

There are grounds for questioning whether convergence as described would occur. There are, for example, many impediments to migration other than government restrictions (e.g. language and cultural differences); also, labour might bring with it capital, thus offsetting the productivity effects described above. The disequilibrium view is that in some circumstances removing migration barriers could lead to a divergence of wage rates because of both the selectivity of migration and the effects of population change on demand. If we abandon the implicit assumption that labour is homogeneous, then migrants might tend to be the younger, more ambitious and better educated people whose loss would reduce labour productivity in the country of emigration and boost it in the immigrant country. Similarly, a loss of population could lead to economic stagnation with a low rate of investment and hence a low rate of embodied technological progress and productivity growth. Again the opposite situation could occur in the country gaining population. Economic convergence in a common market could eliminate the cause of one-way migration flows, but as Krugman (1987) has pointed out, two-way flows of labour with different skills, etc. are large in well-integrated economies like the USA.

We may conclude that removing barriers to labour movements could lead to increased output and a convergence of wage rates, but that this depends *inter alia* on the selectivity of the resource flow. Similar arguments could be made for the integration of capital markets and the equalization of real interest rates. Furthermore, under the standard assumptions, full mobility for one factor is sufficient to ensure full equalization of returns for both factors (Nielsen, Heinrich and Hansen, 1991). The persistence of differences in real wages between countries whose capital markets are highly integrated suggests that the standard assumptions may not hold in practice, in particular countries may not possess identical technology.

Is a common market superior to a CU? This depends critically on the level of the common external tariff (Wooton, 1988). If the common external tariff in a small CU is non-optimal, i.e. non-zero, then moving from a CU to a common market is a move from one second-best situation to another, and this could involve a reduction in welfare. Only if freeing factor movements increases trade with third countries is the movement from CU to common market unambiguously beneficial. To be certain that the move from CU to common market will raise welfare the CU must apply the optimal external tariff.

9.3 MEASURING THE EXTENT AND IMPACT OF INTEGRATION

Quantitative studies of integration arrangements have been concerned with (a) measuring the extent to which the constituent economies are integrated (e.g. by comparing the prices of goods or factors across countries) and, more extensively, with (b) assessing the effect of integration on such variables as the trade patterns of the member countries. The purpose of the latter kind of study is to gauge the impact of integration on the income and welfare of the member countries, a particularly important consideration given the inability of CU theory to provide generalizations on the welfare consequences of union. Much effort has been expended on quantification studies, but it has to be admitted that they have thrown only a dim light on to the economic effects of integration.

9.3.1 The Extent of Economic Integration

As the barriers to the movement of goods, services and factors between the members of an integration scheme are dismantled, theory suggests that there will be an intensification of trade between the economies, permitting greater specialization. In the neo-classical model this should lead to an equalization of prices net of transport costs and taxes, and a convergence of wage and interest rates. However, even in the EC, the most advanced example of regional integration, the evidence for this is weak. A study by Glejser (1972) found, for example, that for a sample of 36 consumer goods, only 21 showed a narrowing of price differences among the member countries of the original EEC between 1958 and 1970 when tariffs and other barriers were being removed. There are, of course, great difficulties in comparing prices across countries because of differences in consumption patterns, quality, etc., and indeed considerable variations in prices occur within countries (see Cecchini et al., 1988, p. 79, for a national/Community comparison). Nevertheless, surveys by the European Commission show an impressively wide dispersion of prices among member countries, with or without indirect taxes. Because the Community market is fragmented along national lines by a variety of non-tariff barriers, firms have been able to practise price discrimination on a major scale. This situation is changing only slowly – between 1975 and 1985 the coefficient of variation of the prices of consumer goods across the EC(9) countries fell from 16.5 to 15.2 per cent (Commission of the EC, 1988, table C.4.2). How far this was due to the EC's efforts to remove non-tariff barriers and foster competition is unclear since other factors such as changes in the distribution systems have also been at work.

The divergence of views on how integration schemes might affect relative wage rates in the member countries (section 9.2.2) makes this an important area for quantification. As with product prices, the difficulties of comparing like with like across countries are considerable. Tovias (1982) found that wage rates in the original EC countries tended to converge over the period 1958–71, but did not demonstrate that this was due to the creation of the common market. Similarly, van Mourik (1989) provided evidence of a gradual convergence of wage rates in the original EC countries between 1959 and 1979 which was mainly attributed to Italy closing the productivity gap with its EC partners. The contribution of the EC itself to this process is uncertain. Evidence of factor price equalization in the Community was claimed by Gremmen (1985) who related the disparity of wages between pairs of countries to the intensity of trade between them during 1959–79.

The mass movement of labour among the EC countries has declined considerably since the early 1970s (Molle and van Mourik, 1988). By contrast, the flow of capital has accelerated and capital markets have become more integrated. Corner and Tonks (1987) have shown, for example, some large increases in the correlation coefficients for stock market prices across the major EC countries between 1973–9 and 1980–8. This was part of a global process of market integration, though for Germany, the Netherlands and Italy integration was more strongly European than in France and especially the UK. The behaviour of European equity markets has been influenced by the stabilizing effects of the European Monetary System on intra-EC exchange rates, and by the general move towards deregulating financial markets. Further indication of the integration of EC financial markets in the 1980s is given by the increasing correlation of interest rate movements among the member countries. One measure of this is the extent of short-term covered interest parity (i.e. an equal price for capital for comparable financial instruments in different markets). Van den Bergh et al. (1987) found that whereas in the 1970s there was little correlation between interest rate behaviour on the Euromarkets and national markets, deregulation in the following decade led to greater integration among most EC countries,[6] except for France and Italy. A similar pattern obtains for long-term interest rates according to Molle (1990) who concluded tentatively that European interest rates had recently shown a clear tendency to converge.

9.3.1.1 Measuring the impact of integration on trade flows

The formation and subsequent enlargement of the EC were accompanied by an increase in the share of the members' trade conducted with each other rather than with the outside world. Thus, in the original EC intra-member country trade grew at 15 per cent a year from 1958 to 1972, compared with 8.5 per cent a year for trade with non-member countries.[7] This raises the questions (a) to what extent the more dynamic performance of intra-EC trade was due to the creation of the EC and (b) how far the strong intra-EC performance was at the expense of trade with non-member countries. To answer these questions requires the elaboration and estimation of a model which incorporates at least the main factors influencing the evolution of trade between the integration partners. Given that a country's trading performance depends upon a constellation of influences which are also interdependent, this is a considerable task made more difficult by the substantial data requirements. Consequently, much of the earlier work on quantifying the trade effects of integration – particularly the impact of EC formation – has adopted the more limited approach of concentrating on the relationship between trade and one or a few key variables which are supposed to influence its development. This relationship is used to assess what would have happened to trade in the absence of integration – this hypothetical alternative scenario is known as the 'antimonde'. The difference between the position in the antimonde and what actually happened to trade is then attributed to integration (the 'EC effect'). The attraction of this residual imputation approach is that it provides a short-cut way of establishing an order of magnitude for the integration effect. The drawback, however, is that since only some of the factors affecting trade have been taken into account, there is a danger that the so-called integration effect is also picking up the effect of other factors such as multilateral trade liberalization or the removal of exchange controls.

Residual imputation models are of necessity *ex-post* (after the event) – they compare what actually did happen with what might have. This has the advantage of making use of the experience with integration. *Ex-ante* (before the event) models are used to generate two hypothetical situations with and without integration; such models could be useful, for example, in the debate about whether or not to go ahead with a proposed integration scheme. Ex-ante studies of integration effects have a long pedigree – Verdoorn (1952) developed a general equilibrium model to explain the effects of a Western European CU on trade flows, the terms of trade and the balance of payments (see also Johnson 1958; Williamson and Bottril, 1971; Petith, 1977; Miller and Spencer, 1977). As Robson (1987) notes, Verdoorn – like most other ex-ante analysts – sidesteps the question of the future values of variables that are determined independently of the integration process – in Verdoorn's case by examining changes relative to the trade matrix of the current year, 1951. Another problem for the ex-ante approach is that using the elasticity of demand to compute changes in imports may be inappropriate in that only part of the tariff change is in practice passed on (Mayes, 1978). To take account of the growing importance of non-tariff barriers (NTBs) by computing the tariff equivalents of NTBs also poses a considerable challenge to ex-ante modellers.

There have been numerous ex-post studies of EC integration, mostly of a residual imputation nature. The simplest approach examines the share of EC imports accounted for by member countries and by the RoW before and after the formation of the EC. Attributing share changes wholly to integration, however, ignores other major factors such as changes in costs. Moreover, trade creation and trade diversion are not separated: by focusing on import shares the effect of trade creation in increasing total imports is ignored. This criticism can be met by measuring the share of imports in apparent consumption (production less exports plus imports) though this also requires data on production. An increase in the share of all imports would then represent trade creation while a decline (increase) in the RoW share would reflect trade diversion (external trade creation). Truman (1969) used this technique with trade and production data for the EC in 1953–68. His antimonde, however, assumed that in the absence of the EC the shares of imports and production in apparent consumption would have remained unchanged, though there was evidence of increased import penetration prior to the EC's formation. More complex antimondes were employed by the EFTA Secretariat (1969) who extrapolated pre-integration trends in consumption shares, Truman (1975) who took account of income trends and cyclical factors, and Kreinin (1972) who used the USA as a 'control' for the changing consumption shares in the absence of integration.

A broader-brush approach is to relate imports not to consumption or expenditure by commodity but to national income or GDP. Balassa (1967, 1975) calculated the ex-post income elasticity of demand as the ratio of imports from a particular source to that of GNP, and constructed an antimonde by assuming that the pre-integration elasticities would have continued into the post-integration period. By comparing these hypothetical elasticities with the observed elasticities he was able to identify an integration effect. Changes in elasticities were interpreted as follows:

> increased intra-area elasticity: gross trade creation;
> increased elasticity from all sources: trade creation;
> decreased elasticity from non-area sources: trade diversion.

Balassa's approach is a simple one and ignores factors like relative prices, but more damagingly, it has been demonstrated by Sellekaerts (1973) that the income elasticities vary widely over the pre- and post-integration periods. The choice of periods for comparison is therefore crucial.

An alternative approach is to build a market shares model which explains each country's share as a particular function of real expenditure and the prices of all supplying countries. Integration effects can be picked up by a dummy variable. Winters (1985) has used this approach to measure the effect of EC entry on UK manufactures trade, basing his model on the almost ideal demand system. The analysis assumes that import share changes due to integration affect neither relative prices (thus ruling out terms of trade effects) nor total expenditure on manufactures. The latter assumption, which is common to all shares-based techniques, abstracts from macro-policy adjustments which might be necessitated, for example, by a growing trade deficit in manufactures caused by EC entry.

A general deficiency of the methods considered so far (except that used by Winters) is that they take little or no account of what is happening in the exporting countries, being focused largely on conditions in the importing country. As Mayes (1978) points out, the neglect of supply conditions implicitly rests on the implausibly strong assumption of infinite supply elasticities. Gravity models have had considerable success in explaining trade flows by relating them to national incomes and population in both supplying and importing countries, and to the distance between them. Estimation uses cross-section data; integration effects can be picked up either by the unexplained residual in the regression or by the use of a dummy variable to represent integration partners. Unfortunately, Aitken's (1973) work shows that these two methods can give widely differing results. Moreover, the results vary substantially from year to year, suggesting a need to take account of business cycle fluctuations. Verdoorn and Schwartz (1972) have developed the approach further by incorporating relative prices into a gravity model, and Prewo (1974) used a general equilibrium approach which linked national input–output models for five EC countries to each other and to the RoW via a gravity model. Taking final outputs post-integration as given, he calculated hypothetical trade flows on the assumptions that (a) trade impediments were unchanged in 1965 and 1970 from the levels estimated for 1959, and that (b) imports from, and exports to, third countries would have kept their 1959 market shares. Since trade barriers were reduced during the 1960s through multilateral trade liberalization, the model probably overstates the integration effects, but Prewo's work is notable for its disaggregated approach and the incorporation of feedback effects through the input–output model.

A further way of formulating an antimonde is to analyse the export performance of the members of a regional group in markets where they receive no preference. Lamfalussy (1963), for example, assumed that exporting countries would have increased their share of the EC market in the same proportion that they increased their shares in third markets. Some empirical support for this approach is given by Williamson and Bottrill (1971) who found that between 1954 and 1961, the actual and predicted shares of EC imports coming from the member countries were closely similar. After 1961, however, a widening gap appears as the actual share exceeds the predicted share, suggesting an 'EC effect'. The method does not, however, enable the effect to be broken down into trade creation and trade diversion, and the implicit assumption that third-country markets were sufficiently unaffected by EC formation to be used as controls is questionable.

The central problem that emerges from the attempts to quantify the trade effects of regional integration schemes is thus computing a plausible antimonde. A wide variety of methods have been employed to this end (see the reviews of Mayes, 1978 and Winters, 1987) but each has drawbacks that result from the incomplete nature of the models used.

9.3.1.2 The welfare effects of customs union formation: the example of the EC

Much effort has been expended in trying to estimate the trade effects of the formation of the EC, using various methods. Mayes (1978) argues that from this work approximate bounds of magnitude can be placed on the 'EC effect': by 1970, intra-EC trade had been expanded by $8–15 billion. This represents an increase of roughly 15–30 per cent of trade in manufactures. Two other general conclusions may be drawn from the many empirical studies (Robson, 1987). First, for manufactures, trade created far outweighed trade diverted. Against this, however, has to be set the substantial trade diverted in agriculture, which Balassa (1975) put at $1.3 billion. Second, there is some indication that the net effect on non-member countries' trade was positive with the external trade created exceeding the trade diverted.

Estimates of the trade effects of integration are, however, of little interest in themselves. Rather, their significance lies in what they might reveal about the effect of integration on economic welfare. Waelbroeck (1976) notes that pre-EC tariffs averaged 12 per cent and the most optimistic estimates of trade creation were approximately $10 billion: this gives the welfare triangles an area of $0.12 \times \$10$ billion $\times 0.5 = \$0.6$ billion, from which it is necessary to subtract the cost of trade diversion in industry and agriculture. At most, the gain in Community GDP would be 0.15 per cent. On this basis the welfare consequences of the formation of the world's most advanced regional integration arrangement appear minimal. Similar results have been obtained from ex-ante calculations making what are argued to be reasonable assumptions about supply and demand elasticities and tariff rates. This suggests that the standard approach to welfare measurement, based on the assumptions of perfect competition and a rising supply curve, may be seriously flawed and quite inappropriate to the assessment needed.[8]

Among the major deficiencies may be: the abstraction from X-efficiency gains due to increased competition (Leibenstein, 1966), the omission of benefits from greater product variety, and the neglect – until the '1992' studies – of gains from the fuller exploitation of economies of scale. Pelkmans and Winters (1988) caution correctly that the cost reduction gains from economies of scale can be no bigger than the barriers which integration dismantles. The crucial point though is that the scale and competition gains apply across the whole of domestic output and not just on the additional trade created by integration. On this basis, the gains could be much greater. Owen (1983), for example, estimated on the basis of his industrial case studies that by 1980 the scale benefits of trade creation in the EC could have amounted to some 3–6 per cent of the combined GDP of the original EC member countries. In general, however, early studies of the formation of the EC, while acknowledging the potentially much greater impact of 'dynamic' factors (such as the pro-competitive effect), concentrated on the static effects using the conventional analytical framework. More recent work on the single European market has pursued a different approach, emphasizing the dynamic effects of the removal of non-tariff barriers to trade and drawing on recent developments in industrial organization theory.

9.3.1.3 Estimating the income effects of 1992: the Cecchini Report

The central aim of the 1992 programme for the completion of the single European market is to achieve the free movement within the EC of goods, services, capital and persons. Free intra-Community trade will stimulate greater efficiency in consumption and production and the effect will extend to non-traded goods and services through the movement of capital, labour and technology. The extent of the potential gains from 1992 has been much debated, the focal point being a major empirical study by the European Commission. This was published in the form of a 16-volume set of reports and papers – *The Costs of Non-Europe*, a comprehensive economic report (Commission of the EC, 1988) and a popular version (Cecchini et al., 1988) known as the Cecchini report. The Commission concluded that if the 1992 programme were fully implemented EC GNP would be raised by about 5 per cent – enough, the cynic might suggest, to represent a useful gain without being implausibly high!

The Commission reached its view by identifying four principal sources of gain from 1992. First, it would eliminate losses due to border controls. Survey data put the administrative costs and delays occasioned by intra-EC customs procedures at ECU 8 billion, or 2 per cent of transborder sales.[9] Second, it would remove or reduce a range of other barriers to trade. Among the most important of these are discriminatory public procurement policies and the proliferation of national technical standards. The potential gains were again estimated from survey data, but it should be emphasized that their full realization would entail major adjustments – for example, ending discriminatory public procurement would reduce the cost of coal to electricity generators by an estimated 25 per cent in the UK (and by 50 per cent in Germany) and the cost of pharmaceuticals to the UK's National Health Service by 40 per cent.

The third source of gain arises from the fuller exploitation of economies of scale. Fragmentation of the market currently allows small firms to survive, sometimes producing at a suboptimal scale and suffering thereby higher costs. Rationalization after 1992 would enable the firms which survived to raise output and cut costs. In the manufacture of electric locomotives, for example, the number of producers could fall from 16 to 3 or 4, reducing costs by an estimated 13 per cent. Gains would arise, fourthly, from a more intensely competitive environment as trade barriers came down. Firms would then be under greater pressure to raise their X-efficiencies and monopoly rents would be eroded.

The Commission's estimates of the economies of scale and pro-competitive effects of 1992 are based heavily on the work of Smith and Venables (1988) (see section 9.2.1.5). The Commission generalized these results to all manufacturing industries by computing the ratio of direct effects (gains from trade barrier removal) to total welfare effect for each of Smith and Venables's sample industries. The ratios were then applied to other similar industries to gross up their direct effects to obtain a total effect. 'Similarity' was based on the extent of economies of scale and industry concentration. On this basis, the Commission estimated that '1992' would generate a gain of ECU 142 billion at 1985 prices, or 4.8 per cent of GDP. A more optimistic variant was also computed by taking the difference between Smith and Venables's results for the segmented and integrated markets as representing the pro-competitive effect of 1992 and adding to this estimates of economies of scale from survey evidence.

Clearly, the Commission's study of 1992 represents a great advance in the analysis of integration effects – it is an ex-ante study which aims to capture not only the traditional static effects but also the pro-competitive and scale effects. It is indeed 'a high point in applied economics' (Winters and Venables, 1991). Nevertheless, some reservations are in order, particularly in view of the great influence which the Commission's work has had on the '1992' debate. First, the work relies considerably on microeconomic modelling which is at a relatively early stage of development, and the results are quite sensitive to the particular assumptions employed. Second, the results for the services sector may be overoptimistic, being based on a limited sample for a single year (Winters, 1991). Third, the emphasis on economies of scale may be overdone. The estimates are based on data from before the advent of computer-aided manufacturing which has made it possible to produce even small runs efficiently. The danger is that too much emphasis will be placed on creating large firms ('Eurochampions') and not enough on the benefits of greater product diversity (Geroski, 1989). The view that there is only limited scope for the further exploitation of internal economies of scale is supported by recent empirical work by Caballero and Lyons (1991). Fourth, the analysis abstracts from the adjustment problems which 1992 is likely to generate and which could be locally severe. Problems are likely to be particularly acute for unskilled labour since integration is likely to reduce the demand for unskilled relative to skilled labour (Gasiorek, Smith and Venables, 1991). Finally, the Commission's study may have neglected two important dynamic effects (Baldwin, 1989). First, by adopting an industry-by-industry approach, beneficial spillover effects between industries as they grow (e.g. through better training of labour) may have been missed; Caballero and Lyons's work provide supporting empirical evidence for such external economies of scale. Second, Baldwin argues (p. 254): 'The one-time efficiency gain implies a higher GDP for any given capital stock, leading to a one-time rise in the GDP–capital ratio. With a constant investment rate this directly raises the rate of investment. Thus the static gain from 1992 generates a permanent increase in the sustainable growth rate'. Certainly, a more affluent EC post-1992 could offer greater rewards to innovation, stimulating R & D and accelerating the growth rate, and these additional effects could be very large. However, the links between market integration and innovation are poorly understood, and quantification remains hazardous.

9.3.1.4 Computable general equilibrium models

Quantitative studies of integration schemes should ideally be general equilibrium (GE) in nature so that they are internally consistent through capturing the many important feedback effects. They should also (a) be disaggregated sufficiently to pick up intersectoral adjustments and (b) reflect the oligopolistic or monopolistically competitive nature of most industries. This is a tall order but some pioneering studies have applied computable GE techniques to integration problems (e.g. Harris and Cox, 1984; Hamilton and Whalley, 1985; Markusen and Wigle, 1987; Gasiorek, Smith and Venables, 1991). For illustrative purposes, the model of Brown, Deardorff and Stern (1991) – BDS – investigating the impact of the North American Free Trade Area (NAFTA) is reviewed briefly below.

BDS model 4 countries: the 3 proposed NAFTA partners (the USA, Canada and Mexico) and an aggregate of 31 other industrial and newly industrializing countries; the remaining countries are included in residual RoW demand and supply equations. There are 23 tradable goods and 6 non-tradables, each being produced under conditions either of perfect competition (PC) or monopolistic competition (MC), the allocation of industries depending on estimates of their economies of scale in production. In PC industries products are differentiated by country, in the other industries by firm. PC firms set price equal to marginal cost, while MC firms maximize profits by setting price as an optimal mark-up over marginal costs. The number of MC firms, and hence product varieties, is determined by the condition that there are zero profits. Consumers are modelled as allocating expenditure in a two-stage process, first among goods, regardless of varieties and then among national or firm-specific varieties. Equilibrium prices are determined in world markets, balancing supply and demand for each MC firm's product, and supply and demand for each country's product in the PC industries. National markets are separated by tariff and non-tariff barriers in the base version but these are then removed or modified to simulate the formation of NAFTA.

Computable GE models do not provide predictions that can be compared with actual outcomes. Instead the numerical results have to be interpreted in the light of their assumptions, parameters and data (Brown and Stern, 1989). For their NAFTA analysis BDS assume that tariffs on intra-NAFTA trade are eliminated and US quotas on imports from Mexico are relaxed. As expected, trade between the member countries is stimulated (by $18 billion) and this takes mainly an intra-industry form between Canada and the USA, but a more inter-industry form between the USA and Mexico, with Mexico specializing more in labour-intensive products. There is a small drop in trade with non-member countries, but the damage to these countries is estimated to be tiny. The welfare effects for the member countries are small but positive, with Mexico making the largest gain proportionately (+ 1.6 per cent equivalent variation). The model also suggests that if Mexico liberalizes its capital imports, as planned, then its benefits from NAFTA will be greatly increased (+ 5 per cent). Wage rates would increase by 9 per cent, deterring illegal migration to the USA. The model abstracts from adjustment problems in that it assumes labour is fully employed and capital and labour are perfectly mobile. The results indicate, however, that the need for adjustment will be modest, with much of the additional trade being intra-industry.

9.4 POLICY ASPECTS OF INTEGRATION

In a world of mixed economies with extensive government intervention, integration involves not just the elimination of barriers to the free movement of goods, factors and services – what Tinbergen (1954) described as negative integration – but also the co-ordination and harmonization of policies, positive integration. The principle of subsidiarity – that for democratic reasons policies should be operated at the lowest level of government compatible with efficient operation – together with the reluctance of national politicians and civil services to relinquish power – means that policy co-ordination occurs only where there is evidence of important efficiency gains. These arise particularly where spillover effects of uncoordinated national policies on other countries cause public goods to be under-or overprovided. Several levels of policy integration can be identified:

1 *Information:* partners agree to exchange information on current and prospective policies but keep full independence of action.
2 *Consultation:* involves seeking the opinions and advice of the partner countries before taking legislative action.
3 *Co-operation:* partners continue to follow their own policies but a mechanism is provided for adjusting them if they clash.
4 *Co-ordination:* requires partners to adapt their policies to ensure that they are consistent internationally but there remains scope for the adaptation of measures to meet the varied requirements of different countries or regions, according to their needs and capacities.
5 *Unification:* involves the introduction of uniform measures among the partner countries.

The weaker arrangements such as information, consultation and co-operation can be handled through intergovernmental actions without the need for extensive central decision-making and administrative institutions (as in EFTA). More ambitious integration plans (e.g. monetary union) require stronger actions – co-ordination and unification – and central institutions (as in the EC).

The functions of public policy may be divided into three areas (Buchanan, 1968; Musgrave and Musgrave, 1985): (a) *allocation:* securing a better allocation of resources and an improved functioning of markets; (b) *stabilization:* achieving an appropriate combination of growth, disinflation and employment; and (c) *redistribution:* securing a more equitable/balanced pattern of income and living standards among social groups and among regions. These three areas provide a useful framework for analysing policy aspects of integration, together with a fourth, *external relations* (Molle, 1990).

9.4.1 Integration and Allocation Policies

The general principle that, in a market economy, economic agents acting in their own best interests will also achieve what is socially desirable commands widespread support in the Western countries. It is also accepted that in some circumstances (e.g. monopolization) markets will fail and government intervention may be superior to unrestricted free markets. Thus, competition policies, regulation of technical standards and industrial/sectoral policies are employed to varying extents in industrial countries. They create spillover effects among partners in integration schemes, and a possible case for policy co-ordination.

Even if the integration scheme is of a relatively loose kind, some element of competition policy co-ordination is probably essential. The case for supplementing national competition/antitrust policies is that state aids and certain kinds of private restrictive business practices (e.g. export cartels) may have damaging effects on other countries which under national policy-making will be ignored. Policy co-ordination may then not only be more efficient because at the regional level the spillovers are internalized but also necessary for the survival of the scheme.[10] Technical regulations are another area where policy co-ordination might be beneficial. National regulations arise for sound reasons (e.g. to protect consumers from dangerous products) but are often captured by domestic producers to create non-tariff barriers against imports. Tax harmonization is a politically sensitive issue, but the progressive reduction of other trade barriers may put pressure on countries with high rates of indirect taxation to cut them, with implications for the structure of taxation and the funding of public services. The pressure for tax harmonization could eventually extend to corporation and income taxation, as countries compete to attract companies and individuals through their approach to taxation and the provision of public services.

National industrial or sectoral policies have a clear potential to frustrate market integration. Well-entrenched interest group pressures may force policy co-ordination/co-operation rather than eliminating the assistance. EC experience with agriculture and steel underlines the importance of defining very clearly the objectives of integration and choosing carefully the instruments in relation to these objectives. An example to the contrary is the EC's Common Agricultural Policy whose principal aim appears to be to support the incomes of small farmers. Instead of making direct income payments to the target group linked to restructuring (Marsh and Ritson, 1973), intervention has focused on supporting farm product prices. The consequences are: (a) over-production of these products, (b) high consumer and taxpayer costs, (c) capitalization of price supports into the price of farmland (the factor in least elastic supply), (d) the creation of a powerful lobby of landowners and large farmers in favour of preserving the system, but (e) the continuation of low returns to labour on small farms. Are the obstacles to rational industrial/sectoral policies any more severe at the international level than nationally? This depends on how well organized the lobby groups are at the international level and also on the decision-making rules. For example, where the costs of a programme are shared in a predetermined way (as with the EC budget), there is an incentive for a government to demand measures – say, a subsidy which benefits largely its national producers – which it would reject if the whole cost had to be met nationally. If decisions are based on unanimity, other governments may be prepared to fund jointly such a subsidy in order to ensure that measures which are particularly important to them are incorporated in a package deal.

9.4.2 Integration and Stabilization Policies

In an interdependent world, national macroeconomic policies have large spillover effects on other countries – e.g. a country contemplating an expansionary policy will find that a significant proportion of any extra demand created will be met by increases in output overseas. An individual country approach to economic policy is unlikely to be optimal, risking either over-deflation or over-inflation, as suggested by game-theoretic studies pioneered by Hamada (1985). Policy co-ordination could make every country better off but runs up against many problems (Artis and Ostry, 1986; Steinherr, 1984). These include the costs of co-ordination (favouring agreement on a set of rules rather than continuous consultation), the possibility of free-riding by non-participants, differences in perception as to how economies operate, institutional constraints on the freedom of government agencies to co-operate internationally, complexity of negotiations, and the absence of compensating mechanisms which might be used to attract countries who themselves might gain little from co-ordination.

The EC's experience with macroeconomic policy co-ordination has so far been limited. Existing policy co-ordination under the European Monetary System will have to be greatly increased under plans for EMU, with irrevocably fixed exchange rates (or a single currency), a single monetary policy and fiscal policy co-ordination. Monetary union (MU) offers a number of potentially important gains for the participants (Commission of the EC, 1990). They include:

1 the elimination of transaction costs, estimated at 0.5 per cent of GDP for the EC countries;
2 the elimination of exchange risk which would stimulate trade thereby raising static efficiency through greater specialization;
3 an increased growth rate through reduced investment risk and lower interest rates;
4 a lower inflation rate (assuming that monetary policy is conducted independently of short-term political pressures);
5 increased efficiency of public expenditure and taxation, through increased competition (but the necessary extent of fiscal policy co-ordination is controversial);
6 increased stability through greater resistance to economic shocks which would be spread among the member states; and
7 international gains through, for example, reduced foreign exchange reserves which would no longer be needed to back intra-EC trade, seignorage gains on foreign holdings of non-interest bearing EC banknotes, and the greater influence of the EC in world monetary affairs.

Opposition to MU traditionally focused on the loss of a macroeconomic instrument forcing one or more countries away from their preferred point of internal balance between inflation and unemployment (Corden, 1972b; Fleming, 1971). The general view is now that nominal exchange rate adjustment has little if any impact on unemployment over the longer term. However, the transitional costs of MU in high-inflation countries might be substantial and there is also a concern that adjusting to country-specific external shocks might prove more costly without exchange rate flexibility. The establishment of MU raises a number of important economic and political issues. First, what preconditions should be required (e.g. *re* the convergence of inflation rates) and, hence, should all countries participate from the outset or should there be a two-tier system?[11] Second, what should be the single currency and how should it be introduced (as a replacement or as a parallel currency)? Third, how far would non-monetary policies have to be co-ordinated, i.e. how extensive would economic union be? Fourth, what safety-net measures should be provided? Fifth, what changes would be needed to EC political institutions in order to maintain democratic accountability?

9.4.3 Integration and Redistributional Policies

Integration schemes may redistribute income between countries as well as within countries. Policies may then seek to offset or reinforce this for a number of reasons. First, schemes will only survive where each country feels that on balance membership increases its welfare. Countries facing severe adjustment costs and/or delayed benefits may need to be given an incentive payment to continue with membership. Similarly, further integration (e.g. EMU) may be acceptable only with 'safety-net' income support measures. Second, income transfers may be used to realize efficiency spillover effects whereby shifting activity from a low- to a high-unemployment region brings additional resources into use, combatting inflationary pressures and increasing the regions' combined output. Third, transfers may occur because of equity spillovers – people in the more prosperous regions derive utility from assisting those in poorer regions.

Within individual countries a high proportion of interregional income differences are eliminated through government action (e.g. through central funding of unemployment benefits). Income transfers between EC members are proportionately much less and the emphasis is on expenditure rather than income instruments (MacDougall, 1977). Thus in the EC income tax and social security measures remain under national control but the European budget finances certain regional development measures. The principles on which the funding of the European budget should be based have been a matter of controversy. One possibility is to assess national contributions according to the benefits received from membership, but many sources of gain are not easily measurable. The most tangible benefits are the national receipts from the budget, but to use this basis would lead to the sterile result that countries received back what they contributed – the *juste retour*. Alternatively, budget contributions could be based on 'ability to pay' so that there is in some sense an equality of sacrifice from the member countries. Again there are severe problems facing any attempt at implementation and actual contributions have been determined in an *ad hoc* way reflecting the bargaining strength of the member countries. Net contributions to, or receipts from, the European budget, as Hitiris (1988) emphasizes, are an incomplete and unsatisfactory basis for assessing the costs and benefits of membership of the EC. Grinols (1984) argues for the use of budget transfers to ensure that no member of a CU suffers a loss of welfare from joining the union. Using a revealed preference approach, Grinols calculates the amount of money an individual would need at the new set of CU prices to be no worse off than before. The aggregate of these individual amounts provides a national estimate. Even after taking account of gains from adjustment of production and consumption to the new set of CU prices, as well as the transfers to and from the EC budget, Grinols finds that the the UK suffered an income loss of 1.5 per cent from EC membership during the 1970s.

9.4.4 Integration and External Relations Policies

How far external relations need to be put on a common footing depends on the nature of the integration scheme. A free trade area, for example, allows its members independence in trade policies whereas a CU obliges members to set a common external tariff and to adopt common measures in a number of areas (e.g. anti-dumping policies). This lays the basis for wider co-operation in foreign affairs. Acting together, the members obtain increased bargaining power on the world stage, though to achieve this may require compromising national interests.

Integration schemes are inherently discriminatory towards non-member countries who face the possibility of trade diversion, trade suppression and worsening terms of trade. GATT trade rules provide some protection against an increase in protection – a CU's external tariff must not be higher than the general incidence of the national tariffs which it replaces. Subsequently, however, there may be a tendency for the more protectionist countries to have a disproportionate influence on the evolution of trade policies, particularly where decisions require unanimity. The outcome depends on the discipline exerted by international trade rules on the one hand and the political pressures to externalize adjustment problems on the other. Jacquemin and Sapir (1991) argue that the level of external protection is a crucial factor influencing competitive pressures within a regional integration scheme. They show that price – cost margins in EC industry are much more sensitive to market penetration by products from outside the EC than from within.

Potential adverse effects on non-members, plus the attraction of better access to a large-market, have encouraged third countries to seek bilateral accords with groups like the EC and EFTA. The EC in the past, mainly for political reasons, has responded by offering varying degrees of preferential access to its market (Hine, 1985). The preferences for developing countries have typically been most generous where these countries have been least competitive, reflecting the influence of EC producer lobbies. As EC integration proceeds, agreements confined to tariffs and quotas may not suffice to give non-member countries access to the single European market comparable to that of the member countries. More importantly, the EC is unwilling to share decision-making on rules which affect trade, such as technical standards. This is encouraging non-member countries to seek full EC membership in order to have the best possible conditions of access. However, if enlargement results in increased diversity within the EC, this may retard policy 'deepening' in other areas.

9.5 CONCLUSIONS

After a period of decline, there is now a resurgence of interest in regional integration schemes, particularly in Europe. Over the last 40 years, economic integration has spawned a substantial theoretical literature, particularly on CUs, but much has been misdirected. The central finding of orthodox comparative static analysis remains that of Viner, namely that it is not possible to generalize about the economic desirability of CU membership. Beyond this, analysis has demonstrated that CU membership may be superior to non-preferential trade policies in some circumstances, e.g. where there are constraints on the use of instruments like subsidies, or where a union can influence its terms of trade with the RoW. The conventional static effects of CUs appear, however, to be very small and it is clear that the most significant gains may be generated instead from greater competition and the fuller exploitation of economies of scale. Empirical work on modelling the effects of integration under these conditions has been developing very rapidly, particularly in the context of the single European market and the North American Free Trade Area. Over the next few years computable GE models promise greater insights into integration effects.

An aspect that has not been emphasized in this new approach is why opening markets to the stimulus of greater competition should be pursued regionally rather than multilaterally. One possible explanation is that this allows partner countries to collaborate in strategic trade policy – a high-technology project for example, will be more credible to rivals if backed by a regional group than by a single country. Also, the adjustment costs associated with increased competition may be more acceptable to powerful producer interests if liberalization is regional rather than global. Within a region, cost differences may be relatively small so that integration brings about intra-industry rather than inter-industry specialization and consequently lower adjustment costs (Greenaway and Hine, 1991). In the EC adjustment costs in some industries (e.g. agriculture and clothing) have been contained by protectionist policies. After 1992, they may be less effective and greater inter-industry specialization may occur, especially in the new member countries. The expected benefits of 1992 are contingent on governments dismantling non-tariff barriers which may prove difficult if adjustment costs are high.

The removal of barriers to factor mobility in integration schemes is conventionally regarded as raising economic efficiency since factors can move to where their marginal productivity is higher. Krugman (1987), however, argues that the main benefits are likely to come not from net resource transfers between countries but from the efficiency advantages of more integrated capital and labour markets. This involves the two-way flow of resources comparable with intra-industry trade in goods. Advantages from this such as increased diversification in capital markets have to be offset against possible losses, for example from capital moving to avoid tax or to exploit loopholes in regulatory frameworks.

Integration increases the interdependence of economies so that without a corresponding increase in macroeconomic policy co-ordination, inappropriate policies may ensue. Interdependence may also have beneficial effects upon national policies (Krugman, 1987). For example, membership of a regional group may act as a buffer against destabilizing shocks since the economy of the group is likely to be less volatile than is a single national economy. Similarly, integration can help countries to increase the credibility of their economic policies by linking them to policies of other group members, and hence achieving their objectives at lower cost. Industrial and regional policies also have spillover consequences for partner countries which are heightened by integration; correspondingly, there is an argument for co-ordination. This implies, however, some compromise of national interests which in turn depends on the decision-making system and how far it is influenced by pressure groups.

The removal of barriers to trade and factor mobility and the co-ordination of economic policies through regional integration schemes are likely to have substantial effects on the economies of the member countries during the 1990s; the consequences of regionalism for the world economy and its institutional framework may also be considerable.

NOTES

1 For reviews of CU theory see Pomfret (1986) and Hazelwood (1987); earlier reviews by Lipsey (1960) and Krauss (1972) provide useful guides to the development of the literature.
2 See O'Brien (1976) for a discussion of earlier contributions.
3 Assuming that the union members are too small to affect their terms of trade with the rest of the world, then the welfare effects for the union of trade diversion and trade creation will also be the effects for the world.
4 Unless the initial tariff is less than $p_1 p_2$ in which case forming a CU would have no effect on H and the initial tariff would also be the appropriate one.
5 Trade modification is illustrated in the Venables (1991) approach outlined below.
6 See e.g. Molle (1990) for discussion of capital market integration in the EC.
7 World trade as a whole also grew at 8.5 per cent a year.
8 Grinols (1984) explored a radically different, but still comparative static, approach. He first asked what additional income would be required to allow consumers to consume their pre-CU bundle of goods at post-CU prices. This estimate was adjusted to allow for changes in consumption and/or production in order to exploit price changes induced by CU formation. A crucial and questionable assumption is that all of the observed price changes after CU formation are due to CU formation.
9 The removal of cost-increasing non-tariff barriers offers greater gains than from tariff elimination, since there is no revenue loss to be set against the consumer surplus gains.
10 See e.g. Tsoukalis and Strauss (1985) on the need for an EC steel policy.
11 Optimum currency area theory aims to provide objective criteria (e.g. factor mobility or the openness of economies) to determine which entities should share

a single currency, but offers little insight into which might form a feasible currency area. See Mundell (1961), McKinnon (1963), Kenen (1969) and Vaubel (1978).

REFERENCES

Aitken, N. D. 1973: The effects of the EEC and EFTA on European trade: a temporal cross-section analysis. *American Economic Review*, 63, 881–91.

Appleyard, Dennis R., Conway, Patrick J. and Field, Alfred J. Jr. 1989: The effects of customs unions on the pattern and the terms of trade in a Ricardian model with a continuum of goods. *Journal of International Economics*, 27, 147–64.

Arndt, S. W. 1968: On discriminatory versus non-preferential tariff policies. *Economic Journal*, 78, 971–8.

Artis, M. and Ostry S. 1986: *International Economic Policy Co-ordination*. London: RIIA/RKP.

Balassa B. 1961: *The Theory of Economic Integration*. Homewood, Ill.: Irwin.

Balassa, B. 1967: Trade creation and trade diversion in the European Common Market. *Economic Journal*, 77, 1–21.

Balassa, B. (ed.) 1975: *European Economic Integration*. Amsterdam: North-Holland.

Baldwin, R. E. 1989: The growth effects of 1992. *Economic Policy*, 2, 247–81.

Baldwin, R. E. 1992: Measurable dynamic gains from trade. *Journal of Political Economy*, 100/1, 162–74.

Bergh, P. van den et al. 1987: Deregulating van de internationale financiele stromen en valutastelsel. In Auctores Varii, *Sociaaleconomische deregulering*, 130e Vlaams Economisch Congress, 843–79.

Berglas, E 1983: The case for unilateral tariff reductions: foreign tariffs rediscovered. *American Economic Review*, 73, 1141–2.

Brown, D. K., Deardorff, A. V. and Stern, R. M. 1991: A North American free trade agreement: analytical issues and a computational assessment. Mimeo, University of Michigan.

Brown, D. K. and Stern, R. M. 1989: Computable general equilibrium estimates of the gains from US–Canadian trade liberalisation. In D. Greenaway et al. (eds), *Economic Aspects of Regional Trading Arrangements*, Brighton: Harvester Wheatsheaf, ch. 4.

Buchanan, J. M 1968: *The Demand and Supply of Public Goods*. Chicago: Rand McNally.

Caballero, R. J. and Lyons, R. K. 1991: External effects and Europe's integration. In L. A. Winters and A. J. Venables (eds), *European Integration: trade and industry*, Cambridge: Cambridge University Press, 34–50.

Cecchini, P. et al. 1988: *The European Challenge 1992*. Aldershot: Gower.

Collier, P. 1979: The welfare effects of customs union: an anatomy. *Economic Journal*, 89, 84–95.

Commission of the EC 1988: Research on the 'cost of non-Europe' – basic findings. Vol. 1 *Basic Studies; Executive Summaries*, Brussels.

Commission of the EC 1990: One market, one money. *European Economy*, 44.

Cooper, C. A. and Massell, B. G. 1965: A new look at customs union theory. *Economic Journal*, 75, 742–7.

Corden, W. M. 1972a: Economies of scale and customs union theory. *Journal of Political Economy*, 80, 465–75.

Corden, W. M 1972b: Monetary Integration. *Essays in International Finance*, 93, Princeton University.

Corner, D. C. and Tonks, I. 1987: The impact of the internationalisation of world stock markets on the integration of EC securities markets. In M. Macmillan, D. G.

Mayer and P. van Veen. (eds), *European Integration and Industry*, Tilburg: Tilburg University Press, 229–46.

EFTA Secretariat 1969: *The Effects of the EFTA on the Economies of Member States.* Geneva.

El-Agraa, A. M. 1984: *Trade Theory and Policy: some topical issues.* London: Macmillan.

Ethier, W. and Horn, H. 1984: A new look at economic integration. In H. Kierzkowski (ed.), *Monopolistic Competition and International Trade*, Oxford: Clarendon Press, 207–9.

Fleming, J. M 1971: On exchange rate unification. *Economic Journal*, 81, 467–88.

Gasiorek, M., Smith, A. and Venables, A. J. 1991: Completing the internal market in the EC: factor demands and comparative advantage. In L. A. Winters and A. J. Venables (eds) *European Integration: trade and industry*, Cambridge: Cambridge University Press, 9–29.

Gehrels, F. 1956: Customs unions from a single country viewpoint. *Review of Economic Studies*, 5.

Geroski, P. A. 1989: The choice between diversity and scale. In E. Davis *et al.* (eds) *1992 Myths and Realities*, London Business School, 29–45.

Glejser, H. 1972: Empirical evidence on comparative cost theory from the European Common Market experience. *European Economic Review*, 163, 247–59.

Greenaway, D. and Hine, R. C. 1991: Intra-industry specialisation, trade expansion and adjustment in the European Economic Space. *Journal of Common Market Studies*, 29, 603–22.

Gremmen, H. 1985: Testing factor price equalisation in the EC: an alternative approach. *Journal of Common Market Studies*, 23, 277–86.

Grinols, E. L. 1984: A thorn in the lion's paw. Has Britain paid too much for Common Market membership? *Journal of International Economics*, 16, 271–93.

Hamada, K. 1985: *The Political Economy of International Monetary Interdependence.* Cambridge: Cambridge University Press.

Hamilton, B. and Whalley, J. 1985: Geographically discriminatory trade arrangements. *Review of Economics and Statistics*, 67, 446–55.

Harris, R. G. and Cox, D. 1984: Trade, industrial policy and Canadian manufacturing. Toronto: Ontario Economic Council.

Hazelwood, A. 1987: Customs unions. In J. Eatwell *et al.* (eds), *The New Palgrave: a dictionary of economics*, London: Macmillan.

Hine, R. C. 1985: *The Political Economy of European Trade.* Brighton: Wheatsheaf.

Hitiris, T. 1988: *European Community Economics.* Hemel Hempstead: Harvester Wheatsheaf.

Jacquemin, A. and Sapir, A. 1991: Europe post-1992: internal and external liberalisation. *American Economic Review*, 81, May, 166–70.

Johnson, H. G. 1958: The gains from freer trade in Europe, an estimate. *Manchester School*, 26, 247–55.

Johnson, H. G. 1960: The cost of protection and the scientific tariff. *Journal of Political Economy*, 68, 327–45.

Johnson, H. G. 1965: An economic theory of protectionism, tariff bargaining and the formation of customs unions. *Journal of Political Economy*, 73, 256–83.

Kemp, M. C. and Wan, H. Y. 1976: An elementary proposition concerning the formation of customs unions. *Journal of International Economics*, 6, 95–7.

Kenen, P. 1969: The theory of optimum currency areas: an eclectic view. In R. A. Mundell and A. K. Swoboda (eds), *Monetary Problems of the International Economy*, Chicago: Chicago University Press, 41–60.

Kowalczyk, C. 1990: Welfare and customs unions. Dartmouth College Working Paper 90–17.

Krauss, M. B 1987: Recent developments in customs unions theory: an interpretative survey. *Journal of Economic Literature*, 10, 413–36.

Kreinin, M. E. 1972: Effects of the EEC on imports of manufacures. *Economic Journal*, 82, 897–920.

Kreinin, M. E. 1974: *Trade Relations of the EEC: an empirical investigation*. New York: Praeger.

Krugman, P. R. 1987: Economic integration in Europe: some conceptual issues. In T. Padra-Schioppa, *Efficiency, Stability and Equity*, Oxford University Press.

Krugman P. 1991: Is bilateralism bad? In E. Helpman and A. Razin (eds), *International Trade and Trade Policy*, Cambridge, Mass.: MIT Press, 9–23.

Krugman, P. and Venables, A. J 1990: Integration and the competitiveness of peripheral industry. In C. Bliss and J. B. de Macedo (eds), *Unity with Diversity in the European Economy*, Cambridge: Cambridge University Press, 56–77.

Lamfalussy, A. 1963: Intra-European trade and the competitive position of the EDC. *Manchester Statistical Society Transactions*, March.

Langhammer, R. J. 1992: The developing countries and regionalism. *Journal of Common Market Studies*, 30, 211–31.

Leibenstein, J. 1966: Allocative efficiency versus 'X-efficiency'. *American Economic Review*, 56, 392–415.

Lipsey, R. G. 1960: The theory of customs union: a general survey. *Economic Journal*, 70, 496–513.

Lipsey, R. G. 1975: *An Introduction to Positive Economics*. London: Weidenfeld & Nicolson.

Lipsey, R. G. and Lancaster, K. 1956–7: The general theory of 'second best'. *Review of Economic Studies*, 24, 11–32.

Lloyd, P. J. 1982: A 3×3 theory of customs unions. *Journal of International Economics*, 12, 41–63.

MacDougall Report 1977: *Report of the Study Group on the Role of Public Finance in European Integration*, Vols 1 and 2. Brussels.

McKinnon, R. I. 1963: Optimum currency areas. *American Economic Review*, 53, 717–24.

Markusen J. and Wigle, R. M. 1987: *US–Canada free trade: effects on welfare and sectoral output/employment levels in the short and long run*. Mimeo, University of Western Ontario.

Marsh, J. S. and Ritson C. 1973: *Agricultural Policy and the Common Market.* London: Chatham House/Political and Economic Planning.

Mayes, D. 1978: The effects of Economic Integration on trade. *Journal of Common Market Studies*, 17, 1–25.

Meade, J. E. 1955: *The Theory of Customs Unions*. Amsterdam: North-Holland.

Miller, M. H. and Spencer, J. E. 1977: The static economic effects of the UK joining the EEC, a general equilibrium approach. *Review of Economic Studies*, 44, 71–93.

Molle, W. T. M. 1990: *The Economics of European Integration*. Aldershot: Dartmouth.

Molle, W. and van Mourik, A. 1988: International movements of labour under conditions of economic integration: the case of Western Europe. *Journal of Common Market Studies*, 26, 317–42.

Mourik, A. van 1989: Countries, a neo-classical model of international wage differentials. In W. Molle and A. van Mourik (eds), *Wage Differentials in the European Community, Convergence or Divergence?* Aldershot: Gower Press, 83–103.

Mundell, R. A. 1961: A theory of optimum currency areas. *American Economic Review*, 51, 509–17.

Mundell, R. A. 1964: Tariff preferences and the terms of trade. *The Manchester School of Economic and Social Studies*, 32, 1–13.

Musgrave, R. A. and Musgrave P. 1985: *Public Finance in Theory and Practice*. Auckland: McGraw-Hill.

Nielsen J. U-M., Heinrich, H. and Hansen, J. D. 1991: *An Economic Analysis of the EC*. Maidenhead: McGraw-Hill Book Company Europe.

O'Brien, D. 1976: Customs unions: trade creation and trade diversion in historical perspective. *History of Political Economy*, 8, 540–63.

Ohyama, M. 1972: Trade and welfare in general equilibrium. *Keio Economic Studies*, 9.

Owen, N. 1983: *Economies of Scale, Competitiveness and Trade Patterns within the European Community*. Oxford: Clarendon.

Pelkmans, J. 1984: *Market Integration in the European Community*. The Hague: Martinus Nijhoff.

Pelkmans, J. and Winters, L. A 1988: *Europe's Domestic Market*. London: Routledge.

Petith, H. C. 1977: European integration and the terms of trade. *Economic Journal*, 87, 262–72.

Pomfret, R. 1986: The theory of preferential trading arrangements. *Weltwirtschaftliches Archiv*, 122, 439–65.

Prewo, W. E. 1974: Integration effects in the EEC: an attempt at quantification in a general equilibrium framework. *European Economic Review*, 5, 379–405.

Rivera-Batiz, L. A. and Romer, P. M. 1991: Economic integration and endogenous growth. *Quarterly Journal of Economics*, 106, 531–55.

Robson, P. 1987: *The Economics of International Integration*, 3rd edn. London: Allen & Unwin.

Sellekaerts, W. 1973: How meaningful are empirical studies on trade creation and trade diversion? *Weltwirtschaftliches Archiv*, 109, 519–51.

Smith, A. and Venables, A. J. 1988: Completing the internal market in the EC, some industry simulations. *European Economic Review*, 32, 1501–25.

Steinherr, A. 1984: Convergence and co-ordination of macro-economic policies: some basic issues. *European Economy*, 20, 71–110.

Tingbergen, J. 1954: *International Economic Integration*. Amsterdam: Elsevier.

Tovias, A. 1982: Testing factor price equalisation in the EEC. *Journal of Common Market Studies*, 20, 165–81.

Truman, E. M. 1969: The European Economic Community: trade creation and trade diversion. *Yale Economic Essays*, 9, 201–57.

Truman, E. M. 1975: The effects of European economic integration on the production and trade of manufactured products. In B. Balassa (ed.), *European Economic Integration*, Amsterdam: North-Holland, 3–40.

Tsoukalis, L. and Strauss, R. 1985: Crisis and adjustment in European steel: beyond *laissez-faire*. *Journal of Common Market Studies*, 23, 207–28.

Vanek, J. 1965: *General Equilibrium of International Discrimination: the case of customs unions*. Cambridge, Mass.: Harvard University Press.

Vaubel, R. 1978: *Strategies for Currency Unification*. Tübingen: J. C. B. Mohr.

Venables, A. J. 1991: Customs union with a continuum of products. Mimeo, University of Southampton.

Verdoorn, P. J. 1952: Welke sijn de achtergronden en vooruitzchten van de economische integratie in Europa en welke gevolgen zou deze integratie hebben, met name voor de welvaart in Nederland? *Overdruk*, no. 22, Central Plan bureau, The Hague.

Verdoorn, P. J. and Schwartz, A. N. R. 1972: Two alternative estimates of the effects of EEC and EFTA on the pattern of trade. *European Economic Review*, 3, 291–335.

Viner, J. 1950: *The Customs Union Issue*. New York: Carnegie Endowment for International Peace.

Waelbroeck, J. 1976: Measuring the degree or progress of economic integration. In G. Machlup (ed.), *Economic Integration: worldwide, regional, sectoral,* London: Macmillan, 89–99.

Williamson, J. and Bottrill, A. 1971: The impact of customs unions on trade in manufactures. *Oxford Economic Papers,* 25, 323–51.

Winters, L. A. 1985: Separability and the modelling of international economic integration. *European Economic Review,* 27, 335–53.

Winters, L. A. 1987: Britain in Europe: a survey of quantitative trade studies. *Journal of Common Market Studies,* 25, 315–35.

Winters, L. A. 1991: *International Economics,* 4th edn. London: Harper Collins.

Winters, L. A. and Venables, A. J. (eds) 1991: *European Integration: trade and industry.* Cambridge: Cambridge University Press.

Wonnacott, P. and Wonnacott, R. 1981: Is unilateral tariff reduction preferable to a customs union? The curious case of the missing foreign tariffs. *American Economic Review,* 71, 704–14.

Wooton, I. 1988: Towards a common market: factory mobility in a customs union. *Canadian Journal of Economics,* 21, 525–38.

10

SERVICES TRADE

André Sapir and Chantal Winter

10.1 INTRODUCTION

Services have generally been ignored by trade economists on the grounds that they are 'non-traded' activities. This lack of interest in services trade by scholars was reflected in the contributions to the excellent *Handbook of International Economics* edited by Jones and Kenen (1984). Ten of its 12 chapters made no reference to services at all. In the remaining two, the space devoted to services was a paragraph in one – by Baldwin (1984) on trade policies in developed countries – and a footnote in the other – by Deardorff (1984) on testing trade theories.

Interest by trade economists in services was prompted in the mid-1970s by policy-makers acting under pressure from practitioners, mostly in the USA, who complained of the lack of international trade rules in services. The early literature was entirely descriptive and policy-oriented.[1] It established that trade in services was not as unimportant as it had been thought. At the same time, it supported the view that trade expansion was hampered by widespread government interventions which fell outside the scope of international arrangements, most notably the General Agreement on Tariffs and Trade (GATT). A second wave of contributions followed rapidly. Although still largely empirical, it had more analytical preoccupations. Its purpose was to examine whether the pattern of trade in services could be explained by the same factors that determine trade in goods.

By the early 1980s empirical evidence seemed to indicate that the theory of comparative advantage applies to trade in services, just as it does to trade in goods. It was not, however, until the mid-1980s that trade theorists confirmed the applicability of the principle of comparative advantage to trade in services.

Meanwhile, important developments were occurring on the policy front. At the 1982 Ministerial Meeting of the GATT Contracting Parties, the US Trade Representative proposed that trade in services figure on the agenda of the next round of multilateral trade negotiations. This objective was reached four years later at the Punta del Este Meeting launching the Uruguay Round. For the first time, the international trading community had decided to initiate negotiations aimed at establishing 'a multilateral framework of principles and rules for trade in services'. These exciting events have generated a vast literature on the methods for trade liberalization and its welfare implications.

Much of it is policy-oriented, but a number of theoretical pieces have also been published.

The recent growth of the literature on services trade was certainly overdue in view of the increasing importance of services. In the domestic economy of all 'industrial' countries, services now account for more production and employment than agriculture and manufacturing combined. Even in many developing countries the share of services in GDP reaches nearly 50 per cent (See Hoekman, 1990). At the same time, the importance of services in the international economy has greatly increased. In the mid-1980s, the recorded share of services in world merchandise and services trade was put at nearly 20 per cent (see Kierzkowski and Sapir, 1987). In reality the importance of services is probably much greater.

This survey begins with a discussion of some of the conceptual issues which are relevant in the context of trade in services in section 10.2.[2] Section 10.3 reviews the trade-theoretical literature on the determinants of trade in services, while section 10.4 concentrates on the empirical work attempting to explain the observed trade patterns. Section 10.5 surveys contributions to normative trade theory devoted specifically to services, whereas section 10.6 is devoted to the more applied literature on commercial policy.

10.2 NATURE OF SERVICES

A central question that arises in the context of trade in services is whether services are economically similar to goods and, hence, whether traditional trade theories apply equally to goods and services. At first sight, the answer to this question would seem to be 'yes'. After all, on the supply side, goods and services use similar factors of production; equally, on the demand side, both goods and services compete for the consumer's income. Although a common approach to both goods and services seems therefore warranted, it cannot be denied that services exhibit certain characteristics with specific consequences for international transactions. The major one is, undoubtedly, that services tend to be less traded than goods both in absolute value terms and relative to domestic output. This situation has generally been ascribed to two factors: the inherent non-tradability of some services, and government restrictions that impose barriers to trade in services.

In the recent trade literature, the issue of non-tradability of services is often related with the fact, noted by Hill (1977), that their production and consumption must, generally, take place simultaneously. This non-storable nature of services implies that production and consumption tend to occur at the same time and in the same location. The requirement of physical proximity between users and providers has been extensively explored by Bhagwati (1984) and Sampson and Snape (1985). These authors distinguish between two categories of services: those that require physical proximity, and those that do not. A typology of international transactions in services based on this distinction is presented in figure 10.1.

	Provider does not move	Provider moves
User does not move	Commodity trade (type 1)	**Temporary movement** Factor trade (type 3) **Permanent movement** FDI/migration (type 4)
User moves	**Temporary movement** Commodity trade (type 2) **Permanent movement** migration	

Figure 10.1 Typology of international transactions in services

Four types of international transactions in services can be distinguished:

1 Immobile users in one nation obtain services produced by immobile providers located in another nation. This occurs, for instance, in financial services and professional services, where transactions flow via telecommunications networks.

2 Mobile users from one nation travel to another nation to have services performed. This situation is most frequent in tourism, education, health care, ship repair and airport services.

3 Mobile providers from one nation travel to another nation in order to perform services. This situation occurs in certain business services, such as engineering, where frequent or close interaction is not required.

4 Providers from one nation establish a branch in another nation in order to perform services. This is the most common pattern of international service competition, involving frequent and close interaction between buyers and sellers. It is the dominant type in most services, including accounting, advertising, banking, consulting services and distribution.

Although only transactions of type 1 resemble international trade in goods, the generally accepted definition of international trade in services goes beyond transactions that require neither the provider nor the user of services to move internationally; it also includes transactions of types 2 and 3. On the other hand, transactions of type 4 fall outside the scope of trade; they belong to the category of permanent factor movements (foreign direct investment or labour migration). Note that there is clearly an asymmetry between capital and labour, with only the latter generally lending itself to temporary movements and, hence, to type 3 transactions.

In the recent literature, types 1 and 2 are sometimes referred to as 'commodity (or product) trade', while transactions of type 3 are called 'factor trade' (see Ruane, 1988). Both transactions involve movements of factor services, but the make-up of these movements differs considerably between the two categories of transactions. The key is the distinction between embodied and disembodied factor services. Commodity trade involves movements of embodied factor services, whereas factor trade implies that disembodied factors of production move internationally.[3]

There are several implications resulting from the distinction between the different types of international service transactions.[4] First, given the prevalence of type 4 situations, foreign direct investment (FDI) plays a crucial role in international service transactions. A report by the US Office of Technology Assessment (1986) indicates that in activities such as accounting, advertising and insurance, sales by US affiliates abroad far outweigh direct exports by US corporations (quoted by McCulloch, 1988). Second, barriers to transactions in services typically involve restrictions regarding establishment (type 4) or the movement of key personnel (type 3). Third, the border between the different types of international transactions, especially types 1, 3 and 4, is not impermeable. In consulting services, for instance, much of the foreign work is provided by local establishments (type 4), but key personnel travel from the home office to provide specialized services (type 3). It may even be that travel is replaced altogether by video conferences or other means of communications (type 1). Finally, the border between the different types of transactions is moving. Complementary innovations in data processing and telecommunications have reduced the need for interaction between consumers and producers in several services such as retailing (tele-shopping) or banking (tele-banking). This has enhanced the tradability of services, partly eroding type 4 transactions in favour of type 3. Many service industries are also witnessing a greater interaction between international trade and FDI.

Another feature of services that bears on tradability is their intangible nature and the resulting problems of asymmetric information. The quality of certain goods can be determined by consumers prior to a purchase. For other goods, the quality can only be learned after they are bought and consumed. In yet other cases, the quality is never fully learned, even after consumption. These three categories of goods have been labelled 'search goods', 'experience goods' and 'credence goods' (See Tirole, 1988, chapter 2). Since services only exist while they are being consumed (i.e. they are intangible), their quality cannot easily be assessed prior to consumption. Services are, therefore, rarely search goods. Most are experience goods, and a few (such as medical services) are credence goods. Thus, a major issue for services is information.

Although it can be argued that the ultimate quality of certain services depends on the interaction between users and providers, it remains that sellers know more a priori about product quality than buyers. Asymmetric information about product quality between consumers and producers creates two types of problems: moral hazard and adverse selection.[5]

The moral hazard problem is present in most services due to the fact that their quality may change over time. Repeat purchases can, under certain conditions, help overcome it by inducing suppliers to develop a reputation. Problems of adverse selection arise in most professional services (such as consulting, legal or medical services), where buyers are confronted with suppliers of various competence.[6] Adverse selection tends to reduce the frequency of market transactions.

The fact that problems of asymmetric information pervade many service industries has several consequences. First, the frequent use of reputation to signal quality implies that service markets are often characterized by non-price competition. Second, reputation, like any other intangible asset, creates an incentive to sell in foreign markets in order to maximize the rent that can be gained. Given the need for interaction between consumers and producers, such incentive usually translates into FDI. Moreover, Sapir (1988) notes that service firms often become multinational in order to follow their customers. These firms tend to acquire a quasi-contractual relation with their customers 'based on trust that lowers the cost of contracting and the risks of opportunistic behavior. If the service firm has such a quasi-contractual relationship with a parent [multinational], it enjoys a transactional advantage for supplying the same service to [its] foreign subsidiaries' (Caves, 1982, p. 11). Lastly, being largely a sunk cost, reputation creates a barrier to entry which may severely reduce the degree of actual or potential competition in services industries.

In almost all countries services are subject to more government regulations than most other activities. In the presence of market failures, such regulations can be justified on the ground of efficiency. The three main types of failures – imperfect competition, imperfect information, and externalities – are relevant to service industries.

Most service sectors operate under conditions of imperfect competition resulting from various degrees of market power on the part of producers (see Sapir, 1991). Some industries are natural and/or public monopolies (railroads and segments of telecommunications), others tend be oligopolistic (certain transportation services as well as banking), while still others are characterized by monopolistic competition (for instance business and professional services). The second type of market failure that prevails in service industries is imperfect information. This often results in government intervention – in the form of occupational licensing and certification common in many professions (as for accountants, doctors or lawyers) – designed to protect consumers from low-quality services. Finally, services may be subject to externalities of different kinds, including network externalities (as in the case of telecommunications services).

Although government regulations of services are generally imposed for purely domestic reasons, they may constitute barriers to international transactions. This is obvious when regulations explicitly discriminate against foreign service providers. Barriers to international transactions in services can be classified into four categories, each corresponding to a type of transaction:

1 barriers to trade;
2 barriers to the movement of service users;
3 barriers to the movement of service providers;
4 barriers to FDI.

The previous discussion on the interaction between the different types of service transactions points towards similar interactions between the various categories of barriers. For instance, unless a foreign bank is granted 'rights of establishment' in a country, it may not be able to export (and indeed to sell) to this country – even in the absence of any other formal barrier.

Government regulations may act as barriers to trade in services even if they are not intended to discriminate between domestic and foreign producers. In telecommunications services, for instance, the divergence of national regulations across countries may be sufficient to prevent international transactions from occurring. This is most flagrant in bilateral situations when one country grants monopoly rights to a (usually state-owned) domestic firm while the other permits competition.

In recent years government regulations, particularly those in service activities, have come under severe attacks. Critics have questioned both the motivation and the effectiveness of public regulation. First of all, economists associated with the 'Chicago School' have emphasized that regulation tends to be captured by interest groups seeking to acquire monopoly rents.[7] More recently, other economists have raised doubts about the basic premise that regulation remedies market failures, or at least that it does so effectively. The result of these attacks has been a widely shared view that regulation often tends to limit rather than foster competition. This view has greatly contributed to the deregulation movement that started in the USA in the late 1970s (see Weiss and Klass, 1986), moved to the UK in the early 1980s (see Kay and Vickers, 1988), and has spread throughout the rest of Europe in preparation for 1992 (See Hindley, 1987). This movement covers nearly all service industries, from transportation and telecommunications services to financial and professional ones.

In a parallel fashion, efforts have recently been launched internationally to reduce discriminatory measures that impose barriers to trade in services. The status of international negotiations on services and their prospects for the 1990s will be examined in section 10.6.

10.3 DETERMINANTS OF TRADE: THEORY

The modern theory of international trade distinguishes two broad explanations of trade patterns. On the one hand, differences across countries in factor endowments, technologies or tastes result in comparative advantages that explain the pattern of trade in activities characterized by perfect competition and constant returns to scale. Such trade is of an inter-industry nature, each country exporting certain commodities in exchange for other commodities. On the other hand, even if countries are identical, there will be international trade flows in the presence of increasing returns to scale (and, therefore, imperfect competition). These are intra- or inter-industry flows, depending upon the nature of commodities. For differentiated commodities, countries will exchange some varieties against others (intra-industry trade). For homogeneous commodities, inter-industry trade will occur.

Do the traditional explanations of the pattern of trade in goods extend to services in spite of their distinguishing features identified in section 10.2?

The first effort of theorists in the field of trade in services has been to verify whether the principle of comparative advantage applies. In an important paper, Hindley and Smith (1984) argue that there is no need for a specific approach to services trade. According to them, the theory of comparative advantage applies equally to services as it does to Brussels sprouts or a bunch of flowers. 'Services are different from goods in ways that are significant and that deserve careful attention, but the powerful logic of the theory of comparative advantage transcends these differences' (p. 389).

The first formal consideration of the applicability of the principle of comparative advantage to services is by Deardorff (1985). The paper uses the traditional $2 \times 2 \times 2$ Heckscher–Ohlin (HO) model, where one commodity is a good and the other a service. It identifies three possibilities that may create difficulties with comparative advantage: (a) complementarity between goods trade and services trade; (b) factor trade; (c) factor trade without physical movement.

Complementarity between Trade in Goods and Services

Some services are supplied only to make international trade in goods possible. This may be the case of specific transport, insurance or legal services. Deardorff analyses the role of such services in three different situations:

1 autarky, where no trade occurs, neither in goods nor in services;
2 free trade, in both goods and services;
3 semi-autarky, that is trade in goods only.

These three situations are denoted by the superscripts 'a', 'f', and 's' respectively.

In autarky, services are not produced since there is no trade in goods. Therefore, the equilibrium in autarky can be represented by a vector (p^a, q^a, x^a), where p^a and q^a are the equilibrium prices for goods and services and x^a is the equilibrium good output. (Since services are not demanded in autarky, their equilibrium level s^a is equal to zero.) Under the assumption of profit maximization, the equilibrium vector is the one which maximizes the value of total output at the given autarky prices:[8]

$$p^a x^a \geq p^a x + q^a s \quad \text{for all } (x, s) \in F \qquad (10.1)$$

Under free trade, the equilibrium vector is (p^d, q^w, x^f, s^f), where p^d is the domestic price, q^w is the world price of services and $p^w = p^d + q^w$ is the price of the internationally traded goods. Let T, V, and U denote the net exports of goods, the net exports of services and the domestic use of transportation services, respectively. Then, the equilibrium vector must satisfy the following three conditions:[9]

$$p^d x^f + q^w s^f \geq p^d x + q^w s \qquad \text{for all } (x, s) \in F \qquad (10.2)$$

$$(p^w - p^d) T^f - q^w U^f \geq (p^w - p^d) T - q^w U \quad \text{for all } (T, U) \in G \quad (10.3)$$

$$p^w + T^f + q^w V^f = 0 \qquad (10.4)$$

The first condition implies that, at the given equilibrium prices, no other output level can be more valuable. The second establishes that, in equilibrium, net exports of services are the most profitable.[10] The third condition requires balanced trade.

Comparing the autarky and free trade equilibria, and assuming the weak axiom of revealed preferences, Deardorff shows that the above conditions imply

$$p^a T^f + q^a V^f \leq 0 \qquad (10.5)$$

'that is, it must be true on average that the goods and services that a country exports must be worth less to it in autarky than the goods and services it imports' (Deardorff, 1985). Therefore, trade in goods and services conforms to the traditional theory of comparative advantage.

Deardorff also analyses the semi-autarky equilibrium, where all the conditions defined under free trade still hold, with the superscript 'f' replaced by 's'. He finds that (10.5) still applies, and since V is zero by definition, that is $p^a T^s \leq 0$. Thus the theory of comparative advantage continues to explain trade in goods, even if the complementary services are not traded but are taken explicitly into account in the model.

The author concludes that the principle of comparative advantage is valid to explain patterns of trade in goods and complementary services. Nevertheless, since, by definition, these services are not demanded in autarky, their autarky prices do not exist. Therefore, autarky prices cannot be used as an indicator of comparative advantage when services are demanded as a by-product of international goods trade. Hence there is a problem in measuring comparative advantage and predicting which country will be a net exporter of such services. One possible indicator of comparative advantage may be based on autarky factor prices, but demand conditions may preclude the validity of this approach.

Trade as Factor Trade

Some services may not be tradable in the traditional sense. For instance, a three-star meal at 'La Tour d'Argent' can only be consumed in Paris.

Suppose, however, that factors of production can move internationally and that a meal at a three-star restaurant requires two primary inputs: skilled labour (the chef) and unskilled labour (his assistants). Furthermore, assume that France is relatively well endowed with skilled labour and that a three-star meal is relatively intensive in unskilled labour. In autarky, France would, therefore, have relatively high prices for its three-star restaurant services. Yet, with skilled labour allowed to move internationally, the French chef may go to New York and combine with local unskilled labour to produce a three-star meal there. Does this violate the principle of comparative advantage? The answer is obviously no, provided one realizes that what is actually traded is not the three-star meal but the service of the French chef, i.e. what takes place is factor trade. The key point is the distinction between embodied and disembodied factor services explained in the previous section. This point is stressed by Jones (1985).

Factor Trade without Mobility

The physical presence of all the factors of production is not always necessary for production to take place. In particular, this may be the case for certain types of skilled labour. A manager can transmit his directives by phone or by fax. Equally, the French chef could instruct his assistants in New York by means of video conference. Although there is no physical movement, such situations would none the less qualify as factor trade. Deardorff (1985) analyses the issue of factor trade without mobility with the help of the following model. There are two countries A and B, which exhibit homothetic identical demands for the two commodities produced. The first one is a traded good denoted by X whereas the second commodity is a non-traded service denoted by S. The production of both commodities requires the use of labour L and management M. The factor of production management is assumed to be internationally traded even if its physical mobility is not required for factor trade to occur. In autarky, the relative price of services is lower in country A than in country B, because of differences in either factor endowments or technology. Differences in the pre-trade autarky prices can arise for three reasons: (1) differences in factor endowments with country A well endowed with management, the factor used intensively for the production of S; (2) differences in factor endowments with country A well endowed with labour, the factor used intensively for the production of S; (3) differences in technology with country A exhibiting a Hicksian neutral technological superiority in producing S.

Under free trade, country A will export management M and import X in case 1, whereas it will export X and import M in case 2. This conforms to the traditional theory of comparative advantage. Indeed, the pre-trade autarky prices which must be taken into account are the pre-trade autarky prices of tradables, that is the price of X and M and not the price of X and S. Therefore, when trade is due to differences in factor endowments, the principle of comparative advantage holds. As Jones (1985) points out, the key is not the extent to which a commodity or a factor is physically traded but who is paid for the provision of the traded commodity or factor.

In case 3, however, Deardorff shows that the principle of comparative advantage may not hold because the country with relatively high services factor prices in autarky may be a net exporter of that factor under free trade. Deardorff considers first the autarky equilibria in the two countries. Among all possibilities[11] he notes that one equilibrium is a situation where 'the salary of management in A, measured in units of X, is higher than in B, but by less than the full extent of A's technological advantage' (Deardorff, 1985, p. 41). Allowing for trade implies that A's managers will, in fact, contribute to the production of S in country B. Indeed, even if A's managers are paid more than B's managers, this difference does not offset the competitive advantage of A's producers due to their technological superiority.

The contribution of Deardorff (1985) is to have formally established that the law of comparative advantage applies to services, provided some of their specific features are properly accounted for. This result appears to apply only when comparative advantages result from international differences in factor endowments. Jones (1985) has refuted the validity of case 3 when there are differences in technology, arguing that Deardorff has implicitly introduced quality differences across countries in production factors, and has failed to correct their prices accordingly.

In conclusion, under perfect competition, the theory of comparative advantage applies to international trade in services (see also Hoekman, 1988b). In many instances, however, service industries operate under conditions of increasing returns to scale and scope and imperfect competition. Therefore, the concept of comparative advantage may not be sufficient to explain trade patterns. Several authors have recognized the role of imperfect competition in services, but none has attempted to examine the implications for the patterns of trade. Instead, they have concentrated their attention on normative issues (see section 10.5).

10.4 DETERMINANTS OF TRADE: EMPIRICAL ANALYSIS

Testing the validity of trade theories has been greatly hampered by the lack of systematic data on international trade in services. The main source of internationally comparable data is the *Balance of Payments Yearbook* published by the International Monetary Fund (IMF). On the basis of the IMF statistics, trade in services is generally defined to include the following 'invisible' (i.e. non-merchandise) transactions between residents and non-residents of a country: shipment, other transport, travel and other private services.[12] These transactions are sometimes referred to as trade in 'non-factor services'.

There are many well-known problems with IMF balance-of-payments statistics on foreign exchange transactions, including the lack of disaggregation by partner-country. In the case of services, these problems are compounded by the 'invisibility' of transactions (at least as far as customs agents are concerned) which leads to gross underreporting and misclassification. As Hoekman (1990) concluded after careful review of the existing statistics, 'data on trade in services are not very reliable and are likely to be biased downward' (p. 44). Data problems in services trade are also examined by Ascher and Whichard (1987).

The first attempt to explain trade in services in a systematic manner was by Dick and Dicke (1979). The authors focused on an aggregate measure of trade in knowledge-intensive services, which they defined to comprise shipment, other transport and other private services (including property income from intangible assets, i.e. patents and licences). In order to test the theory of comparative advantage, they regressed various indicators of revealed comparative advantage on variables measuring factor endowments. The results of their cross-section estimates for 18 OECD countries found no evidence of the role of comparative advantage in determining the pattern of trade in services. Although the result was partly attributed to non-tariff trade barriers, the authors seemed to accept the then widely held view that 'regardless of trade distortions, it is imaginable that factor endowments have no significant influence on trade in services' (Dick and Dicke, 1979, p. 346).

This view was firmly challenged by Sapir and Lutz (1981) in a paper which is probably the best-known empirical investigation of comparative advantage in trade in services. The authors attempted to explain international trade in services on the basis of cross-country differences in factor endowments and technology. The study analysed separately freight, passenger services and insurance. Other private services (including insurance) were also investigated in a companion piece by Sapir (1981). The sample included both industrial and developing countries, and the size varied by sector according to the availability of trade data in the IMF Yearbook.

The main result of this body of work is that '[c]onventional trade theory applies not only to goods but also to services', with factor endowments being an important determinant of trade patterns in both goods and services (Sapir, 1982, p. 79). Regression estimates indicate that countries abundant in physical capital enjoy a comparative advantage in transportation services (freight and passenger services), while those abundant in human capital have a comparative advantage in insurance and other private services. These results suggest that industrial countries have a comparative advantage in services, owing to their physical and human capital abundance. At the same time, however, the net export performance of advanced developing countries (exports to developing countries, and imports from industrial countries) implies that comparative advantages are not static. Instead, developing countries that accumulate physical and human capital are likely to gain comparative advantage in certain service activities. A similar view is held by Lall (1986).

Until better and more detailed international balance-of-payments statistics become available, empirical researchers must turn to other data sources to test trade theories. Two possible alternative avenues are international data on a particular service and national statistics that cover a wide array of services. An example of the first option is the study by Sapir (1986) which offers a detailed analysis of trade in engineering services. This paper confirmed the pertinence of the dynamic view of comparative advantage in services and the potential role of developing countries as exporters of services.[13] The second alternative was adopted by Langhammer (1989) in a study of North–South trade in services which relies on balance-of-payments statistics from four countries (France, Germany, Japan and the USA) that publish bilateral trade data. This work again demonstrated that the pattern of trade in services between industrial and developing countries is related to relative factor endowments. The study also emphasized the limitation of studies based on balance-of-payments statistics with high sectoral aggregation and suggested the need for detailed work on international activities of individual service industries.

10.5 COMMERCIAL POLICY: THEORY

Trade theorists have devoted relatively little attention to the determinants of the patterns of trade in services. In contrast, they have investigated the welfare implications of government policies towards trade in services in some details. Some authors have even argued that (under perfect competition), 'the fact that it may be difficult to develop a convincing *description* of the sources of comparative advantage, . . . does not in any sense invalidate the *prescriptions* of the theory of comparative costs' (Hindley and Smith, 1984, p. 371).

As explained in section 10.2, trade in services can take two forms: commodity trade or factor trade. In the commercial policy literature, these two trade channels are not always considered together. Some authors focus on commodity trade and examine the implications of barriers to trade in services for trade in goods and welfare. Others allow for the possibility of both commodity and factor trade, and investigate the consequences of policies that authorize only one of these two channels to materialize. Unless specified otherwise, the contributions reviewed in this section use a general equilibrium framework.

Models with Only One Trade Channel

The main issue analysed in models with one channel of trade relates to the complementarity between goods and services. Most authors have focused on the complementarity at the level of trade or production, but some have noted that goods and services can also be complementary at the level of consumption.

Three types of models have been considered in the literature to study the impact of barriers to services trade on welfare: (1) models of perfect competition, (2) models of imperfect competition, (3) models whose distinguishing feature is the treatment of reputation.

Perfect competition

The most common approach to the complementarity between trade in goods and services relates to transportation. The early literature on transportation costs in the context of international trade focused entirely on goods. In the so-called 'iceberg model' (Samuelson, 1954), transportation costs are modelled in a mechanical way: the amount of goods reaching the importing nation is assumed to be a proportion of that leaving the exporting country. This popular model served extremely well for examining trade in goods in the presence of transportation costs. It did not, however, enable us to analyse trade in transportation services *per se*, since this activity was not assumed, explicitly, to use productive resources. In particular, it was not possible to examine the impact of commercial policy on transportation services, nor its effect on trade in goods.

Starting with Falvey (1976) and Cassing (1978), authors have developed models of international trade in the traditional HO framework, where transportation appears as a produced activity. Further extensions were provided by Casas (1983) and Melvin (1985). Along the same lines, a recent paper by Ryan considers a three-sector, single factor, *n*-agent economy. Two of the sectors produce consumer goods, while the third provides transportation services linking producers and consumers of goods. The model assumes a perfect complementarity between trade in goods and the provision of services: the quantity of services produced is proportional to the international flow of goods. Ryan shows that free trade in services is optimal. He also finds that liberalizing trade in services is likely to result in a reallocation of resources away from goods, and that the latter's world-wide production may fall if the elasticity of substitution of goods in consumption is greater than unity.

Deardorff (1985) also examines a situation where goods and services are complementary at the level of trade. He shows that if foreign countries do not permit trade in complementary services, the domestic country may not be able to export goods at all. This and the above contributions clearly illustrate, in a general equilibrium framework, the importance of liberalizing trade in both goods and services. Under perfect competition, nothing short of free trade in all commodities will maximize world welfare.

Burgess (1990) studies the same type of problem but allows for greater flexibility at the level of complementarity in the sense that goods and services are not necessarily produced in fixed proportions. In the first part of the paper he presents a model with two goods, a producer service, and two primary inputs (capital and labour). The output of the service sector enters as an intermediate input into the production of both (final) goods, and the service sector uses the same primary inputs as the goods-producing industries. Burgess notes that with identical technologies, free trade in goods only will reduce factor and services prices and will, therefore, reduce the incentive to liberalize trade in services. However, with differences in technology for the provision of services, barriers to trade in services may impede trade in goods. Moreover, in the absence of distortions, Burgess finds that trade liberalization in services is optimal in a world where comparative advantage stems from differences in factor endowments.

The previous model does not differ drastically from models including explicitly intermediate inputs in the production process. However, in the second part of the paper, Burgess considers that the production of producer services requires a specific factor called 'management services', in addition to the primary inputs labour and capital. He also assumes that due to the intangibility of services, 'it is technically impossible to trade services internationally in the sense of having production occur in one country and consumption occur in the other' (Burgess, 1990, p. 134). Therefore, the international provision of services requires the international use of management services. The degree of mobility of factors is larger than in traditional models since capital is assumed to be perfectly mobile across countries and since management service providers, although less than perfectly mobile, can accept employment opportunities abroad. Burgess (1990) shows that his model has the same reduced form as the familiar Heckscher–Ohlin–Samuelson model, with two domestic primary factors (labour and management) and two final commodities. Given this reduced form, the author is in a position to evaluate the impact on welfare of barriers to trade and to confirm the fundamental proposition that trade liberalization in both goods and services will result in a net welfare gain.

Imperfect competition

Jones and Kierzkowski (1989) describe a situation where, like in the models of Deardorff (1985) and Ryan, trade in services may be necessary for trade in goods. The only difference with these models is that trade (in either goods or services) may be intra-industry and not only inter-industry. The conclusion of Jones and Kierzkowski (1989) is an important one: the liberalization of trade in services is crucial to ensure an efficient international allocation of production regardless of whether trade is inter- and/or intra-industry.

Kierzkowski (1986) analyses the issue of economies of scale for transportation services in a partial equilibrium model, where the demand for transportation is derived from that for goods imports. In his model, transportation flows are determined by three factors: the flows of goods, the unit transport costs and exchange rates. The markets for goods are perfectly competitive, but the international market for transportation is assumed to be duopolistic, with one firm operating in each of the two postulated countries. Government intervention in one country in support of its transportation industry will increase this country's share in the world market for transportation, but reduce its export of goods under normal conditions.

Markusen (1989) considers a model with two goods, X and Y, both produced under constant returns to scale and sold on perfectly competitive markets. The model also incorporates n producer services, $S_i(i = 1, 2, \ldots, n)$, which are used as inputs exclusively for the production of X. These inputs are produced under increasing returns to scale and sold on monopolistically competitive markets. Markusen assumes two countries which are either identical in all respects or differ only in their absolute size. Two cases are considered: (1) X and Y are traded, but S_i are not; (2) S_i and Y are traded, but X is not.

In the first case, the modern theory of international trade predicts that if nations are identical, they will not benefit from trade liberalization in X and Y. If the two countries differ in absolute size, the smaller may even lose from trade in this case. This result is obtained by a comparison between the autarky and free trade equilibria, using the market-clearing condition for the latter. Markusen shows that a sufficient condition for gains from trade is that the domestic production of X expands under free trade. In addition, he shows that it may not be so when the small domestic country is at a cost disadvantage relative to the large foreign country because of a distortion between p – the price of X – and the marginal rate of transformation. In the second case, however, the countries will benefit from trade in producer services, since it would allow them to share the fixed costs associated with the production of all varieties of S_i. Although X cannot be traded, the two countries will, none the less, experience a shift outward of their production possibility frontier due to trade in producer services, since more varieties of S_i can be supplied to each country at a lower cost than previously. Markusen shows that under case 2, each country will benefit from a greater diversity of producer services under very general conditions. In fact, the only situation compatible with welfare losses corresponds to unstable equilibria and should not, therefore, be taken into account. Markusen also shows that each country always benefits from a greater variety of producer services under case 2 than under case 1. The conclusion of Markusen (1989) is, therefore, a striking one: trade in producer services is superior to trade in final goods. Note, however, that the key in this model is not so much the distinction between goods and services as that between intermediate inputs and final commodities.

Contrary to the previous model which emphasizes specialization within the services sector itself, Francois (1990a, b) develops a model where services are used for co-ordinating and linking together specialized intermediate producers. In the production side of the model, it is assumed that different firms produce different varieties of a differentiated good x by employing labour l. Production of any variety x_j is subject to increasing returns due to specialization. Many production techniques can be used for producing any variety, each technique involving a different level of specialization (indexed by v) of the production process. Producer services are required for the co-ordination and control of the production process. It is assumed that services are produced internally by the firm, but the model would not be altered substantially if they were, instead, purchased from independent service firms. In the demand side of the model, the Lancaster type of preferences are postulated. Different consumers prefer different varieties of differentiated good. With strong symmetries imposed on preferences, the elasticity of demand for each variety *j* is identical for all varieties and is a function of the number (*n*) of available varieties: $\sigma_j = \sigma(n)$. Because of the symmetries in the model, all available varieties will be produced in identical quantities (*x*) and will be identically priced (at *p*) in equilibrium. The solution of this model is expressed in terms of five variables: *x*, *p*, *v*, *n* and the share of labour employed in the production of services. Changes in the extent of the market resulting from expansion of the labour force result in changes in the size of operations which lead to both an increasing degree of specialization and a growing share of labour employed in producer services.

Suppose now there are two economies, home and foreign, with demand and supply conditions like those presented above. Home country values are indicated by small letters, and foreign country ones by capital values. Francois (1990a) postulates identical technologies, endowments and preferences, so that $x = X$ and $l = L$. If trade is allowed, there will be a consolidation among existing firms, with the remaining firms being larger than before trade. At the same time, the number of varieties available to consumers will increase. The increased size of firms prompts them to apply more specialized methods of production which require more producer services. Expanded opportunities for trade in differentiated goods, therefore, result in increased specialization, a growing production of services and a rise in welfare.

In Francois (1990b), it is assumed that services and goods require different types of labour (skilled and unskilled respectively), with which the two economies are differently endowed. At first, only free trade in goods is allowed, trade in services being impeded by prohibitive restrictions. In equilibrium goods prices are equalized, but services are cheaper in the country which is relatively well endowed with skilled labour. With the introduction of trade in services, this country will, therefore, export services in exchange for goods. Liberalization of trade in services leads to an increase in the number of product varieties produced, an increase in scale and thus a movement towards more specialized production methods in the service-importing country, a movement towards either more or less specialized methods of production in the service-exporting country, and a decline in the price of manufactured goods relative to total factor income. The number of foreign firms rises, while the number of domestic firms declines. The remaining domestic firms end up larger than they were before liberalization. Both service-importing and -exporting countries stand to gain from liberalization of trade in producer services. Liberalization of trade in producer services affects the extent to which specialization is applied to the production process and the realization of returns associated with such specialization. These returns are in addition to the standard comparative advantage-based arguments for liberalizing trade in services.

The role of reputation

Market failures such as imperfect information associated with the intangibility of services have often been presented as arguments in favour of regulation.

In the trade literature, many authors have also stressed that the intangibility of services may require a different approach than for goods. Little effort has been made, however, to formally model intangibility and its impact on international flows of services.

In the field of trade in goods, authors have developed models where informational barriers may justify the infant industry protection in developing services that enjoy comparative advantages in innovative experience goods. Without protection of their domestic market, efficient new entrants may not be able to compete with well-established foreign firms. Such a situation is likely to arise on sophisticated goods markets where consumers are not equipped to correctly determine all the attributes of a sophisticated differentiated product. Before purchase, they must therefore rely on the reputation of firms as indicators of product quality. In services transactions, consumers must often take the producer's reputation as the sole quality indicator since services do not exist prior to purchase. The infant industry argument may therefore be a relevant issue for services in developing countries which explains their reluctance to liberalize international services transactions. Grossman and Horn (1988) have developed a model to determine 'whether the existence of informational barriers to entry provides a valid reason for temporarily protecting infant producers of experience goods and services in countries that are followers rather than leaders in innovative industries' (Grossman and Horn, 1988, p. 3). The originality of their work stems from an attempt to model the intrinsic features of services (i.e. their nature) rather than their economic function (i.e. their role). The model is based on closed economy models of asymmetric information with respect to product quality. It is an open economy model aimed at analysing the opportunity of commercial policy in the case of imperfect information, when the latter materializes in a moral hazard problem in the domestic firms' choice of quality and in adverse selection among potential entrants into the industry.

Grossman and Horn consider a dynamic partial equilibrium model of perfect competition with one experience commodity sold and consumed during two periods. During each period, domestic consumers must choose between a foreign and a domestic commodity. At the beginning of the first period, consumers know the quality level of the foreign products sold by well-established firms, but they cannot distinguish between domestic products above some minimum, threshold quality. Domestic entrants will not therefore supply products below the threshold quality. None the less, their incentive to supply high-quality products is assumed to be positively related to their type (i.e. their cost structure). Low-cost firms are likely to provide high-quality products, that is to behave in a 'reputable' way. These firms act to maximize their intertemporal profit. On the contrary, higher-cost firms maximize their first-period profit because they have an incentive to choose to produce the minimum quality and to supply a non-desirable commodity. Such firms are referred to as 'fly-by-night' firms because once their product quality level is known, they are not able to remain active on the market during the second period. During the first period, the domestic firms' product quality is unknown and cannot be perfectly anticipated because, on a perfectly competitive market, the equilibrium market price does not help to discriminate between the products of 'fly-by-night' firms and that of others. Consumers can, however, determine the average domestic product quality because they know the threshold quality level chosen by 'fly-by-night' firms and the distribution function of efficiency between all potential domestic entrants. The domestic first-period market share is determined by the expected domestic average quality which equalizes the expected hedonic domestic price and the foreign one. Since some entrants are 'fly-by-night' firms, expected domestic average quality is less than the quality supplied by reputable firms. This may preclude the entry of efficient domestic firms, depending upon the form of the profit function and the instrument adopted to solve the asymmetric information problem. Grossman and Horn consider two possible ways of correcting such non-optimal market equilibrium. The first one is government action by way of temporary or permanent tariffs against foreign products. The second instrument is a private one: domestic firms may try to signal their quality level through investment in production capacity.[14]

The authors analyse four cases: (1) a temporary tariff without private investment; (2) permanent protection without private investment; (3) a temporary tariff with private investment; (4) permanent protection with private investment. In the first case, Grossman and Horn show that protection lowers domestic welfare because the first-period tariff does not discriminate between domestic 'fly-by-night' and 'reputable' firms. Protection does not correct for the moral hazard problem because it does not influence the incentive to provide high-quality products. Moreover, it exacerbates the adverse selection problem since the additional domestic entrants are less efficient firms which will provide non-desirable commodities. Permanent protection (case 2) may increase domestic welfare because the second-period tariff only rewards the reputable firms. Therefore, it reduces the moral hazard problem, but it does not necessarily correct for the adverse selection one. With a low market equilibrium price (low quality level), second-period protection causes more firms to enter, but all these additional firms are less efficient. They will, therefore, reduce the average quality level even if they behave like 'reputable' firms. In the third case, Grossman and Horn show that temporary protection along with quality signalling is even worse, because, as in case 1, protection does not correct market failures. Moreover, temporary protection increases the social cost of signalling and generates excess investment capacity. Since the cost of additional investment dissipates the subsidy implicit in the tariff, the number of domestic entrants is the same as without any government intervention. Finally, when the government engages in permanent protection (case 4), the welfare consequences are even worse because it creates excess capacity and encourages additional inefficient firms to enter the market.

In conclusion, the infant-industry argument is only justified in case 2. But such a policy is time inconsistent because 'once the mature phase of industry competition arrives, the government has an incentive to terminate any protection from the infancy phase' (Grossman and Horn, 1988, p. 22). Grossman and Horn therefore conclude that imperfect information does not justify government intervention by way of tariffs since it fails to correct the source of market failure.

Models with Two Trade Channels

One of the characteristics of services is that the choice between commodity trade and factor trade may be more limited than in the case of goods. Recently, trade theorists have developed models that enable us to examine these two channels of trade in services. So far, only situations of constant returns to scale and perfect competition have been considered.

Jones and Ruane (1990) and Ruane (1990) consider a model where production requires the use of specific factors. Labour is assumed to be country-specific but intersectorally mobile, while all other factors are potentially internationally mobile but sector-specific. All countries use labour and sector-specific factors to produce manufacturing and service commodities. Contrary to the situation in most of the models with one trade channel – except for the model by Grossman and Horn (1988) – the distinguishing feature of services in this model is not their complementarity with goods. Instead, in this model services are final commodities which differ from goods by the fact that initially they are not traded. The paper analyses the impact on a small country of an opening to trade in services via two alternative channels. The country can either trade in the service commodity or in the service factor. In this model, trade is driven by international differences in both technology and relative factor endowments. The model of Jones and Ruane (1990) and Ruane (1990) can be examined with the help of figure 10.2, which explains the relationships between the home return to the service factor r_s, the commodity price p_s and the supply for and demand of services x_s.[15] The locus in the left-hand panel of figure 10.2 explains the relationship between r_s and p_s in the home country. Since technology and the skills of factors are assumed to differ at home and abroad, the world values for the service factor return and product price need not lie on this locus. If the home country has a technological comparative advantage in services relative to manufacturing, the locus lies south-west of the world position C^*, with world values for r_s and p_s given by r_s^* and p_s^*, whereas comparative disadvantage would be indicated by a world position such as $C^£$, drawn symmetrically with C^* for convenience. Technological comparative advantage implies that if the home country were to pay the service factor the world rate of return, its cost of producing the service commodity would lie below the world price. On the other hand, in manufacturing, given that commodities are freely traded, prices are equalized internationally.

Even if the home country has a presumed technological advantage in services it will not necessarily either export the service commodity or attract the service factor from abroad, because the pattern of trade also depends on relative factor endowments. Factor endowments determine the location of the

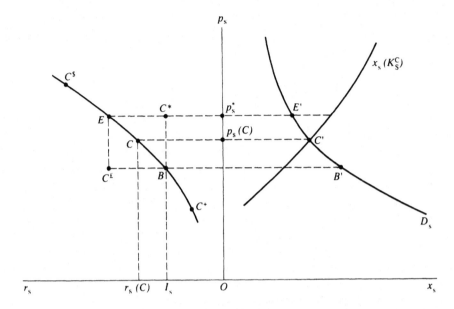

Figure 10.2 Relationships between the home return to the service factor r_s, the commodity price p_s and the supply for and demand of services x_s (Reproduced from Ruane 1990)

pre-trade home values for r_s and p_s along the curve in the left-hand panel of figure 10.2.

The position of the supply curve depends on local technology and the endowment of the specific service factor. The demand curve reflects not only local taste patterns but also the endowments of all national factors. For example, if the demand and supply curves intersect at C', then the initial location is at C on the r_s–p_s locus in the left-hand panel. This represents an endowment position which is 'balanced' relative to the rest of the world, in the sense that if the country has a comparative advantage in the service production, then this results in a relatively low cost of the service commodity $(p_s(C) < p_s^*)$ and a relatively high return to the service factor $(r_s(C) < r_s^*)$. If, by contrast, the home country has an abundance (a scarcity) of the service factor relative to its supply of labour and other specific factors, so that the supply curve in the right-hand side panel of figure 10.2 intersects the demand curve to the right of B' (to the left of E'), then the initial equilibrium would lie at a point such as $C^+(C^s)$. Such endowment positions are defined as 'extreme', in that in these cases technological advantage does not result in a relatively low cost of the service commodity (as at point C^s) or in a relatively high return to the service factor (as at point C^+).

In both cases, the authors show that, while opening up either trade channel will lead to welfare gains, factor endowments are crucial in determining the output adjustment of the local service sector. In the case where endowments are 'balanced' (i.e. the initial equilibrium lies on the range EB in figure 10.2), either trade channel leads to an unambiguous expansion of the service sector if the home country enjoys a technological comparative advantage in services and a contraction if it suffers from a comparative disadvantage. It turns out that the trade channel which brings about the greater output adjustment leads in this 'balanced' case, to the greater welfare gain. By contrast, in the case of more extreme endowments (either side of the range EB on the locus), the two alternative channels point in opposite directions in terms of the adjustment required of the local service sector. For example, assuming the country has a technological comparative advantage, if the autarky point is C^* in the left-hand panel, allowing factor trade leads to an outflow of the service factor which causes output in the service sector to fall. None the less such a decline in output raises local real incomes since each unit of the service factor which exits earns more abroad (r_s^*) than is forgone at home (r_s). On the other hand, if commodity trade is opened up to world competition, output in the service sector would expand. There is an unambiguously larger welfare gain in the latter case as the superabundance of the service factor (which prompts it to exit if factor trade is opened up), combined with the economy's technological advantage in producing the service commodity, results in a substantial expansion in the output of the service sector. Thus, in the model of Jones and Ruane (1990), while there are welfare gains no matter how services are liberalized, such welfare gains and the outcome for the domestic service sector depend crucially on the actual channel through which trade is liberalized.

Melvin (1989) uses a traditional $2 \times 2 \times 2$ HO model where trade is explained solely by differences in relative factor endowments across countries. Contrary to the previous model, here, factors of production are not sector-specific. Labour is assumed to be country-specific, while the capital service factor is assumed to be internationally mobile. With only one final commodity and the capital service factor being traded, Melvin finds that factor trade does not always result in efficient world output. This may be the case when the tradable commodity uses the mobile factor intensively. Under free trade in both final commodities, factor trade does not preclude efficient world output but it may be responsible for an indeterminacy in trade patterns. As a consequence, 'traditional commercial policy may not have the expected welfare effects' (Melvin, 1989, p. 1196). However, the analysis does not differ from standard models dealing with international capital mobility, except that, in this model, capital is called 'capital services'.

In conclusion, whether one or two channels of trade are considered, the general presumption that derives from theoretical models is that freer trade in services is welfare-improving.

10.6 COMMERCIAL POLICY:
THE ROAD TOWARDS LIBERALIZATION

Long ignored by international efforts to liberalize trade, services now occupy a notable place on several policy agendas. In the Uruguay Round, services trade dominates the other 'new' issues for which multilateral trade negotiations are taking place for the first time.[16] Within the EC, the drive to complete the internal market ('EC-92') is also largely motivated by the desire to liberalize transactions in services. This section reviews these current liberalization efforts. It differs substantially from the previous sections where the main emphasis was on the economic literature. Here, the focus is on actual economic events, which are commented through references to the literature.

The presence of services trade on the Uruguay Round agenda owes much to the insistence of the USA over the objections of some developing countries and the early apprehensions by the EC. McCulloch (1990) summarizes the principal motives behind the initiatives by the USA to promote services in the multilateral framework during the early 1980s:

1 the perceived shift in comparative advantage from goods towards services and, therefore, the need to secure increased export opportunities for services;[17]
2 the lobbying by a handful of financial services firms (especially American Express) in order to maintain or improve rights of establishment abroad;
3 the perception by some policy-makers of the need to maintain the momentum in favour of multilateral trade negotiations in the face of anti-GATT sentiments in the United States (the so-called 'bicycle theory'). (On this, see Feketekuty, 1988.)

On the other hand, the lack of enthusiasm of developing countries for including services in the multilateral trade framework stemmed from three concerns stated by Bhagwati (1985):

1 that the benefits from multilateral trade rules would accrue to the industrial countries owing to their comparative advantage in services;
2 that the new focus on services would distract the attention of trade negotiators away from trade in goods, especially those where the developing countries enjoy a comparative advantage;
3 that services include politically sensitive infrastructure activities sectors which developing countries may wish to exclude from trade liberalization.

As already indicated in section 10.4, there is empirical evidence supporting the view that industrial countries tend to have a comparative advantage in services, notwithstanding the fact that developing countries do enjoy a comparative advantage in certain services, particularly labour-intensive ones. Economists have been quick to point out that '[t]here are gains not only for countries which expand their exports but also for those which increase their imports' (Sapir, 1985, p. 40). In fact, the traditional gains from trade would be especially large for services in view of their role as intermediate inputs in most other activities, a function which is especially crucial in developing countries.[18] In this connection, Hindley (1988) provides a useful analytical framework for assessing the cost of protecting the services sector in developing countries. Yet, as both Bhagwati (1985) and Sapir (1985) had correctly predicted, such arguments were unlikely to win the support of developing countries for including services on the agenda of multilateral trade negotiations.

In order to convince the developing countries that bringing services into multilateral negotiations was also in their advantage, it was necessary to demonstrate that it would serve their export interests, i.e. that negotiations would improve their access to industrial country markets. The question then arose as to whether such interests should take into account both goods and services or be confined to services trade. Some authors argued that, given the relative lack of export opportunities for developing countries in the area of services, the quid pro quo should be between goods and services. It was suggested that, in multilateral negotiations, industrial countries should offer to liberalize their markets for agricultural and manufactured goods of interest to developing nations in exchange for gaining better access in the service markets of these nations. 'Thus there need[ed] to be a global approach to trade problems instead of the traditional view which segments the problems into a goods and a services compartment' (Sapir, 1985, p. 40).[19] Other authors, while agreeing that a grand bargain involving both goods and services may be desirable from an economic standpoint, contended that a trade-off within services would be preferable. This view, cogently put forward by Bhagwati (1985), was partly based on the perception that a grand bargain would be unfair to the developing countries since they would be taking on new obligations (in services) in exchange for the rolling back by the industrial countries of violations of existing GATT obligations (mostly in labour-intensive goods such as textiles and clothing).

The disagreement between some developing countries and the USA on the issue of services prevented the launching of a new round of multilateral negotiations for several years after its principle had been agreed at the 1982 Ministerial Meeting of the GATT Contracting Parties. Early on, the battle focused on whether or not to include services in the future round. Later, it moved to the modality of their inclusion, the USA favouring a single-track approach (one negotiation covering both goods and services) while the developing countries preferred a dual-track formula (two separate negotiations) – some developing countries (especially India and Brazil) continued, however, to resist inclusion. Under the compromise finally adopted in 1986, at the launching of the Uruguay Round in Punta del Este, the dual-track approach was selected, but it was agreed that the two negotiations would be conducted within the same framework (Marconini, 1990).

The principle and the modality of the inclusion of services in the Uruguay Round would not have been possible without the crucial role of the EC in promoting a compromise. Its own early apprehensions about services trade liberalization had been overturned in the mid-1980s by the combination of two factors. First, statistical evidence indicated that the Community is the world's largest exporter of services and enjoys a comparative advantage reflected by a consistently positive services trade balance. Second, it was acknowledged that, despite 30 years of efforts to abolish 'restrictions on freedom to provide services within the Community' (article 59 of the Treaty of Rome), little had actually been achieved and that the costs of 'non-Europe' were particularly important in services (Commission of the European Communities, 1988). This gave the necessary impetus towards achieving a single European market in services by 1993. Although there is some disagreement in the literature on the exact nature of the relationship between the EC's internal market programme and the Uruguay Round, the two are generally viewed as complementary liberalization processes.[20]

As predicted by many authors, establishing a multilateral framework of principles and rules for trade in services has been an extremely complex task.[21] After seven years of intense work there is a general consensus that the final outcome of the services negotiations will comprise of three elements:

1 A framework agreement – the General Agreement on Trade is Services (GATS) – laying down general principles applicable to all services. Although it bears some resemblance with the GATT, it was felt that the specificity of services trade (in particular the issue of mode or channel of delivery) required an agreement distinct from that for goods.
2 Sectoral annexes specifying special arrangements covering a limited number of sectors (including telecommunications and financial services).
3 Initial commitments by the participants.

One of the most contentious issues in the negotiations has been the interface between the modes of delivery (transactions of types 1, 2, 3 or 4) and the participation of the developing countries. The problem has centred around two topics: the most-favoured-nation (MFN) principle and labour mobility. In both instances, the problem relates to a major ambition of the industrial nations in the services negotiations, namely to obtain not only improved trade access but also rights of establishment for their services companies in the developing countries. These countries have been reluctant to commit themselves to granting such rights in politically sensitive infrastructure activities. As a result, some industrial countries have sought to deny the application of the MFN principle from the services agreement.[22] Another option for alleviating the reluctance of the developing countries to make concessions in services would be to treat capital and labour with symmetry as far as the concept of 'right of establishment' is concerned.[23] Symmetry should not be interpreted here in the literal sense, i.e. a perfect match between permanent establishment and permanent residence. Rather, as Bhagwati (1987) has suggested, what is at stake is the possibility of temporary residence by foreign labour to execute service transactions. Progress on this issue is considered as crucial by some developing countries in view of their relative endowments. Lack of concessions on the part of industrial countries in services that necessitate substantial temporary relocation of labour would reduce the interest of the developing countries to take part in the final outcome of the services negotiations. In this case, the only chance to get them on board would be to revert to a grand bargain involving both goods and services.

10.7 CONCLUSIONS

As the survey has shown, the past decade has witnessed intense research on trade in services. Much of it has been of a theoretical nature, the main message being that the positive and normative implications of standard trade theories generally extend from goods to services. In particular, the theoretical models have shown that freer trade in services is welfare-enhancing. On the empirical front, contributions have been less numerous, due in part to lack of data. It has been verified that standard trade theories are powerful tools to explain the pattern of trade in services. But, so far, little attempt has been made to provide quantitative evidence on the gains from liberalizing trade in services.

The knowledge gained by economists over recent years has contributed significantly to the process of creating a much-needed multilateral framework for international trade in services. The establishment of a GATS will be an important achievement. The journey down the road towards liberalization has, however, only begun. Even then, much work will remain for both policy-makers and researchers in the field.

NOTES

The authors are grateful to Bernard Hoekman, Harsha Singh, David Greenaway and Alan Winters for helpful comments on an earlier draft, and Cecilia Mulligan for putting it all together.

1 The most notable contributions here include Griffiths (1975), US Department of Commerce (1976), Krommenacker (1979), Sapir and Lutz (1980) and Shelp (1981).
2 Previous surveys can be found in Ryan (1988) and Findlay (1990).
3 Grubel (1987) offers a somewhat different view on embodied factor services.
4 There is a growing literature on multinational corporations as channels for international transactions in services. The reader should refer to Rugman (1987) and Dunning (1989) for an overview of the issue.
5 See Holmström (1985) for an early discussion of the role of asymmetric information in the context of services.
6 See Inman (1985). Adverse selection is also present in financial services. In this case, however, there is an additional problem resulting from the difficulty for the seller to gauge the risk attached to different buyers.
7 See Noll (1989) for an extensive review of the literature.
8 F is 'the set of all feasible outputs of goods and services that can be produced by a country given its technology and factor endowments' (Deardorff, 1985, p. 13).
9 G is the set of all possible combinations of net trade in goods and in services used, when the complementarity between trade in goods and services is accounted for.
10 In each side of the inequality, the first term is the total net value of transportation services, associated with net export of goods, while the second term is the value of transportation services paid to domestic transportation firms. The difference between the two terms gives the net value of transportation services paid to or received from foreign transportation firms and, hence, giving rise to international transactions.

11 Equilibrium factor prices depend on the degree of substitution between goods and services in demand and on the relative factor intensities of the two industries.
12 The last item includes services such as advertising, banking communications, construction, engineering and insurance.
13 This view is derived from Balassa (1979) who proposed the notion of a 'stages' approach to comparative advantage whereby a country's pattern of trade in manufactured goods is presumed to evolve according to its accumulation of physical and human capital.
14 Investment is an indicator of long-term production.
15 The exposition of the model follows that of Ruane (1990).
16 The other 'new' issues are trade-related intellectual property rights (TRIPs) and trade-related investment measures (TRIMs). See Greenaway and Sapir (1992).
17 Balassa (1990) also indicates that the liberalization of trade in services 'conforms to the apparent comparative advantage of the United States in service industries' (p. 131).
18 The key role of services in the development process was pointed out in Sapir and Lutz (1981) and analysed more thoroughly in Riddle (1986).
19 There have been many versions of this grand trade-off between goods and services. One such bargain, proposed by Hoekman (1988b), involves a linkage between services and safeguards (article XIX of GATT).
20 Hindley (1987), Nicolaides (1989) and Messerlin (1990) also attempt to draw lessons from the internal market programme for the Uruguay Round negotiations.
21 Jackson (1988) proposes a number of ways for setting up a legal–institutional structure that takes into account the complexity of services trade.
22 Bhagwati (1990) offers a two-step solution to this problem. During a first (limited) period, developing countries would be granted unconditional MFN rights with no-rules obligations, but with quantity obligations. At the end of this period, they would have to accept rules obligations or lose their rights.
23 This idea has been promoted mainly by Indian economists. Nayyar (1986) has put it forcefully: 'If there is to be a right of establishment, which enables the producer of a service to move to the consumer of a service across national boundaries, there is no reason why this should be confined to capital alone in the form of investment in services. Considerations of symmetry and equity require that such a right of establishment should also be available for labour services.' See also Bhagwati (1987).

REFERENCES

Ascher, B. and Whichard, O. 1987: Improving service trade data. In O. Giarini (ed.), *The Emerging Service Economy*, New York: Praeger.
Balassa, B. 1979: The changing pattern of comparative advantage in manufactured goods. *Review of Economics and Statistics*, 16, 259–66.
Balassa, B. 1990: The United States. In P. A. Messerlin and K. P. Sauvant (eds), *The Uruguay Round: services in the world economy*, Washington, DC: The World Bank and the United Nations Centre on Transnational Corporations.
Baldwin, R. E. 1984: Trade policies in developed countries. In R. W. Jones and P. B. Kenen (eds), *Handbook of International Economics*, vol. 1, Amsterdam: North-Holland, ch. 12.
Bhagwati, J. N. 1984: Splintering and disembodiment of services and developing nations. *The World Economy*, 7, 133–44.

Bhagwati, J. N. 1985: Trade in services and developing countries. Xth Annual Geneva Lecture delivered at the London School of Economics, 28 November.

Bhagwati, J. N. 1987: Trade in services in multilateral trade negotiations. *The World Bank Economic Review*, 1, 549–69.

Bhagwati, J. N. 1990: Multilateralism at risk. The Harry Johnson Memorial Lecture 1990, delivered in London on 11 July.

Burgess, D. F. 1990: Services as intermediate goods: the issues of trade liberalisation. In R. Jones and A. Krueger (eds), *The Political Economy of International Trade*, Oxford: Basil Blackwell, 122–39.

Casas, F. R. 1983: International trade with produced transport services. *Oxford Economic Papers*, 35, 89–109.

Cassing, J. 1978: Transport costs in international trade theory: a comparison with the analysis of non-traded goods. *Quarterly Journal of Economics*, 93, 535–50.

Caves, R. E. 1982: *Multinational Enterprises and Economics Analysis*. Cambridge: Cambridge University Press.

Commission of the European Communities 1988: The economics of 1992. *European Economy*, no. 35.

Deardorff, A. 1984: Testing trade theories and predicting trade flows. In R. W. Jones and P. B. Kenen (eds), *Handbook of International Economics*, vol. 1, Amsterdam: North-Holland, ch. 10.

Deardorff, A. 1985: Comparative advantage and international trade and investment in services. In R. M. Stern (ed.), *Trade and Investment in Services; Canada/US perspectives*, Toronto: Ontario Economic Council, 39–71.

Dick, R. and Dicke, H. 1979: Patterns of trade in knowledge. In H. Giersch (ed.), *International Economic Development and Resource Transfer*, Tübingen: J. C. B. Mohr.

Dunning, J. H. 1989: Transnational corporations and the growth of services: some conceptual and theoretical issues. UNCTC Current Studies, Series A, no. 9, New York: United Nations.

Falvey, R. 1976: Transportation costs in the pure theory of international trade. *Economic Journal*, 86, 536–50.

Feketekuty, G. 1988: *International Trade in Services: an overview and blueprint for negotiations*. Cambridge, Mass.: American Enterprise Institute and Ballinger.

Findlay, C. 1990: International exchange in services in the Asia–Pacific region. *Asia–Pacific Economic Literature*, 4.

Francois, J. F. 1990a: Producer services, scale and the division of labour. *Oxford Economic Papers*, 42, 715–29.

Francois, J. F. 1990b: Trade in producer services and returns due to specialization and the monopolistic competition. *Canadian Journal of Economics*, 23, 109–24.

Greenaway, D. and Sapir, A. 1992: New issues in the Uruguay Round: services, TRIMs and TRIPs. *European Economic Review*, 36, 509–18.

Griffiths, B. 1975: *Invisible Barriers to International Trade*. London: Macmillan.

Grossman, G. and Horn, H. 1988: Infant-industry protection reconsidered: the case of informational barriers to entry. *Quarterly Journal of Economics*, 103, 767–87.

Grubel, H. G. 1987: All traded services are embodied in materials or people. *The World Economy*, 10, 319–30.

Hill, T. P. 1977: On goods and services. *The Review of Income and Wealth*, 23, 315–38.

Hindley, B. 1987: Trade in services within the European Community. In H. Giersch (ed.), *Free Trade in the World Economy*, Tübingen: J. C. B. Mohr.

Hindley B. 1988: Service sector protection: considerations for developing countries. *World Bank Economic Review*, 2, 205–23.

Hindley, B. and Smith, A. 1984: Comparative advantage and trade in services. *The World Economy*, 7, 369–90.

Hoekman, B. M. 1988a: The Uruguay Round of multilateral trade negotiations: investigating the scope for agreement on safeguards, services, and agriculture. Unpublished Ph.D. thesis, Ann Arbor: University of Michigan.

Hoekman, B. M. 1988b: Services as the quid pro quo for a safeguards code. *The World Economy*, 11, 203–15.

Hoekman, B. M. 1990: Services – related production, employment, trade, and factor movements. In P. A. Messerlin and K. P. Sauvant (eds), *The Uruguay Round: services in the world economy*, Washington, DC: The World Bank and The United Nations Centre on Transnational Corporations.

Holmström, B. 1985: The provision of services in a market economy. In R. P. Inman (ed.), *Managing the Service Economy*, Cambridge: Cambridge University Press.

Inman, R. P. 1985: Introduction and overview. In R. P. Inman (ed.), *Managing the Service Economy*, Cambridge: Cambridge University Press.

Jackson, J. 1988: Constructing a constitution for trade in services. *The World Economy*, 11, 187–202.

Jones, R. W. 1985: Comments on A. V. Deardorff, comparative advantage and international trade and investment in services. In R. M. Stern (ed.), *Trade and Investment in Services: Canada/US perspectives*, Toronto: University of Toronto Press for the Ontario Economic Council.

Jones, R. W. and Kenen, P. B. 1984: *Handbook of International Economics*, vol. 1. Amsterdam: North-Holland.

Jones, R. W. and Kierzkowski, H. 1989: The role of services in production and international trade: a theoretical framework. In Ronald W. Jones and Anne O. Krueger (eds), *The Political Economy of International Trade*, Oxford: Basil Blackwell Publishers.

Jones, R. W. and Ruane, F. 1990: Appraising the options for international trade in services. *Oxford Economic Papers*, 42, 672–87.

Kay, J. and Vickers, J. 1988: Regulatory reform in Britain. *Economic Policy*, 3, 286–351.

Kierzkowski, H. 1986: Modelling international transportation services. Washington, DC: IMF research paper, DM/86/35.

Kierzkowski, H. and Sapir, A. 1987: International trade in services: perspectives from the developing countries. Paper presented at the World Bank Conference on Developing Countries' Interests and International Transactions in Services, Washington, DC, 15–16, July.

Krommenacker, R. 1979: Trade-related services and the GATT. *Journal of World Trade Law*, 13, 510–22.

Lall, S. 1986: The Third World and comparative advantages in trade services. In S. Lall and F. Stewart (eds), *Theory and Reality in Development*, London: Macmillan, 122–38.

Langhammer, R. J. 1989: North–South trade in services: some empirical evidence. In H. Giersch (ed.), *Services in World Economic Growth*, Tübingen: J. C. B. Mohr.

McCulloch, R. 1988: International competition in services. In M. Feldstein (ed.), *The United States in the World Economy*, Chicago: The University of Chicago Press.

McCulloch, R. 1990: Services and the Uruguay Round. *The World Economy*, 13, 329–48.

Marconini, M. 1990: The Uruguay Round negotiations on services: an overview. In P. A. Messerlin and K. P. Sauvant (eds), *The Uruguay Round: services in the world economy*, Washington, DC: The World Bank and the United Nations Centre on Transnational Corporations.

Markusen, J. R. 1989: Trade in producer services and in other specialized intermediate inputs. *American Economic Review*, 79, 85–95.

Melvin, J. R. 1985: Domestic taste differences, transportation costs and international trade. *Journal of International Economics*, 18, 237–57.

Melvin, J. R. 1989: Trade in producer services: a Heckscher–Ohlin approach. *Journal of Political Economy*, 97, 1180–96.

Messerlin, P. A. 1990: The European Community. In P. A. Messerlin and K. P. Sauvant (eds), *The Uruguay Round: services in the world economy*, Washinton, DC: The World Bank and the United Nations Centre of Transnational Corporations.

Nayyar, D. 1986: International trade in services: implications for developing countries. Exim Bank Commencement Day Annual Lecture, Bombay.

Nicolaides P. 1989: *Liberalizing Service Trade: strategies for success.* Chatham House Papers, London: Routledge for the Royal Institute of International Affairs.

Noll, R. G. 1989: Economic perspectives on the politics of regulation. In R. Schmalensee and R. Willig (eds), *Handbook in Industrial Organization*, vol. 2, Amsterdam: North-Holland, ch. 22.

Riddle, D. 1986: *Service-led Growth: the role of the service sector in world development.* New York: Praeger.

Ruane, F. 1988: Comment on the papers by C. R. Neu and A. Sapir. In R. Baldwin, C. Hamilton and A. Sapir (eds), *Issues in US–EC Trade Relations*, Chicago: University of Chicago Press, 269–76.

Ruane, F. 1990: Internationalization of services: conceptual and empirical issues. Mimeo, Trinity College, Dublin.

Rugman, A. M. 1987: Multinationals and trade in services: a transaction cost approach. *Weltwirtschaftliches Archiv*, 123, 651–67.

Ryan, C. 1988: Trade in services: an introductory survey. *Economic and Social Review*, 20, 37–48.

Ryan, C. no date: Gains and losses as a result of freer trade in goods and transport services in a model with interregional and international trade. Mimeo, University of Wales, Bangor.

Sampson, G. and Snape, R. 1985: Identifying the issues in trade in services. *The World Economy*, 8, 171–82.

Samuelson, P. A. 1954: The transfer problem and transport costs: an analysis of effects of trade impediments. *Economic Journal*, 64, 264–69.

Sapir, A. 1981: Determinants of trade in services. CEME Discussion Paper no. 8104, Université Libre de Bruxelles.

Sapir, A. 1982: Trade in services: polity issues for the eighties. *Columbia Journal of World Business*, 77–83.

Sapir, A. 1985: North–South issues in trade in services. *The World Economy*, 8, 27–42.

Sapir, A. 1986: Trade in investment-related technological services. *World Development*, 14, 605–22.

Sapir, A. 1988: International trade in telecommunications services. In R. Baldwin, C. Hamilton and A. Sapir (eds), *Issues in US–EC Trade Relations*, Chicago: University of Chicago Press, 231–44.

Sapir, A. 1991: The structure of services in Europe: a conceptual framework. CEPR Discussion Paper no. 498, London: Centre for Economic Policy Research.

Sapir, A. and Lutz, E. 1980: Trade in non-factor services: past trends and current issues. World Bank Staff Working Paper no. 410, Washington, DC.

Sapir, A. and Lutz, E. 1981: Trade in services: economic determinants and development related issues. World Bank Staff Working Paper no. 474, World Bank, Washington, DC.

Shelp, R. K. 1981: *Beyond Industrialization: ascendancy of the global service economy.* New York: Praeger Publishers.

Tirole, J. 1988: *The Theory of Industrial Organization.* Cambridge, Mass.: The MIT Press.

US Department of Commerce 1976: *U.S. Service Industries in World Markets: current problems and future policy development.* Washington, DC: US Government Printing Office.

US Office of Technology Assessment, United States Congress 1986: *Trade in Services: exports and foreign revenues.* Washington, DC: US Government Printing Office.

Weiss, L. W. and Klass, M. W. (eds) 1986: *Regulatory Reform.* Boston: Little, Brown & Company.

11

THE RELATIONSHIP
BETWEEN INTERNATIONAL TRADE AND
INTERNATIONAL PRODUCTION

John Cantwell

11.1 INTRODUCTION

International production is defined as that production which is located in one country but controlled by a multinational corporation (MNC) based in another country. Such production is in large part financed by MNCs through foreign direct investment (FDI). International production has risen steadily in the post-war period, and since the 1960s it has tended to increase faster than trade. As a result international trade and production have become more closely linked. One indicator of this linkage is the high share of international trade that is now controlled by MNCs. Another important consequence is that national patterns of specialization in economic activity have become heavily dependent on international production as well as trade.

Despite the widely acknowledged significance of the phenomenon, economists have been rather slow to analyse the relationship between international trade and production. Historically, in international economics more attention was given to the association between international production and capital movements (Dunning, Cantwell and Corley, 1986). The study of MNCs as a distinctive branch of economics originated in this way. In a thesis originally presented in 1960, Hymer (1976) distinguished FDI from foreign portfolio investment. While portfolio investment flows are motivated by interest rate differentials across countries, FDI is motivated instead by the benefits of gaining control over production and markets, normally in fields of activity in which the firm responsible is already involved. This calls for a theory of the firm and the industry rather than a theory of finance, and this became the major basis for the further analysis of international production.

One implication that was perhaps not fully appreciated at the time is that the relationship between FDI and trade is likely to be much more complex than the relationship between portfolio investment and trade. The traditional discussions had concentrated simply on how capital movements would be likely to respond to trade. In Hume's price–specie–flow mechanism capital flows correct trade imbalances. For the more mercantilist minded Steuart trade imbalances instead tend to be sustained by capital movements, as deficit countries would be short of funds and have high interest rates, thus drawing in capital from abroad and ensuring an overall balance of payments equilibrium; an idea with some modern relevance.

However, most trade theories supposed that trade would automatically balance, in which case capital movements may also be an alternative to trade, reducing its overall level. In the Heckscher–Ohlin–Samuelson (HOS) framework capital movements can be viewed as a substitute for trade once the assumption of international factor immobility is relaxed (Mundell, 1957). Capital moves to a country in which it is initially scarce, and accordingly in which real interest rates are high prior to trade or investment. The movement of capital replaces the movement of goods produced by capital-intensive means. The motivation of capital flows by interest rate differentials is consistent with the theory of portfolio capital movements, although in the financial theory separate allowance must be made for differences in the riskiness of investments between countries and the advantages of portfolio diversification; but the replacement of trade by capital movements is much harder to reconcile with the treatment of FDI provided by the theory of the firm, which emphasizes the motive of gaining control over productive assets (Casson, 1982).

The control of productive assets by MNCs may be itself sufficient to raise the rate of return on their operation, either through increasing the efficiency with which they are used, or by raising the market power of the corporate group. So at a microeconomic or industrial level capital movements that facilitate corporate control may run counter to flows motivated by differences in the general interest rate. Moreover, in a model based on the theory of the firm FDI is as likely to complement trade as to substitute for it, and trade may well result from FDI rather than the other way round. While in the conventional trade model capital movements make countries more similar and so reduce trade, in the firm-based model the creation of an international division of labour within MNCs may increase the extent of national specialization and trade (Markusen, 1983, 1984).

The explanation of this difference is partly that in the theory of the firm the connection between FDI and trade is less direct than is the linkage between capital movements and trade in the HOS model as adapted by Mundell. FDI provides one of the means by which MNCs ensure control over international production, and to secure this objective the transfer of capital resources becomes just part of a broader package. The establishment of international production by firms may in turn replace trade, or it may create trade – where, for example, the imports and exports of an affiliate are increased as a result of its integration into an MNC. National differences in production conditions may be reinforced by the decisions of MNCs. Thus, this chapter focuses on the relationship between international trade and international production, and not the relationship between FDI and trade as such. Indeed, the growth of international production does not necessarily require the growth of FDI, since as affiliates become more mature their sources of funding are increasingly likely to be local (and local borrowing is not included in FDI). In any case, the composition as well as the level of international production determines its effect upon trade. Although much of the empirical literature on the association between international trade and production has proxied MNC activity or international production by using FDI data, it is in this respect potentially misleading from a theoretical point of view.

The relationship between international trade and production does not run in just one direction but is an interactive one. It is more complicated than the linkage between trade and portfolio capital movements, as there are different types of international production and they affect trade in different ways. Broadly speaking, three kinds of international production can be distinguished; namely, the resource-based or export-platform; the local market-oriented or import-substituting; and the rationalized or internationally integrated type.

This typology can be used to help to describe a historical sequence in the evolution of international production. The early growth of international production (from the latter part of the last century to World War II) was principally in resource-based activity in less developed countries, often in colonies, former colonies or dependent territories. International production in the manufacturing sector was mainly local market-oriented, though, and this form came to dominate after 1945 with the growth of investment by MNCs in manufacturing activities in other industrialized countries, led by the rapid growth of US FDI in Europe. From the late 1960s onwards there has been a gradual shift towards the international integration of MNC activity, with affiliates becoming a more specialized part of MNC networks, rather than simply replicas of their parent companies serving their own local markets.

The trade effects of resource-based international production are the easiest to understand, which probably explains why there was little historical interest in the relationship between international trade and production. There are two respects in which resource-based international production and the more recent export platforms (exploiting the availability of cheap labour rather than natural resources) are at odds with the conventional approach to trade as represented by the HOS framework. First, international production promotes trade and does not replace it. It especially promotes the exports of resource-based products from the host country, but it may also increase home country exports. Such home country exports can be created directly (the export of agricultural or mining equipment to the host country) and indirectly (the export of the same MNCs to third countries as a result of their cheaper or better quality resource inputs, and the export of manufactured consumer goods to the host country by other firms). Second, trade becomes intra-firm as well as inter-firm, and so it is partially organized by managerial decision rather than the free market price mechanism. Helpman and Krugman (1985) consider how traditional trade theory can be adapted to encompass intra-firm trade in the context of this type of international production.

The Helpman and Krugman approach relies on the fact that in another respect resource-based international production is consistent with the HOS framework. That is, the direction of trade flows can be viewed as being regulated by relative factor endowments. The less developed country exports resource-based or labour-intensive products, while the developed country exports more sophisticated and capital-intensive manufactured goods. So when international production was mainly of the resource-based kind it could be argued that while it might complicate trade theory it did not warrant a new or separate body of theory.

Matters become more difficult, though, in the case of local market-oriented international production. Two considerations are particularly significant. First, this type of production has both trade-replacing and trade-creating effects, and it is impossible to say a priori which of these effects will dominate. The trade-replacing or 'job export' effect is the more immediately obvious, and indeed local market-oriented international production is often termed 'import-substituting' (from the perspective of the host country). Hirsch (1976) and Buckley and Casson (1981) provided models of this substitution process. However, it does not necessarily follow that trade is actually replaced by local production; where, for example, the host country imposes a tariff or some other trade barrier it is this which displaces its imports, and the foreign firm is merely confronted with a choice between local production and the loss of the market in question. A trade-creating effect may be brought about in a variety of ways (Lipsey and Weiss, 1984). It may happen directly (the parent company or its home country suppliers export components for further processing by the affiliate, and other products for resale which are complementary to those produced locally by the affiliate), or indirectly (the direct presence of the affiliate helps to expand the demand for other home country products in the host country).

Second, and perhaps even more significantly, the pattern of trade established by such local market-oriented international production cannot be easily explained through an appeal to relative factor endowments. This type of investment and trade runs primarily between similar industrialized countries, and involves goods produced by processes with similar factor intensities. This calls for a revision of the theory of trade, and much recent trade theory has been directed to this end, though it has still not often provided an integrated treatment of international trade and production between similar countries. The distinctive issue that is raised by an approach which views exports and international production as combined means of exploiting competitive strengths in foreign markets is that the pattern of international trade and production comes to depend upon the innovativeness of different national groups of firms in an industry. Innovative success embodied in nationally differentiated and firm-specific technology and organization leads to exports and outward international production in the sector concerned. This may create inter-industry trade as well as intra-industry trade, as the cross-sectoral pattern of technological achievements varies significantly between the industrialized countries (Cantwell, 1989; Patel and Pavitt, 1991).

With the growth of local market-oriented international production in the post-war period the earliest attempts to develop a theory of its relationship with international trade can be dated to the 1960s. This took the form of an adaptation of the product cycle model (PCM) by Vernon (1966), Hirsch (1967) and their associates. At that time it was reasonable to depict the USA as the technological leader, and most of the relevant trade and investment ran from the USA to Europe. So the USA exported innovative products to Europe, but as the products matured US companies shifted the location of production to Europe. In the PCM the switch in the location of production was seen as being driven initially by a changing composition of demand as incomes caught up in Europe and US exports had reached a critical level. As the product became fully mature the growth in demand levelled off, and such standardized products were manufactured locally in Europe where production costs were lower. Once international production had been established in Europe exports from the USA continued, partly because the most recent products would still be produced (and redesigned) close to the site of the original innovation in the USA, and partly due to a trade creation effect of the kind described earlier.

One of the difficulties of the PCM was that although it provided an integrated treatment of international trade and production it had little place for a theory of the firm or its industry. It was therefore ill-equipped to respond to the development of a more even balance of this kind of international trade and production between the industrialized countries, running equally between countries rather than predominantly in a single direction. Differences in technological capabilities across companies and industries are regulated by factors other than the total level of home country income and the composition of domestic demand. In addition, international production itself evolved in a new direction as already mentioned, towards the integration of affiliates that had previously separately served their own local markets. The problems that this shift towards integrated MNC networks raised for the PCM were recognized by Vernon (1979).

The rationalized or integrated type of international production has the most complex relationship with trade of all. One reason is that it is trade creating for both the home and the host country, as it deepens the international division of labour. While resource-based production essentially promotes host country exports, and local market-oriented production impinges on the exports of the home country, integrated production promotes both exports and imports and in both the home and host countries. The net trade effects are therefore difficult to determine, but they depend upon the contribution of an affiliate to the overall value added of the MNC network and the relative size of its local market. In addition, the trade implications of different forms of international integration are different.

It is worth distinguishing between vertical integration, in which each affiliate contributes some stage of production to a common process co-ordinated across countries by the MNC; or horizontal integration, in which each affiliate contributes a particular product range that it exports to other countries over some wider geographical area. Vertical integration within the MNC is by definition associated with intra-firm trade. Horizontal integration may be

associated with intra-firm trade if affiliates are responsible for local distribution as well as production, but otherwise it will not. Although horizontally
integrated MNCs do not necessarily engage in intra-firm trade they are likely
to contribute to intra-industry trade, as each affiliate is required to narrow
its field of product specialization within its industry, exporting the varieties it
produces while other varieties are imported. The different types of international production and the form of trade they are associated with are
summarized in table 11.1.

Table 11.1 The evolution of international production and the
development of intra-firm trade and intra-industry trade

Type of international production	Composition of MNC trade
Resource-based production	Intra-firm, inter-industry trade
Local market-oriented production	Some intra-firm, intra-industry trade
Internationally integrated production	Intra-firm and intra-industry trade

As a result of the spread of integrated international production over the
last 20 years economists have begun to devote some attention to the study
of intra-firm trade (see Casson et al., 1986). A common approach is to
investigate the determinants of the share of the overall trade of MNCs
which is intra-firm, and it has been argued that transaction cost-related
factors are especially significant. Some attention has also been directed to
the impact of the closer linkages between international trade and production especially in an integrated region like the European Community (EC)
(Dunning, 1993). This involves an assessment of the total trade position of
MNCs.

Drawing these arguments together, there are four issues that must be
addressed when examining the relationship between international trade and
international production. First, the different types of international production influence trade in different ways. Since at a world level there has been a
historical evolution from resource-based, to local market-oriented, to internationally integrated production, it is possible to depict the structure of the
linkage between international trade and production as gradually shifting over
time. Second, the trade of MNCs may be intra-industry or inter-industry, and
it may be intra-firm or inter-firm. The connection between this second issue
and the first is illustrated in table 11.1. Third, international production may
be trade-replacing or trade-creating depending on the context. Fourth, the
relationship between international trade and production varies with the
degree of maturity and strategies of firms, and with the stage of development
of countries. This is related to the first issue, since a more mature MNC and
a more highly developed country are likely to have a greater proportion of

internationally integrated production, and thus to be associated with a more complex pattern of MNC trade.

The remainder of the chapter surveys these issues in greater detail. In section 11.2 the significance of the trade of MNCs in relation to overall international trade is elaborated upon. Section 11.3 considers the connection between MNC trade, intra-firm trade, intra-industry trade and intra-industry production, with reference to the relevant literature. Section 11.4 assesses the evidence on the empirical significance of substitutability versus complementarity between international trade and production, in the light of recent changes in the composition of international production and in company strategies. Some policy implications of the increasing association between international trade and production are outlined in the concluding section 11.5.

11.2 THE DEFINITION AND SIGNIFICANCE OF THE TRADE OF MNCs

There are various ways of defining the trade of MNCs by comparison with the total international trade of a given country. Four such definitions are suggested by Hipple (1990b), and these might be extended to five. The broadest definition covers all that trade in which part of an MNC network (either a parent company or an affiliate) is involved as one of the parties to the transaction. Defined in this way around 99 per cent of all US trade is related to MNCs (Hipple, 1990b)! Even confining the analysis to US MNCs (US parent companies and their foreign affiliates) they were involved in nearly 80 per cent of US exports and nearly 50 per cent of US imports in 1982. At the other extreme only intra-firm trade is considered, which was responsible for about a third of the total value of US trade in 1982. Intra-firm trade also accounted for about one-third of the total exports of Japan and the UK in the early 1980s (Blomström, 1990). The share of intra-firm trade in the total trade of various countries is shown in table 11.2 (see Dunning, 1992, for a further discussion). It seems unduly restrictive, though, to define intra-firm trade between parents and their affiliates as the entirety of MNC-related trade.

Table 11.2 The share of intra-firm trade in the total national trade of selected countries (%)

Country (year)	Share of total exports	Share of total imports
USA (1986)	36	36
UK (1984)	29	51
Sweden (1975)	29	25
Belgium (1976)	53	48
Portugal (1981)	31	34
Japan (1983)	31	18

Source: Dunning (1992)

The three other possible definitions of MNC-related trade are by parent company, by affiliate (the choice of Hipple, 1989) or by the location of trading firms. From the viewpoint of a given home country, parent company trade encompasses the exports and imports of locally owned parent companies, plus the exports and imports of foreign parents to or from the home country. This type of MNC trade accounted for over 80 per cent of the value of US trade in 1982, and indeed exports from US parents to foreign parent companies alone (the overlap between the trade of the two groups) constituted about a third of all US exports (Hipple, 1990b). Affiliate trade comprises the exports and imports of foreign-owned affiliates located in the home country, plus the home country exports and imports sent to or received from domestically owned affiliates located abroad. This formed about one-half of US trade in 1982. Intra-firm trade is a substantial subset of both such parent and affiliate trade, involving the trade linkages between foreign-owned affiliates and their foreign parents, and between home country parents and their affiliates abroad. Inded, these two definitions are probably most useful as a reference point for considering the significance of intra-firm trade relative to the wider total trade interests of MNCs.

Table 11.3 The significance of MNC trade in the USA (as % of total trade)

Segment of MNC trade	Approximate percentage of total US trade in 1982
All MNC trade	99
Intra-firm trade	33
Parent company trade	80
Affiliate trade	50
Local MNC partner trade	80 (imports) to 90 (exports)

Source: Hipple (1990b)

Alternatively, the MNC-related trade of a country may be defined as the trade of parts of MNC networks located in that country. This is probably the most useful definition from a national point of view, as it relates solely to the trade of domestically located concerns. The exports of MNCs are then defined according to the multinational or domestic status of sellers or exporters, and they include the total exports of locally owned parent companies and foreign-owned affiliates located in the home country. US parent firms were responsible for over 70 per cent of US exports in 1982, and foreign-owned affiliates generated nearly 25 per cent, so between them they took over 90 per cent. MNC imports are treated as the imports of this same group of US-located firms, in their role as local buyers or importers of goods produced abroad. US parents accounted for about 45 per cent of US imports in 1982, and foreign-owned affiliates took over 30 per cent, and so together they bought just under 80 per cent. The implication seems to be that purely domestic firms tend to import less than MNCs relative to their share of local production (which is much greater than 20 per cent), but they contribute to exports even less. The significance in total trade of the various segments of MNC trade is summarized in table 11.3. The dominant position of MNCs in trade is an indication of the now close association between international trade and production.

Another implication of these figures is that parent companies tend to be net exporters from their home countries, but foreign-owned affiliates may be net importers (as in the USA, although this is not the case for every country). The different definitions of MNC trade provide an additional perspective on this. Defining MNC-related trade as all trade involving an MNC partner, or by parent company or by affiliate, this trade is roughly in balance in the sense that (at least in the USA) the MNC shares of exports and imports are roughly equal. However, the trade of US-located firms that are part of MNC networks has been in surplus, owing to the greater volume of trade by US parents than foreign-owned affiliates, but by contrast total intra-firm trade in the USA has been in deficit. This deficit arises because the surplus of US parents is concentrated in their trade with unrelated firms in the rest of the world, but the deficit of foreign-owned affiliates is very heavily concentrated in their trade with their parent companies.

Indeed, the deficit in the overall trade of the USA in 1982 was roughly equivalent to the deficit on intra-firm trade (Hipple, 1990b). So it might be argued that the US trade deficit can be linked with the competitive deterioration of the world market shares of US MNCs in the 1970s and 1980s. The intra-firm trade of US parent firms with their foreign-located affiliates, which shows a moderate surplus, has been relatively reduced; but the intra-firm trade of foreign-owned firms with their parent companies, which is heavily in deficit, has been growing more rapidly (Hipple, 1990a). There is, though, another way to view this phenomenon. Since the early 1970s non-US firms have been catching up with the higher degree of multinationality that had on average been the heritage of US firms (Cantwell and Sanna Randaccio, 1990). Non-US firms have been especially keen to expand their US production, and this has resulted in foreign-owned affiliates assuming an increased share of the MNC-related trade of the USA. This may have contributed to a deficit in the short run as in the early stages of their establishment foreign-owned affiliates may be heavily dependent upon imports from their parent companies. However, as these affiliates develop, their exports might be expected to grow faster than their imports (Lipsey, 1991).

It is also possible to assess the significance of MNC-related trade beyond the perspective of a particular country. In recent years the total value of sales from international production (affiliate but not parent company sales) has been similar to the total value of non-affiliate exports from the major industrialized countries (Cantwell, 1989). As has already been illustrated, though, the two are connected since affiliate exports (included in affiliate sales) and parent company exports (included in non-affiliate exports) are in part directly exchanged in the form of intra-firm trade. At a world level affiliate and parent company trade together account for a substantial share of total international trade. US MNCs alone were responsible for over 17 per cent of the total world exports of manufactured goods in 1977, as shown in table 11.4. Again, US parent companies and their affiliates contribute in roughly equal measure to world trade. MNCs are especially prominent in trade in chemicals, capital goods or machinery, and transportation equipment.

Table 11.4 The share of the total value of world exports of manufactures accounted for by US MNCs in 1977 (%)

	US parent companies	US-owned affiliates	Total US MNCs
Food products	3.18	3.92	7.10
Chemicals	11.86	10.99	22.85
Metals	4.06	3.30	7.36
Mechanical engineering	12.19	10.59	22.79
Electrical equipment	11.50	9.87	21.38
Transport equipment	16.59	15.39	31.98
Other manufacturing	5.34	5.24	10.58
Total manufacturing	9.04	8.34	17.37

Sources: Blomström (1990) for US-owned affiliate and total world exports; US Department of Commerce, *US Direct Investment Abroad, 1977* for US parent company exports

However, the movement towards internationally integrated MNC networks has complicated the empirical assessment of the significance of MNC-related trade. In the conventional case an increase in international trade would indicate that a greater value added or value of production is entering into trade. This need not follow where intra-firm trade is created through affiliates becoming specialized in some stage of production. Such intra-firm trade may represent no new value added entering into trade, but simply that the same value added enters into trade more frequently. So the prominent role of MNC trade may be in part attributable to an increase in intermediate product trade relative to final product trade, and an increase in the value of trade relative to the value of production (or value added) that enters into trade.

11.3 INTRA-FIRM TRADE, MNC TRADE AND INTRA-INDUSTRY TRADE

The analysis of intra-firm trade has normally proceeded with reference to the total trade of the MNCs concerned, using either the definition of parent company trade or affiliate trade (Lall, 1978; Casson et al., 1986). In the earliest discussions the emphasis was on how the internal transfer prices set in intra-firm trade may differ from prices in an external market (Lall, 1973). Companies might set up intra-firm trade and establish transfer prices so as to redistribute declared profits between the parent company and affiliates, in order to take advantage of international differences in tax and regulatory regimes. However, the evidence suggests that the facility for transfer price manipulation is not a very important motive for intra-firm trade (Blomström, 1990). Most intra-firm trade (even relative to the total trade of MNCs) runs between industrialized countries with few exchange controls or regulatory restrictions, and the most important determinants of intra-firm trade seem to be industry-specific factors. Intra-firm trade is responsible for a much higher share of MNC trade in some industries than others.

The most important influence on the propensity to engage in intra-firm trade is the research intensity of the industry in which MNCs are involved (Lall, 1978; Siddharthan and Kumar, 1990). Other considerations that positively affect the share of intra-firm trade in total MNC trade are the average degree of multinationality of firms in an industry, and the extent of after-sales servicing. All these factors affect the degree of co-ordination that is required between trading partners, and thereby determine the extent of intra-firm trade.

It is useful here to distinguish between trade in final products and trade in intermediate products (Casson, 1986). In research-intensive industries the goods that are traded are more likely to embody proprietary technology. If they are intermediate products they are more likely to be sent to affiliated firms for further processing than to independent companies. It is sometimes argued that this is because of the desire of firms to prevent competitors acquiring their technology; but the most significant reason seems to be that the efficient use of such products necessitates the development of appropriate skills through a learning process that is best organized within a firm that has experienced or is experiencing a similar type of learning. In the case of final products it may also be advantageous to arrange distribution through an affiliate where the product design is highly specific and subject to change upon the receipt of customer feedback; and where there are greater uncertainties over the quality, quantity and price of products (so the firm is concerned to reduce the costs of bargaining with and monitoring its trading partner in order to be able to appropriate a full rent on its product innovation).

Similar arguments apply in industries in which the after-sales servicing of final products is important. A regular and significant exchange of information between trading partners is likely to be needed, and it is more efficient to manage this within a firm. Meanwhile, companies operating in industries that have become highly multinational are more prone to benefit from internationally integrated stratetgies, and this raises their intra-firm trade. Where they move towards a vertically integrated corporate structure intra-firm trade in intermediate products increases as a matter of course; but with horizontal integration intra-firm trade in final products may also be created if products continue to be to some extent nationally differentiated, and so require locally integrated adaptation and support services. Intra-firm trade in intermediate products is also likely to be high in resource-based industries in which firms are concerned about the security or the quality of their resource supplies. Intra-firm trade may also be promoted in industries subject to more pronounced fluctuations in demand, where it can be a means of redistributing inputs or products for resale from affiliates with excess capacity to those facing excess demand (Kogut, 1985).

In all these cases intra-firm trade increases the efficiency and lowers the costs of the transactions involving the MNC. Because of this, it can be argued that the growth of such intra-firm trade is likely to increase the market shares of MNCs relative to purely domestic firms, and to increase the overall efficiency of production and thereby raise the volume of output in countries that are linked by it. In this event the efficiency gains or lower transaction costs associated with intra-firm trade can be expected to increase the general level of both trade and production (Gray, 1992b, c). This will occur so long as these efficiency gains outweigh any costs that may be associated with an increased market power of MNCs and a greater capacity for transfer price manipulation.

A link is sometimes drawn between the expansion of intra-firm trade and the similar growth in intra-industry trade (see e.g. Greenaway, 1986; McCharles, 1987). However, some care needs to be taken in identifying the relationship between the two. Intra-firm trade has risen as MNCs have shifted towards integrated structures, as outlined in the introductory section. Vertically integrated production necessarily creates intra-firm trade in intermediate products, but this need not be intra-industry trade; while horizontally integrated MNCs may avoid intra-firm trade, even though the final product trade associated with horizontally integrated production (which includes an intra-firm component) is generally also intra-industry trade. So although the move towards integrated strategies by MNCs increases the trade of MNC networks, this does not always take the form of intra-firm trade, and even where it does it need not be intra-industry trade.

To appreciate that the intra-firm trade created by the vertical specialization of an MNC network need not also be intra-industry trade it is simplest to consider the formerly dominant resource-based type of international production. This involved the vertical integration of resource extraction in one country and further processing in another. However, the intra-firm exchange of minerals or agricultural products for manufactured capital equipment does not constitute intra-industry trade, as was emphasized earlier. This distinction may be difficult to draw consistently in empirical work, though, if all the trade or investment of a company is just classified to its major industry or activity. Although in general trade data are not classified in this way, specific data on intra-firm trade may be. In addition, in any trade data the problem of 'categorical aggregation' may arise where the classes chosen are sufficiently broad, such that dissimilar products are grouped together under the same industrial category. For example, vertically integrated intra-firm trade is very important in the motor vehicle sector, but the various kinds of vehicle components may be very different from one another. In this event the appearance of intra-industry trade may be a statistical illusion. Despite this, Pomfret (1986) still argues that vertical specialization, including intra-firm vertical integration, is a major explanation (at least of measured) intra-industry trade.

Horizontally integrated MNCs generally organize affiliate specialization by product ranges within industries, and so they create more genuine intra-industry trade. However, whether this takes the form of intra-firm trade depends upon the relationship between production and distribution. If the products are not complex but standardized and unlikely to change very much, and there is little need for after-sales servicing, then distribution may well be the province of independent companies. Distribution itself may be subject to economies of scale and scope, but any service MNCs that are established as a result (such as those in retail trade) may well engage in a local market-oriented type of international activity, with each affiliate taking responsibility for its own purchasing requirements. In this case, the affiliates of the horizontally integrated manufacturing MNC may enter into individual contracts with the relevant affiliates of the service MNC (or with purely national distributors) through which to serve final product markets internationally. This kind of MNC trade, then, need not be organized on an intra-firm basis.

Although there is not a complete association between trends in the reorganization of international production and the rise of intra-industry trade, they are surely related. Resource-based international production (and the associated intra-firm trade) was tied essentially to inter-industry rather than intra-industry trade. Local market-oriented international production has ambiguous effects on the industrial composition of trade. The balance between intra-industry and inter-industry trade is most likely to be affected when cross-investments take place between countries in the same industry, leading to intra-industry production. When each affiliate is a replica of its parent company serving its own local market with a full range of products, then it is possible that intra-industry production substitutes for intra-industry trade. However, as argued above, parent companies may still export complementary products to their affiliates (so here intra-firm trade contributes to intra-industry trade), and other home country firms in the same industry might find that the host country demand for their exports is increased. So intra-industry trade may be only partially replaced, if at all.

Once MNCs become internationally integrated then they more clearly promote intra-industry trade (Cantwell and Sanna Randaccio, 1992). Leaving aside the trade of vertically integrated networks, at least some of which is of an intra-industry kind, horizontally integrated MNCs certainly create intra-industry trade on a major scale. To the extent that their activity is industrially diversified they may also create some inter-industry trade, but diversification has tended to decline as part of the same process of rationalization by which integrated MNCs have been established, and at broader levels of aggregation it is not a crucial issue for most companies. With horizontal integration a pattern of intra-industry trade is brought about even at the level of individual companies. Each affiliate produces certain varieties for its local market and for export, and imports other varieties. When this is combined with a system of intra-industry production (MNCs originating from different countries operate similar networks) then international production is likely to become fully complementary to intra-industry trade. The pattern of locational specialization of MNCs may become similar as they each attempt to take advantage of the specific skills, production expertise and local demand characteristics of countries, thereby reinforcing intra-industry trade. While vertically integrated MNCs have promoted intra-firm trade, horizontally integrated MNCs have promoted intra-industry trade. It is the overlap between the two that is more complicated.

Recent developments in the theory of trade (Krugman, 1990, 1991) and the theory of trade and growth (Grossman and Helpman, 1991) which make comparative advantage endogenous offer greater hope for a more satisfactory theoretical incorporation of the impact of internationally integrated MNCs on trade. Integrated MNCs promote intra-firm and intra-industry trade by building upon and steadily reinforcing national differences in production conditions across countries. As originally set out, the theory of intra-industry trade was essentially an explanation of the separate and specific location of the production of different varieties, and hence of the volume and direction of trade flows (Helpman and Krugman, 1985). It was not a theory of the national origins of the ownership of production, nor of the linkage between ownership and location. To accommodate the existence of the MNC trade theorists have normally had to introduce a firm-specific public good, that once created could be utilized freely by the same firm at other production sites (Hirsch, 1976; Markusen, 1984).

What this leaves out of account or at least fails to make explicit, but which is emphasized in the newer theories, is the role of separate path-dependent learning and external spillover benefits in each location. The technology used by different affiliates of the same MNC is locationally differentiated and context-specific, despite also embodying firm-specific characteristics. With local learning the pattern of comparative advantage and intra-industry specialization is endogenous. Since such learning has both location-specific and firm-specific elements this helps to reconcile the determination of national patterns of specialization and the national origins of the ownership of production. Just as countries develop differentiated areas of expertise in the process of accumulating a comparative advantage in some industry (Krugman, 1991), so home country firms build up related advantages (Cantwell, 1989). Integrated MNCs gain economies of scope by contributing to the formation of this international division of labour, but these MNCs are likely to originate from countries that are or have been comparatively advantaged in the same industry.

11.4 THE EVIDENCE ON THE EFFECTS OF CHANGING STRUCTURES OF INTERNATIONAL PRODUCTION ON THE TRADE OF MNCs

The relationship between international trade and international production is an essentially complementary one, and changes in the structure of international production have made this increasingly true. Even in the case of the local market-oriented kind of international production, the empirical evidence suggests that as a rule the trade-creating effect tends to outweigh the trade-replacing effect. This is especially true of the longer-term impact, as opposed to the immediate or short-run effect of international production. In the earliest stages of FDI in manufacturing activity international production is positively associated with home country exports and host country imports. As affiliates become better established a more balanced trade position then tends to develop through the growth of affiliate exports, sometimes back to the home country, but more especially to third countries. This process of adjustment is of course reinforced where there is a shift towards integrated MNC structures, as has again tended to occur. The integration of production has given an all-round impetus to trade throughout MNC networks.

One of the earliest studies of the changing form of the relationship between international trade and production as MNCs develop was carried out by Bergsten, Horst and Moran (1978). They examined the association between US outward direct investment and US exports. Using pooled cross-section data disaggregated by the industry of activity and the geographical destination of exports and outward investment, they found a positive correlation between exports and outward investment which gradually declines as outward investment rises. By employing a quadratic functional form they showed that the positive relationship between exports and international production flattens out once a sufficiently high degree of internationalization is achieved. They suggested that this is because affiliates initially focus on marketing and assembling parent company products rather than producing a full range themselves. In other words, in the first instance international production may substitute for home country exports of the products that are assembled locally, but this is more than balanced by an increase in home country exports of intermediate products and of other final products; while in the longer term affiliates learn and develop a local capability that is less dependent upon supplies from the parent company.

One of the problems with a cross-sectional study of this sort is that there are other variables, such as market size, that influence the extent of both international production and exports. It might be claimed, for example, that there is a net substitution effect between international production and home country exports, but this effect is small relative to the joint effect of market size. Lipsey and Weiss (1981) attempted to control for such other influences in their investigation of the relationship between US exports and US-owned foreign affiliate sales in a cross-section of countries, based on a series of industry-level regressions. In most industries US manufacturing affiliate activity tended to promote US exports, while non-US foreign affiliate activity tended to promote third-country exports, but not US exports. Indeed, in less developed countries US-owned affiliate activity was actually negatively related to the exports of other countries. They concluded that their findings supported the idea that international production is a means by which oligopolistic firms compete for host country market shares; it may adversely affect exports from other countries, but it typically supports exports from the home country.

Lipsey and Weiss (1984) extended their study to the firm level, looking at the cross-country association between US parent company exports and (their own) affiliate sales, for the firms of a given industry. At this level they were able to distinguish parent company exports of intermediate products from exports of final goods. They found that international production was positively related with the firm's exports of finished products from the USA, and that there was an even stronger link between affiliate activity and parent company exports of intermediate products. This is not surprising, as it is reasonable to expect that the scale of intra-firm trade in intermediate products tends to be positively related to the size of affiliates.

Evidence of this kind casts grave doubt on the usefulness of models that rely on a bipolar distinction between their characterization of local market-oriented international production as trade replacing, and resource-based or export-platform production as trade creating (Kojima, 1978). This approach derives from attempts to amend the HOS model to encompass international production, and the presumed substitutability between trade and local market-oriented investments is a result which is peculiar to the basic structure of that model (Markusen, 1983).

The HOS model is therefore an inappropriate starting-point for the analysis of the relationship between international trade and production. The trade and capital flows that are associated with local market-oriented international production are not attributable to national differences in endowments of factors that can themselves be traded or leased as inputs to production (at least between firms, if not between countries). Trade and international production are instead usually a result of a differentiated learning process within the firms of each country and a differentiated institutional structure, that leads to a pattern of comparative advantage in certain kinds of technological capability rather than others (Kogut, 1987). The resulting capability incorporates firm-specific tacit elements that may be imitated (through co-operative arrangements or independently) but not directly traded. In the fields of the strongest firm-specific capability the high degree of technological competence of locally based firms promotes both exports and outward international production. Investment abroad enlarges the firm's foreign market share and widens its capacity for corporate technological learning by operating in a new environment, both of which enhance the export capability of the parent company.

The positive relationship between exports and international production observed by Bergsten, Horst and Moran (1978) and Lipsey and Weiss (1981, 1984) is particularly evident in the earliest stages of international corporate growth. In the 1980s the sectoral distribution of exports and outward international production of Germany and Japan were well correlated, as international production began to follow exports for the fastest-growing German and Japanese firms (Cantwell, 1989). However, this cross-industry correlation was much weaker for the USA and the UK, whose MNCs were already more mature, and had shifted towards internationally integrated strategies. The move to international integration encourages the trade of both the home and host countries, but the scope for such integration differs between industries. In industries in which demand remains highly nationally differentiated or in which there are political constraints due to the role of government-controlled customers (as in aircraft) or official regulations (like in pharmaceuticals) MNCs may be obliged to retain an emphasis on multi-domestic structures and affiliate specialization may be limited.

Apart from this kind of cross-industry variation in the significance of trade relative to international production for more mature MNCs, another interesting development in recent years has been the regional focus assumed by corporate integration strategies. As a consequence, while trade has come to play a dominant part in the international linkages created by MNCs within regions, it has a much weaker role relative to international production between regions. The distinction between local market-oriented and internationally integrated production may now be thought of as a distinction between interregional and intraregional types. In other words, a British multinational might have affiliates in the USA and Canada to serve the North American market, and a US MNC has affiliates in the UK and Germany to serve the EC market, so at an interregional level investments are local market-oriented; but within each region the affiliates integrate their activities and become quite highly specialized.

Because this type of structure is increasingly typical, the use by some authors of the term 'globalization' to describe the emergence of internationally integrated strategies is unfortunate. The integration of corporate activities is instead normally organized at a regional rather than a global level. This has, though, increased the incentive for the major MNCs to establish international production in all the three major industrialized regions (North America, the EC, and Japan and the Pacific Rim). To participate in the new opportunities for regional integration, and to avoid being excluded from markets or new corporate alliances as 'outsiders', it is necessary for MNCs to have affiliate networks in place in each region.

Once again, much of the evidence relies on the more extensive data available on US MNC activity. These data illustrate how, for US MNCs, the trade of affiliate networks has been rising very rapidly, but this trade has been increasingly of an intraregional kind. The nature of this shift towards regionally integrated strategies is shown in the EC case in table 11.5. The value of the exports of US-owned manufacturing affiliates located in the EC increased from 15.0 per cent of their sales in 1957 to 42.7 per cent in 1987. This is only a slightly faster trend than elsewhere, as for all US-owned foreign affiliates in manufacturing the export to sales ratio rose from 15.9 to 38.6 per cent over the equivalent period (Cantwell, 1992). What is still more interesting is that this trend towards the international integration of affiliate activity became regionally oriented in the 1970s and 1980s. The share of intra-EC exports in EC-located manufacturing affiliate sales rose from 21.8 per cent in 1977 to 28.0 per cent in 1982, while the non-EC export share actually fell back. In other words, the shift towards regionally integrated strategies has been at the expense not only of local market-oriented production, but also at the expense of integration outside the EC region.

Of course, it may be that closer regional integration is merely a first step towards the wider international integration of activity in due course. It is simply that regional integration over shorter distances can be achieved most easily in the first stage, in the same way in which in the development of the MNC the first affiliates are often established in countries that are geographically and culturally nearer to the home country. However, it also seems that to achieve regional integration in the first instance may require a sufficient concentration of effort that for the time being interregional trade linkages are generally relaxed. Strategies of corporate integration also involve a greater intensity of linkages than is entailed in the broader process of regional integration to which the new MNC strategies are related. Hence the intra-EC trade of US-owned affiliates has been growing faster than the total intra-EC trade of all companies.

Table 11.5 The share of exports in total sales for US-owned manufacturing affiliates located in the EC (%)

	Total exports	Intra-EC exports	Non-EC exports
1957	15.0	n.a.	n.a.
1966	26.7	n.a.	n.a.
1977	38.6	21.8	16.8
1982	41.9	28.0	13.9
1987	42.7	n.a.	n.a.

n.a. = not available.
Source: Cantwell (1992)

So while international trade and production are closely and increasingly connected through the role of MNC trade, the form of this relationship has come to depend upon the geographical groupings to which the home and the host countries belong. The major regions are becoming linked to one another more by international production than by trade, but the significance of trade linkages between countries in a region is rising and being reinforced by international production and the associated affiliate integration. Investment flows between regions and the investments of MNCs within their own regions promote high levels of intra-regional trade. These new MNC strategies are helping to bring about (and are influenced by) a change in the geographical composition of international trade.

Of course, trade created by MNCs in furtherance of a so-called new international division of labour (Fröbel, Heinrichs and Kreye, 1980) may well be of an interregional rather than an intraregional kind. However, the relative significance of this strategy of subcontracting certain tasks to producers in less developed countries seems to have diminished as technological improvements like those in robotics have gradually led this production to shift back to industrialized countries. Even where this has not happened there is a growing tendency for the production to be located closer to the relevant industrialized region, as in the switch by US MNCs of some low-cost processing activities from South-East Asia to the Mexican border area. In addition, the industrialized regions are themselves coming to encompass some lower labour cost countries or areas. In the EC, for example, investments in this kind of activity may be directed to Portugal or Greece or perhaps in future to Eastern Europe rather than to a less developed country outside the region (Dunning, 1993).

Much MNC trade is intra-firm, especially within regions. About a half to two-thirds of US affiliate exports within the region in which the affiliates are located are intra-firm, although the intra-firm share is only about a third to a half of their exports to countries outside the same region. The greater role of intra-firm trade within regions lends some further support to the view that MNC integration is stronger within regions than between them. The notable growth of intra-industry trade within the EC can be linked to this rise in intra-firm trade in the region (Greenaway, 1986). However, as argued above, the overlap between the two is rather complicated, and in fact the growth of intra-industry trade can be linked even more closely with the other component of MNC trade that is not intra-firm.

Within regions intra-firm trade tends to be associated mainly but not exclusively with vertical integration, or the exchange of intermediate products. This is not necessarily the case with intra-firm trade between regions in which it may be more efficient for affiliates in the host region to maintain contacts with local distributors. As shown in table 11.6, 55 per cent of the intra-firm exports of US manufacturing parent companies in 1977 were final product exports that did not require further local processing. The ratio is below 50 per cent in most sectors, but nearly 75 per cent in transport equipment, which is dominated by MNCs in motor vehicles. Within the EC it is well known that US-owned affiliates in the motor vehicle industry are engaged in a good deal of intra-firm intermediate product trade, but between the USA and the EC the bulk of intra-firm trade involves the exchange of final products.

Table 11.6 The share of the value of exports of US parent companies to their affiliates that is for resale without further manufacture in 1977 (%)

Food products	26.0
Chemicals	41.6
Metals	28.2
Mechanical engineering	39.4
Electrical equipment	31.3
Transport equipment	74.8
Other manufacturing	42.3
Total manufacturing	55.0

Source: Casson (1986)

The changing trade objectives of MNCs as a result of the emergence of internationally or regionally integrated affiliate structures may have little effect in practice on the general determinants of the location of international production. In local market-oriented investment, which arguably is being reconstituted at an interregional level, the major incentive is the size of the local market (see e.g. Scaperlander and Mauer, 1969). For internationally integrated production, though, the greatest attraction is an effective local infrastructure and production capabilities that are complementary to the competitive strengths of the MNC. As a consequence MNCs tend to export from high-wage countries which also happen to be the same countries that provide the largest markets (Kravis and Lipsey, 1982).

Low wages do not in themselves attract even that production which uses unskilled labour intensively. What is attractive is a low ratio of wages to productivity, but in many low-wage economies this ratio is relatively high as productivity and economic organization are even weaker than are wages. For this reason the least developed countries attract little international production (Lall, 1984). From the observation that countries with large internal markets also attract export-oriented investments Kravis and Lipsey (1982) had concluded that local scale economies constitute the basis for affiliate exports. It seems more likely that bigger markets with higher incomes are associated with countries with a better technological and other infrastructure.

It is also reasonable to argue that the type of international production attracted by countries depends upon their stage of development, and different types of production have different effects on trade as suggested earlier. Katseli (1991) proposes a stylized sequence in the course of development over which the relationship between international trade and production changes. In the first stage a less developed country may attract resource-based production if it is rich in natural resources, and local market-oriented production if it is a large country. In the next stage of development it is feasible to attract export-platform production. In the third stage international production in services follows that in manufacturing and extractive activity, and MNCs establish local trading networks. In the final stage production becomes more specialized in accordance with the requirements of integrated regional MNC networks.

Progress from one stage to another is not always achieved, depending in part on whether governments encourage such a development path (Katseli, 1991). In the newly industrialized countries of the Pacific Rim, and more recently in Mexico, international production acted as a catalyst for industrial restructuring, including a gradual reshaping of the pattern of comparative advantage and thus exports. It has also helped to integrate the trade of these countries into new regional networks. By contrast, in Brazil and Nigeria development has not proceeded far beyond the first stage, and foreign MNCs have so far had little effect upon the exports of these countries.

11.5 CONCLUSIONS

At one time the policy-related debate over MNCs seemed largely to divide into two hostile camps. On the one side were the economic nationalists who were wary of foreign ownership and control, and believed that high foreign shares of local production undermined the capacity to take national economic initiatives. Their opponents argued instead that the presence of foreign MNCs increased local efficiency, and provided a means of upgrading local technology at relatively low cost.

Such arguments now seem very dated. Economic interdependence through the combination of international trade and production has now risen to a point where similar new products and processes are introduced at around the same time in all countries with substantial MNC interests. Isolation from the regular innovations developed through the international networks of the worlds' largest firms is widely recognized as a recipe for economic backwardness. However, economic policy cannot afford to ignore the detailed consequences of greater integration in the shape of the varying impact of a changed organization of MNC activity on the development path of different countries. Policy should be concerned with the effects of various possible patterns of affiliate specialization across countries rather than with the share of foreign ownership in a particular economy. The locational specialization of MNCs and the trade it facilitates is of an intra-industry as well as an inter-industry kind. For example, the most technologically sophisticated fields of production in a given industry may be concentrated in some countries and not others, though which countries are favoured depends upon the industry under consideration. The types of activity that a country attracts (and the consequent composition and balance of its MNC-related trade) depend upon its specific local capabilities and institutions, and these are affected in turn by its national policy decisions.

The increasing integration of affiliate networks also entails a theoretical reassessment of the international trade which is thereby created. The existence of the MNC does not remove the need for a theory of trade, as some factors remain immobile across national boundaries (Corden, 1974). However, these are not factors of production in the conventional sense as encapsulated in the HOS model, but instead follow from the national differentiation of technology and work organization. What is immobile is essentially the locationally specific elements of the technological structures and collective skills that are embodied in national organizations. These are tied to the traditions of local educational and training systems, organizational methods, operating customs, business and institutional practices, company exchange arrangements and so forth. Most MNC-related trade is therefore based on technological differences between countries (Dosi, Pavitt and Soete, 1990).

These national differences may be reinforced by the locational decisions of MNCs. While MNCs locate local market-oriented production close to the largest markets, they locate integrated production so as to take advantage of locationally specific production capabilities. The activities they locate in a particular country are those best suited to its existing location advantages, but as MNCs specialize in accordance with established national traditions the country's locational advantages may be consolidated. The MNC has a technological capability of its own which is generally related to that of its home country, but which also includes some firm-specific elements that enhance its operations in all countries. A foreign-owned affiliate is therefore likely to contribute a fresh approach to local production and problem-solving activity that interacts positively with the customs of the more capable indigenous firms and encourages their further innovative development, in part through the competitive challenge that it provides them with.

The integration of affiliate networks tends to reinforce national patterns of specialization and increase trade. There is a continual interaction between the competitive or ownership advantages of MNCs and the location advantages of countries, as they are termed in the eclectic paradigm (Dunning, 1988). The competitive advantages of firms are strengthened through strategies of inter-national integration, and by drawing on differentiated technological develop-ments in a variety of countries. The location advantages or tacit capabilities of countries are not fixed over time either, and they are influenced (among other things) by the types of activity that MNCs decide to locate within their borders. Given this interaction, in its original form, the eclectic paradigm was set out as a reasonable appeal for an integrated theoretical approach towards international trade and production (Dunning, 1977).

In most circumstances, but especially when international production is of an integrated kind, the policies that are most likely to be effective in encouraging a positive interaction between the locational strategies of MNCs and national economic development are those directed at an improvement in the underlying supply-side structure of a local economy. Such policies range from building up and sustaining a comprehensive and modern infrastructure to facilitating the availability of labour with the appropriate skills and training. The specific features of these policies depend upon the charac-teristics of a country's current technological capabilities, and its comparative advantage in innovative methods by comparison with its major trading partners, which are usually in the same region. For the policies to succeed they should aim to encourage home-based and foreign MNCs to locate in the country those activities that help to promote a gradual development of the national pattern of comparative advantage towards the fields in which the country presently enjoys its greatest innovative potential relative to others in the same regional group. Dynamic comparative advantage is used in this context in a broad sense that encompasses the intra-industry technological and organizational capabilities that are specific to local firms, and not just their pattern of inter-industry specialization.

This suggests that governments should focus on the longer-term policy environment for MNCs rather than on short-run policy issues. In the 1960s economists concerned themselves with the immediate impact of FDI on the balance of payments position of various countries; today governments must instead consider how far it is possible to encourage the restructuring of production through the reorganization of the international networks of MNCs in different industries and under various conditions in a fashion which is conducive to both national and international economic welfare (Dunning, 1992). This is a more fundamental question than is sometimes posed in the policy debate over MNCs and trade.

One implication is that policies that directly discriminate against or favour the operations of foreign-owned as against indigenous companies, or policies relating to foreign ownership as such are unlikely to be terribly relevant or helpful. The various regulations or controls that may be imposed on foreign-owned firms can be collectively termed 'trade-related investment measures' (TRIMS), and these may be contrasted with the investment incentives that are usually intended to have the opposite effect, sometimes in a particular area such as an export-processing zone. The three TRIMS that have attracted most attention are local content requirements, export performance requirements and trade balancing measures (Gray, 1992a). Policies of either kind may well prove to be counter-productive, although weighing up all the detailed costs and benefits is complicated (for a survey see Guisinger et al., 1985). Restrictions may only inhibit a beneficial interaction between foreign and indigenous firms by discouraging investments, or (in the case of local content requirements) by persuading foreign manufacturers to bring their component part suppliers with them rather than gradually to develop a new relationship with potential local suppliers. Thus, for example, Japanese component suppliers have followed the Japanese motor vehicle companies to Europe, where there has been pressure over local content issues (Ozawa, 1991; Saucier, 1991). At the other extreme, where countries compete for investments by tax and other incentives the net result may be that MNCs take the same locational decisions but simply capture a higher share of economic rents. In any event, TRIMS seem to be of little significance in practice, as only 3 per cent of foreign affiliates of US MNCs report being subjected to any one of these measures (Gray, 1992a).

One policy issue that arises from the developments described in the previous section is the problem of less developed countries that are excluded from the integration of MNC activity in the major industrialized regions. The best recommendation here seems to be for developing countries to ally themselves with a particular region, if possible as preferential trading and investment partners (UNCTC, 1991). They can then hope to play some role in the future development of affiliate networks, and participate in the growth of MNC-related trade.

Of course, it is also feasible to approach the analysis of the relationship between government policies and MNC behaviour from the other direction. As a result of the closer linkages between international trade and production, and of MNC integration strategies, company managements have begun to make greater efforts to influence trade-related policies. The future success of integration strategies depend on a free trading environment, the harmonization of national regulations, and the free movement of people. It is for this reason that the representatives of some prominent European companies took the lead in initiating the EC's plans for a single internal market. This in turn has further encouraged regionally based integration strategies. If in future such free trading arrangements and associated economic linkages are established between regions as well it is possible that the integration of MNC activity would become more genuinely international, and the scope of MNC-related trade would then expand still further.

NOTE

The author is grateful to Mark Casson, David Greenaway and Alan Winters for helpful comments on an earlier draft of this chapter.

REFERENCES

Bergsten, C. F., Horst, T. and Moran, T. H. 1978: *American Multinationals and American Interests*. Washington, DC: The Brookings Institution.

Blomström, M. 1990: *Transnational Corporations and Manufacturing Exports from Developing Countries*. New York: United Nations.

Buckley, P. J. and Casson, M. C. 1981: The optimal timing of a foreign direct investment. *The Economic Journal*, 91, 75–87.

Cantwell, J. A. 1989: *Technological Innovation and Multinational Corporations*. Oxford: Basil Blackwell.

Cantwell, J. A. 1992: The effects of integration on the structure of multinational corporation activity in the EC. In M. Klein and P. J. J. Welfens (eds), *Multinationals in the New Europe and Global Trade*, Berlin: Springer-Verlag.

Cantwell, J. A. and Sanna-Randaccio, F. 1990: The growth of multinationals and the catching up effect. *Economic Notes*, 19, 1–23.

Cantwell, J. A. and Sanna-Randaccio, F. 1992: Intra-industry direct investment in the EC: oligopolistic rivalry and technological competition. In J. A. Cantwell (ed.), *Multinational Investment in Modern Europe: strategic interaction in the integrated Community*, Cheltenham: Edward Elgar.

Casson, M. C. 1982: The theory of foreign direct investment. In J. Black and J. H. Dunning (eds), *International Capital Movements*, London: Macmillan.

Casson, M. C. 1986: Introduction and summary. In M. C. Casson et al., *Multinationals and World Trade: Vertical integration and the Division of Labour in World Industries*, London: Allen & Unwin.

Casson, M. C. et al. 1986: *Multinationals and World Trade: Vertical integration and the Division of Labour in World Industries*. London: Allen & Unwin.

Corden, W. M. 1974: The theory of international trade. In J. H. Dunning (ed.), *Economic Analysis and the Multinational Enterprise*, London: Allen & Unwin.

Dosi, G., Pavitt, K. and Soete, L. L. G. 1990: *The Economics of Technical Change and International Trade*. Hemel Hempstead: Harvester Wheatsheaf.

Dunning, J. H. 1977: Trade, location of economic activity and the MNE: a search for an eclectic approach. In B. Ohlin, P. O. Hesselborn and P. M. Wijkman (eds), *The International Allocation of Economic Activity*, London: Macmillan.

Dunning, J. H. 1988: The eclectic paradigm of international production: an update and some possible extensions. *Journal of International Business Studies*, 19, 1–31.

Dunning, J. H. 1992: *Multinational Enterprises and the Global Economy*. Wokingham: Addison-Wesley.

Dunning, J. H. (ed.) 1993: *From the Common Market to EC 92: Regional Economic Integration in the European Community and Transnational Corporations*. New York: United Nations.

Dunning, J. H., Cantwell, J. A. and Corley, T. A. B. 1986: An exploration of some historical antecedents to the modern theory of international production. In G. Jones and P. Hertner (eds), *Multinationals: theory and history*, Farnborough: Gower.

Fröbel, F., Heinrichs, J. and Kreye, O. 1980: *The New International Division of Labour: structural unemployment in industrialised countries and industrialisation in developing countries.* Cambridge: Cambridge University Press.

Gray, H. P. 1992a: The role of TNCs in international trade: an overview. In H. P. Gray (ed.), *Transnational Corporations and International Trade and Payments*, UNCTC Series on Transnational Corporations, London: Routledge.

Gray, H. P. 1992b: International intra-firm trade: the marketing and distribution dimension. In H. P. Gray (ed.), *Transnational Corporations and International Trade and Payments*, UNCTC Series on Transnational Corporations, London: Routledge.

Gray, H. P. 1992c: The interface between the theories of international trade and production. In P. J. Buckley and M. C. Casson (eds), *Multinational Enterprises in the World Economy: essays in honour of John Dunning*, Cheltenham: Edward Elgar.

Greenaway, D. 1986: Intra-industry trade, intra-firm trade and European integration. *Journal of Common Market Studies*, 26, 153–72.

Grossman, G. M. and Helpman, E. 1991: *Innovation and Growth in the Global Economy.* Cambridge, Mass.: MIT Press.

Guisinger, S. E. et al. 1985: *Investment Incentives and Performance Requirements.* New York: Praeger.

Helpman, E. and Krugman, P. R. 1985: *Market Structure and Foreign Trade: increasing returns, imperfect competition, and the international economy.* Brighton: Wheatsheaf.

Hipple, F. S. 1989: The changing role of multinational corporations in US international trade. In H. P. Gray (ed.), *The Modern International Environment*, vol. 7 of Annual Series on Research in International Business and Finance, Greenwich, Conn.: Jai Press.

Hipple, F. S. 1990a: Multinational companies and international trade: the impact of intra-firm shipments on US foreign trade, 1977–1982. *Journal of International Business Studies*, 21, 495–504.

Hipple, F. S. 1990b: The measurement of international trade related to multinational companies. *American Economic Review*, 80, 1263–70.

Hirsch, S. 1967: *Location of Industry and International Competitiveness.* Oxford: Oxford University Press.

Hirsch, S. 1976: An international trade and investment theory of the firm. *Oxford Economic Papers*, 28, 258–70.

Hymer, S. 1976: *The International Operations of National Firms: a study of direct investment.* Cambridge, Mass.: MIT Press.

Katseli, L. T. 1991: Foreign direct investment and trade interlinkages in the 1990s: experience and prospects of developing countries. Paper prepared for the UNCTC, United Nations, New York.

Kogut, B. 1985: Designing global strategies: profiting from operational flexibility. *Sloan Management Review*, Fall.

Kogut, B. 1987: Country patterns in international competition: appropriability and oligopolistic agreement. In N. Hood and J. E. Vahlne (eds), *Strategies in Global Competition*, London: Croom Helm.

Kojima, K. 1978: *Direct Foreign Investment: a Japanese model of multinational business operations.* London: Croom Helm.

Kravis, I. B. and Lipsey, R. E. 1982: The location of overseas production and production for export by US multinational firms. *Journal of International Economics*, 12, 201–23.

Krugman, P. R. 1990: *Rethinking International Trade.* Cambridge, Mass.: MIT Press.

Krugman, P. R. 1991: *Geography and Trade.* Cambridge, Mass.: MIT Press.

Lall, S. 1973: Transfer pricing by multinational manufacturing firms. *Oxford Bulletin of Economics and Statistics*, 35, 173–95.

Lall, S. 1978: The pattern of intra-firm exports by US multinationals. *Oxford Bulletin of Economics and Statistics*, 40, 209–22.

Lall, S. 1984: Transnationals and the Third World: changing perceptions. *National Westminster Bank Quarterly Review*, May, 2–16.

Lipsey, R. E. 1991: Foreign direct investment in the US and US trade. *National Bureau of Economic Research Working Papers*, no. 3623, February.

Lipsey, R. E. and Weiss, M. Y. 1981: Foreign production and exports in manufacturing industries. *Review of Economics and Statistics*, 63, 488–94.

Lipsey, R. E. and Weiss, M. Y. 1984: Foreign production and exports of individual firms. *Review of Economics and Statistics*, 66, 304–8.

McCharles, D. C. 1987: *Trade among Multinationals: intra-industry trade and national competitiveness*. London: Croom Helm.

Markusen, J. R. 1983: Factor movements and commodity trade as complements. *Journal of International Economics*, 13, 341–56.

Markusen, J. R. 1984: Multinationals, multi-plant economies, and the gains from trade. *Journal of International Economics*, 16, 205–26.

Mundell, R. A. 1957: International trade and factor mobility. *American Economic Review*, 47, 321–35.

Ozawa, T. 1991: Japanese multinationals and 1992. In B. Bürgenmeier and J. L. Mucchielli (eds), *Multinationals and Europe 1992: strategies for the future*, London: Routledge.

Patel, P. and Pavitt, K. 1991: Large firms in the production of the world's technology: an important case of non-globalisation. *Journal of International Business Studies*, 22, 1–21.

Pomfret, R. 1986: On the division of labour and intra-industry trade. *Journal of Economic Studies*, 13, 56–63.

Saucier, P. 1991: New conditions for competition between Japanese and European firms. In B. Bürgenmeier and J. L. Mucchielli (eds), *Multinationals and Europe 1992: strategies for the future*, London: Routledge.

Scaperlanda, A. E. and Mauer, L. J. 1969: The determinants of US direct investment in the EEC. *American Economic Review*, 59, 558–68.

Siddharthan, N. S. and Kumar, N. 1990: The determinants of inter-industry variations in the proportion of intra-firm trade: the behaviour of US multinationals. *Weltwirtschaftliches Archiv*, 26, 581–91.

UNCTC 1991: *World Investment Report 1991: the triad in foreign direct investment*. New York: United Nations.

Vernon, R. 1966: International investment and international trade in the product cycle. *Quarterly Journal of Economics*, 80, 190–207.

Vernon, R. 1979: The product cycle hypothesis in a new international environment. *Oxford Bulletin of Economics and Statistics*, 41, 255–67.

INDEX